W. T. Dawley

Cosmas Damian William

Yours most truly
John Grice

Yours Ever Sincerely
Jas. W. Jones

Yours truly
W. J. Stone

Yours truly
Chas Moser, O.S.B.

Fred Thornberg

Thos Stockham

Yours truly
Billy August

A. W. Neill
Indian Agent

Voices from the Sound

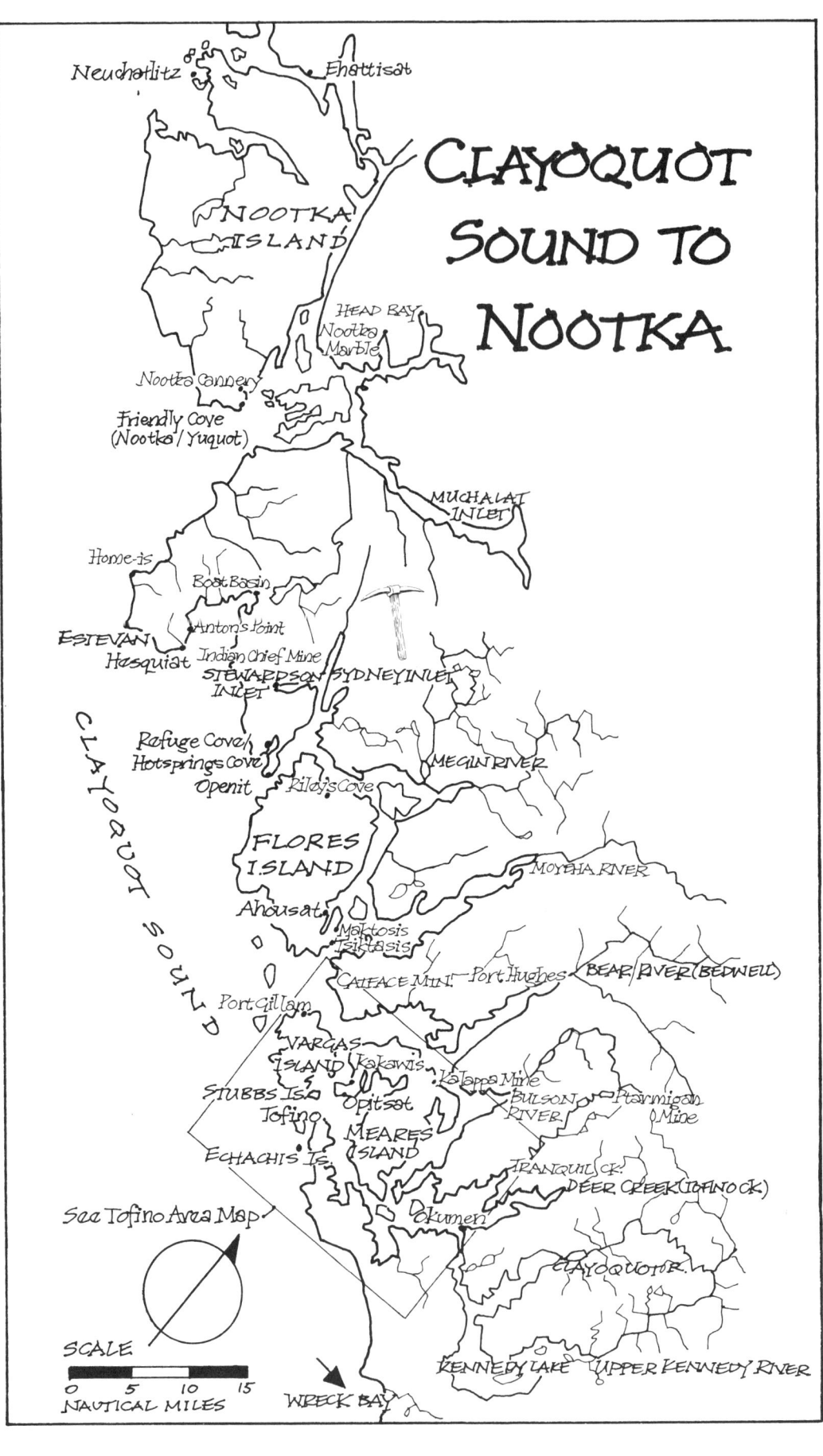

VOICES FROM THE SOUND

Chronicles of Clayoquot Sound and Tofino 1899–1929

Margaret Horsfield

SALAL BOOKS

Copyright © 2008 by Salal Books
First edition September 2008

Published by Salal Books
P.O. Box 1021, Station A
Nanaimo, BC V9R 5Z2
Toll Free Number: 1-888-858-5455
salalbooks@voicesfromthesound.com
www.voicesfromthesound.com

All rights reserved. No part of this publication may be reproduced, stored in a retrieval system, or transmitted in any form or by any means, electronic, mechanical, photocopying, recording or otherwise, without prior written permission of the publisher.

Design and layout by John McKercher
Production by Charlie Clark Books, llc.
Edited and indexed by Audrey McClellan
Copy-edited by Amelia Gilliland
Maps and illustrations by Briony Penn
Cover illustration by Edward R. Turner

LIBRARY AND ARCHIVES CANADA CATALOGUING IN PUBLICATION

Horsfield, Margaret
Voices from the Sound : chronicles of Clayoquot Sound and Tofino, 1899–1929 / Margaret Horsfield.

Includes bibliographical references and index.

ISBN 978-0-9697008-2-1

1. Clayoquot Sound Region (B.C.)—History. 2. Clayoquot Sound Region (B.C.)—Biography. 3. Tofino (B.C.)—History. 4. Tofino (B.C.)—Biography. 5. Christie Indian Residential School—History. I. Title.

FC3844.5.H67 2008   971.1'2   C2008-904394-4

Printed and Bound in Canada by Friesens Corporation.
Printed on chlorine-free paper made with 10% post-consumer waste.

— For Emma, with love —

Contents

List of Maps viii

Acknowledgements ix

Concerning Spelling, Punctuation and Abbreviations xi

Introduction xiii

1 *Up the Coast* 1

2 *A Hot Time in Ahousat* 23

3 *Kakawis* 41

4 *Dear Mr. Dawley* 63

5 *Priests at Sea* 85

6 *A Bunch of the Boys* 109

7 *Around the Sound* 127

8 *Vital Events* 145

9 *Liquid Dominion* 159

10 *Hesquiat Days* 179

11 *A Winter's Tale* 197

12 *Next Boat* 210

13 *Dear Father* 229

14 *A Go-Ahead Little Settlement* 244

15 *Writing Under Difficulties* 259

16 *Affliction* 277

17 *Dearest Girl* 297

18 *Silences* 318

Epilogue 335

Photo Credits 337

Notes on Sources 342

Select Bibliography 351

Index 355

List of Maps

Clayoquot Sound to Nootka   frontispiece

West Coast Vancouver Island Steamer Stops 1899–1929   xviii

North Pacific Sealing Grounds   31

Travels of Father Charles   93

Tofino Area   160

South Hesquiat Peninsula   194

Tofino Harbour   311

About the maps:
All maps are by Briony Penn. As far as possible, names on these maps are consistent with names used in the time period represented in this book. Many place names on the coast have changed over the years, some more than once, so some names on these maps will differ from those on modern maps. Where space permits, variant modern names are provided.

Acknowledgements

Several years ago, Leona Taylor directed me toward the Dawley papers at the BC Provincial Archives. She helped to guide me through these papers, sharing her enthusiasm and her favourite characters. Without her help, and the invaluable database she has created in cataloguing the Dawley papers, I doubt I would have written this book. Leona also has assembled a database of articles about the west coast of Vancouver Island from the *Victoria Times Colonist*, which proved extremely useful. Thank you, Leona, for your unstinting help, your sense of humour and tactful silences, and especially for bringing James W. Jones and the rest of the boys into my life.

A special mention also for Suzanne Mackenzie, the archivist at Mount Angel Abbey Library in Oregon. Suzanne has been constantly helpful, hospitable and kind, far beyond what I could have reasonably expected. I am profoundly grateful. My thanks to Abbot Nathan Zadrow for generously allowing me to use Father Charles Moser's diary, Father Maurus Snyder's papers and a wide array of photographs from the abbey archives.

At Queen of Angels Monastery at Mount Angel, Sister Alberta Dieker arranged for me to see photographs and documents in the archives there and helped with my searches. She and Prioress Donna Marie Chartrau have kindly permitted me to use material from their collection. I thank them both.

Ken Gibson, with his unequalled knowledge of the west coast, sent many sources, ideas and photographs my way and helped me with innumerable questions. I am greatly in his debt.

A number of people open-heartedly trusted me with family photographs and papers. Joan Niblock gave me the memoirs, letters and photographs of her father, Mike Hamilton. Joan and Colin Nicholson shared their memories of Walter Dawley, provided photographs and checked family information for me. Nan Beere provided Brewster family photographs and letters. Ron MacLeod rescued Dr. Dixson's diary and told me about the MacLeod boys. Flora McCue shared information about her grandfather, Edward Gillam.

I am grateful to all the people I interviewed for this book: Dorothy and Edward Arnet, Emma Gallagher, Anthony Guppy, Walter Guppy, Father

Stephen Hofman, Ray Jones, Flora McCue, Harold Monks, Joan and Colin Nicholson, Joan Niblock, Susan Scott, Marian Stocks.

The staff of the BC Provincial Archives, UBC Library, Special Collections, and Library and Archives Canada have been consistently helpful. Thank you all. My thanks also to Dr. Wally Chung, whose collection of CPR material, now at UBC Library, Special Collections, is so extensive and useful.

For commenting on the manuscript at various stages, thanks to Peter Buckland, Cairn Crockford, Sue Davies, Yvonne Hewett, Isabel Gutmanis, Roland Lines, Harold Monks, Brenda Silsbe.

Claudia Cole responded with unflappable efficiency to research queries. Ron Hamilton helped me to a clearer understanding of place names. Adrienne Mason sorted out several knotty questions. Ian Kennedy and I happily discussed pilchards and other puzzles at length. Thank you all, very much.

Mark Kaarremaa remastered many original photographs and photographed a great number of documents, never asking awkward questions like why? or—again? Many thanks also to Peter Buckland for his help with photography.

My editor, Audrey McClellan, guided the book through its final stages with a sure hand and a keen eye; I cannot thank her enough. Thanks also to Amelia Gilliland for her careful copy-editing.

To the book's designer, John McKercher, my heartfelt thanks for his skilful work and calm patience as I sent one problem after another his way. And Briony Penn, who did the maps and illustrations, brought past and present together for me in unexpected ways, for which I thank her.

The Canada Council and the BC Arts Council provided valuable financial support to me in the early stages of writing this book.

My thanks also to Bob Bossin, Jill and Hank Byington, Bill Dale, Brother Cyril Drnjevic, Jean Eastwood, Bev and John Ford, David Griffith, Christopher Hanna, David Klus, Molly Lane, Emily Morgan, Jan Petersen, John and Sarah Platenius, Liza Potvin, Don Reksten, Sister Josephine Schultz, Joan Skogan, Marni Stanley, Edward R. Turner, Susanne Voetmann, Melanie Williams.

Throughout this project, Peter Buckland has believed in me and backed me up. Thank you, Peter, for seeing stories in new ways, for challenging me to do better, for making me think and rethink. You lead, as always, by example.

The last word goes to my daughter. Emma, you have grounded me and educated me more than anyone in the entire world. Thank you. And whether or not you believe books have voices—take a chance on it. This one is for you.

Concerning Spelling, Punctuation and Abbreviations

AN ESSENTIAL NOTE FOR READERS

Prepare for some oddities of spelling, place names, punctuation and abbreviations in the pages ahead of you.

The spelling of place names varies enormously in the original sources for this book. These sources provide at least six variant spellings of "Ahousat," and that is only one example. In my own writing, I use the generally accepted modern spelling of place names, found on current maps and charts. When quoting from sources using variant spellings, I quote the sources exactly. If clarification is required, I place the commonly accepted spelling in brackets.

The original sources often refer to places by names no longer in use. A few examples: Bedwell River is consistently called Bear River; Yuquot is always Friendly Cove; Hot Springs Cove is Refuge Cove. To avoid confusion, I generally stick with the names used in the sources; explanations appear in brackets if required. For further clarification, the maps in this book provide as many variant names as space permits.

Names of people, boats and companies appear differently in different sources. Here again, I use what I judge to be the generally accepted spelling, but when quoting from an original source I use the spelling found there, sometimes placing the accepted spelling in brackets.

In the letters and diaries cited here, many writers use highly creative abbreviations. Schooner appears as "schr" or "sch"; steamer as "str" or "st"; sack as "sk" or "sck"; barrel as "brl"; Indian as "Ind," and so on. The writers, pen in hand, were in a hurry. Abbreviations can vary within the same letter, changing with the whim of the writer. Unless the meaning is entirely obscured, I leave these alone. If necessary, I provide the full word in brackets.

Spelling of common words is unpredictable in the letters and diaries. "Boat" can be correctly spelled on one line and appear as "bot" on another. "Know" can appear as "kno" or "no" in the same letter. I generally leave these spellings untouched, trusting the reader will understand, even enjoy, the variety.

Punctuation in all handwritten originals is extremely erratic and can cause confusion. Some letters have no punctuation whatever; some contain entirely random punctuation. On occasion, to preserve the sense of the writing, I have added or removed punctuation, but I do so as little as possible. When the punctuation or lack thereof adds personal zest to the source—for example, Fred Thornberg's use of the "=" sign to give emphasis or to add pauses in his letters—I leave such idiosyncrasies intact.

I provide the full date and year when citing letters and diaries. The originals contain so many different abbreviations and so many ways of writing dates that standardization was essential to avoid confusion.

Concerning the names of the priests: Members of a monastic order, like Father Charles Moser, who was a Benedictine, are addressed by their first name —in his case, "Father Charles." Diocesan priests, who are not members of a monastic order, like Father Augustin Brabant, are addressed by their surname—in his case, "Father Brabant." Occasionally, Father Charles Moser or Father Maurus Snyder signed their letters "P. Charles" or "P. Maurus" followed by the letters OSB. "P." stands for "Pater"; "OSB" stands for "Order of Saint Benedict."

I use the terms "Indian" or "native" throughout this book when writing of First Nations people, judging these terms to be neutral and broadly acceptable. This allows for consistency between the original sources and my own writing without introducing the confusion of additional terminology that is now in current use. I am aware that language is a sensitive issue here, and I know language is continually evolving. I know of no perfect solution. I trust that readers will find my approach acceptable.

Occasionally the language used in original sources concerning First Nations people seems offensive, troubling and racist. These were the voices of the time. I do not cite such sources lightly.

Introduction

On a grey day threatening rain, try, if you can, to be down near the waterfront in Tofino. Look out over the harbour, over its many scattered islands, into the distance beyond, with Lone Cone Mountain looming in the background.

   Groups of tourists brighten the scene, ungainly in their survival suits as they board specially outfitted boats and head towards the outer coast of Vargas Island to watch for whales. Swarms of kayakers come into sight, paddles flashing in synchronized rhythms. A wide, curving wake divides the water behind an aluminum motorboat that zooms across the harbour, effortlessly avoiding all the navigation buoys. The deep-throated engines of a large new water taxi mutter at the dock, while a handsome old fishing boat motors into its berth. A float plane takes off, its noisy crescendo briefly overwhelming the scene before fading as the plane banks steeply, bearing visitors away on a scenic tour of Clayoquot Sound.

   Silence descends and then the rain starts to fall, an obscuring, misty drizzle. The horizon closes in, blurring in the dull light, and as the view becomes increasingly indistinct, something strange happens. Perspectives shift, perceptions change.

   Through the colourless and transforming lens of the rain, the harbour seems suddenly empty. The contemporary bustle is nowhere to be seen or heard. Present realities dissolve. The kayaks, coffee shops and tourist attractions of Tofino fade away like an insubstantial dream; the sounds of boats and float planes ebb into the distance. Time disappears.

   Look again at this watery coastal landscape, lying before you as it did a century and more ago, and know that, in the rain, much can be seen, much understood.

   As you watch through narrowed eyes, blinking the rain away, a number of small dugout canoes may come slowly into focus. They are arriving from all directions, heading towards the Tofino dock. A black-robed priest awkwardly paddles one canoe. Several native children are in another, racing easily ahead of two unkempt prospectors struggling hard against the current in their canoe. A few rowboats emerge in the distance, joining the canoes, and the harbour fills with activity.

The boats are all coming to meet the coastal steamer, just now entering the harbour, black smoke belching from its funnel. An ear-splitting screech of the whistle announces its arrival, and within moments, dozens of people converge on the dock in a cheerful melee. Schoolchildren shout to each other, running pell-mell along the muddy, stump-strewn trails of the rough settlement on their way to the harbour. The steamer comes alongside, the gangway lowers with a clang, greetings fill the air, passengers disembark and the children scramble on board, heading for the commissariat to buy comic books and treats. Wooden crates swing overhead as they are winched off the ship and onto the dock, and people eagerly open their parcels amid a hubbub of news and gossip.

A short distance across the water, over at Clayoquot on Stubbs Island, the portly storekeeper checks his pocket watch and waits his turn. He stands behind the store counter, writing a last-minute letter to send on the steamer up the coast to his branch store at Ahousat, along with an order of groceries and some empty barrels for dogfish oil. Soon the steamer will call at Clayoquot, and sales will be brisk in the hotel saloon, next to the store, while goods are unloaded. The storekeeper expects a new bull calf to arrive on this boat—poor creature, it is tethered on the deck of the steamer right now, over at Tofino, plaintively bawling—along with several tons of flour and a large order of fresh produce. He must remember to check the oranges right away to see if any have spoiled; the last batch was mouldy. The Chinese kitchen workers gather on the hotel porch in anticipation of the steamer's arrival; he can hear their chatter and their laughter from the store.

From where you stand you can see, you can sense, all of this, and just for a moment—suspended in the eternal rain—times past and people long gone are visible, audible.

Such moments cannot last. They are fleeting, ephemeral—some might say imaginary. Yet the people you have glimpsed, and their stories, were once all real —as real as rain. And sometimes, truly, they can be heard.

A mixed crowd of people vie for attention in this book, striving to be glimpsed and to be heard. All of them are from the west coast of Vancouver Island. Some of them were friends, some strangers, some had nodding acquaintance with each other or did business together. Only a few of these people are well known in the annals of British Columbia's coastal history, and many were obscure figures even in their own day.

Their lives intersected during the early decades of the twentieth century. They drifted in and out of the same territory, often just on the periphery of each other's vision, inhabiting many different realities within the small world and the vast distances of Clayoquot Sound. Frequent travellers and fellow travellers on the west coast, the lives of these people are linked by accidents of timing and geography; they are also connected, unknowingly, by various papers they left behind—letters, diaries, scraps of memoir, disjointed notes.

Dozens of names come tumbling from these documents. Here are storekeepers, settlers and sealers; First Nations residents and their children; priests, prospectors and fortune seekers. With few exceptions, the documents these people left behind were never intended for posterity; few had any official role or purpose, and their very survival has been largely a matter of chance. They have shown up in widespread and random places: in dusty boxes in a hotel basement, in a monastery archive, in a farmhouse attic, in public archives, in scrapbooks, shoeboxes and dark cupboards. Many of the letters were laboriously composed by people for whom writing was a severe struggle; their vocabulary, spelling and punctuation can be baffling. Yet as difficult to decipher as they may be, these documents are all vital strands in the fabric of West Coast history. Detailed, gossipy and colourful, they reveal long-lost stories of lives lived on the coast, radiating a sense of immediacy that is irresistible.

To touch the thin onion skin of a letter written over a hundred years ago by an infuriated storekeeper at Ahousat; to pore over a barely legible love letter sent out in haste from Tofino aboard the coastal steamer *Princess Maquinna*; to turn the pages of a crumbling diary written at Hesquiat by a doctrinaire and lonely priest; to learn, in a perfectly penned letter from a native student at Christie School on Meares Island, that he is spitting blood; to find a letter written on a First World War battlefield by a soldier worrying about an overdue account at the Clayoquot store—to view any or all of these documents is to be drawn into the past and to hear the writers as clearly as if they are speaking aloud, here and now. Laughter erupts in one letter, seething fury in the next, confused sadness in another. In a terse diary entry, the keening of an anguished mother is heard as her child is taken away to school; in a file stuffed with business letters, a storekeeper complains loudly because a box of raisins is spoiled by salt water; in a letter to his fiancée, a hard-working settler is pleased to report selling an island near Tofino for $150. A cacophony of Clayoquot characters emerges—people who seem just as vital and alive, just as cantankerous or pitiable or brave or eccentric as they were on the day they wrote their letters or diaries.

Chief amongst these are the Clayoquot merchant Walter Dawley and the missionary Father Charles Moser, who lived and worked at many locations in Clayoquot Sound. These two men kept records and preserved their documents; their papers cover the same era and the same area, and they often feature the same personalities. These two collections of documents provide the essential foundation on which this book is constructed. Immensely rich and detailed, the Dawley papers and the diary and papers of Father Charles have not been explored in much detail until now. Their usefulness and their historical value are such that they merit much greater attention in future.

Walter Dawley's papers consist of a vast array of inbound correspondence, addressed to him, covering a period of more than thirty years from the mid-1890s onward. Over fifteen thousand letters swell the files of this collection in the British Columbia Archives, many of them personal letters to Dawley, handwritten by customers and suppliers. Very little written by Dawley himself survives, certainly nothing of a personal nature.

By contrast, the single most important document left by Father Charles Moser is his extensive diary. Beginning the day of his arrival on Vancouver Island's west coast in May 1900, and continuing until his departure thirty years later, the diary is an unparalleled source of information. Other papers of Father Charles, and those of his fellow priests—the correspondence addressed to Father Maurus Snyder in particular—are similarly valuable. All of these, along with a large collection of photographs taken by the priests, are located in the archives of Mount Angel Abbey in Oregon.

Sometimes these parallel sources of information dovetail perfectly, presenting different viewpoints of similar events or the same people. Sometimes they represent two starkly different realities. Either way, they offer continuous streams of information, remarkable for their detail and consistency, and they offer perspectives on the early twentieth century in Clayoquot Sound that become even more vivid when considered alongside other sources, other first-hand documents.

My aim in this book is to provide a sense of the vitality and humanity of the early twentieth century on the west coast of Vancouver Island, to people the landscape and to bring personal stories into focus. On the whole, the individuals who appear in the following pages are not movers and shakers, not decision makers or policy shapers; they were simply living on the coast and trying to make a go of it in a rapidly changing environment. They are also among the ones who left behind some sort of paper trail, some sort of documentation, however faint and incomplete it may be. Not everyone did so. Many who lived around Clayoquot Sound in the early twentieth century cannot be represented here in any detail, simply because few documents have survived—at least not in sources I have had access to—that allow their voices to be heard. Contemporary documents written by women, by Chinese workers and Japanese settlers, and most particularly by First Nations people are difficult to come by. The presence of all these people, especially First Nations residents of the area, can be strongly felt, their influence intuited, but they have left behind few, if any, papers. These few, however, are powerful: letters from native children at Christie School; requests for medicine; lists of goods purchased by sealing crews at the local stores. Although such scraps of information are partial and fragmented, they are unquestionably valuable, and I hope I have made good use of them.

This book does not pretend to provide a definitive history of the area, the period or the people. Here is simply a point of entry, a window onto one era in the history of the coast, a means of meeting some of the personalities who were part of that history and to hear what they have to say. A great deal remains to be discovered and written about coastal history; many sources are yet to be examined, many stories are still untold. The business of recording and assessing this history has only just begun.

Any mistakes in interpreting the material I have used, from whatever source, are my mistakes and my responsibility alone. I only hope I have represented fairly the people I am writing about, and that to some extent I have succeeded in letting their voices be heard.

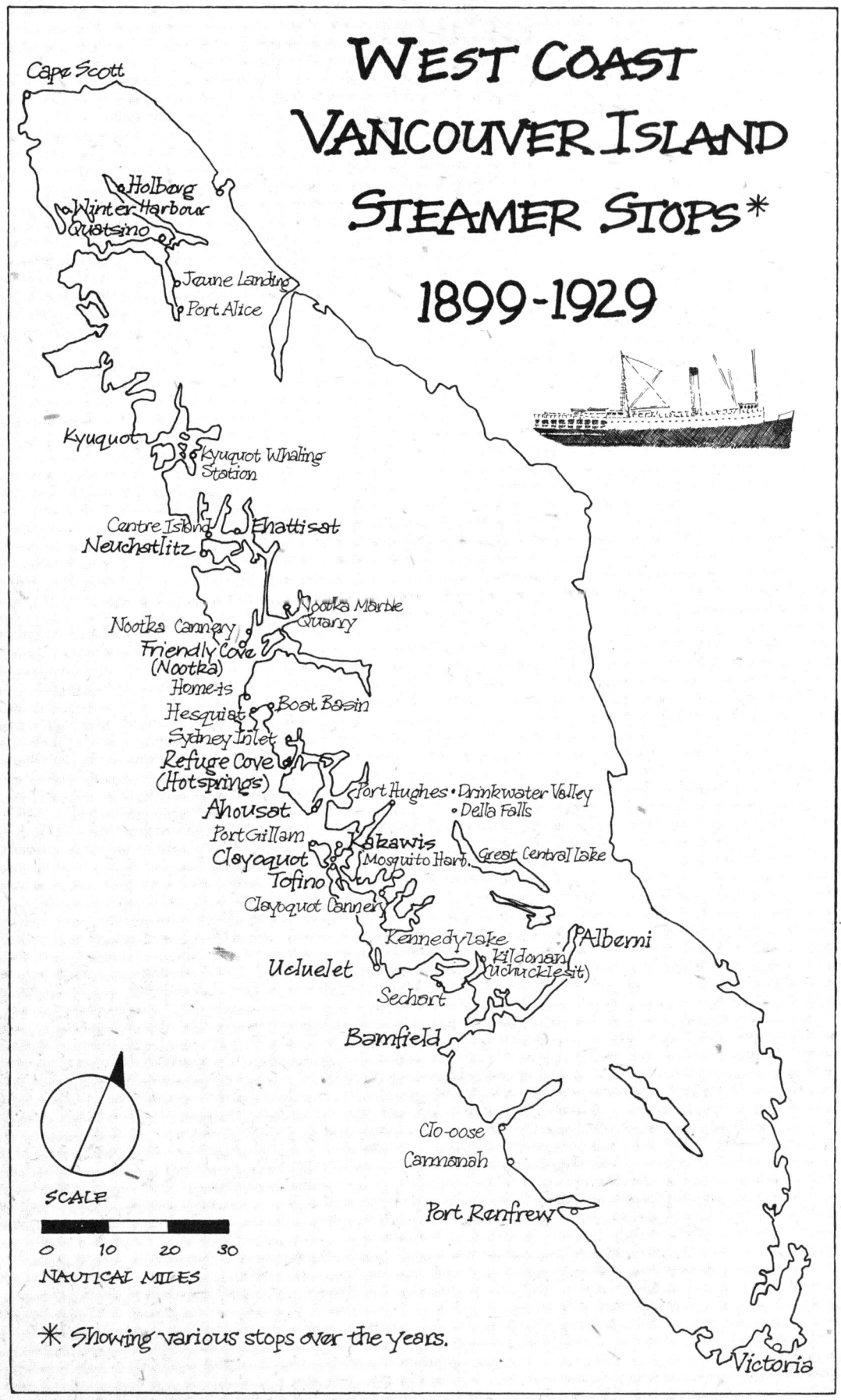

— 1 —

Up the Coast

Ahouset March 8, 1899

Mr Dawley:
Your letter to Hand = no chance here for to get good Hunters = all of the good Hunters have signet artickles in the 2 sch that was here, each of the sch had 15 canoes = and bothe of them went to sea this morning…take my advice dont send another sch to Ahouset for a Crew she would only be disapointed = the would have to reese price to $4.00 for seals before the would get them to goe = and then it would only be second class hunters and old men for steerers.

This letter is one of many thousands swelling Walter Dawley's files of inbound correspondence. Carefully preserved from the late 1890s onward, these letters contain a wealth of vivid detail about everyday life in Clayoquot Sound during the early decades of the twentieth century. Now neatly corralled in archival boxes, all of this correspondence originally travelled by boat to reach Walter Dawley at his store on Vancouver Island's west coast. Stuffed into heavy sacks, heaved on board steamers or schooners, the letters addressed to Dawley eventually spilled onto his roll-top desk behind the counter of his store in a chattering flood of correspondence.

In this letter of March 8, 1899, Dawley's correspondent is Frederick Christian Thornberg, the storekeeper up at Ahousat. Preoccupied by vexatious details concerning the sealing schooners on the coast, and by the demands of their captains, Thornberg vented his concerns, as usual, by writing to Dawley:

> Cpt Sieward has been a-jawing me again about getting a discount on his orders…[He] said I ought to write to you about it = don't give him or enny one sealing out of Ahouset a discount on there orders = if you do you will ruin your Business here…Capt Seeward is a hard man to please = he has got his back up again about something…[he] has been growling the whole time he was here. [Capt] Peppett so fare, in his dealings with me…or with the Indians, has ackted a gentleman.

By the time Walter Dawley received this letter, these sealing captains had already set sail with their crews of native hunters on board, heading for the distant sealing grounds offshore. After long, arduous journeys, the vessels would finally return, each one laden with hundreds of sealskins, bringing a hubbub of commercial activity with them as the crews disembarked at their home villages, determined to enjoy spending their seasonal earnings. For now, Fred Thornberg could put behind him all the bothersome details of outfitting the sealers, pricing sealskins and dealing with ill-tempered captains, and could turn his attention to the immediate, mundane issues of storekeeping:

> I am run out of Potatoes (I had 10 sck) send me a sck Potatoes pr next St if you have enny to spare = I believe the HBC [Hudson's Bay Company] made a misthake in price of Chewing Tobacco, the first Box

Walter Dawley and Thomas Stockham's first store was on Stockham Island, seen here from the northwest. From the early 1890s until 1902, this was the centre of their business empire, which included stores at Nootka and Ahousat.

A view of the hotel on Stockham Island, looking south. Built in 1898, this hotel was the first in Clayoquot Sound.

Feb 14, 21 @44¢—the second Box on Feb 20, 21@ 72¢ it is the same quality of chew Tobac Mahogany T&B Chew.

Walter Dawley and his business partner, Thomas Stockham, were Fred Thornberg's employers; they owned the store he ran at Ahousat and provided him with all his goods. From their headquarters on Stockham Island, about a mile across the harbour from where Tofino now stands, Stockham and Dawley together ran a tightly controlled business empire, provisioning the coast and trading with the native people from three different stores: their main store on Stockham Island; the store at Ahousat, ten miles to the northwest; and their more distant store at Nootka, nearly forty miles up the coast.

Anchored solidly in place behind his store counter on Stockham Island, Walter Dawley was an imposing figure, large and inscrutable, no detail ever escaping his attention. His ambition was as expansive as his waistline; he intended his business to prosper, to grow and eventually to dominate the coast. He overlooked no opportunity and brooked no opposition. In charge of all the paperwork for the partnership, Dawley conducted business almost entirely by mail. All but a very few of his own outgoing letters have been lost, but letters written to him, and in response to him, survive in the thousands. These letters provide an intricately detailed, revealing picture of how his business operated, and how the area around him developed, over nearly three decades.

Dealing with the incoming mail, which arrived in waves aboard various coastal vessels, absorbed a great deal of Walter Dawley's time. Meticulous in all business matters, he neatly annotated and filed his letters, deliberately preserving every imaginable piece of paper: promotional leaflets, hurried notes from friends, pleading letters from customers who could not pay, carefully composed orders in copperplate handwriting, orders scrawled in pencil on scrap paper, fawning letters from wholesalers and large piles of correspondence from his storekeepers up the coast, particularly Fred Thornberg.

In the late 1890s, Thornberg was easily the most voluble letter writer on the entire west coast of Vancouver Island. His letters to Walter Dawley are outpourings of business minutiae mingled with grievances both real and imagined. Nearly indecipherable, they are peppered with wildly original spelling and punctuation and are hurried along with bizarre abbreviations. Tiny crabbed handwriting covers both sides of sheets of onion skin paper, filling even the margins with extra jottings as he wrote of store business, of his neighbours, of the sealing schooners and their trade, and as he placed orders for merchandise, extravagantly underlined and spiced with double dashes, exclamations and asides. Asking for "5 Box Pilot Bread," he remonstrated, "I dont want burnt Biscuits"; ordering shoes, he irritably stressed that they must be size nine, "no other size is wanted…dont send me no more No 6=7=8 shoes."

Thornberg was frequently outraged by the goods Dawley sent: "What made you order the same kind of Tin Dishes (wood Hdl) I wrote to you it was a poore seller" and "Your shaving brushes is to good for Ind trade a cheaper one to sell @ 25¢ would be better for this trade." But apart from such mercantile considerations, the single most persistent subject recurring in Thornberg's letters is the fur seal trade.

By the late nineteenth century, sealing had become a huge business, the economic lifeblood of the coast. In earlier decades, a few white traders purchased whatever sealskins they could obtain from native hunters who paddled their canoes twenty or thirty miles offshore to hunt seals in their feeding grounds. Hunting methods changed after 1868, when the fur trader William Spring attempted a new, innovative method of offshore sealing aboard his schooner *Surprise*. With four large canoes on her deck, and twelve hunters from Clayoquot aboard, *Surprise* took the hunters out to the seals. The idea was to increase efficiency and maximize the kill, sparing the hunters long and often dangerous journeys by canoe. Once in position offshore, the natives launched their canoes from the deck of the schooner and set out on the hunt, usually with two or three men in each canoe. Provided with basic supplies in case they were separated from the schooner, and armed with harpoons and spears—in later years with rifles—they paddled away, their tapered blades entering the water silently so as not to alert the seals. After a day's hunting, they returned to the schooner, skinned the seals, salted the skins and stowed them away.

In the mid-1870s, nine schooners based out of Victoria employed this method of sealing, and by 1882, this number had increased to fourteen. The larger vessels could take up to twenty canoes on their decks and some forty or more native hunters; one such boat could arrive back in Victoria at the end of the season with well over a thousand sealskins.

The comings and goings of the sealing schooners provided the main source of income for Stockham and Dawley's three stores and the main source of cash income for the Indian population on the coast. For many years, sealing was arguably the single most important industry consistently fuelling the economy of the city of Victoria; eventually scores of sealing schooners were based there. These schooners relied heavily upon the services of skilled native seal hunters from up the coast—the most renowned hunters were men of Opitsat and Ahousat, closely rivalled by hunters from Hesquiat, Nootka and Kyuquot. The schooner captains competed fiercely to have the best of these hunters sign on to their vessels as crew —to sign "artickles," as Fred Thornberg put it—for the annual seal hunt. Many of the individual captains depended on the local storekeepers to help them obtain the best crews—after all, the storekeepers knew the hunters, lived amongst or near them and did business with them continually.

The storekeepers not only acted as procurers for the sealing captains but also paid wages to the hunters on behalf of the captains when the season ended—wages that were quickly spent at the store or sometimes already forfeited by earlier debts. In addition, the storekeepers bought many types of skins and furs from the natives, as well as dogfish oil, fish, baskets and carvings. Their stores became essential hubs of communication for everyone on the coast. The Indian Agent, the sealers and visitors from villages along the coast would leave messages for each other with the storekeepers. "Crazey Jack says to tell Whiskey Charley that he will come to Clayoquot...providing he gets a wife but not else," declared one such message from Nootka in 1898, "write and let him know by return." From Ucluelet in 1899 came another message: "Tutube's wife could like TchTchpia's wife to come down to Ucluelet to visit her. She is quite ill and she thinks TchTchpia's wife can help her."

The cash economy had taken firm hold amongst the native people of Clayoquot Sound by the end of the nineteenth century. For several decades, they had been inexorably drawn into the commercial web of white traders, largely due to the income generated by the fur sealing industry. In 1881, Harry Guillod, the Indian Agent for the area, observed in his annual report that "the Indians are large consumers of flour, biscuit, rice, sugar and print, while the demand for soap, good class of clothing and boots and shoes for adults and children is steadily on the increase." Without the sealing trade, this demand for consumer products would never have arisen so rapidly. According to the *Victoria Daily Colonist* of January 8, 1882, the offshore sealing industry directly employed some four hundred Indians. "Probably nearly $200,000 will be paid out by Victoria firms for native wages and supplies," states the newspaper, "to say nothing about the expenditure of the American vessels, some of which finds its way to Victoria directly, and indirectly through the west coast Indians." Given these impressive figures, Stockham and Dawley could confidently expect tens of thousands of dollars to filter through their stores every sealing season.

Walter Dawley originally came from Morrisburg, Ontario. As a young man he left his family's farm, seeking his fortune in wider, more distant horizons. No account survives of how he and Stockham met, but because they each had considerable expertise in handling furs, they could well have been drawn together by connections in the fur trade. Stockham was the first to spot the potential of the west coast when he was a member of a survey party scouting out timberland at Trout River in Clayoquot Sound. Since his arrival in Canada from his native England in 1879, Stockham had worked at many trades, and here he sensed a golden opportunity, realizing that with the traffic of sealing vessels, the expanding consumer market and the rumours of mineral discoveries, the setting was ideal for a pair of ambitious merchants. He and Dawley went into business together, establishing themselves as traders on Stockham Island in or shortly after 1891. In all likelihood, Dawley, then in his early thirties, was the main investor; in later years he described himself as the head of the business and Stockham as the partner. Dawley recalled their early days in a laconic scrap of unpublished memoir:

> [Stockham] told me that the Clay[oquot] Indians had plenty of furs so we decided to go into the fur business together. We built a store on Stockham Island opposite the Clayoquot Indian village…with shipwrecked lumber from Schooner Cove on Long Beach, rafted it and towed it down with a canoe nine miles, not even a row boat available.

At their store on Stockham Island, very near the Indian village of Opitsat, the two men set out to dominate the local fur-buying market, and before long they were seeking furs from more distant locations on the coast. Shrewdly, they set up satellite stores, first at Nootka in 1894 and then at Ahousat in 1896. Fred Thornberg was their first storekeeper at Ahousat; John W. Goss was the first at Nootka. These stores firmly established Dawley and Stockham's presence on the coast, giving them significant control over the spending power of native people in the area and ensuring them a high volume of trade with the sealing schooners.

The two men proved adept at gathering local power and influence. Dawley became mining recorder in 1898, and a regular, profitable traffic of prospectors came by the store on Stockham Island to record their mining claims and hear the latest about mining developments. Not long afterward, Dawley became Justice of the Peace. He corresponded at length with politicians, developers and speculators, and he kept abreast of developments concerning the telegraph line that by 1899 stretched beyond Alberni to Cape Beale and might one day extend all the way to Clayoquot.

In 1898, Stockham and Dawley expanded their Stockham Island operation by building a hotel, the first one in Clayoquot Sound. They catered largely to prospectors and sealers, renting out six rooms and offering the amenities of the dining and sitting room—complete with two spittoons—to their guests. On October 7, 1898, the *Colonist* heralded this as a "fine new hotel lately opened by Stockham and Dawley, [where] the travelling public can be accommodated in first class style…the starting point for those looking for mines or pleasure resorts."

From this vantage point, the two men kept a suspicious eye on any and all commercial competitors. Their real bugbear was the long-established store about a mile away from theirs on Stubbs Island (sometimes called Clayoquot Island or just Clayoquot). This store was on the site of the earliest fur-trading post in the area, dating back to the mid-1850s. By the 1890s, Thomas Earle, a well-known Victoria merchant and member of Parliament, owned the Clayoquot store, employing Filip Jacobsen as manager. Stubbs Island had several advantages over Stockham Island: it had a more protected anchorage; it was headquarters for the provincial police constable for Clayoquot Sound; a post office had been based there since 1890; and just across the water from the Clayoquot store, on the Esowista Peninsula, a scattered handful of settlers, slowly increasing in number, provided an expanding market.

Despite Stockham and Dawley's successes over on Stockham Island and up the coast, the store on Stubbs Island reigned supreme, widely acknowledged as the commercial and social centre of the area. Dawley and Stockham found this grimly unamusing. They could only look on with chagrin when Thomas Earle financed a large dock at Clayoquot in 1898 to accommodate the increasing coastal steamer traffic. Later the same year their chagrin increased tenfold when Earle decided to build a hotel at Clayoquot, in direct competition to theirs and constructed only a few months later. But, watchful and opportunistic, the two men bided their time, convinced their day would come and that eventually they would dominate all commercial activity in the area, by whatever means available.

An estimate of the population living in Clayoquot Sound at the turn of the century yields figures of about eight hundred native people and probably fewer than a hundred white people. Scattered thinly throughout the Sound, these people lived on islands, up inlets, near good beaches or streams and in a number of native villages, the largest being Opitsat, Kelsemat, Ahousat and Hesquiat. The only means of travel on the coast was by water, sometimes on schooners or coastal steamers, but much more commonly by dugout canoe or rowboat.

By 1899, settlers had hacked a handful of homesteads from the bush at the head of the Esowista Peninsula, and a few buildings could be seen near the waterfront. Graceless and raw, these buildings perched awkwardly in the middle of rough clearings joined together by even rougher trails. The widely separated dwellings, initially isolated from each other by dense forest, coalesced over a number of years into a messy, unofficial settlement, loosely defined at first as

Starting in 1898, the steamer *Queen City* made twice-monthly trips up the west coast from Victoria to Nootka. She could carry up to 100 passengers.

"the townsite." By 1904 the place was becoming known locally as Tofino. Just as Dawley and Stockham had kept a wary eye on Clayoquot from their stronghold on Stockham Island, they also kept this upstart community in their sights, even though in the early years it did not trouble them unduly. They reckoned the place would never amount to much.

A crude trail extended from the nascent Tofino townsite toward the village of Ucluelet by the end of 1899, but the idea of a road link to the rest of Vancouver Island was inconceivable. The wildest dreamers never imagined such a thing; they lobbied instead for an improved steamship service from Victoria, although some dared to imagine a railway might one day reach the coast. The potential of the area fired many fertile imaginations. Hailed as a territory bursting with resources, fit for exploitation and development of all types, it inspired much hyperbole. "According to published accounts the West Coast lands teem with riches in the shape of gold, copper, coal, iron and other metals, whilst the fertile lands add to its value," Victoria doctor J.S. Helmcken wrote in a letter to the editor of the *Victoria Daily Colonist* on May 24, 1899.

The *Colonist* never flagged in reporting hopeful mining schemes, happily noting every glimpse of quartz, copper, gold or silver. Its writers commented approvingly on the movements of prospectors, the growing fishing industry supplying small coastal canneries, the small-scale logging and sawmills opening

By the end of the nineteenth century, the steamers *Willapa* (shown here with her crew and passengers) and *Queen City* were sharing the west coast route. *Willapa* continued on the route only until 1902. From 1903, the steamer *Tees* regularly served the west coast, along with *Queen City*.

up. Movements of the sealing ships, the departures and arrivals of the coastal steamers and detailed lists of passengers travelling up the coast appeared in the newspaper year after year. No event was ever too small to report. The celebrations held at Clayoquot on Queen Victoria's eightieth birthday in 1899 received detailed coverage that included everything from the canoe races to the segregated foot races for whites and Indians, the sack races, the "whites versus Indians" tug-of-war and the evening dance at the Clayoquot store "for the whites," which concluded with everyone singing the national anthem.

In the winter of 1899, most of the goods for Stockham and Dawley's stores travelled on board the Canadian Pacific Navigation Company's *Queen City*. This staunch little steamer called twice a month at scattered communities between Victoria and Nootka, and once a month extended her run to settlements farther north. On the coast only since December 1898, the 116-foot-long *Queen City*, able to accommodate up to a hundred passengers and three hundred tons of freight, was a marked improvement over the older, more cramped steamers *Maude* and *Willapa*. With her electric lights shining through the dark and the rain of winter, *Queen City* was a welcome sight, a valued contact with the outside world whenever she appeared at remote locations. The *Colonist* hailed her arrival on the coastal run on December 9, 1898, as a positive sign of things to come:

> Interest in the development of the numerous industries of the West Coast is being manifested now among shipping men as it never was before…at Clayoquot—in fact all along the Coast—new mining properties are opening up…Five years ago the principal trade done was with the sealers, and there was no farming, canning or mining along the West Coast. The change has brought a marked improvement in the transportation facilities.

Up at Ahousat, Fred Thornberg found little to please him in all this talk of increased activity. Even the improving steamship service met with no approval because, from his point of view, the steamers were little more than unpredictable beasts that often made his life miserable. Due to the perils of travel on the exposed and storm-wracked coast, the steamer schedule was highly erratic, and Thornberg took personal umbrage when the steamer arrived, as it often did, in the middle of the night or during a deluge of rain. No matter what the weather or the hour, whenever the steamer arrived and sounded its whistle, Thornberg was obliged to paddle out into the harbour of Ahousat to unload goods from the steamer into his canoe and to load his outgoing freight onto the steamer. Because there was no dock at Ahousat, this process was extremely laborious. Often Thornberg had to leave newly arrived goods in a freight canoe overnight, at anchor and covered with a tarpaulin, to be taken ashore the following day. Time and again this awkward handling of freight led to calamity and left Thornberg compiling aggrieved lists to send to Dawley. "1 Box Macaroni total damaged, 1 50# box Muscatel Raisins total damaged, ⅓ of C [case] of Tea damaged, all of the foregoing damaged by salt Water…" began one such doleful litany.

Receiving or sending goods by the sealing schooners going up and down the coast was another option, but it was even more chancy than the steamers. The schooners kept to no schedule at all; they came and went at the whim of their captains and owners and in pursuit of their own interests. Walter Dawley strongly favoured using the sealing schooners to transport goods, for the captains sometimes obliged him by providing a free service. In Fred Thornberg's jaundiced opinion, it made little difference who carried freight up and down the coast or whether or not it travelled for free. He knew only one thing was certain: when it came to handling the freight, a great deal of gruellingly hard work was guaranteed, and far too often he had to do it all by himself.

January 12, 1899

Mr Dawley
St arrived here at dark to night & blowing a gale & raining = could not land goods to night but will do so in the morning = you sent me to menny Boston Pilots 15 Boxes so the Bill sais = the Potlash [potlatch] is over but eaven if the had come last trip of St I could not have sold half of them... after this trade will be very small until the sch comes for sealing.

On this occasion, the steamer arrived late at Ahousat, in foul weather and at night, so Thornberg did not manage to paddle the cargo safely ashore. It remained overnight in his dugout canoe. To make matters worse, when he examined the freight, he found too many boxes of pilot biscuits and far too much fruit. "<u>I dont want enny Fruit pr next St</u>," he declared testily, with his characteristic underlinings and abbreviations, adding, "if you send Apples = I shal reaturn them no sale for them here." Thornberg was particularly annoyed about these apples, for he had ordered them much earlier from Dawley, but they did not arrive in time for the potlatch.

Canoe loaded with goods, alongside *Queen City*.

Potlatches, the lengthy and lavish ceremonies so central to the native culture on the coast, traditionally brought large numbers of people together for feasting and sharing. The host of a potlatch spent money abundantly on gifts of food, clothing and household goods to be given away to invited guests from far and wide. Storekeepers could rely on making ample profits from potlatches, and Fred Thornberg knew exactly what to order for his store in advance: popular items included print fabric and ribbon, blankets and shawls, raisins and rice, soup plates and washtubs, biscuits and, very importantly, apples. But this time the apples were late, the four-day potlatch at Ahousat was over and all the visitors had dispersed back to their home villages. No one was at Ahousat to buy the excess apples.

To add to his gloom, Thornberg knew that trade would now be slow until the seal-hunting season opened in the spring. The dreary days of winter stretched ahead, and he was completely out of sorts. Cheerlessly, he passed on the bad news that the recent potlatch brought the store far less money than expected: "as for the Potlatch Cashe from the Ahouset was about $200.00 = most of the Indians here are dead broak = wants goods on trust I wont give trust = so the trade is not much = about $30.00 a Day for 4 dayes."

To Thornberg's disgust, he faced a lot of particularly hard work in January 1899, repeatedly having to load heavy sacks of ore, totalling a ton or more at a time, onto the steamer from his freight canoe. Shipping ore was a regular headache for him, thanks to the buoyantly optimistic prospector James W. Jones, who was busily working a mining claim up in Sydney Inlet—a green, silent arm of water, flanked by steep mountains, a few miles northwest of Ahousat. Enthusiastically convinced that when he and his partner found the right investors, a large and prosperous mine would open at Sydney Inlet, Jones regularly shipped quantities of ore to Victoria and from there to smelters at Everett or Tacoma, in Washington. Jones brought the ore from Sydney Inlet to Ahousat by canoe, anchored it in the harbour to await the next steamer and then headed back to the inlet, leaving Fred Thornberg to load the ore onto the steamer. Never pleased about handling this heavy and unwieldy stuff, Thornberg referred to it glumly as "Jones Oare."

"It was freezing very hard here last night and so to night," commented Thornberg in a hurried note to Dawley on January 2, 1899, marked "Late at Night." "By tomorrow I expect the Harbour frozen over = if so I can't ship the Oil and Jones Oare." Despite this, Fred somehow managed to get the ore out on the next steamer, and its safe arrival was duly noted in the *Colonist* on January 7, 1899: "Steamer Queen City returned from Ahousett and intermediate West

Coast points Thurs night, bringing as freight a ton of ore from Ahousett." A less successful performance with another shipment of Jones's ore occurred later that same month:

> This afternoon I launch the large Canoe and put Jones Oar in the Canoe = could not thake the Oil = to much ice on the Bay if it dos not friese to night and if the St comes to morrow it will be alright as we can break the Ice yet, and get to the St = it is open Water yet, where the St stops but if it freases to night hard I expect I will have to leave the Canoe with the Oare in it frozen up in the Ice and it will have to stay there.

No "Oare" left Ahousat this time. The laden canoe sat frozen in Ahousat Harbour until the weather warmed up. The oil mentioned by Thornberg also went out later.

This dogfish oil was a highly saleable commodity, frequently shipped to Walter Dawley from Ahousat and Nootka and then sent on to dealers in Victoria. The demand was steady, for dogfish oil was needed as an industrial lubricant and for lighting; in the coal mines of Nanaimo and elsewhere on Vancouver Island, the open-flame pit lamps all burned dogfish oil. A clear oil, extracted by pressure and heat, it was an important trade item on the coast for over fifty years. The Indians extracted the oil, usually gathering it in one-gallon tins, and sold or traded it to the storekeepers and the sealing captains. Prices fluctuated: Dawley's correspondence reveals prices from twenty-five to forty cents a gallon.

Fred Thornberg was only too familiar with storing and shipping dogfish oil and wrote of it often. The usual practice was to collect it in forty-gallon wooden barrels and ship as many as fifteen or more barrels at a time. Hoisting these barrels into dugout canoes and paddling them out to await the steamers was an unwelcome exercise, fraught with peril in the dark of winter and downright dangerous in the heat of summer.

> August 6, 1899
>
> Mr. Dawley: I would be pleased to know at what Date of the Month can I be sure of St calling at Ahouset…ones a Month would be fare preferable, than to be foolet like I have bean several times = I was working on the canoe, and was about half finisht = but had to launch her as 5 Brls of Oil had to goe up = and as the Oil is heavy, have to get it loadet in Canoe the Day before St arives here, no St came = so now it has put me back not alone in fixing up and painting the Canoe = but

> I expect that my work is ruint on the Canoe = paint not perfectly dry under the Copper that I am fixing the Canoe with, have to keep her half full of Water or ells the Barls will burst in this hot Weather.

On this day, no steamer came, the barrels of oil nearly burst in the heat, and the paint job on the canoe was almost certainly ruined.

Sometimes Thornberg tried a different tactic, rafting the barrels together and floating them out to the steamer. "On Sept 3rd I had 15 Brlls in the Raft," he wrote, "it was a very dark Night when I took them to St = 3 got out of the Raft and I could not find them again that night = I thought it was 3 of the largest Brlls that had got a drift…but in the morning I found it was 2 large & 1 smll." Keen to inform Walter Dawley that the loss of these particular barrels was entirely his responsibility, Thornberg pointed out: "It is too risky to raft Oil at Night & dark but you sent word…to ship to night = and that is risky = Barlls often slip under Booms." The letter ends with the emphatic instruction "Order 20 emty oil Barls."

No white trader had lived longer on the west coast of Vancouver Island than Fred Thornberg or was more colourful a character. Erratic and contrary, he first arrived in the sound in 1874 to work as a fur trader and to run the original store and trading post at Clayoquot on Stubbs Island. "I Fred Thornberg," he wrote in his memoirs, "took charge of Clayoquot Station in 1874 buying furs, Seal and Dogfish Oil…" Originally from Denmark, Thornberg found himself the only white man for many miles around, doing business every day with native people, whom he continually feared would kill him. "I traded through a hole in the End of the Building," he wrote, "two Indians could just stand and look in." Thornberg had a reputation for keeping a loaded rifle by his side at all times, and his shrill distrust of almost everyone became legendary on the coast.

Married to an Ahousat woman named Lucy, Thornberg eventually left Clayoquot in 1889 to live at Ahousat with his family. Lucy bore him six children in all; the youngest, Freddie Junior, was born in 1900. Yet even though his wife was Ahousat, although he spoke the local language fluently and his children were half-Indian, Thornberg neither trusted nor liked the Ahousats. He lived amongst them in an atmosphere of continual conflict and confrontation, convinced that everyone in the village was against him, even plotting to murder him. He wrote to Dawley on April 10, 1899, declaring, "I expect it wont be long before this Divels of Ahouset Indians will have me and Children poisened." He accused the Ahousats of sprinkling blood contaminated with tuberculosis on his door handles and in his water barrels, "so that in opening the Dore a person could hardly help it but he would get some of the Blod on his Hands and in that way swallow some of the poisoned blod and catch the disease." Several days later, Thornberg wrote that he had been very sick: "The Ind nearly got the best of me this time = I must have swalowed some of that poisent Blood." Alongside such persistent fears and mistrust, Thornberg clung obsessively to the idea that Ahousat people planned to rob his house and store: "Have you enny strong <u>Iron dore bolts</u> in stock if so send me 2 as I want them for the Dores in the Store, the must be at least 8 inch long." The Ahousats cordially disliked Thornberg in return, to the point of lodging official complaints about his presence as a trader on their reserve land. Instead of being driven away by this atmosphere of dissension, Thornberg stubbornly remained at Ahousat for well over twenty years, although in the early 1900s he did move off reserve land, relocating across the inlet, away from the main village site.

Back in 1874, in his early days as a fur trader at the Clayoquot trading post, Fred Thornberg met Father Augustin Brabant for the first time. A large, powerful man, possessing overwhelming energy and confidence, Brabant was a Roman Catholic priest born and educated in Belgium. Driven by the unshakeable conviction that he must work as a missionary amongst the native people of the region, Father Brabant possessed the ego as well as the physical strength essential for this self-imposed challenge.

"We left Victoria on Whitsunday at 8 in the morning on the schooner Surprise," Brabant wrote in his diary on April 12, 1874, on his first trip up the coast. Travelling in the company of Bishop Charles Seghers of Victoria, he was searching for a site to establish a permanent Roman Catholic mission. This was to be the first permanent Christian mission of any kind on Vancouver Island's west coast.

Neither Brabant nor Seghers knew much about the territory ahead of them: it was a vast *terra incognita*, a pagan expanse on the extreme western edge of North America. They did know, however, that they were not the first ambitious outsiders to arrive here. Other parties, with commercial rather than religious interests, preceded them, and from the outset their priestly mission had close connections with these others. Their mode of transport on that first trip makes this clear, for they were aboard *Surprise*, the sealing schooner that, six years earlier, had been the first vessel to take native hunters and their canoes offshore. Father

Brabant arrived on the coast just as the sealing industry began a rapid acceleration. His presence at such a time fits into a widespread pattern: all over the colonized world, missionaries appeared on the map in conjunction with, or shortly after, traders. Time and again, exploitation of natural resources was accompanied by attempts to convert native peoples to a new religion.

In September 1874, five months after their initial voyage, Father Brabant and Bishop Seghers returned on their second mission-scouting expedition. This time they travelled aboard *Surprise* as far as Ucluelet, then transferred into a sealing canoe and set out for Clayoquot. "Now we were on the open ocean in a small sealing canoe with two Kyuquot and one Ehattisat Indian," Brabant wrote later. "The sea was heavy and no wind. An occasional wave broke over our bows and did considerable damage to our stock of provisions, especially to our biscuits and our sack of flour."

It was on this trip that Brabant and Seghers sought out Fred Thornberg, who was at Clayoquot, and passed a night in his home. "He was a Dane," wrote Brabant, "and had taken an Indian woman for a wife. Together they made us most comfortable." By stages, and in several different boats, the two men continued all the way up to Kyuquot, visiting as many tribes and villages as they could and teaching "the Lord's Prayer, the Hail Mary, the Creed, Ten Commandments and Seven Sacraments in their own language."

On their return voyage down the coast, the priest and the bishop stopped at Hesquiat for a repeat visit. "We found the chief's house, where we stayed for four days, cleanly swept out, and mats laid all over the floor, and the Indians full of joy to see us again." According to Brabant, this warm welcome determined the outcome of their search for a future mission: "It struck the Bishop that this tribe would be a good place to start a Mission, being the most central and the Indians of the best good-will." Having made their proposal to the Hesquiat chief, Brabant wrote, "We were informed, in the presence of the whole tribe, that land would be given for Mission buildings…that we could have our choice as to locality." Over the following months, plans progressed quickly to build a substantial church, measuring sixty feet by twenty-six feet, and a house for the priest. Less than a year later, in July 1875, the first Mass was said in the new church, dedicated to St. Antonine, and Father Brabant took up residence in the village. "I was left alone," he wrote, "…in charge of all the Indians from Pachina to Cape Cook."

For more than three decades, Father Brabant remained on the west coast, never hesitating to assert his authority and impose his formidable will on the native people. He regarded the Hesquiats in particular as "his" people, and in his missionizing zeal he outfaced all opposition and feared no enemies. In 1876 he was attacked and seriously wounded at Hesquiat by Chief Matlahaw, at least in part because Matlahaw was crazed and terrified by the smallpox running rampant along the coast, claiming many victims. He shot Brabant twice, seriously wounding him, and disappeared into the forest, where he was later found dead.

Fred Thornberg achieved local notoriety for flatly refusing to go to Brabant's rescue. Convincing himself that the priest was already dead, and fearing for his own safety, Thornberg dismissed the Hesquiat men who came to the Clayoquot trading post and asked him to come and help. Magnanimously, he provided twelve yards of white cotton for the men to take back to Hesquiat to wrap Brabant's corpse. "The Priest and me the writer," stated Thornberg in his memoirs, "several times had a good hearty laugh about the 12 yards of cotten I sent by the Indians for a shroud for the death [dead] Priest & now he was OK talking and laughing with me. But he said the same piece of cotten came later on very handy & usefull to him—he cut it up in propper length and uset the pieces for dish cloths."

Once recovered from his injuries, Father Brabant continued at Hesquiat, his fervour to establish his mission undiminished. He remained there, a massive and dominant presence, determined to change an entire way of life, to convert a people he considered brute savages to the one true religion, which he believed he represented, and he did so with the absolute, unswerving conviction that God was on his side.

In his memoirs, Fred Thornberg claimed that in their early years, he and Father Brabant were the only two white men living on the coast north of Clayoquot. Over time, the Danish fur trader and the Belgian priest developed a strong personal bond, helped by the fact that Thornberg was Catholic.

Thornberg and Brabant both arrived on the coast nearly two decades before Walter Dawley and Thomas Stockham and well in advance of other early settlers. By the end of the nineteenth century they had overseen and witnessed immense social and economic changes in the area, and they had also seen the coming of many previously unimaginable services. Coastal steamers now came by twice, sometimes more often, each month; schooners called in regularly; mail delivery extended to Clayoquot; and, amazingly, stores on the coast now carried a good array of merchandise and were within comparatively easy range. In his earliest days in Hesquiat, Brabant claimed that five or six months could pass without his receiving news of the outside world, or without seeing another white man. By the turn of the century, all of that had changed forever.

In 1899, William Netherby became the storekeeper at Stockham and Dawley's Nootka store. A good correspondent and sharp-witted in his dealings with the sealing schooner captains, Netherby was highly organized, a great contrast to the distracted Fred Thornberg at Ahousat. "Well I did a pretty good business while the schrs were in & have now some $400 on hand," he wrote on July 8, 1899. "Will ship on this boat 126 gals oil…I have only 1 more empty barrel so you had better send some more & for the Lord's sake don't send such ones as was sent last time they nearly all leak."

At first Netherby seemed the ideal employee, but as the months passed during his first year at Nootka, he began to show signs of discontent. "What did you want to send any more flour for," he snapped at Dawley. "I have enough to last for about 2 yrs now they are not buying much flour at present." By December 26, Netherby no longer even pretended to enjoy the life of the storekeeper at Nootka, writing: "I cant stand the pressure of this place…there is not enough in it for one thing & another thing is that I am not cut out for a treader I have not the patience that is necessary to have to trade with Siwashes." Mindful of the winter potlatch season coming up, Netherby dutifully added a postscript to this letter of resignation: "Don't fail to send Shawls & Print & wht ctn." He had purposely kept the price of print cotton up during his time at Nootka, knowing, as he said to Dawley, "The potlatch season always takes that."

The generous spirit of potlatch season never rubbed off on the storekeepers on the coast. They gave nothing away, holding prices high for potlatches and sometimes trying to sell inferior products or outdated merchandise just to be rid of it. As a result, potlatches usually yielded generous profits. "I expect a potlatch will be held tomorrow so will take in some money I hope. Everything is OK & am getting on fine with the Natives," William Netherby wrote confidently in his early days at Nootka.

The Canadian government banned potlatches in 1884, decrying them as pagan events encouraging immorality and wastefulness, but periodic attempts to enforce this ban proved largely ineffectual on the west coast, at least during the late nineteenth century. The Indian Agent, Harry Guillod, was keenly aware of this. By law, he should have been enforcing the ban, but in his annual reports during the 1880s and 1890s, he seems half-hearted in his efforts. In 1885, Guillod told of a memorable encounter at Nootka with the renowned Chief Maquinna and other coastal chiefs, all gathered to discuss the potlatch. "Moquina, the chief of the Moo-a-chaht or Nootka tribe, who also claims headship over the Ehattisahts, brought out his mask and paraphernalia used at potlaches, and made a long speech." Among many salient points raised by Maquinna in this speech was his insistence that the potlatch was "an incentive to industry, a great help to the white man's trade."

Guillod knew this point was unarguable. In his 1885 report, he described the nature and volume of goods given away at potlatches, telling of vast numbers of blankets, bolts of fabric and beads being distributed, and he concluded, "No doubt there is some waste at these meetings, where a canoe full of cooked rice and several sacks of sugar, or six or eight boxes of biscuits are distributed, but the poorer Indians reap some benefit from it, and all carry away what they cannot eat."

From the point of view of the storekeepers, some potlatches were better than others. The Ahousat potlatch in January 1899 disappointed Fred Thornberg, but he wasted no time trying to understand why the returns were so poor, commenting only that "most of the Indians here are dead broke." In his 1898 annual report, Harry Guillod agreed, remarking that young men in his area were making less money than they did previously because sealing seemed to be in decline: "The fact of there being less money earned affects the old and sick most, as friends are not so able to help, and there are not so many potlaches and feasts given." The *Victoria Daily Colonist* concurred, reporting in an article on January 16, 1898, that sealing had fallen on "evil days" and, six months later, in July 1898, commenting on the "now declining industry."

Yet despite such doom-laden comments, catches improved the following year, to the point that on January 1, 1900, the *Colonist* greeted the new century with the comment: "Sealers have great success. Fair catch and good prices give renewed life to industry." In the ensuing years, the sealing trade lurched erratically onward, its future the topic of avid speculation amid growing apprehension about its much-feared demise.

In his store at Ahousat in the winter of 1899, Fred Thornberg never doubted the future of the sealing industry. He awaited the return of the sealing schooners with the same confidence he awaited the springtime. In all his years on the coast, the sealing schooners had arrived every spring in search of native crews and supplies, and they surely always would. To Thornberg they were an entirely reliable phenomenon, as certain as the pilchard runs or the herring spawns on the coast.

So Thornberg drifted away from the subject of the unprofitable potlatch in his correspondence with Walter Dawley, instead focusing his attention on the crafty details of daily business. Gleefully, he reported success in selling salt-water-damaged raisins, charging five or ten cents for undisclosed amounts: "I wrote to you that one Box Raisins was total damaged...I turnet the wet side down and...I opened the box at the other end (top) and found that I could sell some of them = I sold half of them the other half I had to throw away." Thornberg also thought up an excellent scheme to help sell flour. "I want a tin Flour sifter," he announced. "Mice get in the Store some time and dirty a sck of Flour = I have nothing to clear the Flour with sometime I have had to throw out of Dor a whole pan of Flour full of Mice dirt but if I had a sifter I could easy clean it & put it back in sck."

Sifter or no sifter, the mice at the Ahousat store persisted. They liked flour. Some time later, William Netherby replaced Thornberg at the Ahousat store, only to be equally plagued by mouse droppings. "Send two cats," he wrote testily, "mice in the flour."

WM. MUNSIE, PRESIDENT. CAPT. WM. GRANT, MANAGING DIRECTOR. RICHARD HALL, TREASURER.

The Victoria Sealing Company, Limited.

ADDRESS COMMUNICATIONS TO
F. ELWORTHY, SECRETARY.

OFFICE: BOARD OF TRADE BUILDING,

VICTORIA, B.C.

Mess. Stockham & Dawley
 Clayoquot

Jan 11/01

Dear Sir

This will be handed to you by Captain D. McPhee of the schooner Eva. Kindly advance him what

— 2 —

A Hot Time in Ahousat

Victoria December 8, 1898

Dear Mr Dawley:
Captain Haan of the schooner Victoria and I have been talking about going to Clayoquot or Ahouset if we feel sure of getting Indian crews for our vessels at 3.00 per skin the same price as I paid this year…Please let me know which vessel the Dora Sieward or the Ida Etta had the best Indian crew out of Ahousett this year. And which vessel had the best crew out of Clayoquot…No doubt the Carrie CW would go to Ucluelet if the Umbrina would go to Clayoquot but I suppose it would be easier to get the Ahousett Indians at 3.00 per skin per Canoe than it would be the Clayoquot Indians…

yours etc.,
JW Peppett

THE HUSTLE, ANXIETY and backroom dealing so integral to the business of sealing permeate Walter Dawley's files through the late 1890s and early 1900s. Letters arrived for him on every steamer coming up the coast, crammed with information about the movement of sealing schooners and urgently requiring information about crews. He heard from the schooner captains, the owners

Opposite:
Sealing schooner *Favorite* around 1901.

of the vessels, the insurance companies, the brokerage firms and the commission merchants, all of them edgy about who was getting the best hunters and the best deals, what the hunters were doing, who was trying to influence them, who was purchasing which sealing schooner and where they were going.

Dawley knew all the answers and dispensed information as he saw fit, generally in return for the lucrative business of outfitting the sealing schooners. He would provide the food, harpoons, guns, ammunition, coal oil, lanterns, rope, oilskins and all the gear necessary for the long sea voyages. For a commission, he would also find crews of native hunters, and at the end of the season he would issue their pay, guaranteeing their trade in his store.

> February 10, 1899
>
> Gents! I have secured 13 canoes try and secure me Kelsamat Jack to go at once on the coast with us, get him somehow but get him—send word pr steamer—clinch him with an advance.
>
> In haste yours etc,
> Sieward

The intensity of the phrase "get him somehow but get him" is echoed in letter after letter from the sealing captains. The captains were out to "sign" the best hunters by whatever means they could, fair or foul. "I am afraid that with 3 schooners…there will be a hot time in Ahousat," Captain Sieward confided in a letter explaining that he did not plan to compete for hunters at Ahousat in the upcoming season. "I have concluded to go to Neuchatlitz where I am to get 15 canoes."

By contrast, Captain Peppett seemed untroubled by the prospect of confrontation with other captains that season. "I had about made up my mind to place the Umbrina in Clayoquot rather than Ahousett," he wrote in November 1899, "and compete for hunters against Capt Campbell in the E. B. Marvin and Capt Gosse in the Otto knowing full well that three crews of fairly good hunters cannot be got there." Although he was prepared to compete with two other captains for Clayoquot crews, by which he meant men from Opitsat, Peppett decided to head for Ahousat after all. "I would like to get Jimmy Jim as Boss and I will be pleased to give him one of the boats with two men and give him a first class gun to use on the Coast, I have ordered four new first class guns from Montreal. If I am obliged to make a fight for hunters I want to be in the hottest part of the fight."

Judging by the letters to Dawley, the hottest part of the fight for the best hunters was always at Ahousat, although the most able men from every village were snapped up quickly each season. Sealing captains unfamiliar with the coast sometimes made the mistake of hesitating, taking their time in seeking out a crew. "Which Indians are the best hunters the Ahousetts or the Clayoquots?" one asked tentatively in December 1898. The more experienced and wily captains knew exactly what and who they wanted, although they did their best to outwit their native crews, never letting them feel they were valued, encouraging them to sign poorly understood agreements that obliged them to return, unwillingly, to the same vessel season after season, and tirelessly disputing the amount owed at the end of the season.

The names or nicknames of certain hunters appear regularly in letters to Dawley: Jimmy Jim, Boss Kitla, Bighead, Atleo, Jumbo, Police George, Chief Billy and many others. Even the schooner owners in Victoria, men who stayed in offices and never saw, let alone skinned, a seal, knew these hunters by name and reputation:

> Victoria [undated—early 1899?]
>
> Dear Sirs:
> I want you to send word to Fred to secure Atleo of Ahouset for the Otto without fail. There is now signed on the Otto articles...Jimmie—Jumbo—Bighead—Isaac Bishop—Campbell Willie...But Atleo, Paul, Charlie, Bishop and any other good hunters we are after.
>
> Wm Munsie
>
> PS Give Atleo an advance to hold him of say $25 or $30 untill the schooner goes down.

The influential William Munsie was the head of the Victoria Sealing Company, formed in 1891, which represented most of the sealing schooners based in Victoria. He constantly demanded detailed information from Dawley. On March 20, 1899, he wrote: "Please let me know by return mail just how many canoes each schooner secured out of Clayoquot...also how many hunters there are still left for another vessel providing any other should wish to go there." The letter has a postscript: "Did they get a good crew each or has the best hunters kept back?"

Captain McPhee was one of many sealing captains working for the Victoria Sealing Company, and, like all the others, he had no hesitation in trying to subvert the company. He wrote a personal appeal to Walter Dawley on June 1, 1901, asking for his help and telling him that he wanted two particular schooners, the *Florence M Smith* and the *Triumph*, to be based out of Clayoquot that season.

McPhee added that he had no intention of taking the schooner *Viva* out that season, even though the Victoria Sealing Company wanted him to do so. "I want you to write to me and say that the Indians object to the Viva (of course confidential) and I will make it all right...You will get your share this time if we get in there together. Try to keep the Indians from coming down here." He signed off: "PS This company is no damn good."

Repeatedly, the sealing captains demanded that Dawley intervene on their behalf. "You will tell all the Indians that [illegible] will come next boat...if they [interfere] with my crew you will see hell up there...You will please tell Joe Jim to have his eyes open...I am in a hell of a hurry." This scrawled note, dated May 14, 1900, and signed only DMG, is similar to many others: hasty, peremptory and uneasy. Even William Munsie issued harried, conspiratorial orders to Dawley: "Don't let anybody else in Clayoquot this year," he commanded in a letter of April 29, 1899, meaning that no other schooners should be allowed access to the Clayoquot hunters. Dawley knew it behooved him to pay attention to such demands; men like Munsie could, through their arrangements with the native crews, significantly affect his business.

Victoria February 21, 1899

Mr Dawley:
The schooner Viva sailed for Clayoquot on the 16th hoping she may get out OK. The Otto also sailed for Ucluelet but I fully expect she will have to go to Clayoquot the Ucluelets made good money last

Native girls wearing new shawls. Walter Dawley stocked what he termed "Indian trade shawls," popular giveaway items at potlatches.

A HOT TIME IN AHOUSAT

year consequently are independent. I thought best to continue our arrangements of last year so you can have more control over the Indians by doing all the business through your store.

Wm Munsie

All the storekeepers, whether at Clayoquot, Ahousat or Nootka, engaged in small-scale conspiracies and shifting allegiances with the sealers. Dawley and his employees favoured one schooner one season, another the next; they would share information with one captain but not another. Month by month this could change. The people who never received favours or inside information from the storekeepers were the hunters themselves. "I did not tell the Indians that the sch Otto would come to Ahousat," Fred Thornberg wrote. "I only askt Boss Kitla if he thought that enny of the sealers that was left would be willing to goe sealing with the Clayoquot Indians in the sch Otto = he said = no Look out how you trust Kitla his a/c with me was Dr. $57.50."

Amongst Dawley's papers, a ledger survives from 1898–1900 showing details of trade with some of the hunters. The ledger lists goods sold on credit to men employed on the schooners. Their names, or nicknames, appear along with dates and lists of merchandise. So, for example, on May 26, 1898, Police George totted up a substantial $23.50 worth of merchandise. The priciest items he bought were two ladies' shawls, costing $3.00 each. These were expensive, probably the best quality available. The ones ordered for potlatches at Ahousat at that time cost a mere $1.25. Police George also purchased firecrackers, a penknife and a long list of food. Other names in the ledger include Ucluelet Willie, Jasper, Pretty Charlie, Long Jim, Old Custer, Massa Jack, Fat Jackson and Young Joseph. They purchased everything from buttons to shingles, oranges, shoes, silk handkerchiefs, coal oil, dishes, tobacco, hats, grapes, butter, painkillers, a looking glass, velveteen and oilskins—all on credit against their sealing wages.

At Ahousat, Fred Thornberg kept an equally close eye on the spending habits of the seal hunters. In April 1899 he sent Walter Dawley a list of the accounts of the crew on the sealing schooner *Walter L Rich*. Among others, he named Fat Sam, Little John, Old George, Short Charley, Chips and Jack Dearskin, indicating that their credit was, on average, twenty dollars per man. The man in charge of the crew, Boss Kitla, had a large credit of $63.75. These men were all out sealing, but Thornberg had to deal with

Fred Thornberg's accounts for the Ahousat sealing crew of the schooner *Walter L Rich*, April 1, 1899. Names on the list include Boss Kitla, Kelsemat Tommy, Jack Dearskin, Chips and many others. Crew members were often known only by nicknames.

their wives. The women knew that their men would have money coming to them on their return, and they wanted credit right away, not just at Ahousat but at Stockham and Dawley's store on Stockham Island as well. Thornberg was not happy about this.

"The wifes of the men out sealing may want some goods for part of amt still due = and if you pais or trust them I may be the looser on ac of not knowing what you do at Clayoquot," he wrote plaintively. In truth, he knew full well that the women of Ahousat had every reason for wanting to look elsewhere for their goods. The Ahousat store offered much less choice of merchandise, and the prices were always higher, for Thornberg had no compunction in marking goods up. The coffeepot he ordered in April 1899 is a good example: having paid fifty-eight cents, he sold it for seventy-five. This strategy did not work in his favour, for Thornberg's customers were experienced comparison shoppers. Word spread quickly about price differences between the stores on the coast, and Thornberg lamented bitterly if he suspected Dawley was underselling him or if his Ahousat customers went elsewhere. Stubbornly insisting on selling off his old stock of print fabric, he bemoaned Dawley's cheaper and newer stock: "The Women here are [talking] very much lately = the say you sell good English print that cost 14¢ @ 6 yds for 1.00 other prints that cost 14¢ you sell a 10 yds for 1.00 = the buy very litle Print from me now."

As he worked to establish his mission up at Hesquiat, Father Augustin Brabant gave his wholehearted support to the sealing industry. Such employment accorded with the formal diocesan instructions for the missionary at Hesquiat: "Let him see to it that the Indians themselves shall acquire property and settlement and improve their condition of life, so that with the improvement of their temporal and physical conditions their minds and hearts may be raised to higher and better things hereafter."

Given such instructions, sealing seemed like a godsend. Here was wage-earning employment that allowed the Indians to acquire property and possessions, taking them away from what Brabant decried as their indolent and pagan ways into a world where hard work was rewarded with hard cash. With this cash, the natives could purchase the accoutrements of the Christian civilization the priest promoted so strongly. They could buy stockings and hair ribbons, shawls and shoes and hats, patent medicines and soap, sugar and tea and flour. The men could purchase trousers to cover their naked "lower limbs," deemed so indecent by Brabant that he would not allow a man to enter his home, let alone the church, unless he were wearing pants. This money could also provide furnishings for individual Christian dwellings, for Brabant was determined such homes would replace the communal, and in his eyes sinful, way of life in the traditional longhouse. He envisioned rows of nice little houses at Hesquiat, houses equipped with stoves, tables and chairs, with separate bedrooms, curtains at the windows and possibly even white picket fences. Brabant liked picket fences.

Men from Hesquiat first participated in the offshore sealing industry in 1880. "Two years ago," Brabant wrote in his diary in 1882, "I persuaded the young men to try their luck as fur seal hunters. From the beginning, their success was such that they now seem to be determined to prosecute this lucrative work and leave the dog fish business to the old people." Their first season was highly profitable. Hesquiat hunters brought in nine hundred sealskins, and money poured into the community. As the trade became established, each hunter could hope to earn as much as $500 in a good season. Granted, it was almost impossible for them to arrive home with their earnings intact, for the sealing captains perfected the art of paying out as little cash as possible and keeping their crews indebted: they charged for food eaten on the voyage and they required the hunters to outfit themselves. In addition, the gambling that occurred on board many schooners could drastically reduce the earnings of the hunters. Whenever possible the captains gave credit at the coastal stores and trading posts rather than paying cash, but the hunters' families sometimes used up this credit by the time the men returned from the seal hunt. Some men returned home to find themselves deeper in debt to the storekeeper than when they left.

By 1882, scores of natives from the west coast of Vancouver Island were employed by fourteen Victoria-based schooners for the seal hunt. That year, some of the hunters agreed to participate in a hazardous new venture that would radically transform the industry. Knowing that seals were abundant in the Pribilof Islands in the Bering Sea, at least two Victoria-based captains decided to seek out this distant sealing territory, far beyond their usual offshore grounds. They were the first Canadian sealers to profit from what rapidly developed into a wholesale, multinational slaughter of the huge numbers of seals that converged in this area every year. Japanese, American, Russian and British interests all vied

The view from Opitsat, looking south towards Clayoquot, with the steamer *Queen City* and two sealing schooners, probably around 1905.

for this largesse, and before long most schooners out of Victoria joined in avidly. The seasonal norm for Victoria-based schooners became a spell of offshore coastal hunting relatively close to home, followed by the arduous trip up to the Bering Sea, to arrive just as the seals settled into their island rookeries.

In 1884, Father Brabant noted: "Last June seventy young men went on a sealing expedition to the Bering Sea. They did very well and arrived home highly delighted with the success of their long voyage. They had killed 1400 animals, receiving two dollars per animal." The decade following saw the fur seal industry reach its peak.

The loss of the schooner *Active* hit the sealing community hard. The vessel disappeared while heading to offshore sealing grounds south of Clayoquot in March 1887. Everyone on board perished—twenty-four Kelsemat hunters from Vargas Island and five white men—in one of the worst storms to hit the coast in years. Nineteen widows and forty-two orphans were left behind, and the comparatively small Kelsemat tribe was devastated. Fred Thornberg was then at Clayoquot, and he had arranged for the Kelsemat crew to sign on with the *Active*. "If I had not askt them to goe sealing they would not be drownet & lost," he wrote sadly in his memoirs. As the *Active* set sail, her sister schooner, the *Dolphin*, lay at anchor in front of the Clayoquot trading post. Her crew from Opitsat refused to go out that day because of the bad weather.

"I seen the Cpt & Mates of the two schooner waving ther hats at one another," wrote Thornberg, recalling the departure of the *Active*. When word spread of the loss of the *Active*, the Kelsemats held Thornberg responsible. Two furious men burst into his home, bent on revenge. "I tried to argue with them & not to blame me, but it was no use me talking to them, because they know that I was the one that don all the talk & agreement." Thornberg managed to appease the men by promising that he would arrange with the Indian Agent and the Catholic priest for relief for the families.

The sealing captains feared that native crews would now refuse to go hunting. The *Victoria Daily Colonist* quoted the experienced Captain Peppett on April 16, 1887: "Capt Petit [sic] predicts trouble if the Active has been lost, as the Indians are now so frightened that it is with difficulty they are induced to go out." But such fear, however real, did not endure. The fur seal industry continued to flourish.

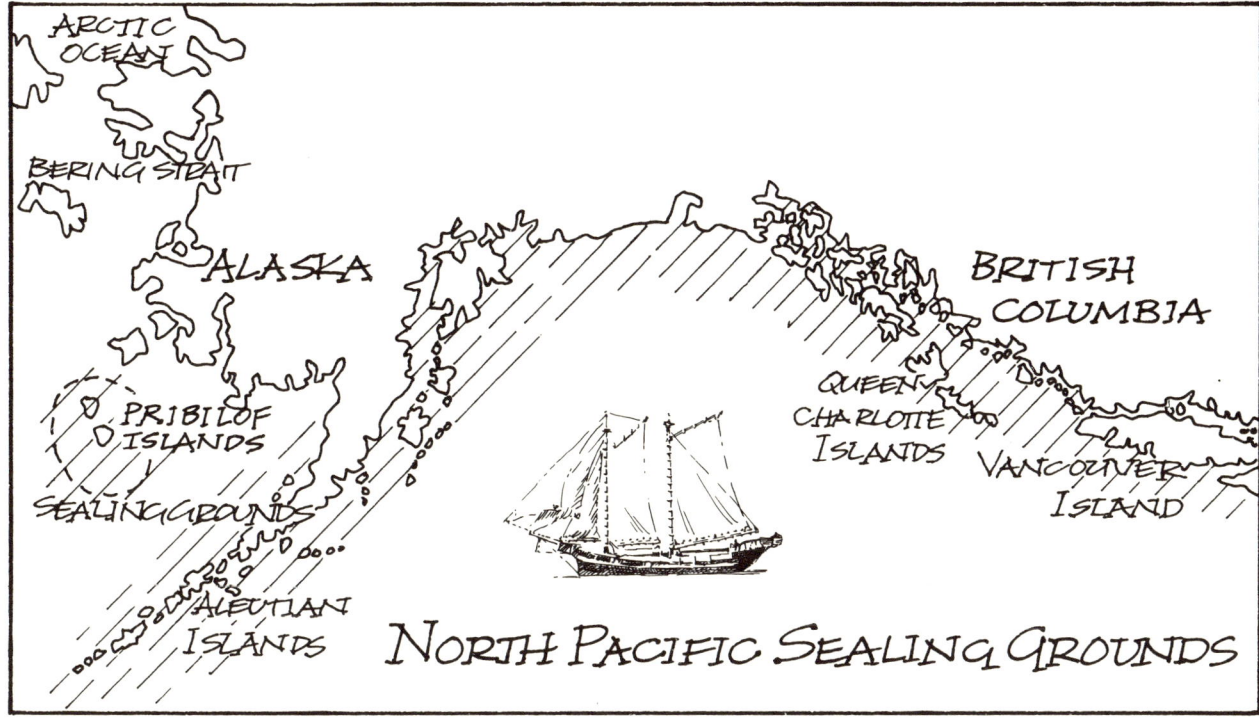

"Two schooners are in the harbor," reported Father Brabant at Hesquiat in March 1893, "...each will take on board about twenty or twenty-four young men, besides their canoes...For each animal they kill they are paid two dollars to the man...They will be back home about the middle of July...The money thus made is used to buy clothes, flour, sugar, etc." This annual exodus of seal hunters from Hesquiat continued to please Brabant. Families were now building their own "Christian dwellings," and in his eyes, Hesquiat was becoming a "nice little village with its white painted cottages and its fine little church."

Within a few years many of these cottages housed an impressive array of consumer durables. According to the *Colonist*, in an article dated October 21, 1899, the amount of personal cargo carried by native people on board the coastal steamers had increased dramatically in recent years, "the Indians having 'hi-you-ictis' [many possessions] these days, acquired in sealing...Organs and other musical instruments are becoming an article of furniture in nearly every house... Sewing machines are also to be seen in almost every West Coast residence."

Father Brabant became a firm ally of the native seal hunters in their business affairs. As the official shipping master at Hesquiat and Nootka, he did battle regularly with the sealing captains, or with any other authorities, demanding that the natives be properly paid and that signed agreements be honoured. "The

Indians cannot go to law about it," he declared in a letter of July 1898, "it would be of no use for no notice would be taken of them. Since the Dominion Government has seen fit...to remind the Indians that they must stick to their contracts, I sincerely hope that steps will be taken to remind owners of sealing vessels to do their duty also."

Infuriated by Brabant's frequent interventions on behalf of the sealing crews, John Goss, who was then storekeeper at Stockham and Dawley's Nootka store, appealed to Dawley at the end of 1898. Following a terse order for milk, apples, pilot bread and flour, he wrote: "Try and have me appointed shipping master for Nootka let us get Brabant out of here he is doing all he can to hurt us so it behoves us to get back at him."

Comments about Father Brabant continued to come Dawley's way from Nootka when William Netherby took over from Goss at the store: "The Schrs have all gone," he wrote, "as you can suppose the [illegible] got 12 canoes and had a hard job to get them, if it had not been for Brabant he would have only got about 8 but Old B. persuaded them to sign."

"Old B" fell in and out of favour with the storekeepers. They were pleased when he encouraged hunters from Hesquiat and Nootka to sign on with the sealing vessels, outraged when he insisted that their contracts be honoured to the letter and the penny. Brabant was massively indifferent to both their anger and their goodwill. These storekeepers and captains were white men, and non-Catholics to boot. He had no particular interest in them.

"A tall, lean man, he always seemed to be under some driving force which kept him on the move continuously. He regarded all Indians between Clayoquot and Nootka Sounds as his own particular responsibility. They feared him too, in his later years." This description of Father Brabant, written by Frank Kelley in 1951, is borne out in every available source. Having been at Hesquiat since 1875, Brabant was a near-legendary presence on the coast by the turn of the century. He had survived the deadly attack by the Hesquiat chief Matlahaw in his early years; had dealt with outbreaks of smallpox by insisting on vaccinating hundreds of Indians; had proven his physical courage and strength of will time and again in various conflicts with "his" Indians, as he called them; and had earned both respect and fear up and down the coast. In matters related to the sealing industry, he was typically implacable and uncompromising. He commanded attention whenever he intervened, and however unpopular the interventions may have been, no one cared—perhaps no one dared—to cross him.

In the heyday of the sealing industry, native hunters came to realize they held a powerful bargaining position: without them the sealing industry out of Victoria would be in grave trouble. They knew they could pick and choose which sealing vessel to go on, quite naturally preferring the larger and better-equipped schooners, the ones with better food, the ones with more amenable captains, the ones on which their wives could accompany them as paddlers or cooks. They also wanted a greater share of the profits and shorter voyages. They learned to play one sealing captain against another, rarely settling for the first offer they received for their services, and frequently changing their minds. "I don't think that sch Victoria would get a Crew from Ahouset," Fred Thornberg wrote in a letter of January 1899. "Jimmy has changed his mind he is trying to get the Libbie."

Some hunters went directly to Victoria to seek the best possible schooner, and there they drove hard bargains with the captain or the owner. For them, this was infinitely better than waiting passively in the villages for the storekeepers to broker deals for them or for the captains to seek them out. Those in charge of the sealing vessels disliked such initiative intensely. If they came across one of the hunters in Victoria seeking a schooner, they did their utmost to send him back to his village.

June 14, 1899

Dear Sirs:
I found 4 Indians here the other day hunting a schooner they said they had 10 canoes. Albert and Joseph Jackson belong to Otto I gave them $24.00 each and signed them before Capt. Lewis = George and Tommy Curly I did likewise with…I had to do this to get them out of the way, they go home tonight on "Willapa."

Wm Munsie

On another occasion, the exasperated Munsie wrote from Victoria: "For heavens sake don't allow Jimmy to come up here as soon as anything is known we will act at once and advise you."

Despite such directives, a growing number of natives chose to travel to Victoria to hunt out the best schooners, and, protest as they might, the sealing company and captains had no power to stop them. More than once, Walter Dawley advised the captains to make the best of it and to hire crews when and where they could. Captain D.G. Macaulay of the schooner *Carrie CW* commented on this on April 7, 1901, in a letter from Victoria. "I am not in favor of signing Siwashes up here at all. But I may have to sign this crowd as all the other

Siwashes from other tribes who are in town now are being signed on their respective vessels."

The *Victoria Daily Colonist* kept a close eye on the sealing schooners. An impressive sight when they massed in the city's Inner Harbour, by the mid-1890s there could be up to sixty or seventy of them there at once. Victoria residents knew these boats and watched them coming and going, and the newspaper reported all of their catches and any adventure or misfortune involving them. On occasion, the crises at sea were all too real, but the newspaper often dramatically overplayed even the slightest hint of disaster.

On March 1, 1904, following a report that a schooner had gone ashore in a gale on the west coast, the *Colonist* was obliged to admit that the vessel had merely touched bottom, only to float off safely at the next high tide. The officers on board the coastal steamer *Queen City*, asked to comment on the perpetual misadventures of the schooners, merely shrugged, saying that the schooners always ran aground and that one had recently been grounded six times on one journey along the coast of Vancouver Island. "Seemingly, according to the Queen City officers, it is a kind of habit the schooners have got into, hitting the Vancouver Island coast here and there, neither the schooners nor the Island seeming to mind it much."

The newspaper noted the movements of the sealing captains as well as their schooners. Often the captains travelled up the coast by steamer in search of a crew, and on February 20, 1904, the *Colonist* reported that *Queen City* was en route to Victoria with "quite a list of passengers, including eight sealing captains who went up to look for Indian crews for the schooners." These captains are identified as McLean, Burns, Pettigrew, Baker, DeLouebray, McKiel, McDougal, Gullin, William Heater, and Macaulay, most of whom at one time or another wrote letters to Walter Dawley, alternately badgering, cajoling and pleading with him to get them good crews for their schooners, preferably at low cost and with exclusive attention, and never mind if this meant betraying or double-crossing every other sealing captain in the game.

Imagine these eight captains aboard the *Queen City* on a dreary February trip down the coast. They would be smoking in the saloon, arguing in the dining room, trying to outwit each other and undercut each other's influence with the native hunters at every port of call. Stuck together for endless hours, they would disembark at Clayoquot, Ahousat, Hesquiat and Nootka to pitch their offers to the hunters, most of whom were fully capable of striking their own deals with the owners of the schooners in Victoria, but who, perhaps, would hear out the captains impassively. The best hunters could decide to go, or not go, on whatever schooner they chose, and they knew it. No matter how the captains pretended that the bargaining power was theirs, the sealing industry out of Victoria ultimately depended on signing up native hunters.

❦

In the end, however, what the sealing industry really depended on was the seals, and on that front the industry had been in trouble for many years. From the killing fields to the boardrooms, alarm bells sounded from the mid-1880s onward about the very nature and existence of this hunt. As the nineteenth century drew to a close, the effect of the massive annual slaughter in the Bering Sea, and the methods used, drew increasingly sharp criticism. For every seven seals shot, some critics said, six sank before the hunters could retrieve them. The decks of the schooners ran with blood and at times flowed with the milk of the nursing mother seals. Tiny pups in the rookeries were left abandoned and condemned to die. Urgent questions arose about the fate of the seal population. Would fur seals become extinct like the doomed sea otter? In the period between 1872 and 1891, nearly a million and a half seals are estimated to have been killed, including the unborn and the abandoned pups. Fisheries inspectors, scientists and politicians all asked how the seal population could possibly survive.

Political arguments about the hunt were equally pressing. The waters of the Bering Sea had become an international battleground of sealers. Every spring the hunters arrived from Canada, the United States, Japan and Russia to vie for furs in these treacherous and foggy waters. Angry jurisdictional disputes flared up. In 1886, American authorities in Alaska, incensed by the number of Canadian sealing schooners working in what they claimed as American waters, seized several Canadian schooners, launching a lengthy political controversy that dragged on for decades. Complex attempts to impose international arbitration or to regulate the hunt were largely ineffectual; diplomats and politicians from all four nations weighed in, repeatedly attempting and failing to reach some kind of accord. The acrimony and the disputes continued year after year as rumours swelled about the imminent, inevitable collapse of the entire industry. Finally, in 1909, negotiations amongst the four sealing nations began in earnest "to protect and preserve the seals" and to establish an international moratorium on the seagoing seal hunt.

Yet despite all the warning signs, despite all the evidence, a stubborn coterie within the sealing industry could not accept that their trade was at risk or that it would ever cease. Throughout the first decade of the twentieth century, as dire predictions about the sealing industry eddied up and down the coast, many sealing captains carried on regardless, writing to Dawley and fretfully demanding the usual information, suspicious of each other and the Indian crews and the sealing company, blindly determined to head up to the Bering Sea. The years ticked by, and as a diminishing number of sealing schooners doggedly continued to head north in search of a disappearing species, their captains' letters became increasingly shrill. These are the anxious missives of men striving to protect themselves from commercial disaster, men willing to make almost any kind of opportunistic deal to ensure their ships are manned and equipped for the sealing season immediately ahead of them, men entirely unwilling to think any further than that.

As owner and captain of the *Umbrina*, Captain J. W. Peppett had for many years relied on Dawley to find him hunters. From 1907 through to 1909, Peppett's letters to Dawley increased noticeably in number and in length, at times arriving on nearly every steamer. Agitated to the point of incoherence, Peppett feverishly pumped Dawley for information: What were the other captains doing? Where were the good hunters? What did Dawley think about hiring white hunters? In a barely rational letter dated February 16, 1908, Peppett pondered which hunters he should try to obtain:

> …as I do not see many good white hunters in sight I thought of taking first class Indian Hunters in the place of White Hunters…You might have a talk with Thompson; Jasper; Yeskin Jack; Chipps; Kilsemat Tom; Robert; Jimmy Jim; Johnson; Philip Johnson & Joe Jim…and I may tke 4 White Hunters and 4 Indian Hunters; there are 8 berths in the hunters room 4 on each side; or I may take 8 Indian Hunters…

After several inconclusive pages of such ramblings, Peppett mustered enough sense to say, "I expect you will get tired reading this letter." Despite all his indecisions and anxieties, Peppett did send the *Umbrina* up to the Bering Sea in 1908 with a native crew, returning with 460 sealskins.

The following season, Peppett again decided to send the *Umbrina* to the northern sealing grounds, this time with Captain J. Searle at the helm. Unfortunately, just before departure, Searle disappeared on an extended drinking spree. Peppett discovered this shortly after he arrived in Victoria aboard the *Tees* from a trip to Clayoquot, and he relayed the sad tale to Dawley in a letter dated June 1, 1909.

> I…went to the Empire Hotel on Johnson Street and found that [Searle] had been drinking since I left the night of the 20th for Clayoquot…[and] has not been since last Thursday seen or heard from…I don't know of anyone that I can get to take charge of the Umbrina…I will make every effort to find Searle and if I think that I will be able to get him sober you will get a telegram from me.

Searle did not sober up in time, so the *Umbrina* did not go sealing in 1909. Captain Peppett sent an embittered letter to Dawley at the end of the year, fed up with the entire business and blaming the native crews for all his misfortunes:

> December 20, 1909
>
> The reason of the very small catches that has been taken the last two years is on account of the large advances being paid to the Indians and the large amount of slops [provisions] being sold to them on the way to Behring Sea so that when they reach there they are so heavily in debt that they don't care whether they get seals or not.

Typical of other sealing captains, Peppett never commented on the root cause of the demise of the sealing industry. The captains rancorously blamed the company, each other or their crews for the hard times facing the industry. Intent on their own problems, never once did any one of them mention the systematic destruction of the fur seal population; never once did any one question his own role in that destruction.

The diehards still persisted in plying their trade, each year fewer than the year before. Thomas Stockham's vessel, the *Thomas Bayard*, made a successful trip to the northern sealing grounds in 1908, returning with over six hundred seal pelts and twenty-eight sea otter pelts. Two crew members were swept overboard on that particular voyage, and an Indian couple from Kyuquot nearly perished when their canoe drifted away from the *Bayard*. They spent twelve days at sea with no water, surviving on a few pilot biscuits and the carcass of a seal, before rescue came. The schooners *Umbrina* and *Dora Sieward* also went up to the Bering Sea in 1908, with native hunters from Ahousat and Clayoquot on board.

The following year the struggling Victoria Sealing Company was on the verge of collapse. Captain George Heater kept Dawley abreast of developments.

> March 1, 1909
>
> Dear Mr. Dawley:
> The Company has had its meeting and have decided not to send schooners out this year. So I have to do the next best thing. I will buy the Vera If you think I can get a crew at $8.00 per skin. The Vera is the best sealer there is and she is in good shape and light to handle on the sea otter ground. She is built of oak and all copper fastened and a very nice little schooner for the inside ground so old friend if you can give me any encouragement I will get her ready will come up next bot [boat] and sign them black devils.
>
> Hoping to hear from you by return mail.
> Geo Heater

For the 1909 season, the Victoria Sealing Company eventually decided to lease five of its schooners to individual sealers, including George Heater, so instead of buying the *Vera*, he chartered her, heading north to Clayoquot in mid-April to sign "them black devils," as he called his crew of hunters. Heater depended on these men for his livelihood; he had worked with them and travelled with them for many years on sealing vessels, yet still he wrote of them as an alien species.

In May 1910, Heater again wrote to Dawley, hoping for the best, hoping for one more season: "I will tell you all about my trubles when I gets up so tell the boys I had a terrible Job to get a schr for them." Later that month, Heater faced defeat:

> Dear old Frend: I am home now & got no ship on the beach I have been to Vancouver and Seattle looking for a Schr but cant find eney thing that will do as yet...so you see I am up aginst it...I would like to have got to Bearing Sea this year or I kno skins is goen to be a good prise But I suppose I will have to com up and dig Clams.

George Heater was spared the ignominy of having to dig clams at Clayoquot, for in 1910, against all odds, he managed to make a highly successful sealing voyage up to the Bering Sea in the schooner *Jessie*. The *Victoria Daily Colonist* of October 14 took due note: "One of the biggest catches made for some seasons by any of the sealing fleet has been made by the sealing schooner Jessie, Captain George Heater…with 878 sealskins, making a total of 1,110 for the season."

Captain Peppett also succeeded in reaching the Bering Sea one final time, in 1910, aboard the *Umbrina*. He died three years later. The *Colonist* eulogized him as one of the best known of the sealing captains, renowned for the ingenious methods he used to coax Indian hunters to sign on to his vessel. On one occasion he took each hunter aside and, as an incentive to join the crew, presented every man with a gold watch, each time taking the watch off his own fob and saying it was his. After a few weeks at sea, all of these watches needed another coat of gold paint.

Long before the seal hunt in the Bering Sea came to a halt, Victoria buzzed with talk of compensation, of how, when the seal hunt closed, those in the industry could claim recompense from the government for their lost livelihood. For years, rumours spread about potentially lavish compensation, and speculators like Thomas Stockham paid close attention, positioning themselves for a different type of kill. Scenting a future profit, he and others began to purchase old sealing schooners.

A depleted fleet of bedraggled sealing schooners soon lay morosely at anchor in Victoria's Inner Harbour, many of the vessels changing hands frequently. Eventually they degenerated into "rotten old hulks…herded up in Victoria harbour for a number of years for the express purpose of claiming compensation," according to one exasperated commentator. An era dragged slowly and painfully towards its inevitable close. Finally, on July 7, 1911, all four nations that had participated in the seal hunt in the much-disputed waters of the Bering Sea signed an international treaty agreeing to a moratorium. The massive, indiscriminate slaughter in the northern sealing grounds had come to an end.

Christie School boys with their band instruments aboard a canoe, probably 1901. Father Brabant returned from his fundraising trip to Europe in 1900 with musical instruments for the school.

~ 3 ~

Kakawis

In the year of our Lord 1900 on May 16th there arrived at Clayoquot on the West Coast of Vancouver Island, B.C. Canada the following Benedictines: Rev. P. Maurus, Rev. Chas. Moser; the Ven. Bros. Leonard and Gabriel, also the Benedictine Sisters: Sr. M. Placide, Sr. M. Frances and Sr. M. Clotilde. We were to take charge of the recently built Christie School, a boarding school for Indian children…

THE OPENING of Christie School at Kakawis on Meares Island in May 1900 was a dream come true for Father Augustin Brabant. He first proposed the idea of a Roman Catholic residential school for Indian children to the bishop in Victoria in the mid-1890s: "a boarding school," he wrote, "is the only means to save the fruits of my labours of more than twenty years."

Brabant believed he must take forceful pre-emptive action in the face of an increasing Protestant presence on the coast. "Their efforts to invade the coast are very pronounced," he wrote in 1895. "A monthly steamer now

41

visits the coast...When a man's life was in danger and when the only means of travelling was an Indian canoe, when the mails reached us only once or twice a year...we were welcome to do alone the work of converting the natives. Now with the present facilities and the absence of danger, the ministers come in sight to give us trouble and pervert our Indian children."

Father Brabant scorned and despised all Protestants, profoundly fearing their influence. Only a school, in his view, would ensure a means to win the hearts and save the souls of young natives, laying claim to them for life and giving the Roman Catholic Church the supremacy on the west coast that he so passionately desired. In 1899 he at last heard from Bishop Alexander Christie in Victoria that the construction of a school could go ahead, with a per capita government grant to finance the education of fifty children. "If we do not accept the grant," warned Bishop Christie unnecessarily, "it will be given to one of the sects; your children will be perverted and you will lose the fruit of all your labours."

Brabant had no intention of letting this happen; the successful establishment of this school became his entire aim. Construction began in the summer of 1899, and by October the school neared completion. An imposing wooden building, shining with white paint, it stood fifty feet up from a sheltered bay on a deeply forested stretch of land at the foot of Lone Cone Mountain on Meares Island. A long and lovely curve of beach lay in front of the school. The place was known to native people as Kakawis, meaning "a place of berries." "The location is an ideal one," wrote Father Maurus Snyder shortly after the school opened, "central from the coast, secluded from the nearest Indian reserve, Opitsat, and the Clayoquot trading post, and well-sheltered from cold winds."

Father Maurus became the first principal of Christie School. Originally from Switzerland, he arrived fired with enthusiasm for missionary work among the Indians because he had read and reread James Fenimore Cooper's *The Last of the Mohicans* at an impressionable age. A less effective preparation for Vancouver Island's west coast can hardly be imagined. His colleagues at Christie School—the brothers, the nuns and Father Charles Moser—knew equally little about the area. When they arrived in May 1900 to take up their new positions at the school, they had no idea what lay ahead. The very idea of being on the sea, at the mercy of wind and weather, was utterly foreign to them.

These were not seafaring folk. They were all from Europe—from landlocked Switzerland and

Christie School in 1900, before any gardens were created. The following year, Father Maurus reported that "the land connected with the school is not cultivated as yet, but with the help of the senior boys [we] succeeded in clearing a few patches this spring for raising vegetables. Some of the boys prepared the place in front of the building for a lawn, and planted it with roses and other flowers."

from Germany. They left their homes prepared to dedicate themselves to mission work among the settlers and Indians of central Oregon, within safe range of their Benedictine headquarters at Mount Angel Abbey, situated on the gentle hill called Mount Angel, which rises above the serene expanse of the Willamette Valley. Little did they know that Bishop Christie, recently arrived in Portland from Victoria, would broker a deal with their Benedictine superiors at Mount Angel and arrange to send a number of their order to a mission field far more adventurous than Oregon. Until they saw it with their own eyes, they could not have dreamed of a location so isolated, so wild, so frighteningly seabound—far from their peers, far from the steadying routines of their monastic life. When they travelled together from Mount Angel to Victoria and there embarked on the *Willapa*, these priests and sisters travelled entirely off the edge of their known universe.

Father Maurus Snyder (left) was the first principal of Christie School, a role he filled from 1900 to 1911. Father Charles Moser (right) was missionary at Opitsat, nearly two miles away from the school. He remained there for ten years before replacing Father Brabant as missionary at Hesquiat.

Father Charles Moser decided to keep a diary from the day of their departure from Victoria:

> The trip from Victoria to Clayoquot was rather a rough one, and seasickness was prevalent on the wooden steamer Willapa of the Can. Pacific Navigation Co…It was early in the morning of the 16th of May when the engine of the steamer stopped…Upon inquiry I was told that the coal bunkers were on fire but also received the injunction not to tell anybody nor to wake up anybody.

None of the other priests or sisters kept a regular diary; their memories of life on the coast can only be gleaned from letters, articles and scraps of memoir. In later years Sister Mary Placide wrote to Father Maurus, recalling their arrival far more acidly than Father Charles: "We left on the old Willapu, or wash tub, for Clayoquot, where we arrived about 11 AM Wednesday, the 16 of May, on the way that morning the steamer took fire."

With characteristic lack of emotion, Father Charles remarked: "The fire was soon under control and the ship continued to Clayoquot where we arrived about 7 AM. By rowboats we and our baggage and freight were transferred from the wharf to Christie School a distance of over 2 sea miles." According to Sister Mary Placide: "We were met at the wharf in Clayoquat by all the white settlers…and all the Indians and canoes of the village."

Father Brabant was not on the dock at Clayoquot to meet the new arrivals, nor did he greet them when they finally reached Christie School. He had left on a fundraising trip that would last several months and was in New York City, about to set sail for Europe. Keen to keep in touch with the school even from such a distance, he wrote to Father Maurus Snyder from New York, expressing his best wishes to all the priests and sisters, and his pleasure to hear of their safe arrival. "I congratulate you…for your courage and sacrifices in venturing so far from your Confratres and Sisters to devote yourselves and spend your lives for the conversion of the poorest of God's poor and the most despised…I am impatient to see you all." He added a warning note: "Like all new beginnings the work will be heavy and perhaps a little discouraging at the start; but I am convinced that with patience and perseverance the school will be a success and a means to save many souls."

Following their arrival at Clayoquot, the newcomers experienced one shock after another. For the first time, Sister Mary Placide fully understood what she must endure to reach Christie School: she had to clamber into a dugout canoe with as much grace and dignity as she could muster, hampered as always by the full, flowing black habit of her order. Before embarking on this final hazardous leg of the journey, she and her fellow sisters stood in an uneasy black huddle, observed from a safe distance by the usual lineup of laconic, tobacco-chewing men who lounged around the Clayoquot store at the far end of the long dock. Travelling by canoe across waters churning with treacherous currents was sufficiently unnerving for the sisters, but on arrival at the long sandy beach in front of Christie School they faced the awkward dilemma of how to disembark. They realized that salt water would soak the hems of their black robes as they made their way through the shallows from canoe to shore unless they received a polite piggyback ride from one of the fathers. Father Maurus later described how, on his first arrival, even he "straddled an Indian brave, thus making the shore without getting his feet wet." On that final segment of the journey over to Christie School, Father Maurus, black-clad and behatted, rode in a freight canoe, sitting bolt upright on a steamer trunk, one of sixteen trunks landed that day at Christie School. He explored his new domain with interest: "Everything was in order; the chapel, classroom, kitchen and dormitories."

Once ashore, Sister Mary Placide and the other sisters had the leisure to look around the large, new, white building that was Christie School. The smell of sawdust and fresh paint filled the air. Many years later, Sister Mary Placide described their arrival in detail in a letter to Father Maurus:

> All we found in the house for dinner was a lot of peeled potatoes, and an immense pan of clams all prepared for cooking, but none of us knew how as we never had seen clams before…and with these two dishes and the immense lunch the good Sisters in Victoria had put up

for us, we gave dinner to 39 that first day, among them Chief Joseph and Queen Mary who arrived to welcome us.

Chief Joseph and Queen Mary were elders of Opitsat, longstanding Catholic converts, and helpful friends to Father Brabant. They became regular visitors to the school, were the best friends the missionary fathers and sisters could have hoped for in the area, and on the inaugural evening, at the feast of clams and potatoes, they were the first Opitsat people to greet the newcomers. Watching the arrival of the sisters provided Chief Joseph and his wife with a novel experience. Black-robed priests were nothing new, but these nuns—their faces framed in tight white bands, their hair hidden beneath a black headdress and their bodies invisible beneath long habits—were unfamiliar creatures.

Roman Catholic priests had been settled in various locations on the coast for a good many years by the time Christie School opened. Following Father Brabant's arrival in 1874, Father Joseph Nicolaye arrived, initially stationed in Barkley Sound and later at Kyuquot. Father Aloysius Stern and, later, Father Emil Sobry came to work at Nootka, and at Opitsat, Father Van Nevel succeeded Father John Lemmens, who later became the bishop in Victoria. By the beginning of the twentieth century, Catholic churches stood at Opitsat, Hesquiat, Ahousat, Nootka and Kyuquot. The largest of the churches was at Hesquiat, the most strongly Catholic of the villages on the coast.

"The school was here," wrote Father Maurus Snyder in an article recollecting his early days on the coast, "but where were the pupils? Children had to be sought after." He wasted no time. Only days after his arrival he was on board the next steamer up the coast, fetching children to the school from the nominally Catholic villages:

> Canvassing parents for children proved no easy task…In many cases the Indians were reluctant in sending their children to school…Their medicine men and Indian doctors and sorcerers spared no pains in discouraging the parents sending the children to school. They even spread evil rumours about the school. They said the boys would have to wear pants all the time. For them pants were an abomination…Also they would have to work and get sick from working…They would be given bread with fine glass and sand mixed up in it to eat.

Despite these warnings, a few parents from Hesquiat and Opitsat agreed to send their children to school. At Kyuquot, "after much pow-wow the chief signed up his two sons Michael and Felix," according to Father Maurus, and a third boy, Leo, also came from Kyuquot. None came from Ahousat, at least not initially. Father Maurus met more resistance at Ahousat than anywhere else. "A burly fellow wanted to shoot me for going on the Ahousat reserve for children for the school," he wrote years later. "I outbluffed him and he did not shoot me."

Classes began May 28, 1900, only twelve days after the priests and sisters arrived. Thirteen children attended on the first day, having first submitted to what Father Maurus termed the "bathing, currying and clothing" process, mandatory for every child. "The Sister matron rang the bell for the girls to assemble. Father Maurus took the boys under his tutorship... The boys looked wide-eyed as Father Maurus spoke a language sounding strange to them."

The first children at the school included Katie Michael, from Hesquiat. Half a century later, in 1950, she wrote to Father Maurus at his request, providing a list of the first group of nine children to arrive at the school. She named Leo Dick, Mick (also called Mike) and Felix Michael from Kyuquot, also Dan Frank, Dionys, Stanish Amoda, William Jones, Nonat John and herself, the only girl. Within days, nine other girls arrived from Opitsat, and following their arrival, Chief Joseph went up to Hesquiat to fetch Jessie and Eustace Andrews. A boy named James and another girl, Eudoxia Charleson, also came then or slightly later. "I do not remember," Sister Mary Placide wrote to Father Maurus, "when Eudoxia came to school, they had her in hiding when you called at Hesquiat."

Harry Guillod, the local Indian Agent, also compiled a list of the first children at the school for his annual report of 1900 to the Department of Indian Affairs, mentioning three boys from Kyuquot, two of whom were sons of the chief; a girl and a boy from Hesquiat; and the rest from Opitsat. The agent saw this as "a good beginning, as it is a new thing to the Indians and they are very loath to part with their children."

The faces of these first children are among those looking out from the earliest photographs taken by the priests at the school. Many group photographs of the children survive, all of them undated. One can guess the approximate dates by the style of the children's clothing, by the age of the priest standing with them, by the structures in the school and how these are described in diaries and letters, but the process is

One of the earliest group photographs of students at Christie School, perhaps taken in 1901.

inexact at best. The identity of the children is even more difficult to determine. Over a hundred years later, the faces of the sombre young girls and boys seem to speak volumes, but they do not speak their own names.

By July 1, 1900, twenty-eight pupils had registered at Christie School, with more coming throughout the year, bringing the official registration in the first year up to forty-four. These children found themselves in an overwhelmingly new world, removed from their parents and villages, hedged in by strict rules, controlled by strangely clad nuns and initially puzzled by strange furnishings and clothing. The oddities were striking, as Sister Mary Placide related in a letter to Father Maurus:

Christie School boys, with Father Maurus in the centre of the second row, date unknown.

> I think I made an effort to teach the children something the day after their arrival, but I don't know whether you would call it school or not, and they were so silly and tickeled over the beds and all the new ideas, we could hardly get them to go to bed the first nights, they would sit on the beds, laugh and talk then get down and look under the beds etc., until poor Sister M. Clotilde was almost beside herself.

The notion of sleeping in beds, so high off the ground, was entirely new to children accustomed to sleeping at ground level; some parents complained to the Indian Agent, fearing their children might fall from these dangerous platforms. Strictly segregated, the girls and boys were never allowed in each other's dormitories and were forbidden to share beds; even same-sex siblings could not sleep together.

Father Maurus described the dormitories in his report to the Department of Indian Affairs, the first of many annual reports submitted every June. The report of 1900 says little about the students, who had been there for only one month at the time, instead describing the school itself, its size, its facilities, even its "charming view of the varied scenery of Clayoquot Sound."

> The building, 40 × 60 frame, is divided into two separate equal parts, one for boys and one for girls. On the first floor are found the parlour, the office, the kitchen, and separate dining-rooms and classrooms for boys and girls… The second floor comprises the chapel, two officers' bedrooms and two dormitories with twelve beds each. In the attic are two more dormitories with thirteen beds each, and two small

bedrooms. The children's bedsteads are all iron, white enamelled, and each bed is furnished with excelsior mattress, two heavy woollen blankets, double sheets, one feather pillow and one white spread. All the rooms are high, airy and well-ventilated; the class-rooms are provided with large windows, admitting a flood of light.

On September 26, 1900, the entire population of Christie School set out in several heavily loaded canoes for a day trip and a picnic at Ahousat, more than eight miles away. The weather was not promising. Father Maurus and Father Charles took charge of the expedition, assisted by Brothers Gabriel and Leonard, none of them familiar with these waters and all of them inexperienced with boats. On board were some thirty children and a visitor, Bishop Orth from Victoria, who perched uneasily in one of the canoes; this trip had been laid on as a special treat for him. In his diary, Father Charles recalled how events unfolded:

> [Father] Maurus with the whole school, Bishop Orth and myself went to Ahousat…for a picknick in our rowboats and canoes. A Mr. Russel, a lay man, was teaching a day school and preaching on Sundays under auspices of the Presbyterian Church. At his invitation we all visited his school and Fr. Maurus had his children sing some songs for the entertainment of Mr. Russel's day scholars.

In 1896 John Russell had opened his day school at Ahousat, swelling the number of Protestant schools in the region to four: besides Russell's school there was a Presbyterian residential school in Alberni, a day school at Ucluelet run by the Methodist preacher Melvin Swartout, and another at Clo-oose in the charge of William Stone.

Sisters and students in a rowboat, perhaps going on a "picknick," date unknown.

Father Brabant observed the opening of these schools with unmitigated horror. If Father Maurus had asked for advice about visiting the school at Ahousat, Brabant would have vetoed the entire expedition. He never gave Protestants the benefit of the doubt, nor did he ever associate with them; the notion was inconceivable. But Brabant was away, still travelling in Europe to raise funds for Christie School. He had recently written a letter to Father Maurus from Lourdes, where, he said, "With tears in my eyes I have prayed—in our own Indian language—for you all and all them committed to our care. Never before had the Blessed Virgin been invoked at this place in the language in which I addressed her." Meanwhile, back at Kakawis, Father Maurus was in charge, optimistically taking everyone on an all-too-memorable "picknick" to Ahousat.

Father Charles recorded in his diary what happened on the return journey to Kakawis:

> At our departure from Ahousat we encountered big breakers and 2 of our boats got swamped and washed back to shore. All occupants of these boats were wet. We almost lost one boat, it being half filled with sand and half buried in sand. After shovelling sand inside and outside the 2 brothers Leonard and Gabriel rode it home, one rowing and the other bailing it, as it was leaking badly. A big Indian canoe was hired to bring the Bishop and others of the incapacitated boat home, where we arrived 9:30 PM.

Arriving at Kakawis late and in the dark, everyone was cold and many were soaked to the skin. It was a thoroughly wretched and hazardous return journey. But worse was to come because, tragically, one child contracted pneumonia on this trip and did not recover. Father Charles explained the circumstances in his diary: "Mike, the son of the Indian Chief of Kyuquot had entered the Christie School in the early part of the summer as a sickly boy. At the swamping of the boat he got wet and from the next day on he was a sick boy. As the days went on he got worse." At 8 AM on October 5, 1900, Mike died. The school had only been open a few months: this was a calamity.

> The first death of a pupil in the school. There was danger that this might wreck the school because the Indians in their superstition were terribly afraid of death or a corpse. Even the name of death was avoided by them. The death of Mike was kept secret and classes went on as usual. The following night coffin and body was moved into a shed on the beach which shed served as a carpenter shop and in the morning of Oct 7 the children were informed of his death. Funeral

services were arranged for 3 PM Oct 8th; children were given the option to take part in the procession or to stay away. For the protection of the school and for moral support white people of Clayoquot were asked to attend and five prominent people responded: Constable Spain, Dr. Rolsten, W. T. Dawley and Mr. Brewster and also Shipping Master Grice.

How the priests felt about having to ask for support from the citizens of Clayoquot, and from non-Catholics, so openly and so soon after their arrival on the coast can only be imagined. But they feared repercussions from the native community at this funeral, so "for the protection of the school and for moral support" they called upon Walter Dawley and other prominent citizens for help. Neither Dawley nor the others failed the priests. They all attended the funeral: Frederick Stanley Spain, the policeman; William Rolston, the doctor; Walter Dawley, the merchant; Harlan Brewster, the owner of Clayoquot Cannery; and John Grice, the shipping master. Three of the men—Grice, Dawley and Rolston—were also Justices of the Peace.

Walter Dawley may not have cared overmuch about the fate of the school or, indeed, about the death of the little boy, but he cared greatly about the future of the Clayoquot area, and he knew that a show of solidarity among white people was important at such a sensitive time. By appearing at Kakawis for the funeral, these local citizens proffered a strong statement of support for the Roman Catholic school and an unmistakable display of white authority.

Father Charles noted: "Most of the children attended the funeral service and accompanied the body to the grave which had been dug in the woods close to the beach on the West side of the school." His diary makes no mention of the little boy's family or his father, the Kyuquot chief Hackla, who "after much pow-wow" only a few months earlier agreed to send two of his boys to Christie School. Perhaps Mike's brother Felix was among the schoolchildren, dressed in their Sunday best, who looked on as the little boy was given a Christian funeral

Boys and brass band in one canoe, girls in the other on a school outing, probably in 1901. Christie School is in the background.

and his body placed in the ground. This was likely the first such ceremony the children had ever witnessed, a ceremony radically and frighteningly different from native rituals surrounding death. Traditionally, bodies were never buried; they were laid in boxes that were placed in specially located trees. In some instances, bodies were placed in burial caves.

Rumours flew up and down the coast about the picnic, the death of Mike and the funeral, eventually coming to the attention of Father Brabant when he returned from Europe. In a letter to Father Maurus on February 18, 1901, as he described a "Nootka boy" he wished to send to Christie School, Brabant harked back to the events of the previous autumn. Many disquieting accounts had reached his ears, and some parents had told him they thought the trip to Ahousat was dangerously ill-judged. "This is I am sure exaggerated," Brabant assured Father Maurus, not very convincingly, continuing with a firm warning against "going out in canoe or boat in dangerous weather—or overloaded… around Clayoquot the currents and sea are very treacherous and therefore I would advice you to give the parents no reasons to complain or to be uneasy—there is no end of talk even now about their experience in Ahousat."

Brabant did not say so directly, but he evidently felt that the new priests at Christie School had not handled Mike's death appropriately:

> First I am asked to tell you that in case any of the children should die, this Nootka boy should not be compelled to kiss the corpse and say "take me along to heaven" as all the children were compelled to do when the Kyuquot lad died—(according to the report of the Ahousats.) Second—in case the boy gets sick you are supposed to send him home as the grand father and father etc think it very wrong to be asked to pay one hundred dollars to have their boy returned as you asked the Kyuquot chief to pay when he proposed to take Felix [his older son] along for safekeeping.

The school learned a sharp lesson from Mike's death. In future, if children were seriously ill and near death, they were sent home. Time and again, Father Charles's diary contains reports of sick children being shipped home to die. Deaths at the school, the priests had learned, were not good for the school.

In his first annual report of June 1900, Father Maurus commented briefly on moral and religious training, saying, "Particular attention is given to this branch of education." An unwaveringly strict eye was kept on moral conduct and on the contact between boys and girls; they were not only in separate dormitories but also in separate classrooms and, in the early years of the school, separate dining rooms. Girls and boys could speak to each other or play together only with permission from the nuns or fathers. The children received daily religious instruction for an hour and attended morning and evening services every day. Many of them were preparing for their first communion; all of them learned church music. They also learned that only a Christian marriage was acceptable to God and that should any of them follow the marriage customs of their native villages, or bear a child outside Christian wedlock, they risked being damned for all eternity to the fires of hell.

Christie School girls, date unknown. As well as learning English, doing lessons and helping with general housework, these girls assisted in preparing meals and learned to sew, mend, knit and do "fancy work."

Concerning the general education of the children, Father Maurus briefly reported at the end of the first year that the girls were gaining a "thorough knowledge of housekeeping," while the boys undertook carpentry, farming and gardening. As for classroom work: "The course of studies outlined by the department is followed as closely as possible under the circumstances. For the present, as all the pupils are new, unable to speak English, attention is given mainly to reading and writing."

The children coming to Christie School had to learn English. "The correct use of English, in clear enunciation, in distinct articulation" was an absolute requirement, as central to the principles of the school as attending chapel. The children had no choice; the school forbade them to speak their native tongue. "Most of the pupils come to the school not knowing a word of English," Father Maurus wrote in an undated memoir, "but in a short time they pick up the English, speaking and understanding the language very well." In the winter of 1901, when Father Maurus was on a fundraising trip to Europe, he left the school in Father Brabant's hands for several months. Brabant wrote to him describing progress in English at the school: "Without boasting I may say that now in all the establishment you do not hear one word of Siwash. At first it was very hard on the boys; there was very little noise in the house…but now they are getting accustomed and speak out like good fellows."

In the early years of the school, the children learned English from nuns and priests for whom English was, without exception, a second language. On festive occasions the children, who were not permitted to say so much as "pass the bread" in their own language, listened politely to folksongs in German. "Sunday evening we had a little programme for the Fathers," wrote one of the girls in a letter to Father Maurus. "After the little programme was over Right Rev Father Abbot played on the piano and Rev Father Henny sang German and Swis songs. We did not understand a word, but all the same we enjoyed it very much."

Commenting on a visit he made to the school in December 1901, when Brabant was in charge, Indian Agent Guillod wrote of "particular attention being paid to the speaking of English, and…the pupils use that language only in their intercourse with each other…The pupils are polite and well mannered and can answer a question in English intelligently." The following year the annual report from the school made sweeping claims for the progress of the students, declaring: "Their mother tongue has been entirely eradicated, and English is spoken by all children in the school." It continued:

> The past year has been characterized by a spirit of devotedness, contentment and cheerfulness on the part of all pupils without exception, beyond the most ardent expectations…especially in the acquisition of the English language…to the Rev AJ Brabant… our most grateful thanks are due, as through his untiring energy and ardent zeal marked progress in English conversation has been made, and a deep filial love implanted in the hearts of the dear little children…We offer him our thanks also for providing the school with a milk cow and calf, and for a neat picket fence which now adorns the front part of the grounds.

After 1905, the use of English at Christie School attracted no further comment in the school's annual reports or in the Indian Agent's reports. The imposition of English was standard practice at all residential schools for native children, and by 1909, eighty-eight such schools existed across Canada. For those in charge of the schools, the mandatory use of English was not a particularly noteworthy issue; it was normal practice, taken entirely for granted. "Violations of the rule not to speak their native language," wrote Father Maurus in one of his final comments on the matter, "have been very rare and insignificant."

For the children, the issue of language was huge. To be removed from home and then not permitted to speak their own language often left them miserably confused and unhappy. Dominic Taylor started at Christie School in 1922, and he recalled those days in an interview for the book *Indian Residential Schools: The Nuu-chah-nulth Experience*: "I couldn't speak a word of English. Didn't know how, year 1922…we were not to speak Indian, anytime, we're in that school. No Indian. Never talk our Indian language! That's where we lost everything! And I learned how to speak English." Maurus Mclean, who arrived at the school in 1925, recollected: "I couldn't understand the English the Benedictine priests and nuns [used] the first day, the first day I went to classroom…My parents and grandparents used to tell me 'some day you will be meeting white people, that society—society of white people. Someday, you'll need that, to learn whiteman's language.'"

Problems posed by the enforced use of English received no open acknowledgement at Christie School. Indeed, few problems were ever acknowledged, at least not in the relentlessly enthusiastic annual reports. "Verdure-clad mountains and mighty veterans of primeval forest afford [the school] cozy shelter against the prevailing winds," Father Maurus rhapsodized in 1901, carrying on to describe the boys' carpentry, the girls' sewing and cooking, and important details such as the "first-class" sewerage, the "crystal water," the football and croquet games, even the planting of roses in the garden enclosed by a white picket fence. The confused incomprehension of many children, adrift in a strange syntax and a stranger environment, had no place in such a report.

The boys in the band, probably 1901. In later years the band expanded. In his annual report of 1903, Father Maurus Snyder wrote: "Music is by no means neglected in our institution. Some of the children are gifted with an extraordinary talent for music…To the band… were added this year piccolo and clarinets."

Following the opening of the school, Father Brabant wrote frequently and at length to Father Maurus. The tone of his letters is often testy, for as much as Brabant longed for Christie School to succeed, he found it difficult to trust these young priests to do their work properly. Yet in many respects, Father Maurus was fortunate to have Father Brabant's advice because Brabant had the huge advantage of experience. Still working at the missions on the coast after nearly three decades, he was fluent in the Indian language, he knew the people in each of the villages, he knew the children and he knew the complex interrelationships between different families and villages. As a result, he was able to provide a great deal of specific information to the new priests.

Initially, Father Maurus peppered the older priest with questions. "With the best will in the world I could not answer all the questions you wish to have explained," Brabant replied, continuing as best he could: "About the totem poles on the coast I know that Maquinna placed one at Clayoquot as a reminder that some of his ancestors came from that locality, and one was placed at Hesquiat by a chief representing an ancestor of his who is supposed to have been the first chief of that tribe." Brabant also answered questions about traditional clothing, about how to form the plural of certain nouns in the Indian language, about adultery—a subject guaranteed to arouse the ire of the priests—and he repeatedly delivered firm, practical advice. "Be sure not to fast during Lent," he wrote. "You need all the nourishment you can take."

Brabant deluged Father Maurus with detailed information about the families of the Indians along the coast. This exchange of coastal gossip had one purpose: to inform Father Maurus about the children who might come to the school, about their families, their social positions and their relationships. Writing from Hesquiat in June 1901, Brabant said:

> If Mr "Swan" comes with his children be sure to take them—his wife's father owned all of Flores Island and the boy is in the regular order of things called to become one of the Ahousat Chiefs! If Jacob comes with his little girl she is a first cousin of Callista and Dan and as she is small she might be put to bed alongside of Callista—she is a very interesting child.

In the case of the boy called Sennen, from Hesquiat, Brabant wrote: "He is the uncle of Eudoxy and the first cousin of your new acquisition Elizabeth—it is safe to let him sometimes have a talk to the two little girls." Then there were "three little fellows" featured in a letter of March 23, 1901:

> I have three little fellows—one is Constant's little boy—Constant is afraid that there will not be any room left for his son and as soon as the weather is warm enough to allow his wife to go along with her infant on a visit to Eudoxie he intends to pay you a visit leaving his young son with you... The other little fellow is called Didacus and as soon as his mother dies Didacus will go to Kakawis. The poor woman... has received the last Sacraments but she does not seem to die as soon as we all expected. The third boy, 8 years, is a Nootka

In the early years at Christie School, Brother Leonard enjoyed hunting and fishing. The older boys at the school assisted and instructed him. Note the watch chains on the boys' waistcoats; such fashions caught on rapidly.

boy and Ubaldus is going on the steamer to take him to Hesquiat… Ubaldus is also trying to get his little niece, 9 years, to go and I think he will succeed—she is an orphan of both parents and so is Paul and when Mary Ann dies Didacus will also be parentless.

Many of the children Brabant sent to the school had lost one or both parents. He did not consider this in any way remarkable; for years he had seen tuberculosis ravaging the native population on the coast, breaking up family groups. In telling Father Maurus about a Hesquiat child called Agnes, Brabant explained that the parents were anxious she be accepted though she was just seven years old: "She is very bright for her age—one of the reasons for the parents sending her at so early an age is because the mother is sick and spits blood from time to time." Repeatedly, Brabant described the health problems of various individuals:

> I am glad that you accepted the boy Sennen. However I am now informed that he has not been very well since last sealing season and if you should notice that he is really sick it will be in order to send him back…He belongs to a sickly family but I always found him to be an exemplary young fellow. He never missed being at church twice every Sunday.

Sennen did not last long at the school. His name surfaces in Harry Guillod's report of 1902: "The majority of the pupils seem strong and healthy. One discharged pupil, Sennat [Sennen], a good Christian lad and promising scholar, died at his father's house at Heshquiat of consumption, but he was not a strong boy when admitted to the school." Guillod was also all too familiar with the prevalence of tuberculosis. In his report of 1899 he commented wearily that "the death-rate for the past year has been exceptionally heavy; as usual, tuberculous diseases prove the most fatal."

Behind Christie School, a field of stumps emerged as the land was cleared. This view is probably from 1904–5.

In Brabant's estimation, the little orphans or semi-orphans of tubercular parents were logical candidates for the school, for he believed them to be defenceless and poorly provided for in the villages. He did not hesitate to employ every possible guile to entice such children to Kakawis. Writing from Nootka in February 1901, he said:

> I met here a little girl…and I was promised that she would come also—she is an orphan of both parents…I bought a pair of shoes, a little print and a woolen hood for her so as to excite the enthusiasm of the children of her tribe…I will try to send her per next boat although her relatives would like to keep her for some time yet as her mother, the sister of Joe the Ehattisat chief, died only a couple of weeks ago.

Two decades later, the same reasoning still applied. Children without parents were often sent to Christie School whether or not they wanted to go. Dominic Taylor recalled this only too well:

> I lost my father in 1922, that's when my father died. I was living with my Grandmother, born 1850. I was gonna grow up with her, my Grandmother. And they came! Like they used to send over to the reserve and pick up the children that…lost their father or mother, you know… And they took me away, Arthur Nicolaye, he was goin' around, sent by the Christie School. Sent up there, and they know, they know where I live with my Grandmother. They went there, they come in… he caught me, he says, "You gotta go Christie School, Kakawis," and he brought me back.

In all his letters to Father Maurus, Father Brabant generally referred to the children only by the Christian names he gave them at the time of their baptism, with little or no indication of the family names or the Indian names of the children. He wrote of them with the ease of familiarity, for he had known most of them, and their parents, all their lives. In one letter he enclosed a dollar from Emily for her sister Agnes at the school, specifying that it is to purchase hair ribbon, and he conveyed to August the message that he had a new little brother who was four days old. Brabant also wrote about a girl—unnamed—who wished to attend Kakawis, identifying her entirely through her family connections: "She is the aunt of Louis but younger than Louis's sister now with you." If this girl was not accepted at the school soon, he feared that "the Methodists will have hold of her."

Christie School laundry. In 1904, Father Maurus reported that "the boys are taught to wash their own clothing; the girls…receive special instruction in all the details of laundrying…without machinery in as far as practical, in order to train the pupils in accordance with their home conditions, after leaving school."

Sister Mary Placide (also called Sister Placida) with some of the girls. The school's reported aim in 1904 was to "prepare each girl to become a practical, all-round, general housekeeper."

Every child he sent to Christie School represented for Brabant a triumph, a soul saved from perdition and, most importantly, from the Protestants. His letters repeatedly reveal the depth of his fear and mistrust of all Protestants. Whether Presbyterian or Methodist, they were all the same to him. In May 1901, writing from Hesquiat, Brabant raged about an upcoming meeting at Christie School. The Roman Catholic bishop from Victoria was due to attend, along with John Russell, the Protestant missionary at Ahousat, and Harry Guillod, the Indian Agent.

> I little thought that the building I was collecting for would be used in its very infancy by a preacher of error and a mercenary of the Government to try and make arrangements whereby a number of poor Indians would be cut off from the ministrations of the Church!…I will not be at that conference—and I notified the Bishop to that effect. If Mr Russell gets admittance into the house I shall take up my hat and walk out of it!

Brabant continued at length, regretting that a number of Indians would witness this meeting, for "when my people see signs of friendship between Catholic Clergymen and sneakish preachers it upsets them and they take scandal."

Harry Guillod picked his way carefully between the sparring Catholics and Protestants, using whatever sources he could for information about the ongoing battles. He wrote to Walter Dawley in September 1901: "There is quite a war going on between Mr Russell & Father Maurus about the Catholics getting

Undeterred by their cumbersome habits, the first sisters at the school learned to enjoy their surroundings. They explored the beaches, handled small boats and even accompanied students on expeditions up Lone Cone Mountain.

Mr Russell's school children for their school, have you heard anything about it?" Whatever Dawley may or may not have heard, he avoided allying himself openly with either the Protestants or the Catholics: after all, why alienate potentially good customers for mere matters of religion?

Purposeful as ever, Father Brabant continued sending children to Kakawis from the Catholic missions up the coast—from Hesquiat, Nootka and Kyuquot—tireless in his efforts to outdo the Protestants. "The Methodists are hunting for children, like madmen, during the fishing season at the Fraser Canneries," he wrote in January 1904, adding that he had enlisted a little girl, aged seven, for the school. "I could not refuse her," he wrote, underlining the words firmly, explaining that this child, a "poor little outcast half-breed," was the half-sister of Paula, who was already at the school. Her mother had died, and her foster father could not look after her. Brabant wrote angrily: "The real father is Mr Hooper, an architect in Victoria, a leader in the Methodist Church who made the plans for the Carnegie Library in Victoria. We may be able to make him pay for the education of the poor child." No one now knows if this allegation of paternity was true or what became of the little girl. A prominent architect, Thomas Hooper designed many significant buildings, including the Metropolitan Methodist Church on Quadra Street in Victoria (now the Victoria Conservatory of Music). Perhaps Father Brabant did vent his wrath on Hooper, demanding money for the support of the child. Perhaps not. As a rule, he never hesitated to impose his forceful morality on others, and if this meant thundering disapproval at a well-known Methodist, he may have relished the challenge.

Remastered from a glass slide used in magic lantern shows, this photograph probably dates from around 1901. Although the sisters travelled short distances by canoe without assistance, surviving accounts indicate that the priests or native students did the paddling for longer canoe trips.

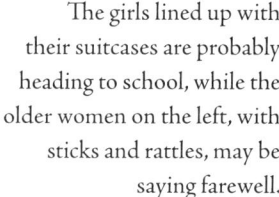

The girls lined up with their suitcases are probably heading to school, while the older women on the left, with sticks and rattles, may be saying farewell.

Occasionally Brabant sent a child to Christie School who was, in his view, of particular significance, like thirteen-year-old Joseph, the first Nootka child ever to attend the school:

> The boy deserves credit for his efforts to get to the school—the opposition of Grandparents, parents and especially distant relatives was something terrible: but the boy conquered them all; and at the date that I write consent of nearest relatives seems to have been obtained…I can say for the boy that I consider him the best here; he is intelligent and of a very kind disposition.

Once Joseph declared he would go to school, his parents, his grandparents and the venerable Chief Maquinna of Nootka all called on Brabant. "[They wished] to enlist my sympathy and ask my services to see that the boy be well cared for." The grandfather even offered Brabant ten dollars to take special care of Joseph. Brabant refused the money. "Be very kind to the boy," he cautioned the priests at the school, "as from his report will depend the getting of candidates from this part of the coast." Later that year, Joseph returned home for vacation with favourable reports, and soon more children from Nootka headed down to Kakawis. Brabant described some of them in a letter dated August 21, 1901:

Christie School girls lined up on the beach. This was their playground. Father Brabant recommended that the sisters lead a regime of daily exercises for the girls on the beach.

Paul is a holy terror full of life and mischief...August is more quiet and very intelligent—he is stronger than he looks...Little Joseph is a hunchback...he will be the pet of the whole establishment...smart and intelligent he is a most lovely little fellow...Mamie is coming but she is very young yet and I am afraid that there may be trouble when the time for leaving comes.

"There may be trouble when the time for leaving comes," Brabant predicted. He was right. Within a few days, little Mamie went away to school. On August 29, 1901, Brabant wrote again: "You have no idea of the distress the mother of Mamie is in since the little girl left. I am sure she would do anything to have her back. But it will wear off." Setting aside this mother's grief, he resolutely continued, "I am promised that the other girl I spoke of, a first cousin of Mamie, will come this fall when her mother returns from Behring Sea—But it is much harder to get girls than boys!"

In his report of 1900, Indian Agent Guillod wrote that parents "are very loath to part with their children." Father Brabant knew this well. He counselled Father Maurus to try to understand the viewpoint of the Indian people. "Rev'd Father, it is terribly hard for the parents to part with their children and you will have to...give them a good chance for visiting them now and then." Brabant advised Father Maurus to provide accommodation for visiting parents, to give long holidays to the children and to allow children of the same family to have special time together at the school. Yet despite such avowedly good intentions, Brabant was able to dismiss the grief of a mother, like the mother of little Mamie in Nootka, with the phrase "But it will wear off..."

Time would prove him wrong. Such sorrows kept coming; they did not wear off readily.

Girls eating herring roe.

Walter T. Dawley

– 4 –

Dear Mr. Dawley

Victoria January 20, 1902

Messrs Stockham & Dawley

Sirs:
I left to your account…$130.00 that is all I can pay on my account at present…Tell Stockham that he sold me a Bogus Clock. I have spent $1.50 on her already for when I went to hang the Pendelum on there was not any thing to for it to hang on to so I had to send her down town and get something put into her and she don't strikes so tell him I am going to bring her back when I come and for him to keep out of my way.

Receiving such a complaint from the aggrieved Captain A. K. St. Clair of the sealing schooner *Allie I Alger* did not worry Walter Dawley overmuch. Even though "she don't strikes," other clocks that did strike sat on the high shelf behind the store counter, and St. Clair's annoyance with Thomas Stockham could be eased with a drink or two. More to the point, the captain revealed in his letter that he hoped to bring his sealing schooner to Clayoquot once again that season, and with any luck he would outfit the ship through Stockham and Dawley. Placating him for the "bogus" clock would probably pay off.

While many of the letters to Dawley are strictly businesslike, dealing with suppliers and freight and orders and bills, a parallel personal world exists amidst all these papers. This is the real heart of his correspondence: the handwritten letters from customers and colleagues, laced with personal comments and asides.

The very ordinariness of the subject matter brings the letter writers to life as they comment on merchandise, negotiate time to pay their bills, order potatoes and eggs, request oilskins to keep out the everlasting rain, offer hides for sale, ask for special treats—peppermints, perhaps, or whiskey—to be sent up the coast "next boat."

Fleeting personal glimpses enliven many letters. A proud new father, Victor Gullin, writing in his stilted English in December 1905, says, "I am very thankfull to you for letting me have $50.00 dollars...you know the Babyes cost money and quait a bit I tell you, but for all that it is lots of fun having them." In contrast to the fun of "Babyes," other letters bristle with irritated questions—about that renegade prospector Pete Brennan, for instance, missing in action somewhere on the coast. Where is he? Did he rent a boat from Dawley? demands one correspondent, adding tiredly, "I hear he is on a drunk and up at Head Bay. Kindly let me know particulars if you have any concerning him."

❦

By the turn of the century, Stockham and Dawley's was the best store on the west coast of Vancouver Island. Nothing north of Victoria could compare, not at Ucluelet, not the stores in the growing community of Alberni, not even the store at Clayoquot on Stubbs Island. So in October 1901, when Mrs. Guillod, the Indian Agent's wife from Alberni, wished to purchase fabric and notions for her sewing society, she set out for Stockham and Dawley's store. Small matter that this meant a sea voyage of up to twelve hours, a distance of over eighty miles, some of it in rough open water. The return journey required several days to complete, given that she would probably spend at least two nights at Clayoquot before the return steamer could take her home. Yet such a voyage seemed unexceptional to her husband, Harry Guillod: "My wife would like to be able to

View of Clayoquot on Stubbs Island in 1905, three years after Stockham and Dawley moved here from Stockham Island.

visit Clayoquot to see your goods," he wrote placidly, "as you have a much better line than the storekeepers here. Thanking you on behalf of the Ladies Sewing Society."

Whether providing goods for the Ladies Sewing Society or for a rabble of sealing schooners, Dawley and Stockham succeeded in making themselves indispensable. They could and did procure anything their customers desired: Singer sewing machines, finest muslin and buttoned boots; stumping powder, picks and dynamite; Castoria syrup, Pink Pills and rum; tea, tinned butter and fruit trees; livestock on the hoof, soup plates and prunes; hay, lace curtains and hired men. If there was a limit to what they could obtain, no one knew it. But they aspired to greater things, and their wishes came true in the winter of 1902. On February 26, the *Victoria Daily Colonist* took note: "Messrs Stockham & Dawley have bought all of Mr Thomas Earle's stock, stores, hotel and wharf at Clayoquot. This will practically give this enterprising firm a monopoly of the West Coast trade beyond Ucluelet."

Rumours about Thomas Earle were in the wind for several months before Stockham and Dawley purchased all the facilities on Stubbs Island. Everyone knew that Earle faced bankruptcy. The grain supplier R. Baker and Son, in a letter to Dawley in early December 1901, mentioned Earle was going into receivership, and in January 1902 the Hudson's Bay Company informed Dawley that Earle's entire place and all inventory were definitely up for sale.

Stockham and Dawley acted fast. Within a few months they had transferred their entire operation over to their new home on Stubbs Island. Their buildings on Stockham Island passed into the hands of the newly arrived Methodist medical missionary, Dr. McKinley, who established a small hospital there that lasted several years.

With the move to Stubbs Island, the business horizons of Stockham and Dawley widened magnificently. To have "a monopoly of the West Coast trade beyond Ucluelet," as the *Colonist* stated, only partly expressed the scope of their enterprise. In their new location they became the communications and transport centre for a large area. The coastal steamer from Victoria called several times a month at their dock, directly in front of their store and hotel, and they had a good anchorage. The

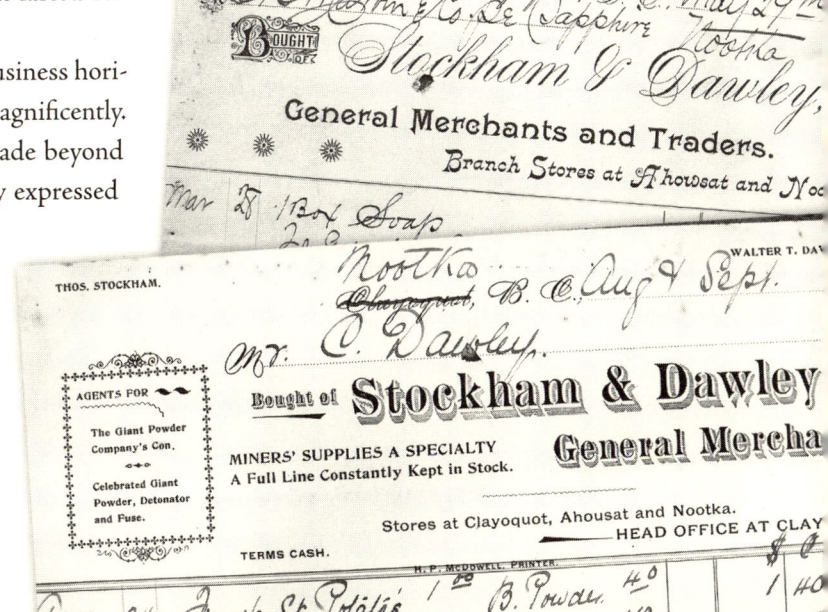

store housed the Clayoquot post office, an enormous asset to the business, and Dawley immediately became postmaster, drawing the princely salary of $80 per annum. He was a Justice of the Peace, as well as mining recorder. The provincial police constable lived on Stubbs Island—by 1902 it was Daniel McDougall, who had succeeded Frederick Stanley Spain—and ever since 1898 a Methodist medical missionary also lived there, first William Rolston, then Charles Service and now Dr. McKinley. All these services and amenities in one location guaranteed a continual procession of customers, and this traffic would only increase, for Stockham and Dawley also set their determined sights on the new telegraph line stretching its way from Alberni toward Clayoquot Sound. They decided it should extend all the way to Stubbs Island.

Inside the store on Stubbs Island, tall glass cases enclosed many items; most others were behind the counter, everything from ice-cream dishes to shotguns.

Time and again, the surviving papers from their business provide evidence of the vastly different personalities of these two merchants. Dawley was imperturbable, deliberate and calculating in all his business dealings, clearly the more educated of the two. Stockham was impulsive and hot-tempered, wily in business but unpredictable. His character comes through most clearly in a handful of letters from 1902, many of which concern negotiations about the telegraph line.

During that summer, Stockham was in Victoria for much of the time, dashing off impetuous letters to Dawley, complaining about the cost of telegraph cable, aggrieved that they might have to pay for a telegraph operator if the line came to Stubbs Island. He suspected everyone of business conspiracies, peppering his letters with comments like "He is no friend of ours," "He may get us in trouble," "Don't say too much," "I know he is working against us." But the telegraph line was Stockham's dominant concern: "I was just talking to the foreman that is putting in that line…I think it would be a good plan to have a little privet talk with him…we might get this thing fixed. I am afraid they will get ahead of us yet."

The cloak-and-dagger negotiations to have the long-awaited telegraph line from Alberni extended to Stubbs Island met with a good deal of local opposition. John Chesterman and several other influential settlers who lived over on Esowista Peninsula wanted the telegraph to terminate at the emerging townsite on the peninsula rather than on Stubbs Island. Chesterman was certain that a community of some size would emerge at the townsite and that investing in future development on Stubbs Island was unnecessary. Stockham and Dawley were unwilling to concede anything to the townsite.

Stockham's letters concerning the fate of the telegraph line became increasingly agitated, written in such haste they are almost indecipherable. A letter dated July 8, 1902, veers crazily from one subject to the next, exhorting Dawley to remember the "ankring" of the telegraph cable, agitating about a special deal to buy a hundred cheap sacks of sugar, warning Dawley of a man called Croft, who Stockham believed was out to cheat them—"he is a crooked bugar we had better look out for him."

By September, Stockham was in a fever of excitement because William Henderson of the Dominion Government Telegraph Service would soon be at Clayoquot to determine the fate of the telegraph line. "Mr. Henderson says he is going to Clayoquot perhaps on the next boat so make it as pleasant as you can for him," he wrote gleefully on September 8. "Keep one of the best rooms for him have it cleaned in good shape also look after him at the table…Stool him out hoor him…Stir him up." Stockham advised Dawley to have Henderson check some surveyed parcels of land over on the peninsula, "on the Town Site on top of the hill no streets opened or any clearing," and to do this "before Chesterman gets a hold of him." This entire letter is a jumbled outpouring of shady suggestions, ending with further instructions for Dawley to keep Henderson happy any way he can: "Hoor Walter. Take him fishing or shooting if he will go make it as pleasant as you can for him do not charge him for board and be free with them best cigars."

Whether or not Dawley followed Stockham's advice—*did* he "hoor" Henderson and ply him with "them best cigars"?—the outcome was satisfactory. On September 22, William Henderson wrote to Stockham and Dawley to say that their application "for Telegraph connection to the Alberni-Clayoquot Telegraph line by cable from Stubbs Island to the terminus of the line at Clayoquot Townsite had been granted by the Department at Ottawa." On December 12, 1902, the

Colonist announced: "Today or tomorrow Victoria will be placed in communication with Clayoquot, on the Vancouver Island coast, the telegraph line having been extended to that place, and instruments installed at the store of Stockham and Dawley, on Stubbs Island, the commercial settlement of Clayoquot."

The installation of the Alberni-Clayoquot telegraph line provided employment to a number of different crews of surveyors and workmen over an eighteen-month period. Dawley's mail reflects the tangled arguments about which local men should be awarded contracts to do this work. Thomas Stockham, writing from Victoria, stoutly supported the reliable Norwegian settler Jacob Arnet or a man named Grant for the sought-after job of foreman for the portion of the line between Kennedy River and Clayoquot. In Stockham's view, anyone was preferable to John Chesterman.

> There is 3000.00 for Canady [Kennedy] river this summer could you not get som one to get out a petison to get [Grant or] Arnett boss up there I spoke to Neal about it I told him Chesterman did not understand the work…and I said that Grant [or] Arnett was far better men…we must do all we can to down Chesterman.

This plotting was to no avail. The job went to Chesterman. Writing from Kennedy Lake on an unspecified date in 1902 after he had taken up the job, he commented on the quality of the dynamite Dawley sold him:

> Mr Dawley: I have tried the Dynamite and find that we have to use twice as much as we do of Giant to get the same results and then it gives us all a headache to handle it, and I would just as soon not have it at all, but if you want to send 2 cases at the price of 1 you may…also one box of 60% Giant as I must have some Good Powder for the Solid Rock.

As foreman of the telegraph crew at Kennedy Lake, Chesterman was in charge of provisioning his men. In one of his letters he ordered dynamite and electric fuses alongside large kettles and nails, raisins and beans, "Jap" rice and yeast cakes, coal oil and lengths of pipe—a typical order for men out in the bush on a construction crew. Chesterman was efficient and well-organized, and Dawley had known this all along, not sharing Stockham's desire to "down Chesterman."

For over a decade, John Chesterman's activities on the west coast can be roughly traced through his letters to Dawley. From 1900 onward he wrote from different locations, going wherever his diverse jobs took him. At various times he was employed on the road to Ucluelet, at Bamfield, on the telegraph line at Kennedy Lake, at the Clayoquot Cannery, on the construction of Estevan Point lighthouse, as a prospector, a miner and a farmer. His letters reflected his needs and his changing fortunes wherever he was. Always well-written, on lined foolscap, they invariably ended with his formal signature, "I Remain Yours Sincerely John Chesterman," the words spaced evenly and carefully over three lines. As an afterthought, he sometimes added a postscript, often a gossipy detail, and signed this merely "Jack."

Anyone looking for Chesterman could be sure Dawley knew where to find him. He always knew where the men in the area were working; after all, he outfitted most of them, and he would see them when they came by to get mail or to board a steamer or send a telegram. "I happened to see Joe Drinkwater who had been up your way," wrote James Thomson on September 2, 1910. One of Dawley's most faithful correspondents and suppliers, for several years Thomson was the manager of the Hudson's Bay Company in Victoria. He continued: "[Drinkwater] said that Chesterman had gone on the Govt Steamer to work on the Trail...I will feel obliged by your letting me know by return of steamer what you know of the matter as it is not likely he has gone to work there without your supplying him with the needful."

Chesterman's name frequently appears in letters from prospective employers asking if he is available for work or if Dawley would recommend him for certain projects, or making sure that Chesterman has collected the paycheques for "the boys" from Dawley's store. In his own letters, Chesterman often made offhand, illuminating comments. "God and the liberal government have been good to me," he said wryly, referring to the number of jobs he had with various government-funded projects. He landed the best of these jobs, and he always ensured that Dawley's store profited from his employment. Writing from Estevan Point in the spring of 1910, Chesterman submitted a long, unpunctuated list of highly technical provisions—"...3 boxes caps and 3 coils fuse 2 7lb striking hammers with handles 1 keg of 6 in hammers with handles 1 keg of 6 in spikes..."—telling Dawley to make out the bill in triplicate and recommending that he keep the charges reasonable in order to hold on

Clayoquot Hotel on Stubbs Island in the early 1900s. With sixteen rooms to rent and a dining room capable of seating twenty-six people, the hotel also housed the only beer parlour in the area. The word "Bar" is barely visible, written on the ground floor window, far right.

to this lucrative government contract. A cryptic comment appears at the end of this letter: "I gave you a good send off with Killeen [his employer] but you have a friend somewhere who is not a good one."

Chesterman and Dawley developed a good business relationship, helped by the fact that Chesterman paid his bills on time. "There was a time when I did not understand you (owing I believe now to T. Stockham's actions)," Chesterman wrote in March 1911, "but since I have got to understand you I have always found you courteous, obliging, and willing to accommodate every-one, and I wish to sincerely thank you for all your known favors to all of us in Clayoquot, and to assure you that as long as you continue to do as you have been doing you need not fear much competition in our district."

This unusually formal letter concludes with an apology for Mrs. Chesterman's shopping habits. During Chesterman's frequent absences, his wife sometimes disregarded her husband's instructions to place orders only at Dawley's store. "I told her I wanted her to trade with you and she promised she would but I suppose it is difficult for her to get around but I will soon be home and will fix this again." If her husband's letters can be believed, the unfortunate Mrs. Chesterman often failed to do the right thing. "I asked my wife to get this statement some time ago," he complained in a letter from Bamfield in 1911, "so I could have included it with this cheque, but she does not seem interested in anything but getting a cheque for herself." That same winter, when his family joined him in Bamfield for Christmas, he wrote, "Enclosed find cheque for $50. The wife and the children arrived all safe and sound and are enjoying it down here immensely and I don't know when I will get rid of them." Chesterman's most acid comment is in a postscript to a letter dated November 7, 1910: "I am glad you think my wife's looks were improved," wrote the loving husband, "as there was room for improvement." Poor Mrs. Chesterman.

Nineteen-year-old Elizabeth Anne Adams married John Chesterman, then aged thirty-four, in Victoria on February 16, 1901. Less than two months later, she arrived on the west coast with him, and they registered for a night at the

Clayoquot Hotel in early April. Chesterman was well known at Clayoquot, for he had been in the area a number of years before his marriage. The *Victoria Daily Colonist* took note of him on January 17, 1896, describing a New Year's gathering, a "magnificent banquet," hosted by Filip Jacobsen on Stubbs Island, which some thirty people attended. After a toast to the Queen and a speech by John Grice about the glorious British Empire, "Mr Chesterman...materially added to the enjoyment of the evening by his humorous versatility and his impersonation of the time honored 'Santa Claus.'"

Six months after Elizabeth Chesterman's marriage, her first child was born at Clayoquot, soon followed by three others. The family lived on a tract of land spanning the Esowista Peninsula, about four miles away from the townsite and accessible only by a rough trail through the bush or by boat. The property fronted on a long sandy beach facing southwest, now called Chesterman's Beach; on the northeast it looked onto the mud flats of Tofino Inlet. Chesterman cleared about half an acre of land and built a small house on the inlet side of his property. When work took him away from home, Elizabeth remained at her lonely homestead with only the company of her young children. Details of their life together are long lost, but a sales ledger for Dawley's store notes that in April 1907, John Chesterman purchased a yard and a half of velveteen at the store. Why? What colour, and for whom? Who can tell, but this small luxury may, perhaps, have cheered Elizabeth.

Their home was anything but luxurious. In 1921, when the place was long abandoned and falling into disrepair, Robert Guppy and his family leased it. After forging their way along the overgrown trail from Tofino to the Chesterman place, the Guppy family faced a "weathered wood-frame building in the middle of an untidy mess of stumps, bushes, logs and small outbuildings...a roughly-made unfinished house." Outdoors, Chesterman's work on the property was still in evidence: the remains of a wooden dyke on the mud flats, and a homemade stump puller, rather like a ship's windlass, mounted on logs. The place had been empty since 1913. John Chesterman died suddenly that year in Alberni, at the age of only forty-six. Mrs. Chesterman left their homestead soon afterward and resettled in Victoria with their children.

Most of Walter Dawley's customers lived in challenging circumstances, in remote places, struggling to clear land and build cabins, working hard to keep boats afloat and food on the table. Few had any money to spare, so in their transactions with the storekeeper, all kept a close eye on cost and quality. "One of them boxes of powder was not quite full," declared one customer suspiciously. "Not pleased with the last order of meat…We had to put it in pickle," wrote another. Complaints about pricing were fairly common. Even the easygoing Willie Rae-Arthur, writing from Boat Basin, questioned the price of feed: "Your price for Scratch feed per 90 lb sack is exactly one dollar more than I have been & am paying Victoria people for the best brand in 90 lb sacks." Willie bore no ill will, placing a generous order, starting with a hundred pounds of flour and continuing "a pound of tobacco, 40 lbs sugar, 50 lbs of Siam Rice, 3 pounds of <u>fresh</u> [underscored four times] creamery butter, four pounds <u>fresh</u> [underscored only once] Canadian Cheese, please be sure this is new & fresh as I do not care for nutty cheese." At the end he asked for two dollars' worth of Scotch peppermints. Willie was partial to peppermints; he sometimes ordered several pounds at a time.

Dawley's customers could be a demanding lot, many of them expecting him to have intimate knowledge of their needs without providing much information at all. Orders sometimes arrived for a pair of shoes or for a sweater with no size specified, let alone colour or style. The customers expected Dawley to know. He also had to match wallpaper samples and shades of paint, to store boats and guns and stoves in his storage shed, to forward personal possessions and to relay detailed messages.

On occasion, Dawley could be surprisingly generous, and at Christmas a spirit of good cheer occasionally overwhelmed him. He would send hampers containing ducks or brant to favoured suppliers and friends in Victoria and Alberni, with a note expressing seasonal good wishes. The sealing captain George Heater thanked Dawley for one such Christmas gift in December 1910. "Mr Dawley, Der Friend," he wrote cheerily, "I received you letter to day glad to hear you are doing so well I hope you will keep it up, I received you ducks which I am very thankful for you kno I like ducks." George Heater pops up regularly in Dawley's papers, writing frequent and friendly letters over the years, on occasion addressing him as "old friend," "my old tillicum" and even "Charley"—a nickname used by only a few of Dawley's inner circle.

From the time it opened, Christie School represented a ripe new market for Stockham and Dawley's store. Taking into account the children, staff and visitors, at least sixty or seventy people lived at Christie School in the early years, and as time passed and the school expanded, there were considerably more. This translated into important local purchasing power, and the two storekeepers did what they could to secure the custom of the school, even extending special favours and dispensing advice.

June 13, 1900

Gentlemen:
Please deliver to bearers George and Justin 1 pc Print just like sample, 1 cs evap. Apples, 1 cs Evap Prunes (the cheap kind mentioned by Mr. Dawley)…We have a few deer skins on hand and wish to tan them and if you can send us instructions how to do it we shall be obliged to you…

Truly yours
P. Maurus

Please accept best thanks for use of canoe.

Yet despite this evidence of goodwill, Dawley had reservations about these Catholics, for they did not prove to be particularly faithful customers. To be sure, they ordered considerable quantities of goods: a typical order, from April 1901, requests a ton of flour, a ton of potatoes, a pail of Royal Mix candy, kegs of nails, sacks of beans, 1,000 envelopes, ten sacks of sugar, overalls and shoes. Letters also survive in which the priests request materials for a hot-water copper, ask advice about purchasing an engine and broach the delicate subject of bringing their cows over to Dawley's to meet with his bull. Yet Dawley was grimly aware that the priests often circumvented his store and ordered directly from suppliers in Victoria. He knew this because his suppliers told him so; J. W. Mellor's glass company was one of several. Writing in September 1902, Mr. Mellor anxiously informed Dawley: "We have received an order from…the Christie Indian Boarding School…If you could manage it we would much rather fill orders of this kind through you." This letter ends by informing Dawley that the priests want to buy paint, suggesting that perhaps Mr. Dawley could "chase up" that business for himself.

Despite such transgressions, Dawley had to acknowledge the school and the Catholic missions up the coast as a determined and highly organized presence. They commanded attention and, furthermore, they usually paid their bills promptly. On the whole, Dawley avoided arguments with them, although he never hesitated to charge interest on overdue accounts or to send peremptory notes demanding payment. He certainly never offered them a bargain. On a buying trip to Victoria in July 1904, Dawley discovered a disturbing price discrepancy. He wrote to Stockham at once: "That Duck print we sold to [Sister] Placida at 12¾¢ is now worth wholesale here 13¢…raise it up on her (mark it at once) 13½¢." Sister Placida would not have been pleased, for the sisters and the priests kept a sharp eye on the price and the quality of their purchases. Father

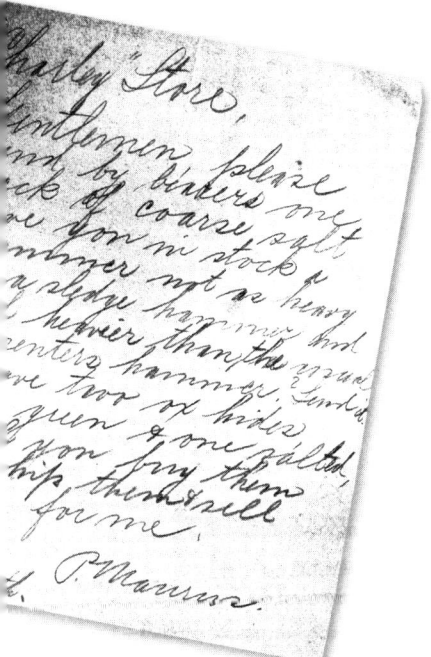

Maurus once returned defective lamp chimneys, pointing out they cost too much in the first place, for he previously bought good ones for $1.00 a dozen and these were $1.50 a dozen. Another time, on December 31, 1909, he composed a forthright letter daring to question Dawley's right to charge interest on a short-term debt:

> Don't you think you got your interest when you charged us 5% commission? And have you forgotten that through your own fault we had to pay a big price for the hay and also that you did not keep your part of the agreement to order your supply jointly with us to secure a lower freight rate? I just mention these things to convince you that to charge us interest is not fair in my opinion. But if you insist, we will pay it and, please God, at an early date.

Infuriating as such comments were, Dawley knew the importance of keeping significant customers like the priests reasonably content. For their part, the priests were equally aware that they needed to be on the good side of prominent Clayoquot citizens like Walter Dawley. As a result, relations remained cordial. Father Maurus came to know Dawley well enough to address him as "Friend Dawley" in one of his rapidly penciled notes, and another is simply addressed "Charley Store." Dawley sent boxes of apples to the school one Christmas and received in return a polite invitation to come and visit. Some years the sisters would send little Christmas gifts; in 1902 a sample of their "Mince Meat" arrived for Dawley, with instructions that he should "thin it with a little spirits."

Letters from his suppliers account for the bulk of Dawley's correspondence, providing a positive orgy of detail about the merchandise he handled: prices and brands of pilot bread, varieties of flour and rice, the cost of women's shawls, the trials of shipping gunpowder and blasting caps, even the types of gumboots sold. Yet alongside endless detail about stolid products like lumber, dynamite and coal oil, many tantalizing wisps of information drift through these letters, reminders of long-forgotten and intriguing consumer items. When the Hudson's Bay Company apologizes for being unable to provide the candy Dawley ordered and offers a different type, with or without "Cupid's Whispers" and costing merely twenty cents per pound, a sugary treat from more than a hundred years ago suddenly, distractingly, surfaces. What *were* "Cupid's Whispers"? And what was in a box of "favourite Prescription," costing $1.00? Was the "red frilled elastic" for a particularly dashing customer? What were those shoes like, costing $1.40 and described so deliciously as "Chocolate Romeos"?

Although he placed orders with suppliers in Ontario, England, Scotland, New York, California and elsewhere in the United States, Dawley gave his closest attention to a group of suppliers in Victoria and Vancouver: the Hudson's Bay Company; Kelly Douglas & Company; Simon Leiser and Company; J. Maynard Shoes; W&J Wilson; the Singer Company; Turner, Beeton & Company; Beckmann Ker Millers; Popham Brothers Biscuits; Weiler Brothers Furniture; Burns Meats; and E & G Prior. These and other regulars appear consistently in the correspondence, but some highly unlikely companies also crop up in Dawley's files, including the gentleman's tailor Curzon Brothers in London, England. This company optimistically offered the "latest London and New York fashion plates" in 1908 on the off-chance there were fashion-starved customers in the remote reaches of Clayoquot Sound. Dawley likely paid more attention to the comments of the McClary Manufacturing Company in its letter of April 1906 from Vancouver. Under the masthead declaring "Manufacturers of Stoves, Ranges, Furnaces, Enameled and Tinwares of all Kinds," the McClary correspondent commented: "We have been hoping to hear from you with an order for your Spring requirements in all of our lines. We understand there is considerable activity on the West Coast...and trust you will not pass us when you require any lines that we can handle."

Dawley was a tough customer. He fired furious volleys of words at his suppliers, demanding reparation for damaged goods, short measure or inferior quality. If the oranges were soft, if the bacon order was short by a pound or two, if one spool of thread or one pair of shoelaces was missing, Dawley immediately sent off a protesting letter. He double-checked everything; no missing inventory ever escaped him. "On counting the packets [of seeds] over carefully twice," he wrote to Messrs Rennie and Company in Vancouver, "I find there are only 342 five cent pkts whilst your invoice calls for 350. Kindly adjust this difference." Counting hundreds of packages of seeds carefully, and twice, was clearly worthwhile if eight packages (five cents each) were missing.

His correspondents took refuge in the flowery commentary of their trade. "We are indeed grateful for the very genial nature of our business relations with you in the past, and hope to merit a continuance of your patronage in the future," declaimed Kelly Douglas & Company. The suppliers Jenner, Roxburgh & Company in Toronto, whose letterhead described them as "Wholesale Importers Laces, Fancy Dry Goods & Smallwares," purred reassuringly that they were

"Trusting you find all to your satisfaction & awaiting your further esteemed commands."

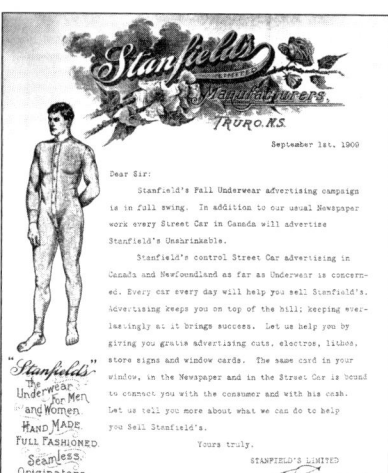

In return for such civilities, Dawley demanded free samples and multiple quotes, and he frequently threatened to send his custom elsewhere. "We are very sorry you do not see fit to favor us with a continuance of your patronage," mourned R. Baker and Son, grain merchants in Victoria. For Dawley, this was entirely normal. Finding fault with his suppliers was simply part of the job, as he saw it, and he did so with relish. In a period of only two weeks in November 1906, Dawley received some eight letters of apology from various suppliers, including James Thomson and Son, who "regret exceedingly the disappointment the shortage in the hose is giving you," and Turner, Beeton & Company, who "had a new packer in the store, and we were very much rushed that day, consequently there was a mix up on your stuff, which we exceedingly regret."

A few notable suppliers fearlessly stood up to Dawley. Gault Brothers of Montreal, dealers in dry goods, commented caustically, "It would be very much more satisfactory if you would write us and say wherein the amount is wrong… when a client says our account is wrong without stating where, it is hard for us to make it satisfactory." When Dawley returned a barrel of salted pork to Burns Meats, saying it arrived spoiled, Mr. Burns retorted, "You must have got this pork the fore part of July as that was the last lot…you had from us. Could it be that this has been laying around for two months?…the brine has been changed and almost pure water put on it…we feel that the fault does not lie with us in this case." Similarly, when Dawley shipped back several sacks full of mouldy onions, the supplier Geo. N. Owen in Victoria testily replied, "I wish to goodness you had dumped them before sending them back. I expected to hear from you about them, as I discovered when too late that the boys had shipped you the wrong Onions." Having neatly deflected Dawley in this manner, Mr. Owen

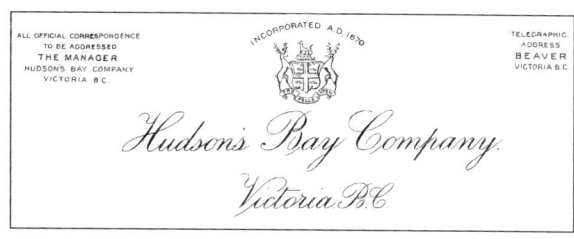

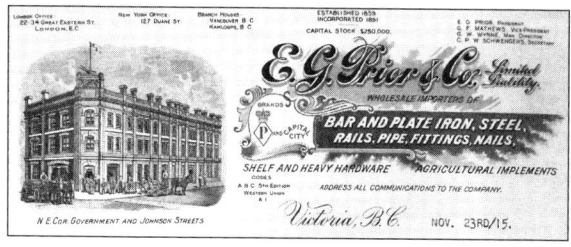

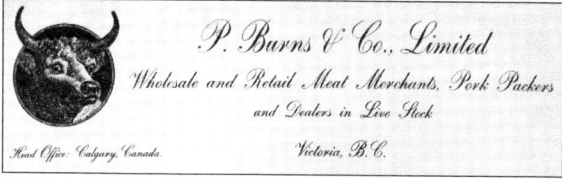

concluded magnanimously, "I am not worrying about your bill, only wish it was twice as big." Another of Dawley's suppliers, Mr. F. W. Fletcher of Fletcher Brothers Music Dealers, paid no attention whatever to Dawley's bluster. He breezily commented, "Well, there is nothing but trouble…I suppose it is raining as usual down there." Ignoring Dawley's business entirely, Mr. Fletcher went on to describe a boat he wanted to sell, "Just the Boat for your place…a Bargain," concluding, "I hope you are as fat as ever I know you are well my regards to [the] Boys."

The most spirited of all Dawley's suppliers was Simon Leiser, the well-known Victoria wholesale merchant. For nearly twenty years, from the late 1890s onward, Leiser shipped groceries up to Clayoquot and purchased considerable quantities of dogfish oil from Dawley. During the many years the two men did business together, they never tired of bickering, and year after year Simon Leiser's buoyant responses came bouncing back in reaction to Dawley's letters. These make it abundantly clear that Leiser was not one to be bullied, no sir, not he, not even if he *had* made a mistake.

> We are in receipt of yours of 16th inst and in reply beg to say that we only shipped you what was ordered…Regarding the Corned Beef to the best of my belief Mr Stockam told me Corned Beef. We would just as soon have sent Roast. It makes no difference to us whatever… it cannot be helped now…However it is not a very big mistake.

This letter briskly acknowledged another oversight; no crackers had been shipped to Nootka in cartons, but Leiser gave a dismissive shrug, saying, "You can send them from Clayoquot."

The two men knew each other well and did not trust each other one jot. Leiser knew that Dawley would go behind his back to another supplier in an

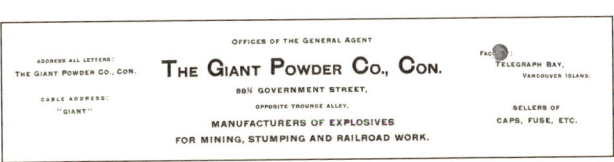

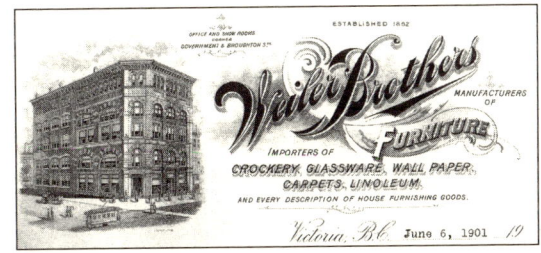

instant, and Dawley knew that Leiser would tell any engaging story to get out of a tight spot, outfacing complaints with admirable sang-froid. When Dawley complained that a whole order of potatoes had gone bad and that the coal oil he ordered had not arrived, Leiser vowed to get even with the man who sold him the potatoes and declared that the sealing schooner *Dora Sieward* used up the entire case of coal oil destined for Clayoquot. At the end of this letter, in which all the blame was laid on others, Leiser cheerfully added, "Why don't you send us some orders. We are the best friends you have, but you think we are trying to do you."

Quick to take offence and equally quick to forget an entire argument, Simon Leiser dashed off impetuous letters continually: "It is some time since we have received an order from you, and do not know why you cannot buy from us. Not that we care very much, but we think we are entitled to some of your trade… It seems to us the best we treat you the worse you treat us." He tirelessly badgered Dawley to place more orders: "Can you not use some Navel Oranges, very cheap…Send us some orders every steamer." "Could you increase the order for us and at the same time order some Tea?" He commented on one occasion that if Dawley would not place an order, he would come to Clayoquot to take an order in person, adding candidly, "I do not want to make the trip. I suppose if I come, you will have a place for me to stop."

Leiser became inured to Dawley's repeated threats to cut off all trade with him. "We are very sorry indeed to see that you have thrown off on us after dealing with us so many years," he wrote in February 1906, "and can assure you it is no fault of ours…we cannot help it if…others come and buy goods from us. We are not dealing with Indians." Dawley bitterly opposed his suppliers dealing directly with natives, several of whom opened small stores in their villages over the years. Doing business directly with the school at Kakawis was almost as bad in Dawley's eyes, but Leiser had no hesitation in that respect. "In regards the Industrial School we cannot refuse to sell [to] them as every person in town sell to them."

Leiser remained in business a long time, becoming well known in Victoria as a philanthropist. He was the prime mover behind the Victoria Opera House Company, and when the Royal Victoria Theatre opened in

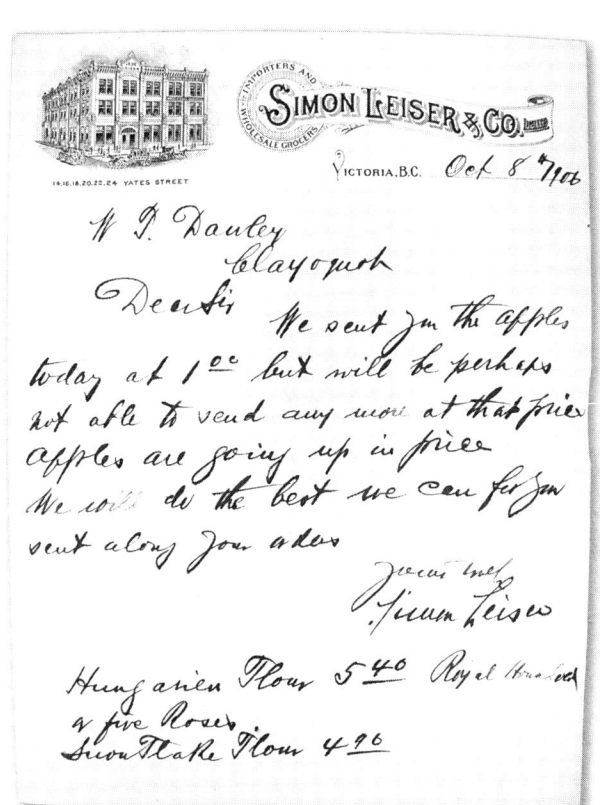

1913, Leiser's bust was placed in the foyer to honour his services. Despite gaps in their correspondence, he and Dawley remained in contact for many years, and Leiser's style never changed: "We want your business and we will do almost anything to please you," he declared in November 1916, in the same breath chivvying Dawley to buy apples at $1.00 a box and oranges at $4.75 a case.

This letter ends by reiterating an old and stubborn argument, dating back to 1898, concerning the price paid for dogfish oil and the method for gauging the amount in the barrels. "Your remarks as regards the quantity of oil are entirely uncalled for as we cannot pay you for more than the tanks or barrels contain," Leiser wrote. The men remained locked in this dispute about measuring dogfish oil for their entire working relationship. The final letter surviving from their correspondence is, unusually, from Dawley to Simon Leiser, dated May 4, 1917: "As for the dog fish oil I certainly feel you are trying to do me out of the value of the full quantity I sent...I was not paid the full market price per gallon for the oil as this oil was worth at that time 37 to 40 cents per gallon...I can hardly trust myself to describe your conduct."

Leiser may never have received this letter. He died unexpectedly on a visit to Vancouver on May 12, 1917. Eulogized for his "unbounded optimism as to the commercial and industrial aspects of this city," Leiser achieved lasting recognition as a pioneer merchant in Victoria. He and Walter Dawley never finished their argument about dogfish oil.

Walter Dawley made a point of being on good terms with the native people in his area, and he stocked large quantities of merchandise with them in mind: Singer sewing machines; "Indian trade" shawls; soup plates, apples, blankets and print fabric for potlatches; white blankets for burials; certain types and styles of sewing notions, as well as particular brands of flour, sugar and pilot biscuit.

The storekeepers at Nootka and Ahousat kept Dawley abreast of the tastes and preferences of the people in the villages. Fred Thornberg repeatedly reproved him for sending the wrong merchandise: Dawley could send men's sweaters to Ahousat but only in "blue and cardinal color...none of the Football jerseys they don't sell here"; he could send cheap men's suits ($7.00) but *not* blue serge. No Ahousats wanted those old-fashioned knitted woollen drawers—they preferred cotton flannel—and as for shoes: "not one out of 20 women...can use the Shoes that Tom bought last year," and the problem was style, not size. The ladies wanted the fashionable shoes with "buttens around the Ankle," but not the really narrow ones. None of the ladies could do them up.

BILLY AUGUST
DEALER IN
GENERAL MERCHANDISE

Opposite: Pages from the 1907 ledger for the Clayoquot store. Note the letters "S& D", meaning "sick and destitute," and the Indian Department entries. Providing basic necessities for native people in need, on instruction from the Indian Agent, was part of Dawley's business.

At Hesquiat, Constant Charleson set up his own small store, hoping to undercut the local store run by a settler, Anton Luckovitch, about a mile from the village. Neither of these Hesquiat enterprises troubled Walter Dawley, for they were very small, and besides, Constant Charleson obligingly provided details about the stores' operations, even ordering many of his goods through Dawley.

In a distressed letter dated November 23, 1900, Constant poured out his retail problems to Dawley: "I cannot understand why the Antoine Lockovich sale the biscuit at $1.70 although that kind biscuit he sold it cost $1.50 at Victoria, the freight fron Vic cost 25¢ each box…I am sorry I cant sale my biscuit as I cant make it cheap more then $2.00." Constant listed the prices of several items in Anton's store, comparing them to his own: "corned beef 35¢, Anton, four for a dollar; soda creakers 75¢ Anton 55¢ each box; rolled oats 40¢ per sack, Anton 25¢ a sack." He concluded sadly that local customers "say they like best Antoines store as he sale the goods very cheap… I am Indian yet I know this is not right what he doing with his goods."

Several native storekeepers followed Constant Charleson's example and set up small stores in their villages. By 1911, Father Maurus Snyder proudly commented in his annual report to the Department of Indian Affairs: "Our ex-pupils are giving a good account of themselves…three conduct stores successfully on their respective reserves." Billy August, the redoubtable Ahousat chief, became the best-known native merchant. On November 7, 1905, Dawley's Ahousat storekeeper, Thomas Gardhouse, wrote: "August has started a store. He is trying to form a company." Billy August printed his own letterhead and set up shop, his declared aim being to get rid of the white man's store at Ahousat. He and Walter Dawley had never been allies; now they became foes.

"By this last mail we received a letter from Billy August, Ahousat, whom, I presume is an Indian. I have however, declined to supply him with goods, a fact that I am sure you will appreciate," wrote the Hudson's Bay Company on December 31, 1907. Two years later, on March 24, 1909, Johnston Brothers Dry Goods Wholesale, in Vancouver, also assured Dawley that "sales to Billy August will cease." Dawley must have instructed his suppliers not to ship goods to his Ahousat competitor. He and Chief Billy had been at odds for years, ever since the days when Billy would go to Victoria with other Ahousat hunters to find their own sealing schooner, not wanting to sign on through Dawley.

No documents survive to show if Chief Billy tried to sell furs directly to the many fur buyers in Victoria, but given his entrepreneurial skills, this seems likely. On the whole, though, Walter Dawley confidently controlled most of the fur buying at Clayoquot, Ahousat and Nootka. From the outset, he and

July 1904

Indian Department

To Kashlia Destitute Kelsmar
- 1 pr Blanket
- Hoopyah Sec & Destitute Clayoquot
- 50 Flour
- 4 Sugar
- 1 Tea   2 mos
- Soo-ook-lal Sec & Sec Clayoquot
- 50 Flour
- 4 Sugar   2 mos
- 1 Tea

B. C. School
To 11 pr 2" Butts

C. P. R.

July 4 To 1 ca Mill ahouer
        " Freight
Aug 22 " 1 Sk Hung Son
        " Freight
    12 " 1 ca Peaches
        " Freight
    22 To 1 ca Beef Clayoquot
        " Freight

                                  14 78

Indian Department

4 To Soo-ook-lal Sec & Sec Clay
   " 50 Flour
   " 1 " Tea   1 60

January. Expenses &c

	1 Bear Skin trade	4 00
		1 25
	Paid siwash bringing goods from Clay	3 00
	1 Land Otter	2 25
5	Handling Frt	2 00
	1 Deer	90
	1 coon 1", 1 martin 75 1 coat & vest	14 00
	Thos Stockham on acc Scholarie C#	2 25
	2 martin 1 coon 1 mink	75
14	Handling Frt	45
	fish	2 50
22	Handling Freight	1 80
31	18 Coons	
		181 82
1	Invoice S & D Clayoquot	68 90
18	"	2 70
22	Doas	1 33
26	Jas & Iron	31 77
2	Invoice Wieler Bros	37 71
	" Turner Beeton & Co	150 58
	" Simon Leiser & Co	80 00
2	"	111 00
18	R Baker & Son	41 50
3	"	
10	"	

Stockham took fur buying very seriously, and whenever Dawley hired a storekeeper, one of the most important qualifications was the man's ability to judge furs. Dawley's own reputation as fur buyer was extremely sound, although even he made mistakes. One of his fur brokers, Mr. G.R. Thompson, crowed with delight on hearing that Dawley had purchased substandard skins. "It breaks my heart, Dawley," he wrote, "to tell you how much you have gone down in my estimation recently…McCulloch tells me you have been had. One of [your skins] had small pox the other the mange. You are henceforth mortal."

Dealers regularly approached Dawley, wanting to purchase furs. "At any time if you have furs for sale," wrote Turner, Beeton & Company in November 1903, "we will be glad to handle them for you free of charge, putting them up for tender, and disposing to the highest bidder. There are seven fur buyers in Victoria now, and it is looked upon as the best market on the coast." Individuals on the lookout for specialty furs also approached Dawley, and an unusual request for four sea lion skins once came his way. "I do not mean the skins of hair seals but the skins of regular Sea-Lions," wrote Sprott Balcom of the Pacific Whaling Company in October 1906. He was making this query on behalf of a friend who wished to cover his "travelling boxes" with sea lion pelts. "If it is too troublesome to get 4 skins, I think 2 will do," he added, suggesting that the price should be around $5.00 per skin. Dawley also undertook to provide highly coloured elk teeth to one collector, "panther skulls" to another and "Fine Black Bear Cub" skins to another. He knew the native hunters who could help him fill such special orders.

The Indian Agent based in Alberni understood the extent of Dawley's knowledge of and connections with the natives and to some degree relied on him for information and assistance. Harry Guillod was the first Indian Agent for the coast, holding the position from 1881 until 1902, when he was succeeded by A.W. Neill, who later became a Conservative MP for Comox-Alberni. These men wrote to Dawley frequently.

The Indian Agency ran an account at Dawley's store for provisioning the most needy natives in the area. Although this was an ongoing and regular source of business, the records of these transactions are meagre. "Jim Tkeetstkia and Kwiyatookhilth…they are in sore need," wrote Harry Guillod on one occasion. "I do not understand…whether they are man and wife or living together or whether they are two old men in different houses if the first give them a box of pilot bread if separate cases a box for each." Guillod later wrote, "Will you please send a pair of red blankets to Clayoose directed to Agnes, care of Mr Stone. They need not be very large they are for a girl of 13. If you have not red send grey you did not write last boat." A.W. Neill sent a note to Dawley asking that the Indian Agency be charged for a "cloth supplied to bury destitute Indian Hashilth of Kelsemat band found dead on Vargas Island—$1.25 I think it was."

Such requests were the exception rather than the rule. Usually Dawley merely handed out basic foodstuffs on behalf of the Indian Agent to people classified as "sick and destitute." Judging from Dawley's papers, the usual offering was a fifty-pound bag of flour, required to last two months. Some of the destitute natives also received a pound of tea and four pounds of sugar, though Neill stressed that sugar must only be given to the sick. Neill took Dawley to task more than once for trying to change the orders, for making substitutions and for giving sugar to people who were, apparently, not sick enough to deserve it.

"It is not your fault," Neill wrote wearily to Dawley in January 1904, "but the order is all wrong. I have strict orders not to give sugar to anyone that is not sick as well as destitute. Please make the a/c out again." On another occasion: "Re: July a/cs Mrs. Kitsasuse, Mrs. Moses, and Sei-ya-nacha being only one person each and getting 50 lbs should have been entered as 'two months supply'. Please do not give them any more until the expiration of two months respectively. I see you tried to improve on some of them by reducing the tea from 1 lb to ½ lb and giving 4 lbs of sugar. That would only do if they were also 'sick.'"

An order book from 1906–7 survives, a large leather-bound volume with thick creamy paper, its edges beautifully marbled. This book contains immaculate records of every purchase, every customer, every penny spent at Dawley's store that year and briefly lists the amount of relief given to sick and destitute natives, all of whom are named, or at least identified, their names sometimes followed by the letters "S & D." "To Jeanie old and destitute Moochalatt Band 50 lb flour; to Sam Preather S & D 2 children Muchalatz Band 50 lb flour, 1 lb tea, 4 lb sugar; to Maggie Bishop, destitute, Ahousat, 50 lbs flour; to Oomis & Wife, old & dest., Neuchalatz, 50 lbs flour…"

With their flour, tea and, if they were lucky, sugar loaded into their canoes, these people would return to their homes to eke out their supplies. Not for them the untold luxuries Dawley's store could provide to his more fortunate customers. Not for them the lemons, tins of cream or Japanese oranges; the grapes, tinned butter and Cupid's Whispers were entirely out of their reach. When the coastal steamers arrived with such bounty, it was not for everyone within Dawley's domain.

Right: Father Charles and Father Maurus on the beach at Friendly Cove.

Below: Father Charles in his canoe, Union Jack mounted behind.

— 5 —

Priests at Sea

November 6, 1902: After I went to bed we had a big thunderstorm. Several times the lightening caused the telephone bell to ring…This storm made me pray for I felt very uncomfortable. Then came a lightning, a flash through my telephone that lit up my room with a report as if a gun was fired off. I had an idea that the lightning struck Christie School & reported through the line. I rang them up several times but no one answered. This only confirmed me in my opinion. They were in trouble and needed help. I dressed took my lantern and started off through the trail. It was pitch dark and a heavy rain falling 10:30 PM.

Father Charles hiking.

FATHER CHARLES MOSER never spared himself. If he believed duty called, he would respond. To set out on the rough trail and trek nearly a mile and a half across Meares Island, from Opitsat to Christie School, in the middle of a pitch-black November night, and in a thunderstorm, was entirely foolhardy, but he did not hesitate.

I had gone halfways when I stumbled over a root and fell into a swollen creek; the light on my lantern was out, all I could do was to get out of the creek and remain there standing, sitting and standing again. I was getting cold very cold. When standing I tramped the mud and water under me to keep the circulation of my blood going—praying loud and singing sacred songs aloud to keep wild animals from me.

This misadventure ended in pure bathos. Nothing whatever was wrong at Kakawis other than the telephone line being out of order. Father Charles arrived there in the early morning, cold and wet and miserable. "They only laughed at my terrible experience of the night," he wrote in his diary. "So I went back to Opitsat and taught school."

Unlike his colleagues at Christie School—the sisters, the brothers and Father Maurus Snyder, who were always in each other's company—Father Charles was in a lonely position. Appointed as the missionary at Opitsat, he lived alone there for his first decade on the coast, running a small day school and linked to Kakawis by the often-malfunctioning private telephone line "installed by P. Maurus between Christie School and my house with dry batteries and extended to Stockham and Dawley's store." Although frequently required to help out at the school, Father Charles was something of an outsider there in his early years.

The village of Opitsat from the water, 1919.

Born in Switzerland in 1874, Father Charles was a small, spare man. Zealous, dogged and stern, he seems to have been odd man out amongst his peers on the coast. In the brief account of a celebratory dinner to mark Father Brabant's birthday in October 1901, Father Maurus failed to mention Father Charles. Walter Dawley and Thomas Stockham attended this birthday dinner, but apparently Father Charles did not. He often escaped mention in the writings of the other priests, seemingly the one easiest to ignore, a workhorse rather than a leader, easily overshadowed by Father Brabant and Father Maurus. Both these men were his superiors: Father Brabant by virtue of his towering and longstanding reputation on the coast, his years of experience and his boundless self-confidence; Father Maurus because of his role as Christie School principal and his personal popularity with sisters, brothers and students alike. The reserved and uncharismatic Father Charles could not compete. His solution was to work ever harder and more stoically at whatever tasks came his way, and from the outset, stationed as he was at Opitsat and set apart from his fellows, Father Charles found his work difficult and lonely.

> After unpacking and arranging my house I opened my day school July 23 [1900.] I rang the Church bell three times, but no body came. All the children went to the Methodist preacher. He took advantage of the change of priest and opened a school which he had not done before. This was a sad commencement for me and I felt bad. Next day I rang the bell again but only once I was ashamed to ring more times and not to be able to get someone for my school. Again nobody.

I was discouraged and went to Kakawis to report to Fr. Maurus. He consoled me and towards evening I went back again to try anew with Gods help.

Even though a Roman Catholic church was built at Opitsat in 1886, and although Father Lemmens and Father Van Nevel had lived and worked there in earlier years, Father Charles soon discovered that he held no religious monopoly. The Methodists had established themselves in the area, and for years they ran their day school at Opitsat in direct opposition to the Catholic day school—neither of them attracting many students. In 1905 the Methodists went further and purchased a house at Opitsat where they held regular religious services. Unlike his counterparts at Kakawis, who lived at a Catholic school safely distanced from the nearest village, Father Charles faced the daily reality of trying to maintain a mission in a village where the religious competition was stiff, and response was tepid at best and occasionally hostile:

> *June 21, 1908:* Sunday and Feast of Corpus Christie. At Mass with exposition of the Blessed Sacrament I explained the doctrine of the real presence of Jesus in the holy Eucharist. When I finished speaking someone in the rear of the church said in a loud voice that I could hear it at the altar "eita-eita" (lies).

Father Charles rarely allowed himself to express discouragement in his diary, but on occasion he could not help himself. "These people have no love for their priest, for their church and for their religion," he declared on December 13, 1908. "It is sad and for 20 years now they had a resident priest doing all kinds of material favors for them, not to speak of the spiritual advantages they received."

Although based at Opitsat, for his first ten years on the coast, Father Charles was continually on the move. As well as his incessant travels back and forth to Kakawis, he regularly visited and stayed at native settlements and seasonal encampments throughout Clayoquot Sound. Year after year, he followed

The village of Echachis, which Father Charles called "Echachislet," is on a small island south of Wickaninnish Island.

the people of Opitsat as they moved to and from their fishing grounds, spending weeks or months at a time at Echachis, which he called Echachislet, a seasonal village site on an island south of Wickaninnish Island. He even ran a day school at Echachis for a handful of children, and in July 1910 he built a small church there, only months before hearing from the abbot at Mount Angel that he would be moving permanently up to Hesquiat to replace the aging Father Brabant.

> *November 17, 1910:* Left Kakawis for my new Mission field at 1 PM with Hesquiat Indians divided in two canoes carrying my iktas (belongings). Rain and south-east Wind. For one hour we had good sailing around Catface Mountain. Later on we had to pull against an outgoing tide. At "Tsiktasis" we made for shore, started a fire in an empty Indian shack…We refreshed ourselves with hot coffee and sandwiches. Then we slept or rather tried to sleep on bare boards for two hours when all hands were called for more coffee with bread and butter. After this we started off again and after a long pull in darkness and heavy rain showers we reached "Owpenit"…We went on shore and as the houses [were] uninhabited at this time of the year we entered one of the open shacks where we enjoyed hot coffee again with bread and butter. Here we waited till daylight…At 7 AM we hoisted sails and sailed out…into the broad Pacific Ocean. A rough sea was running… but further on we had a calm sea with big heavy waves but no choppy sea. At 10 AM we arrived at Hesquiat. The whole village came down to the beach to welcome their new Missionary.

Father Charles remained at Hesquiat for seven years, travelling frequently to the Catholic missions up the coast at Nootka and Kyuquot. In 1917 he was summoned to work at Kakawis, and from 1917 to 1922 he served unhappily at Christie School, the last three years as principal. During the remainder of the 1920s he led a peripatetic existence, shifting unpredictably between Kakawis and the coastal missions, never fully at ease, eternally unsure how long he would be in any given location. Even in his earliest years on the coast, Father Charles expected to be recalled imminently to the monastery at Mount Angel: "My superior [said] he would call me home before September," he wrote in June 1902, but by August he received instructions to remain on his mission. He never imagined, when he first arrived, that he would continue on the coast until 1930, or that he would outlast all of the others who arrived with him.

In his diary, Father Charles stoically chronicles his daily life over the course of thirty years. He provides a consistent voice, recounting many changes, many developments on the coast, in a manner unparalleled by any other document. Despite his overwhelming, often alienating, religious preoccupations, despite his clipped descriptions and generally unrevealing prose, Father Charles is an invaluable witness to a long-lost era of coastal history, providing details and insights unavailable in any other source.

> *June 6, 1902:* For 2 yrs now I used a small canoe and learned during this time to handle it well—so that I am now as safe in my canoe as an Indian is in his. Jimmy Jim is making a sail for me; I never sailed before but now I must try and learn it.

Having never been in a canoe before his arrival on the coast, Father Charles conscientiously set about learning how to paddle. In short order he was travelling confidently by canoe through the at times treacherous waters of Clayoquot Sound, proving himself far more able than the brothers and Father Maurus at Christie School. None of them took kindly to the sea. Recalling their early horrors in handling boats, Brother Leonard commented in a letter to Father Maurus: "It was customary to me to fall into the water every other day, when attempting to pull out the anchor."

Christie School students at work, passing firewood up the beach. Lessons occupied only half a day; chores took up the rest of the children's time.

During his years at Opitsat, Father Charles frequently paddled his small dugout canoe to Kakawis and back, over to Echachis, to Kelsemat and up to Ahousat. When he made longer trips, to Hesquiat or Nootka, he went in larger canoes with the help of Indian paddlers and often with a sail. His many descriptions of canoe travel inspire a sense of baffled amazement. Either he was entirely fearless or he considered himself invincible, for he never hesitated to take on the most challenging journeys, often in terrible weather, finding himself in danger time after time.

> *June 3, 1906:* Pentecost Sunday and steamboat day. Since yesterday strong South-East wind with heavy rain showers. At 3:30 PM SS Queen City passed Echachislet. The sea was going too high for my little canoe hence some Indians who were going to Opitsat took me in tow. But soon the tow line broke and I ventured to proceed alone. It was a terrible sea…and I recommended myself to God, to his Holy Will. When I was about a quarter of a mile from Clayoquot wharf I could see the steamer there when I came to the crest of a wave but down again I went between waves and I could not even see the top of her masts. I made the wharf alright and got the mail which I brought to Kakawis.

Prone as he was to seasickness, Father Charles found the journey between Hesquiat and Nootka particularly challenging, for it meant braving the huge, queasy swells around Estevan Point. During his years at Hesquiat, he undertook this trip frequently, on one occasion with a man he called "Jimmy Codfish," who came to Hesquiat to fetch Father Charles because Jimmy's mother was dying.

> *March 13, 1911:* Jimmy got a canoe with two Hesquiat Indians and we left for Nootka at 9:30 AM. Sea was running very big though the wind from the S East was light, the weather was very thick. It took us fully

View from Christie School of *Princess Maquinna* arriving.

six hours, an open sea trip, and I was very sea sick...I visited the sick woman whom I baptized intending to administer Extreme Unction the following day.

March 14: Had a bad night, not much sleep. Mass at 7 AM with Jimmy present. During my thanksgiving Indian came to announce the death of the woman. She had died during holy Mass. I burried her. In the evening had five Confessions.

March 15: Mass at 6:30 AM. At 8:30 I with the Hesquiat Indian left for home again. Sailed out of Nootka with a northerly wind. Beautiful day, not much of a swell, hence I was not sea sick. After sailing for about an hour we were becalmed and had to pull with the oars. At Estevan Pt caught a slight Westerly breeze. Arrived at Hesquiat about 3 PM after an ocean trip of six hours and a half.

The voyages Father Charles most frequently described were those between Hesquiat and Kakawis: this was commonly "a pull of nearly nine hours," as he put it on March 18, 1911. This long journey could follow different routes, going "inside" around Flores Island, a distance of some forty miles, or "outside" in more exposed waters, which shortened the journey to just under thirty miles. But even taking the inside route meant facing many long miles on the open Pacific, often over menacing swells and along a rocky stretch of shoreline offering no possibility of a safe landing.

January 14, 1911: Left Kakawis for my home at Hesquiat by Indian canoe with two men and two women at 9 AM. There was no wind, pulled with the oars as far as Vargas Island Pt. then sailed with a northerly wind against the incoming tide to open sea...Calm but sometimes a big, funny looking wave came. Off Sidney Inlet rather rough. S. East wind. At 3 PM a gale of wind sprang up suddenly.

By the end of the first decade of the twentieth century, travel on the coast in small boats involved sail, paddle and gasoline motors. Some vessels used all three.

Indians shouted as only Indians can shout. Two men were stearing now with their paddles, sea tremendous big. We had already taken down one sail and the jib and reefed the smaller sail. Indians kept up their shouting—I prayed. Shipped water twice. Reached Hesquiat 4 PM. Deo Gratias.

Risky sea voyages by canoe were something of a Roman Catholic tradition by this time on the coast. A generation earlier, in the days before regular steamer traffic, Father Brabant described voyages that were even more arduous. His story of the three-day trip by canoe from Victoria to Hesquiat in April 1880 is epic: "Both the Indians and myself had given up. The waves were immense and, rising like mountains, threatened to engulf us at any moment. We all lay flat in the canoe, save the man in the stern. At times our frail skiff stood almost perpendicular."

"Sea tremendous big," waves "mountain high," "high running sea": such dramatic descriptions appear occasionally in Father Charles's diary, but in keeping with his usual laconic style, his most challenging canoe trips often receive only cursory attention.

July 19, 1916: Rain at night, and drizzling during forenoon. At noon it brightened up with Westerly Wind. At one o'clock left [from Hesquiat] with two Indians for Kakawis. We took the outside route. Off Sidney Inlet wind failed and we had to pull the rest of the way. It took 8½ hours in all.

Father Charles never revealed how he felt about all these voyages, except for a rare "Deo Gratias" when it was all over. He even wrote of some of his long canoe trips in such flat terms they seem almost dull.

February 18, 1912: Sunday Low Mass at 8:30, no sermon, but announcement of coming Ash Wednesday. At 10:20 left with 2 Indians per canoe for Kakawis. Weather: light westerly wind with hail and rain squalls. Off Sidney Inlet strong West wind and big sea. Took inside passage. No wind on the inside. Pulled all day with the oars and arrived at Kakawis 9:20 PM.

Christie School boys, probably in 1901. The priests relied on the boys for help in handling canoes, especially in loading and unloading freight from the coastal steamers.

This description reduces an eleven-hour canoe trip from Hesquiat to Kakawis in mid-February, in the rain, at times in wind and big seas, the last four hours paddling in the dark, to an entirely unremarkable experience. Yet anyone who has attempted anything remotely resembling such a journey knows how daunting this coastline can be for paddlers in small open boats. Often Father Charles's writing requires a second glance in order to understand properly the extent and the nature of his travels.

Consider a ten-day period in April 1911. Father Charles first set out on foot from Hesquiat to Home-is, north of Estevan Point, a distance of nearly six miles. He walked back to Hesquiat on the same day, stopping in for dinner at Estevan Point. The following day, after saying Mass at 6 AM, he left with four Indians in a canoe for Kakawis. "No wind, pulled for one hour; then a light breeze, slow progress. Big swell. Later on had a good breeze and with two sails up made good progress." Six hours after leaving Hesquiat, the canoe arrived at Kakawis. The following morning, Father Charles paddled to Opitsat and back, and within a day or two he was

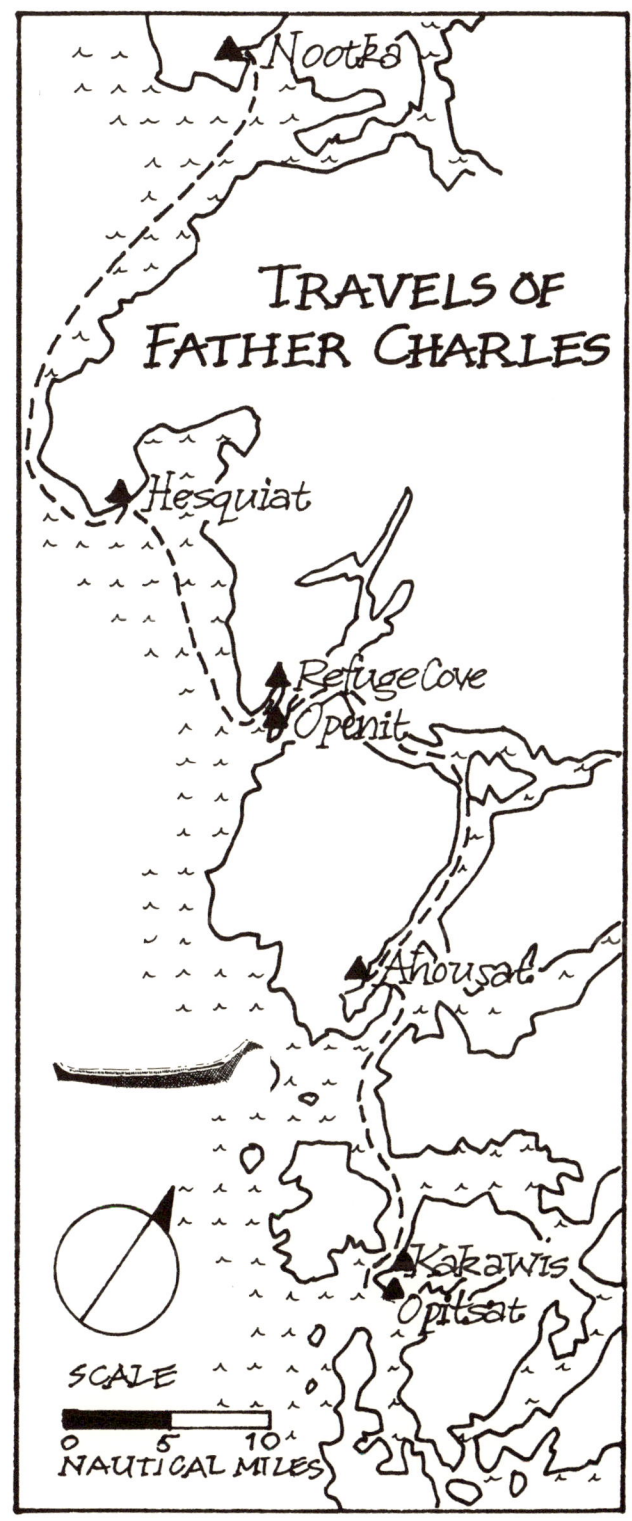

From Father Charles's diary, accounts of a few voyages:

Kakawis to Hesquiat, November 17, 1910: "Left Kakawis…at 1 PM…At 10 AM we arrived…"

Hesquiat to Kakawis, December 26, 1910: "5 hours in open ocean and 4 hours in inside waters."

Nootka to Hesquiat, March 15, 1911: "an ocean trip of six hours and a half."

Hesquiat to Kakawis, March 18, 1911: "a pull of nearly nine hours."

Hesquiat to Kakawis, February 18, 1912: "At 10:20 left with 2 Indians per canoe…Pulled all day…arrived at Kakawis 9:20 PM."

Kakawis to Hesquiat, February 10, 1917: "Left Kakawis by Indian canoe at 9:30 AM and arrived at Hesquiat 5 PM…it rained the whole way."

Kakawis to Hesquiat, October 30, 1919: "Left with Matthias in his canoe at 9 AM…arrived at 3 PM after a stormy outside passage…we shipped a lot of water."

on board a steamer heading up to Nootka. He stayed there for two days and was awoken in the middle of his second night by the whistle of the steamer. He went on board, heading back to Hesquiat. Because of poor weather, the steamer could not stop at Hesquiat but discharged Father Charles at Anton's Point, a more sheltered spot inside the harbour, from where he walked over a mile back to the village, arriving at three in the morning. Within a day he set out for Estevan Point on foot, and after one night there he walked back to Hesquiat. In ten days he had travelled 139 miles: 22 on foot, 33 by canoe and the remainder by steamer.

Over time, Father Charles gained recognition as a seasoned traveller on the coast, prepared to clamber aboard whatever vessel was heading in the right direction at the right time to take him where he wanted to go. Between early June and mid-December 1918, he made seven return trips by steamer from Kakawis to Hesquiat; one trip by fishboat from Kakawis to Friendly Cove, returning by steamer; and three motor-launch trips between Kakawis and Hesquiat. Compared to his early days, this was easy travelling. The long treks up and down the outside coast by canoe were becoming a thing of the past, far outnumbered now by trips in motor launches or by steamer.

Father Charles regularly escorted children to or from Christie School on his travels; groups of students travelled with him, by coastal steamer or canoe, at the beginning and end of school terms. "Steamer here at 7 AM," he commented on April 22, 1924. "As usual I accompany the children to their homes; this time I had 2 children for Hesquiat, 7 for Nootka and 17 for Kyuquot. Hesquiat was reached 1 PM and Nootka at 5 PM." Supporting the work of the residential school in this or any other way was central to his role as a priest on the west coast. Almost equally important, his role as priest implied opposing the Protestant missionaries and teachers at every turn.

By the turn of the century, the religious competition between Catholics and Protestants in Clayoquot Sound reached a new level, particularly at Ahousat. When he was first on the coast, Father Brabant felt confident that Ahousat could be counted as one of "his" villages. He wistfully recalled, in a letter to Father Maurus Snyder, how he "baptised 135 children including the Kelsamats" at Ahousat on his first visit there in 1874. Seven years later, Brabant built a small church at Ahousat with "the generous assistance of the natives," as he stated in his diary, and in 1885, Fred Thornberg built a house there for Father Lemmens on his periodic visits. Despite this, the Catholics were outmanoeuvred by the more persistent Presbyterians, who established a day school in the village in 1896, and later a residential school.

Brabant blamed Father Van Nevel, who succeeded Father Lemmens. He was in charge of both Opitsat and Ahousat during the 1890s, but according to Brabant, Van Nevel never visited Ahousat at all, leaving it "abandoned and neglected." In the long run, this served Fred Thornberg nicely, for he ended up living many years in the abandoned priest's house. But in a letter to Father Maurus in 1901, Brabant indicated he had not lost hope for Ahousat, declaring: "If I were at the head of affairs in the diocese and had the means I would first place a priest in Ahousat and show the heretics [Presbyterians] that we are not dead yet!" The bishop disagreed and wasted no more manpower at Ahousat, instead repositioning Brabant, moving him from Hesquiat to Nootka in June 1901 to counter yet another Presbyterian minister who had recently arrived and set up shop in a cottage belonging to Stockham and Dawley.

At Nootka, Brabant was on familiar ground, for he had been coming there since 1874, sometimes for long stretches of time, and he had built the small church at Friendly Cove in 1888. He knew all the families, he knew the renowned Chief Maquinna, and he knew the storekeeper, William Netherby. Early in 1901, Netherby wrote to Brabant with news that John Russell had come from Ahousat to hold a potlatch for the children at Nootka, purportedly to bribe them over to the Protestant side. Furthermore, Netherby reported that Mr. Swartout, the missionary in Barkley Sound, had said he was prepared to "fight the priest" at Nootka "and make it hot for the Catholics." Worst of all, the venerable Chief Maquinna had invited Mr. Russell into his house and had been talking to him.

This came as a severe shock to Brabant because the chief had told him he favoured the Catholics. "Maquinna and his strong men told me that I need not be uneasy, that no minister will be accommodated here." But now, instead of spurning the newcomer, many locals in Nootka Sound "made it very plain to me that they consider it a very nice thing to have a priest and a preacher." To complicate matters even further, as this denominational conflict was heating up, Chief Maquinna became gravely ill. As Maquinna lay near death, Brabant was at his side, still hoping he might talk the old chief into being baptized:

> After I left him he was quite cheerful and apparently getting better—he continued so till shortly before he died: then his abdomen began to swell and something burst inside and the end soon came—his inside must have been quite rotten and the gas produced by the decaying

inner organs caused the swelling and death...I could do nothing for him before I left and if I had been here it is doubtful that I could have baptised him or been of any assistance as his death was sudden and he was even then in the hands of two medicine women.

The death of Chief Maquinna was a momentous event. The *Victoria Daily Colonist* paid due tribute on April 30, 1901:

> News was brought by steamer Queen City of the death of one of the most noted Indian chieftains of the province, Maquinna, chief of the Nootka Indians...There is weeping and wailing at Friendly Cove and...at Nootka night and day there was a wailing cry from the huts, and the Indians were dancing their sorrow dance and otherwise mourning their dead chief. On a point looking out to sea they have erected a large cairn, the totem, from which they hold the spirit of Maquinna is to look out to sea.

The memorial to Chief Maquinna. Father Brabant's photographs are in poor condition; this sketch is based on one of them.

Brabant was not present when Chief Maquinna died, but he arrived back at Friendly Cove the following day and wrote to Father Maurus from there on April 24, 1901. "I arrived here yesterday—Tuesday—at noon. From quite a distance we noticed a number of Indians on a prominent rock putting up a 'Ka-mat-a' in memory of Chief Maquinna who had died the day before...I am supposed to take a picture of it tomorrow." A month later, Brabant wrote about this photograph of Chief Maquinna's memorial: "I got a lot of pictures from Victoria: they are quite a success—the canoe and Indians are beautiful and so are the decorations on Maquinna's grave, and as these decorations have been destroyed by the storms a week after they were put up my picture is the only souvenir in existence."

Maquinna's nephew, Napoleon, succeeded him as chief, and Brabant was confident he had the support of "the young chief," as he called him. "Napoleon seems to have great confidence in me and must have been instructed by his late uncle to that effect—Next Sunday all the Indians will assemble in the large house of the late Maquinna—I understand that the young heir is to address me and of course I must address all the savages."

Without the support of the old chief, Brabant feared the Protestants would gain a significant foothold in this changing local scene. Determined not to be worsted, he opened a day school at Friendly Cove in the summer of 1901 to provide competition to the recently opened Presbyterian day school, and he set out to make life as difficult as possible for the opposition. Later that year, Brabant triumphantly announced: "The preacher is gone! and no one here, Indians or whites, regret it." He remarked later, in another letter, that the preacher was totally defeated and discouraged, adding a happy outburst of Latin: "He can say: 'Veni Vidi' but he must leave out 'Vici'!" Having trounced the enemy, Brabant reverted to his previous pattern of sending children from Nootka to board at Christie School.

Despite Brabant's momentary jubilation, the Roman Catholic monopoly on the coast was ending. Although the documents and letters of the Catholic priests continue to speak of outfacing the Protestant "heretics," their assumption of superiority was ever less tenable. On October 29, 1905, reporting on the opening of the Presbyterian residential school at Ahousat, the *Colonist*, no supporter of Rome, was openly delighted:

> A day school established at Ahousaht developed in a few years into the present large boarding school. The Roman Catholic Church built an industrial school at Clayoquot [Kakawis]...and their aggressive policy was such as to leave no alternative to the Presbyterian Church but to

take the advance step. To sound the retreat and hand over the ground to Romanism was not the spirit of John Knox, and the presence of the boarding school is an effective check against Romanish aggression.

This conflict between "Romanish aggression" and "the spirit of John Knox" is a perpetual theme in Father Charles's diary. He had a particular dislike for the Methodist Reverend William Stone, who had moved from Clo-oose to Clayoquot in 1902. The two men frequently collided during Father Charles's years at Opitsat, as they competed for the same souls:

> *April 25, 1906:* Last night Dora Sieward arrived bringing the body of Tlaghshiet. He had died aboard on Easter Sunday after an illness of 2 days. Though not yet baptized he was one of my best Indians, always sticking up for the priest and a great help in the fight against the Methodists and attended our Sunday Services regularly. After my Mass I went in my little canoe to the schooner which was anchored off Leonard Isld, but I came too late, Mr. Stone, the Methodist preacher, had been there before me with his launch and was towing the body in a canoe to the burial ground. I followed in my canoe. After hard rowing I reached the Island on which he was to be buried. A dispute followed as usual on occasions like this but this time Mr. Stone departed and I held the services at the grave.

Christie School girls preparing dinner.

Even though the deceased Tlaghshiet was not a Catholic, Father Charles never doubted his right to take charge at this funeral. He regarded the man as one of "his" Indians, perhaps on the pretext that while Tlaghshiet had not been baptized, he was friendly, even inviting Father Charles to his home for a meal only the year before, in May 1905: "Took dinner with Tlaghshiet and his family. We had canned salmon, potatoes, butter, hot biscuits, tea and stewed peaches. It was more and better [than] I would have had in my house."

By 1907, Dr. H. Raynor was the Methodist missionary for Clayoquot and in charge of a small hospital on Stockham

Island, which by then had been renamed Mission Island. The hospital was housed in Stockham and Dawley's old hotel. Father Charles found nothing to admire in this set-up. On November 14, 1907, he wrote that he "was refused by Dr. Raynor (Methodist) entrance to the Hospital to visit Georgie Matthew, a Clayoquot boy, baptized by the priest, but afterwards attending the Presbyterian school at Ahousat. This was the third refusal."

The Presbyterian residential school at Ahousat provided serious competition for native students; more than twenty-five registered during its first year of operation in 1904. Finding and keeping students at the Catholic schools, whether the day school at Opitsat or Christie residential school, was an unceasing challenge, as Father Charles reported, with tired resignation, year after year. By September 1909 he commented that, because of the Methodists' school at Opitsat, he had only "3 or 4 pupils"; nine days later he had only one boy at school. The trend continued. Even bribery failed Father Charles.

> *November 8, 1909:* Had five children in school. From the beginning of October until today I had empty school days. Nobody would come, they all went to the Methodist school. On All Saints day I offered an Indian 25 cents each day whenever three of his five very near relatives would come to my school. In spite of this offer I had none of them till today and then only one of the five.

Observing the Methodists' tactics a few weeks later did nothing to lift Father Charles's spirits. Their attempts at bribery were more lavish and more successful than his:

> *December 2, 1909:* The Methodist minister (Dr. Raynor) called the Indian men to a meeting and in order to get them all he announced a mak-mak potlatch for them. His church bell rang 3 times for the meeting about 20 men attended. They were treated with coffee, bread, crackers, pies and fresh pears which latter were furnished by John Grice of Tofino who himself was present and in a speech exhorted the Indians to join the Doctor in school and church and for so doing were promised free medicine when sick and the best kind of medicine.

As the Opitsat day school floundered on, the priests aggressively sought children for Christie School at Kakawis; whatever happened in the villages, this school was their crown jewel on the coast, the focus of all their efforts. But as

Indian Agent Harry Guillod commented in 1900 when the residential school first opened, the parents were "very loath to part with their children." Families' unhappiness at being separated is abundantly clear in various documents. Even the annual reports of the school, while straining for a tone of buoyant optimism, strike a jarringly artificial note on this subject.

> The parents who, with much reluctance and many misgivings, consented to place their children in the school a year ago, now express satisfaction with their action. Others, who threatened to withdraw their wards, to-day are loud in their praise of the good the school is doing. The children themselves have undergone a wonderful change for the better. The eyes once filled with tears, now beam with joy; and the poor little hearts aching under the weight of homesickness but a year ago, to-day swell with delight at having found in the school a new and more comfortable home. Surly looks yielded to sweet smiles, and sounds of complaint to ripples of merry laughter.

The relentless good cheer of this report of June 1901 fails to mask the unsettling details beneath the surface. In mentioning "reluctance and many misgivings," threats to withdraw children, "surly looks" and "eyes once filled with tears," Father Maurus glosses over a world of unacknowledged problems. His report continues: "The promptness, and the joy, with which they return to the school, when allowed to visit their homes, best prove how much they have grown attached to the school, which they regarded a prison in days gone by."

Whatever Father Maurus chose to say, the evidence to the contrary is sombre and stark: some children were painfully homesick, and some bitterly resented

Girls at Christie School helped to tend a garden enclosed by a white picket fence. It featured a fountain, roses, and flower beds edged with white rocks.

attending the school at all. This reality breaks through in Father Charles Moser's accounts of children who ran away from school or who painfully resisted going to school. The first such description appears in his diary after the school had been in operation only two years.

> *May 25, 1902:* Sr. Placida comes to Echachislet to get Emma [Peter] whose father had signed her for school a week ago. The child don't want to go and hides under blankets. The parents of course side with the daughter. Sister grabs the child and carries it in spite of howling and kicking like a wild animal down the beach and deposits it in the boat. Hayan wawa [much talk] and demonstration from all quarters of the village, with bad talk and lies against the Christie School. Next day Mrs. Peter with relatives fetches the Policeman stationed at Clayoquot and they go to Kakawis to rescue the girl. The Policeman rightly informed turned against the Indians and sent them home minus Emma who is to stay in school.

Nothing of this nature ever appears in the official reports. Instead they focus on the trades and skills being imparted to the students. As well as carpentry, the boys learned plumbing, pipe fitting, shoemaking and net making. Both the boys and the girls worked in the school laundry and learned to make bread. In his report of 1904, Father Maurus listed every single piece of sewing and handwork done by the girls at the school that year: "New garments: thirty-one shirts, thirty pairs of overalls, forty-two jumpers, twenty dresses, seventy-two aprons, forty chemises, thirty-five pairs of drawers…" continuing through all the household linens, surplices, altar cloths, embroidered doilies, handmade rugs, underskirts

Learning the skills of shoemaking.

and on and on. The girls also produced a profusion of tatting and crocheting and quantities of torchon and Battenberg lace, for the school had a lace-making machine in addition to its Singer sewing machines. The sisters ensured the children dressed properly and insisted that they wore shoes, for shoes—surely a mark of Christian civilization—were mandatory, and Brother Leonard operated an excellent shoemaking shop at Kakawis.

The penmanship of the children also received lavish praise. In tandem with learning to read and write in English, all the students learned the "Palmer Method" of handwriting, which involved repetitive written exercises and considerable arm and shoulder movement. In all surviving letters written by students at the school, the Palmer Method of handwriting appears, every child producing almost identical handwriting, uncannily uniform. Developed in the United States by Austin Palmer, the editor of *The Western Penman*, and made famous in his 1888 *Palmer's Guide to Muscular Movement Writing*, this form of cursive writing became all the rage in American schools and businesses. The students at Christie School were one of Palmer's great success stories. In 1904, at the Louisiana Purchase Exposition in St. Louis, samples from Christie School attracted notice in a large exhibit of Palmer Method penmanship. Two years later, six hundred letters written by senior Christie School pupils were circulated as examples to thousands of public school teachers in the United States. Professor Palmer was delighted by these and awarded a certificate of excellency to three students.

Father Brabant greeted this calligraphic achievement dourly. "I am not one of those who believe," he declared, "that reading and writing, in the case of

In the shoemaking shop at Christie School.

Indians, will advance to a great extent the cause of religion; but, to keep our Indian children from perversion, we must follow the trend of the times." Father Maurus disagreed. He was proud of the handwriting of the students, making sure to photograph his three prize pupils with their Palmer certificates.

Particularly in the early years of the school, the priests took many photographs of the children at work, at play, in groups. The sisters at Kakawis printed multiple copies, often in postcard format, of certain photographs. "I printed 2 gross of postal cards," Sister Mary Sophie wrote on one occasion, adding "sold $7 dollars worth of postal cards." She does not reveal where she sold them; possibly through Mount Angel Abbey, or even at Walter Dawley's store, for he certainly did sell postcards. On lucky occasions, parents back in the villages received copies of photographs of their children. Father Brabant wrote from Hesquiat in 1901, describing how "the countenance of Louisa, the mother of Lisa was beaming with happiness when she delivered the letters and pictures."

Many photographs survive of the children at the school, but they reveal no identities. Which one is Emma, who fought so hard against returning to school? Is she there? Is Paul from Nootka amongst the boys? What are they thinking, those boys in the shoemaking shop? The photographs may be speaking likenesses, but the voices of the children cannot be heard, and their names are unknown.

Three boys with their certificates for excellency in the Palmer Method of handwriting, 1904.

Even during the first year of the school, disquieting rumours began to circulate on the coast—rumours about how the children were treated at Christie School. Father Brabant heard all manner of accusations and murmurs at both Hesquiat and Nootka. He blamed the other tribes, particularly the Ahousats, for these rumours, suspecting that the Ahousats were influenced by their resident Protestant missionary.

Stories spread that children were flogged at the school. From the outset, Brabant warned the new priests to avoid this practice. "Be sure to abstain from bodily punishment," he cautioned Father Maurus in a letter dated February 13,

Father Brabant to Father Maurus, February 13, 1901: "Be sure to abstain from bodily punishment— Indians never resort to it and do not tollerate it on their children…"

1901. "Indians never resort to it and do not tollerate it on their children." The old priest was adamant—he knew from his long experience on the coast that this particular taboo should never be breached. According to Brabant, Chief Maquinna originally supported the school because he believed that no child would ever be flogged there, trusting that Father Brabant would direct the other priests never to lay a finger on any child. Nonetheless, alarming rumours persisted, as Brabant recounted in a letter to Father Maurus:

> That little boy Willie has been made to tell things which are not true. Last night I asked a woman to let us have her little girl [for the school] and she told me in unmistakable terms that we could not have the child because the school at Kakawis was bad; the Ahousat little boy had told her that the children were flogged etc etc. However Maquinna told me to say that he would see that the child would come as he knew the accusations to be false.

In his annual report to the Department of Indian Affairs in 1905, Father Maurus made an admission, the first of its kind in all his reports:

> The discipline is mild, but firm. The pupils are under constant supervision and their conduct is watched most carefully. Religious persuasion is the most effectual means of correction with these children; only once during the year, in fact, for the first time in five years, was corporal punishment resorted to.

In his 1906 report, Father Maurus commented, "During the whole year I have had no occasion to apply corporal punishment to any of the pupils." In the following few years, his reports make no reference at all to corporal punishment; indeed, the 1908 report states the school's intentions in the loftiest of terms:

> We are trying to the best of our ability to make the school for its inmates the cradle of civilization, the nursery of faith, the home of industry, the vestibule of Catholicity, and the open door of self-respecting and self-supporting citizenship. Our efforts are therefore directed toward enlightening the mind by the teaching of the truths and precepts of the Christian religion and, in a greater measure towards strengthening the will of the children, by exhorting them to well-doing and guiding them in the daily practice of virtue. The conduct of our children has been highly satisfactory during the past year.

Father Maurus and Father Brabant at Christie School.

Despite such elevated sentiments, snippets of contrary evidence surface in Father Charles's diary:

June 9, 1905: End of vacation for Christie School children. All return to school except one girl from Opitsat.

June 10: With Christie School's boat went to Opitsat to get the missing girl. Her father was absent, the girl did not want to come along, her mother protested—but finally the girl gave in, but started to cry aloud and her mother crying aloud in the same manner as Indian women cry when somebody is dying. It was a pitiful sound and scene.

Father Charles did not name the crying girl central to this "pitiful sound and scene." He took her from her keening mother, and they set out for Kakawis. After about half an hour in the boat, paddling away from her home, she disembarked, tear-stained and silent, on the beach in front of Christie School. Looming above her was the school, white and imposing and larger than ever.

Two new wings expanded the original box-like structure in 1904, one wing for boys, one for girls. The school shone with a fresh coat of paint, and the fenced gardens had increased season by season. Eleven acres of land were

Christie School, 1905.

cleared around the school, and work was underway to build a gymnasium and install shower rooms and indoor water closets. The "sewerage is perfect," Father Maurus reported cheerfully. By the time the unhappy, unnamed girl from Opitsat arrived in June 1905, some sixty children were at the school, ready to start the new term.

Confidently, Father Maurus described their enthusiasm: "Of painstaking application and of lively interest in their studies our pupils seem never to grow weary." None of this would have made sense to the unhappy girl from Opitsat as she faced the school. She did not want to be there. Yet as isolated and abandoned as she may have felt, she was not alone in her resistance to attending Christie School.

In Walter Dawley's collection of documents, two slightly crumpled search warrants survive, dated 1905. Father Maurus requested these, and Walter Dawley signed them in his capacity as Justice of the Peace. The subjects of these warrants were two students who failed to return to the school. With the warrants, either Father Maurus or Constable McDougall from Clayoquot had the right to search for the students in private homes and bring them back to school, with or without their or their families' consent.

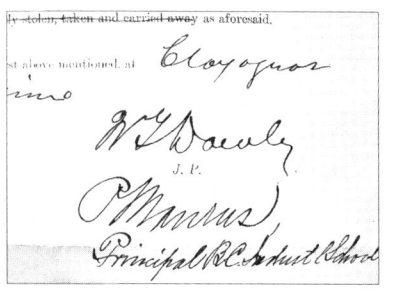

This July 15, 1905, search warrant for Susan Cecil, "unlawfully absent" from the school, was found in Walter Dawley's papers. It is signed by Dawley, as Justice of the Peace, and by Father Maurus.

The search warrant of July 15, 1905, granted Father Maurus permission to search for Susan Cecil at Kyuquot at her own house, for, as the document declares, "Susan Cecil is unlawfully absent from my charge and refuses to return." On November 27, another search warrant issued to Father Maurus enabled him to seek Dennis Jacob, "concealed in the house of Harry Ishka at Hesquiat." Again the reason was that "Dennis Jacob of Hesquiat is unlawful absent from my charge at school."

An angry exchange of letters ensued between Father Brabant and Father Maurus on account of "Dennis Jacob," whom the priests called "Dionys." When Constable McDougall went to Hesquiat to apprehend Dionys and bring him back to the school, he stayed for twelve days at the house of Anton Luckovitch, just outside the village. Eventually McDougall took the unwilling Dionys in charge and returned him to the school, but the school had to pay all the expenses incurred in this incident, including the constable's travel, board and lodging. The school insisted that Dionys's father, Harry, should pay this sum. Several months after the event, nothing had been resolved.

"Anton charged Mr McDougall seventeen dollars for the 12 days he boarded and lodged him," Father Maurus wrote to Brabant on April 21, 1906, "thus the expenses amount to twenty-three dollars…Kindly inform Harry that if he wants Dionys home the balance of thirteen dollars has to be paid immediately else Dionys will not go out before the end of June." Having effectively declared he was holding the boy for ransom, Father Maurus then took aim at Brabant, accusing him of working against the interests of the school, deliberately preventing the constable from apprehending Dionys, and supporting Dionys and his father because he disagreed with the public way in which the case was being handled.

Brabant was furious. His letter of May 1, 1906, is barely coherent with rage:

> From the first week I have met you, you have…always thought it in order to snub me, snap at me and treat me with contempt…the objects of your rage are myself and my handful of Catholic Indians. But such as you fancy us to yourself we do not exist and like the delirious drunkard you are exhausting your temper against imaginary foes! In order to escape further annoyance I must notify you that for the future any and all letters from you will be returned unopened.

Intent on their own heated argument, the two priests never examined what lay behind this episode. Neither of them questioned nor explained why Dionys and his father, Harry, acted as they did. Brabant apparently opposed the use of the search warrant, probably because he disliked any authority to be exercised at Hesquiat other than his own, and Father Maurus infuriated him by bringing in an outside authority. Brabant's resolution never to read any more of Father Maurus's letters and to return them unopened eventually weakened; certainly they corresponded further, but no letters survive for several years following this particular exchange.

No other search warrants surface in Walter Dawley's papers telling of runaways from Christie School, but many stories of runaway students appear in Father Charles's diary as his years on the coast unwind. Repeatedly, he makes terse references about fetching children back to school, sometimes seeking them out with the help of the police constable or the Indian Agent. He comments on unruly behaviour, on disturbances, on punishments at the school. Over the years, such comments become increasingly frequent. "It was a pitiful sound and scene," Father Charles wrote after he witnessed the girl from Opitsat resisting her return to school in 1905. His experience of such sounds, such scenes, had only just begun.

6

A Bunch of the Boys

SS Umbrina
June 23, 1900

To Mr Walter T Dawley, Clayoquot, BC

Dear Friend
You will be know doubt surprised to learn that I have left South Africa and that I am now only a days ride from Southampton…I'll be glad however to reach old BC once more…Give my kindest regards to all the boys…Remember me most kindly to Old Tom and tell him I shall be able to see myself reflected once more on his pate. Is he still using that patent hair elixer. Well I must say good bye for the present. I shall write again soon.

Yours Ever Sincerly
Jas W Jones

"JAS W JONES," signing his name with a grand flourish, swashbuckles his way into the Dawley correspondence in the late 1890s. Then in his early thirties, Jones was a committed risk-taker, a man with a quick eye for good times, ready laughs and likely opportunities. His cheerful insouciance, his unflagging belief that a fortune would emerge from his mining interests, and his readiness to ask for a loan or a favour reveal a devil-may-care, mercurial character. His name first appears in the *Victoria Daily Colonist* on April 7, 1897, in an article discussing the

Opposite: Some of the boys outside the Clayoquot store.

merits of his various claims. "The country about the Sound is, according to Mr Jones, exceedingly promising," the newspaper declares, going on to say Jones had been prospecting on the west coast of Vancouver Island for three years, and that he was taking fifty pounds of ore from Sydney Inlet for a smelting test.

The early years of his acquaintance with Dawley find Jones at his happiest. "Dear Friend Charley" his letters begin, or "Dear Charlie." Few people felt free to address Dawley by his nickname, but Jones was a breezy soul, much chattier than most of the boys who came and went at Clayoquot. "Excuse this writing as my only table is a gold pan," he announced cheerfully in a letter from Sydney Inlet in July 1898, requesting that "prospecting shoes" be sent up to him on the next steamer. In his letters, Jones joked with both Walter Dawley and Thomas Stockham, chaffing "Friend Tom" about his bald head and always passing on regards to any of the boys who happened to be around.

Jones worked on mining claims in several locations over the years: the Pete and Iron King claims on Vargas Island, the Ace of Spades near Alberni, the Hetty Green at Deer Creek in Tofino Inlet, and the Beshalam group of claims in Sydney Inlet—a property owned by Walter Dawley. But it was another group of claims at Sydney Inlet that truly fired Jones's imagination: the Indian Chief group. He worked this mining property in partnership with James Kincaid, convinced that here at last was a wealth of ore liberally laced with copper. The *Colonist* newspaper concurred, hailing Jones as "'Black Jones' than whom there is no better prospector in the district," and describing his find at Sydney Inlet as "the prettiest peacock copper seen in Victoria during recent months."

From July 1897 onward, Jones and Kincaid laboured continually at their mining claims situated on Peacock Mountain in what is now called Stewardson Inlet on the west side of Sydney Inlet. Eleven men had joined them by mid-December, and according to the newspaper, "They have put up a blacksmith shop and cabins and are now driving in a tunnel on the mine." The mines inspector's report of 1898 describes the site: buildings perched on the mountainside 1,000 feet up, and a tunnel extending into the rock some 265 feet. Great expectations abounded, with Jones pinning all his hopes on this venture.

He was not alone in having such high hopes; many others shared his faith in the mining potential in the area. "The coast is overrun with American mining speculators looking for 'good things,'" the *Colonist* reported in December 1899. At Bear River, a mining community called Port Hughes scrambled into existence, complete with a post office and a hotel, to service the needs of a number of new and promising mining ventures. The coastal steamers *Willapa* and *Queen City* were often overwhelmed by all the freight awaiting them; they could barely manage the tons of ore from various mining claims, along with the hundreds of cases of canned salmon from Clayoquot Cannery, all the lumber heading up and down the coast, and the ever-increasing passenger traffic.

James Jones's mining activities are faithfully mirrored in his correspondence with Walter Dawley. Like countless other prospectors, Jones kept in close touch with the storekeeper because, as mining recorder for the west coast of Vancouver Island—later called the Clayoquot Mining Division—Dawley recorded all their mining claims, issued certificates of work and recorded abandonment of claims. In the process, he received a commission of 20 percent on all the moneys he collected, and he became the supplier and confidant of many prospectors. No one knew the lay of the land, in terms of mining claims and interests, better than Walter Dawley. He knew every discovery, every hopeful tale, every hint of a good showing or a rich vein or a promising outcrop, and he knew personally all the boys working the claims in his area and what they were up to.

Yet in the autumn of 1899, when James Warren Jones took it into his head to enlist as part of the Canadian contingent leaving Victoria to fight in the Boer War, all of his friends, including Stockham and Dawley, were taken aback. After all, Jones was American, not Canadian; patriotic fervour for the glory of the British Empire certainly did not inspire him. His reasons for enlisting were quite different. Like many of the young men who went to South Africa, he sensed adventure and fresh challenges, thinking that when the conflict ended he might stay and settle in this exciting new land. This quixotic decision surprised everyone, even Jones's partner James Kincaid, who wrote to Dawley on December 6, 1899, enclosing a payment of $8.90 on his account and adding: "I was much surprised to receive communication from Jones that he was on his way to the Transvail and fear he will get more than he expected."

Leaving his claims and mining interests for Walter Dawley to manage, and turning his back on the busy west coast scene, James Jones set his sights on South Africa. He was one of some fifty volunteers who enlisted in Victoria; of these, twenty-five were selected to make up the Canadian contingent from the city. At first this was high adventure for Jones, chronicled in a number of exceptionally vivid letters to Dawley and Stockham. But however far James Jones travelled, and whatever he experienced, he never escaped the spell of his mining claims.

> Steamer Sardinia, Cape Varde
> November 12, 1899
>
> Dear Friends:
> You will see by my letter I have arrived so far safely on my journey we are now 3060 miles from Quebec and about 8000 from Clayoquot… Let me know when you write how Sidney Inlet is looking and give me all the news you can… It will be full three weeks before we arrive in Cape Town this steamer only makes about 10 miles per hour it was a horrible sight the first two days out from Quebec nearly three quarters of the men were sea sick…about 100 men are layed up with the Clap and about 50 with the old roll. Crabs are numerous.

In the following months, Jones went through many horrors fighting in South Africa, to the point of wondering why he was there at all. His partner Kincaid was right: Jones got more than he expected. In December 1899 he wrote soberly to his friends at Clayoquot from Belmont:

> I tell you these boores are good fighters and brave men… In the last battle they nearly cut to pieces one of our best regements the black watch and a [portion] of the Gordon Highlanders. I fancy there will be quite a few of us missing from Victoria before this is over as we are in the front rank and the right half company however we will die game… the boores say we have no business coming over here to take part in this and when they catch us they will make it hot if they take any prisenors.

The following month, sad news arrived at Clayoquot in a letter to Stockham and Dawley from the teenaged Stuart Stone of Clo-oose. Stuart knew and liked James Jones, and he was shocked by some news he had just received. For the storekeepers' information, Stuart copied out by hand an account from the *Daily Star* newspaper, dated January 25, 1900:

> Word reached here last night that Private J. W. Jones of the First British Columbia Contingent of the Canadian force had been killed

in action at Dover's Farm. Jones was a graduate of West Point, although of Scottish birth, and one of the best known mining men of Vancouver, "Black Jones" being his common title.

"We all feel very sorry if that is true about Mr. Jones," Stuart commented in his round, schoolboy handwriting. "I hope it is not…Mr Jones lost his life when he was fighting for our country, but those Boers may surrender yet." Stuart then moved on to other matters, thanking Dawley and Stockham for the firecrackers and describing the frustrations of duck hunting. "The river is too high this winter and we see hardly anything but butterballs and golden eyes and a few mallards but one day we saw a lot of geese but you cannot get near enough to them with a shotgun. I think we will have to get a cannon and some grape shot for it to kill them."

Rumours of James Jones's death were greatly exaggerated. Indeed, every detail circulating about him proved unreliable: he was not of Scottish birth, nor had he graduated from West Point Military Academy, and he definitely was not dead. The *Colonist* set the record straight in an article headlined "Rumoured casualty" and subtitled "Report in English Papers led to Belief that a Victorian had been killed." "In the list of casualties published in the English papers of those killed at Dover's Farm appears the name 'Private Jones, Victoria,'" the paper reported, going on to say that no Canadians were killed in this engagement and in all probability another Private Jones was killed, a young man from Victoria, Australia.

On May 4, 1900, the newspaper printed one of James Jones's letters, written on March 22 and sent to Mr. W. J. McKeon Jr. of Victoria: "I have time now to drop you a few lines to let you know that I am still in the land of the living, and was not killed at Sunnyside, as reported" is the good-humoured opening. A few days later, another of Jones's letters appeared in the paper, this one addressed to James B. Thomson:

> Dear Friend: I thought I would drop you a few lines to let you know I am still alive and kicking. I have been through some pretty tough places since I last talked to you in Trounce Alley…The rheumatism is much better, but I am afraid, it will take some time before my back is in good shape again. I hurt it carrying a wounded soldier off the field…As strong as I am, or rather was, it was too much for me on top of forced marches and I was knocked out. Well, old chap, how is mining going? I hope Sydney Inlet is turnout all right. I have heard nothing these last 4 months…Remember me to the boys in Victoria.

I remain yours truly
Stuart Stanley Stone

Jones wrote to Walter Dawley from an infirmary at Deelfontein, explaining he would be out of action for some weeks. In this and other letters he thanked Dawley for sending money to his aunt Lucy Jones, a maiden lady in Cumberland, Maryland, who relied on Jones's regular financial support. He reassured Dawley that this would be repaid when Jones returned to Clayoquot, adding hopefully, "I shall probably be in Old BC again about the first of June. Give my kindest regards to Tom and all the boys. Please renew my license."

Jones was overly optimistic thinking he would be back in British Columbia in early June, and the longer he had to cool his heels waiting in South Africa, the more his thoughts turned to home.

> Maitland, May 26, 1900
>
> Dear Friend: Your most welcome letter dated Feb 1st reached me today…It is often three months after a letter is written before we get it…I am glad to here that Sidney Inlet is still being worked and looks well…I hope the west coast will turn out something. I would rather live in British Columbia than in any other part of the world I know of, so far I am simply fed up on this country it is a regular graveyard there are now only five hundred men left fit for duty in the 2nd contingent.

By June 23, 1900, Jones had boarded the SS *Umbrina*, heading to England. He sent Dawley a long and barely legible letter written in grey pencil on notepaper with a maple leaf insignia in the top left corner and the words "Canadian Contingent 1899–1900" printed on the opposite side of the page. After only seven months away, Jones was heartily sick of the war, trusting it would end soon. As he peered through the fog for a glimpse of the shores of Spain and Portugal, his thoughts reverted to their constant theme:

> It is hard for a man to appreciate British Columbia until he goes to S Africa. We are all fed up on this country and I fancy there will be very few that stay…I had quite a few talks with men who have been mining in the country for years they all say it is no…mans country for prospecting…I shall arrive in time in Clayoquot for some good trout fishing I hope.

In this letter, Jones reassured Dawley that he would have "about two hundred or a little over coming to me from various funds, so I will not arrive busted." Some two weeks later, he wrote once again from Gosport, in England, this time with less financial confidence. He was on furlough and had only thirty-five dollars to spend. Could Dawley please help? "You know now how Sidney Inlet is turning out if it is all right and you think Mr. Dewdney will take up the bond...I wish you would kindly send me a money order for ten pounds I could not very well borrow it unless things are booming up at Sydney."

Travelling back across Canada by train, the invalided soldiers returning from the Boer War received an enthusiastic welcome along the way. In Winnipeg, great crowds gathered to cheer them at the train station, and when they steamed into Victoria Harbour on board the *Yosemite* from Vancouver on September 5, 1900, a guard of honour, city dignitaries, a brass band and a cheering crowd of hundreds greeted them. James W. Jones had returned.

Throughout the period Jones was in South Africa, a flurry of correspondence arrived for Dawley from a variety of Jones's relatives in the United States, including his sister Anne, his brother-in-law Samuel Pollard Carusi, his aunt Lucy and his uncle William. They knew that Dawley was handling Jones's affairs, and they deluged him with questions. "The report of my brother-in-law's death," wrote Samuel, "has caused a great deal of sorrow to his sisters and aunts—two of whom, the Misses Jones, of Cumberland, Md., U.S.A. were, in a measure, beneficiaries upon his generosity. May I request an early response?" Jones's aunt Lucy wrote repeatedly, and with great agitation of spirit, touchingly eager to be in touch with someone who knew Jones and could share news of him. Amid anxious queries about Jones's well-being and about the payments she hoped to receive, she also thanked Dawley for sending a photograph of Jones early in March 1900. "I thank you very much for the photo enclosed which I think already shows hardships endured." Later that month, Jones's uncle William wrote to ask Dawley's opinion of the Sydney Inlet property—"Are they working the property strongly?"—and Anne also inquired about her brother's affairs: "My brother's letters were never very much given to detail and we are all greatly in the dark concerning his business affairs."

In all likelihood, Jones was "greatly in the dark" about his own business affairs. Back in British Columbia, nothing prospered as he hoped. His plan to sell his interests in Sydney Inlet at considerable profit met many roadblocks, and on January 22, 1901, he wrote to Dawley in frustration: "The Dewdney Syndicate failed to make the payment due this month I fancy I shall have to hunt for another party now. It is possible that Marshall might take the property for a lump sum... There is full ten thousand dollars worth of ore mined if we can not make terms with either Dewdney or Marshall, Kincaid and myself will ship the ore."

By early April, Jones was much happier. A deal had been struck, and he was enjoying a prolonged visit to the bright lights of Victoria.

> Dear Friend: As you will see by this letter I am still in the city of convivial companions and you will here suppose that I have been trying to paint the city a cardinal hue. Well Sidney Inlet is no longer our property. We sold out to Dewdney at a great sacrifice. If he makes a hundred thousand out of it I am satisfied because there was no possible chance for me to do so with my limited [amount] of credit and Kincaid was in no better shape.

On his visits to Victoria, James Jones always found good company, not only the "convivial companions" with whom he tried to paint the city a "cardinal hue"—presumably in the vicinity of Wharf and Pandora streets where most of Victoria's brothels could be found—but also in bars and hotels around the city where he would find any number of like-minded men, mining men obsessed by the dream of striking it rich, fellow seekers dreaming of precious minerals, particularly gold. Gold fever flared up many times in Victoria in the latter decades of the nineteenth century; ever since gold was discovered on the Fraser River in 1858 and soon afterward in the Cariboo, rumours of gold discoveries continually filled the air. Over the years, enormous numbers of would-be gold miners swarmed through the city on their way to and from the various gold fields, and in the late 1890s, Victoria once again thronged with miners, this time outfitting themselves to head north to the Yukon.

Meanwhile, expectations also ran high about possibilities closer to home, especially on Vancouver Island's west coast. The number of mining claims staked there increased rapidly during the 1890s. The colourful names were all familiar to Walter Dawley and to his younger brother Clarence, who joined him in Clayoquot Sound in 1900: the Iron Duke and American Wonder claims at Tranquil Creek, the Rose Marie on Elk River up above Kennedy Lake, the Indian Chief group in Sydney Inlet, the Iron Cap and Kalappa prospects on Lemmens Inlet, the Brown Jug up at Hesquiat Lake, the Stermont and Glengarry at Nootka—on and on the list continues. The names are mesmerizing, pregnant with potential, each one representing high hopes and boundless optimism. In the long term, most of these claims proved disappointing, for the area never lived up to the wildly heightened expectations that were common currency around the turn of the century. At the time, though, the atmosphere was electric with anticipation, and every coastal steamer carried prospectors, men just like James Jones, heading up the coast to seek their fortunes.

Up at Clayoquot, newly arrived and amazed by all she saw, Mrs. William Rolston, the wife of the Methodist doctor, commented on the steady stream of prospectors passing through. "Every day," she wrote in her diary in 1898, "brings fresh miners and prospectors who with feverish desire to get gold and other precious metals will push their way through mountains of difficulty, and the country will soon be opened up."

The *Victoria Daily Colonist* described a comparable crowd of prospectors on April 21, 1897: "Those who take an interest in the West Coast mines would have appreciated the scene down aboard steamer Tees just before she took her departure for Ahousett and way ports last evening. With very few exceptions, every passenger was a prospector, with a formidable looking pack at hand's reach." In column after column, year after year, the faithful *Colonist* kept its readers abreast of mining developments on the West Coast. The writing is tirelessly enthusiastic and often highly technical, giving mathematically precise descriptions of the angles of a body of ore alongside delighted descriptions of "coppery pyrite" showings, "large bodies of magnetic iron" and "fine grained gabbro and delomite."

The *Colonist* also paid close attention to the human face of mining. "Indians, klootchmen, Chinamen, white men and in general every resident of Clayoquot is a prospector and a firm believer that a great future for that section as a mining country is not very far distant," the newspaper pronounced on June 10, 1897. Yet even while crediting everyone with being a prospector, the *Colonist* had a particularly soft spot for the true "mining men" who spent months out in the bush on the "wild West Coast," tirelessly searching for valuable minerals. Their arrival back in Victoria on June 15, 1897, was typically exciting.

> Steamer [*Maude*] was filled with passengers, but unlike the well-dressed travellers they neither waited for gangplank nor stoppage of steamer before all, or nearly all, were scrambling upon the wharf from all parts of the ship, several of them with a suggestive sack in one hand and pack on the back. These were prospectors, of course, and all were just returning from hunting over the country about Clayoquot for the precious metal, finding in return for their labor what each expects will prove a mint of gold.

No one was immune from gold lust, not even that dour and experienced old priest Father Augustin Brabant. He wrote to Father Maurus Snyder from Friendly Cove on August 29, 1901, in a fever of excitement about a discovery made by a Hesquiat man:

> A beach three miles long covered with black sand and gold! shining in the rays of the sun is the last discovery made by Constant—I am applying for a licence. I am in for a claim; Constant of course comes in for one, and the Indian who showed him the locality and also Sennen at my suggestion, then Rev'd Maurus and Rev'd Charles…
> I understand that it takes eight men to form a partnership. Do not get excited, but the prospects are good.

In another letter Brabant spoke of the "locality where our future fortune lies buried," but he cautioned that they must "let the mining business rest till next year." What became of this priestly flurry of interest in a reportedly gold-strewn beach "shining in the rays of the sun" at an undisclosed location remains unknown. Brabant never mentioned it again, and the subject disappeared like smoke.

This passionate hope of finding "a mint of gold" on the west coast of Vancouver Island predated even Father Brabant, going back to the summer of 1865, when the "newly discovered goldfield of Bear River" stirred a wave of excitement in the newspaper. Scores of avid men jostled for space aboard schooners on their way to Bear River, angrily refusing to allow any Chinese gold seekers to come along with them. On one occasion, six Chinese prospectors were "unceremoniously bundled out of the ship" because "feelings of antipathy to the Chinaman setting foot on white men's diggings is too general." The initial surge of interest in this area soon flickered out because so little workable gold emerged from the sand and gravel bars of the riverbed near its entry to Bedwell Sound.

Twenty years later, in 1886, Chinese prospectors returned to the area, travelling from their settlement at China Creek, near Alberni, where some 170 Chinese immigrants could be found by the late 1870s, working at the mines in that area. The *Colonist* kept a wary eye on the activities of the Chinese at Bear River. "Apparently the Celestials have struck a good prospect," stated an article on October 24, 1887, indicating that seventy-five Chinese were sluicing and prospecting for gold at Bear River. Jealous suspicions soon surfaced about these persistent Chinese. "It is regrettable," the newspaper declared, "if the diggings are as rich as it is now supposed they are, that they should be exclusively controlled by the Chinese." But yet again, reported findings of gold proved to be exaggerated.

Back in the news in the late 1890s, Bear River was by then attracting a steady number of mining men, both white and Chinese. Hopes ran high once more, inspired by promising findings of copper and silver and veins of gold-bearing quartz. An eight-mile trail up the river valley enabled prospectors to access their claims, and speculators formed ambitious plans to develop a townsite in the vicinity of Bear River. According to the newspaper, the townsite, called Port Hughes, was sure to have a good wharf, decent roads and many other services. Very little of this ever came to pass, although a post office opened at Port Hughes in the autumn of 1899, and Mr. Moses McGregor of Victoria financed construction of a fourteen-room hotel at the head of Bedwell Sound, "a commodious building...which would not be out of place in any city." Despite such amenities, Port Hughes never became much more than an overgrown mining camp and, for a few years, a regular stop on the steamer route.

By the middle of 1899, heightened hopes for a gold rush shifted to the promising sands of Wreck Bay, north of Ucluelet. As always, the *Victoria Daily Colonist* revelled in the very mention of gold. "While all the world has been looking to Klondike...for gold," an article announced in July 1899, "the precious dust has...been waiting to be won at a point on the West Coast of this Island, not a hundred miles from Victoria by direct line—and if reports be true, in quantity sufficient to bring ten thousand miners to the field in half a year."

Mercifully, ten thousand miners did not descend on Wreck Bay, but the area was quickly staked, and strenuous efforts ensued to extract what the newspaper called the "flaky, floury gold" from the sand. Thomas Stockham, quoted in the newspaper on July 13, 1899, declared that he "look[ed] upon the latest discoveries

Not all of the boys who came and went on the west coast were prospectors. Pictured here are unidentified workers from the telegraph line construction. Clayoquot was connected to the Dominion Government Telegraph line in 1902. Ahousat, Hesquiat and Nootka were connected in 1914.

of gold in the black sand at Wreck Bay as likely to induce a wholesale exodus to that locality."

By April 1900, up to ten tons of gravel were being sifted each day in Wreck Bay, and miners confidently awaited large returns. That summer they constructed a flume, one and a quarter miles long, to transport water to the workings, and the newspaper excitedly reported shipments of gold arriving in Victoria from Wreck Bay, hundreds and even thousands of dollars' worth at a time. But then came the autumn, and the season of storms and heavy weather wreaked its toll. Work came to a complete halt as the flume and various bits of machinery suffered damage.

In the spring of 1901, diehard optimists resurfaced, and work resumed. Meanwhile, other hopefuls staked out the entire length of adjacent Long Beach, just in case its sands might also be gold-bearing. By this stage, even the *Colonist* admitted that mining at Wreck Bay was only an "indifferent success." The operation limped along until the spring of 1902, when an American syndicate, headed by one Mr. Starbuck from Seattle, acquired the Wreck Bay mining interests. This was not a good idea, for as the *Colonist* ruefully reported on June 9, 1902, "Mr Starbuck, of Seattle, who since cannot be found...has neither paid for the property nor left money for the wages of his miners." Despite the efforts of a group of miners to track down Mr. Starbuck and recoup their money, and despite a few more mutterings in the newspaper, speculation about gold at Wreck Bay ceased.

In September 1902, Thomas Stockham dashed off a nearly illegible letter to Walter Dawley, issuing an outburst of typically unclear instructions:

> Tell Clarence to be ready on the 20th to go to Nootka Mr Swaney is going to send a man up to look at his property, Drinkwater['s] rock is not copper [illegible] it is iron and gold the assayers had not made the assay yet I paid the freight bill 35 cents charge it I did not order the ginger ale.

The "Clarence" who was to head up to Nootka was Clarence Dawley, whose name often appears in letters concerning mining interests. Together with his brother and Thomas Stockham, Clarence had financial interests in a number of mining claims; he is described as a "mine owner and expert" in Henderson's 1902 *British Columbia gazetteer and directory*. Clarence frequently travelled up and down the coast to check out various claims and to assist when needed in the stores at Nootka and Ahousat. Although he arrived on the coast several years after his brother, Clarence knew all the boys in the mining game well, including Joe Drinkwater.

Drinkwater was a prospector from Alberni, a regular amongst the young men working mining claims in the early 1900s. His name shows up regularly in the Clayoquot Hotel register for 1901–2, and on one occasion the entry reads "Joe Drinkwater & wife." Joe married Della Fayette in Victoria in 1899, and Della usually remained behind in Alberni while Drinkwater travelled far and wide on Vancouver Island on his prospecting ventures; this trip to Clayoquot may have been a special treat for her.

One of the most experienced prospectors in the business, Drinkwater could easily outsmart a part-time player in the mining game like John Russell, the Presbyterian missionary at Ahousat. Dawley received an aggrieved letter, headed "Strictly Private," from Russell in early October 1899. "I understand that Drinkwater and Peterson are playing sharp about the Sydney Inlet Hot Springs," wrote Russell. "They have re-staked in their own names shutting me out I believe." The letter ends with a petulant request that Dawley have a man re-stake the property yet again, this time in Russell's name. Such small-time shenanigans occurred frequently when claims were staked.

Joe Drinkwater ran an account at Dawley's store that often proved a bit awkward to deal with. He was always sure he could pay it, just as soon as he found financing for a promising claim, or just as soon as he received payment for the ore he had shipped, or just as soon as his luck turned. In a characteristic letter of October 10, 1905, from Alberni, Drinkwater apologized for not settling his bill and brought Dawley up to date with his improving prospects. "I struck a lot of very high grade ore this year and where we drove the tunnel it looks well. The parties I had in says if the property is half as good as I represent it they will take up at our cash price." A few months later, he wrote again, radiating optimism about another venture, convinced his gold claim was at last about to prove itself: "Everything is looking very bright for me at present I expect we will have small mill working on the gold claim about the first of July it will onely take a few days to get gold enough to pay all my dets, it is free gold & runs four hundred dollars in gold across 16 ft."

This hopeful venture, like so many others, faded to nothingness; Drinkwater's fortune remained unmade, his debt to Dawley unpaid. A great outdoorsman, Drinkwater generally preferred pursuing his own adventures to such mundane matters as paying bills. Shortly after his marriage, he challenged himself to hike across Vancouver Island to the Alberni Valley by going through Bear

Pass from Bedwell Sound. His journey led him from the west coast up into the high country where, on the flank of Big Interior Mountain, he came upon a remote and beautiful lake. He christened it Della Lake in honour of his wife. Discovering that the lake drained over a series of cliffs in three spectacular cascades, he promptly named the waterfall Della Falls. This waterfall, which descends 1,444 feet, is the highest falls in Canada. It tumbles into a creek now known as Drinkwater Creek, situated in—unsurprisingly—Drinkwater Valley. Finding himself eventually at the head of Great Central Lake, Joe built a raft and sailed twenty-four miles to the far end; from there he hiked the rest of the distance back to Alberni. The journey took longer than he expected it would, and Della had almost given up hope of seeing him again.

Joe and Della were not destined to enjoy a long and happy marriage. Too often left on her own, Della fell from marital grace. Joe Drinkwater shared the sad story with Dawley in a mournfully unpunctuated and misspelled letter written in March 1906:

> I supose you have heard all about my good friend Ward and Della their work had been going [on] for over a year I knew it but did not catch them it was quite a releaf to know for sure…she left without me saying one cross word to her I asked her why she left she said that she knew what was comeing I came home about one in the morning and saw Ward runing away from the house she did not deny Ward being their she knew it was no use I have heard since that Ward was not the onely one that has been seen comeing out of my house in the morning…I don't know where Della went that is not bothering me but very little when I see you I can tell yo all so you will know what kind of a man Ward is…

Two years later, in December 1908, Drinkwater wrote to Dawley from Bear River, explaining that he still could not pay his account. Apparently this was due to the machinations of his former partner, Mr. F. P. Nichols:

> He has tied up five thousand seven hundred dollars of my money he is claiming a half intrest in all the timber I located he was a pardner in the mine at that time so he thinks that he can make the pardner ship business stick the trile will not come off untill some time in January we never had eny pardnership agreament between us I did all the work and everything is in my name so I cant see where he will beat me… I will have money to pay my bils as soon as the trile is over.

Woefully for Drinkwater, when his "trile" was over, Nichols had won the case. Nichols also owed Dawley money. This was normal: most of the prospectors on the coast were in debt to Dawley—just like everyone else. Customers generally took their debts seriously and paid up when they could, but a significant few were skilled in the art of evasion. When pressed too far, Dawley turned to his lawyer, Sydney Childs, in Victoria, instructing him to pursue the miscreants. Mr. Childs enlivened his letters to Dawley with trenchant comments on the characters in question.

> Re Nichols. He has got his action settled with Drinkwater, but went away to Omineca Country. I am to get this money on his return…Re Whitwell, Gullin, Neilson, Gwin and Gosse. Are in the same position as when I wrote last. Cant locate Gullin do you know where he is. Gosse wont take any notice of letters. Gwin is no good, but may get it later on. Whitwell I cant find…Neilson, at Clayoquot, is he now working, if so, and available I might garnishee wages. Am afraid the above are a hard bunch.

One of this hard bunch, F.P. Nichols, evidently settled his debt, for within two years he was back in touch with Dawley, seeking help in collecting one of his own debts. Dawley suggested Nichols should settle for the cabin of the man owing him money. "Well, Mr. Dollie," wrote Nichols, "…he shurly is breaking his heart but I don't want it I got all the shack I want…he better cough up or I will land him yet, so if you will oblige me in sending me his adress…I will get him after a wile."

Walter Dawley was of similar persuasion. He usually collected his debts "after a wile," and generally without recourse to the law. He wrote cold, accusatory letters to his debtors, cutting off all further credit without compunction. No one was spared. Making himself unpopular, which he did with unswerving constancy, never troubled Dawley. The prospector W.N. Kenyon was devastated by Dawley's scathing letters concerning his debt and lashed back furiously in a letter dated June 12, 1906, writing from the safe distance of California, where he had retreated to seek his fortune growing oranges.

> Dear Sir:
> As I do not intend going to Clayoquot this year I will undertake to answer your letter thus, but I should have preferred to talked with you over the matter. I do not intend to abuse you in this as you did me. That would be cowardly.

...to receive a letter like you wrote me hurt about as much as you probably intended it should...you have called me a "traitor" and having "no gratitude"...I stuck to you as hard and as faithful as any customer you ever had...and I never dealt with any other firm while there to amount to any thing and you know that is true now that was not treason was it.

...During the six years I paid you ever[y] cent I owed you and my account never ran for long excepting the once...I paid you near $2600 in that time (6 years) and I never complained at your prices but I knew your profits were quite liberal...

Kenyon wrote to Dawley several times from California, full of grievance, bitterly disappointed at his inability to finance a tunnel on his mineral claim, angered by would-be investors, defeated by nearly seven long years of prospecting on the west coast. Yet in his time on the coast, Kenyon was, like Jones and Drinkwater, one of the boys, one of the regulars at the store and the hotel, one of the eternal optimists staking mining claims with such high hopes. Not one of them achieved his wild aspirations of gold and riches, but given the atmosphere and expectations of the time, it is small wonder these men were so consumed by gold-struck, mineral-inspired dreams. Such dreams were in the very air they breathed on the coast.

Correspondence from mining men and prospectors was always sporadic in Walter Dawley's papers. The men would write numerous letters in one short period and then nothing at all as they drifted up and down the coast like fog, employed first on this, then on that project or mining claim. Only a few of Dawley's prospecting correspondents wrote at all regularly.

James W. Jones was one of these, a regular and cheerful correspondent for several years. But when he returned from the Boer War in 1901 and sold out his mining interests, he wrote nothing to Dawley for nearly two years. The two men had some kind of a falling-out. On November 2, 1903, a chilly and formal note arrived from Jones, then at Ahousat. First he informed Dawley he needed no more coffee or tobacco, and then: "In the future if any orders are not attended to I shall deal in Victoria...if you are afraid to leave us full credit and that is your reason for not sending the articles ordered say so. Yours Jas. W. Jones."

Dawley evidently refused to extend full credit. Another silence fell until May 1904, when Dawley received an almost illegible, pencilled letter from Jones, now back at Sydney Inlet. The tone is less frosty, but the letter is still a far cry from the early days, when Jones wrote so jauntily to his "Friend Charley."

> Dear Sir:
> Will you kindly see that the transfer I left with you is recorded and a copy of same with the original sent up on the boat of the 7th. I will settle with you some time in August. I wish you would also send me a pair of boots no 8 about medium weight not those heavy affairs if they are not nailed send a packet with them also five pairs of socks and four plugs tobacco. I do not want the boots to cost over $8.00 socks 40 cents.

Jones's list of supplies is the usual required for men working out in the bush: baking soda, lard, raisins, five dozen eggs, one steel pick without handle, twelve tins of Jersey cream, eight pounds of bacon. All seemed to be well; back at his beloved Sydney Inlet, Jones was again in touch with Dawley, presumably still hoping for a lucky strike. But Jones had not reckoned on his health failing. The following year he wrote to Dawley from Victoria, back on the old friendly footing, but with sobering news.

> September 20, 1905
> Hotel St. Francis, Victoria
>
> Dear Friend:
> I arrived here yesterday evening and saw Dr. Hall he gave me a thorough examination and said he would have to operate tomorrow. I will have to have the testicle removed in order to save the good one. Hall said I would be just as good with the one as a dozen as the one left is well developed and perfectly sound whereas if I leave the injured one in it is apt to affect the good one so when I return to Clayoquot I will be cut proud. He is only going to charge me $20 for operating and attendance and I will be back to Clayoquot and ready for work in a month time. In fact I will only be in the Hospital two weeks so I shall leave here on the boat of the 10th for Clayoquot.

The determined optimism of this letter rings hollow. This was a serious illness, likely testicular cancer or possibly testicular tuberculosis.

In the months following this letter, Walter Dawley received repeated requests for information about Jones and his whereabouts. "When you next see J Jones (Black Jones)," wrote W.B. Garrard in mid-October, "will you tell him

I am expecting to hear from him and to receive samples of ore and description of some of his claims also." The mining investor Edgar Dewdney sent two queries about Jones. The first was a terse telegram in November: "Must have Jones to Sidney Inlet send Jensen with launch if necessary party leaves this evening answer." An equally curt letter came from Dewdney in December. He claimed that Jones should have been in Victoria to meet him and that he had sent several wires to Dawley directing him to contact Jones and put him on the appropriate steamer, so where was Jones? Dawley wired back to Dewdney: "Jones not available."

The west coast was a bustle of enterprise that autumn of 1905. At Mosquito Harbour in Clayoquot Sound, an impressive new sawmill was under construction, "the largest cedar mill in the world" according to the *Colonist*. At Sechart, the new whaling station was up and running: "On the next trip of the steamer Queen City it is expected that 100 tons of guano and 300 tons of whale oil will be received from the whaling station," the newspaper reported on September 13. Shipments of ore regularly showed up on the steamers from various mining claims on the coast; some sixty tons emerged from Deer Creek on a steamer in late August. The fisheries expanded continually, with new plans under discussion for everything from fertilizer plants to oyster propagation, and enormous tracts of timberland were being staked by investors for future exploitation. For any of the boys seeking new horizons in the area, the potential seemed boundless.

Never one to miss out on likely prospects, James Jones would surely return to the coast. Yet in the autumn of 1905, immediately following his surgery, no one heard from him. Nothing at all. Several months would pass before Jones resurfaced, and when he did, nothing would ever be quite the same.

— 7 —

Around the Sound

May 7, 1906

Dear Sir:
I have received your [letter] of 27th April asking for a Boy at $20.00 to help the Cook and wash dishes. I got one for you and he put his blanket down in the steerage of the Queen City he got his blanket back and is going to one of the Canneries. I have got another boy for you and he goes on the Queen City to-night.

Yours faithfully,
Wing On

24 Cormorant St., VICTORIA, B.C.
July 22nd 1903
Stockham & Dawley Esq
Clayoquot
B.C.
Dear Sir
I wish to notify you that the wages of the cook who has been working for you and you have paid ...

WING ON,
Pioneer Grocer & Provision Dealer
INTELLIGENCE BUREAU,
ALL KINDS OF CHINESE HELP FURNISHED.
24 Cormorant St., VICTORIA, B.C.
Sept 30th 1903.
Stockham & Dawley
Clayoquot
B.C
Dear Sir
You hired a Chinaman cook from me a short time ago, in the first time You wrote me a letter to promise to pay the commission and you have neglected to do so therefore if it is not paid by the end of two weeks. I shall place it in the hands of lawyer for immediate collection. Kindley answer at once or forward the same and oblige.
Yours truly
Wing On
$1.50

VICTORIA, B.C.
May 14th 190
Stockham & Dawley
Clayoquot B.C.
Dear Sir
Will you kindly remit the fare for a passage and you will guarantee this fare one way. But he cannot come unless you pay his fare to and from Clayoquot, If you able to pay more than 25.00 per month You will get a first class cook, to your mining Camp. please answer and You will oblige
Yours truly
Wing On

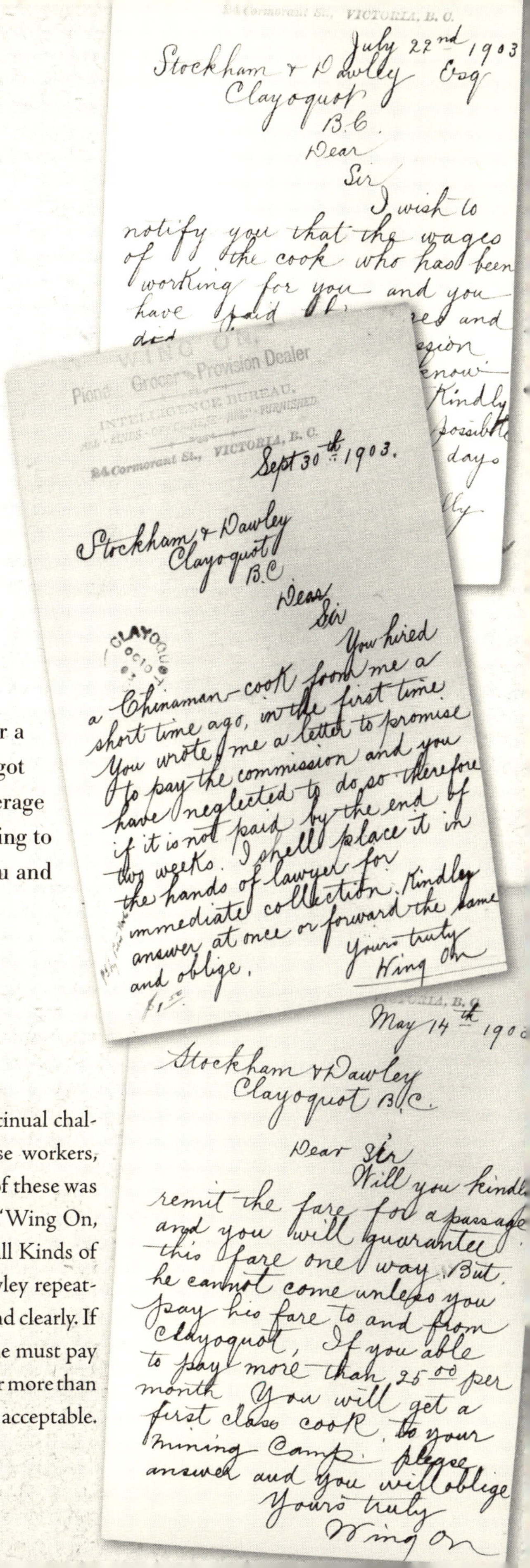

Finding workers for the Clayoquot Hotel was a continual challenge for Walter Dawley. He relied largely on Chinese workers, locating them through Chinese merchants in Victoria. One of these was Wing On, whose faded business stamp declares him to be "Wing On, Pioneer Grocer and Provision Dealer, Intelligence Bureau All Kinds of Chinese Help Furnished." Wing On was in touch with Dawley repeatedly between 1903 and 1909, always setting his terms firmly and clearly. If Dawley wanted Wing On's workers to come to Clayoquot, he must pay their steamer fares. If he wanted a first-class cook, he must offer more than twenty-five dollars per month. Thirty-five dollars would be acceptable.

If he wanted a "China boy" for kitchen help, he must be prepared to wait because many of the boys were working in the canneries. Wing On's letters show him to be entirely in command, never one to be hurried or chivvied by Dawley.

January 3, 1906

Dear Sirs: I cannot get a good boy under $20.00 New Year time... Chinamen here will not work for less now.

Your resp
Wing On

If he wanted Chinese workers, Dawley needed to conciliate Wing On. By contrast, Wing On did not need to kowtow to Dawley, for compared to the canneries or the Victoria hotels, Dawley did not hire many Chinese workers; in short, he was not a particularly important client. Besides, with other employment options available, why would a Chinese worker choose to travel to lonely and distant Clayoquot? Should a comparable job be available in Victoria, or with a group of fellow Chinese workers at a cannery, there could be no contest. Yet over the years, many Chinese employees did board the coastal steamers and set off to work at Clayoquot. When they decided to leave, Dawley immediately wrote to Wing On, requesting replacements:

March 3, 1909

To Wing On, Esq.
Victoria

Dear Sir:
Kindly send a cook and helper by return steamer on the 10th. Will pay cook $35.00 helper $20.00 and pay their fare of $3.00 each providing they stay six months or longer. I have spoken to the Purser on the steamer Tees to bring them and I will pay their fare to him here. The work is very easy especially for the cook as there is only an average now of eight boarders.

Yours truly,
Walter T. Dawley

Even during their early years, at their first establishment on Stockham Island, Dawley and Thomas Stockham employed at least one Chinese worker. This worker makes a cameo appearance in the inventory for the hotel, dated

September 28, 1898, shortly after the hotel opened. Crammed with faded, pencilled lists, the nine-page inventory describes every single item the place contained: cutlery, bedsteads, spittoons and even "1 Pelican (stuffed)" in the dining room, where two tables and fifteen chairs could be found, not to mention a cruet stand and a sideboard. Three full pages deal with the contents of the kitchen, and following the saucepans, the meat saw and the sacks of beans, hard on the heels of the scrub brush, the tomato catsup and one sack of potatoes, comes the entry "1 Chinaman." The list carries on to mention "½ venison" and concludes with a tiny sketch of a bird in a cage and the note "1 Canary Bird & Cage, Dogs by the Gross."

So there, on equal footing with the pelican (stuffed), the countless dogs and the canary—which was lucky to be in the fresh air of Clayoquot Sound rather than in the coal mines of Nanaimo—the "1 Chinaman" was briskly recorded for posterity. That he should be counted amongst the potatoes and the saucepans as an asset of the hotel simply indicates the general attitude of the time toward the "Celestials," as the Chinese were frequently called. Their labour, often indentured, was a nameless, faceless commodity; one such worker was very like another.

The presence of this unnamed Chinese worker is again sensed in the description of the hotel's bedrooms. Most of the ten bedchambers had a bed or beds, a washstand, a chair, a chest of drawers—some even with a looking glass—curtains and a blind, candlesticks and a "chamber set, complete." Room One boasted a carpet. The linens were carefully counted: counterpanes, blankets, pillows, towels, sheets and pillow slips in every room but one. No pillows or linens graced Room Nine; its furnishings were spartan, just "1 Blanket Red," along with a chair, a mattress, a table and a bed. In parentheses following this list for Room Nine is the word "(Chinaman)." This "Chinaman," if he remained a few years at the hotel, may have been Fung Ma, who appears in the 1901 census as a "domestic," resident at the hotel.

Dawley's Chinese workers assisted with maintenance, land clearing, cutting cordwood—for which they were paid $1.50 per day—and sometimes they helped to take inventory in the store. Occasionally a Chinese worker found himself heading up the coast to help the storekeepers at Ahousat or Nootka. "PS Send that Chinaman up next str," William Netherby wrote impatiently in a terse postscript to one of his letters from Ahousat in the winter of 1900. But the greatest need for Chinese help was always at the hotel, and this need increased considerably after Stockham and Dawley took over Thomas Earle's establishment on Stubbs Island in 1902.

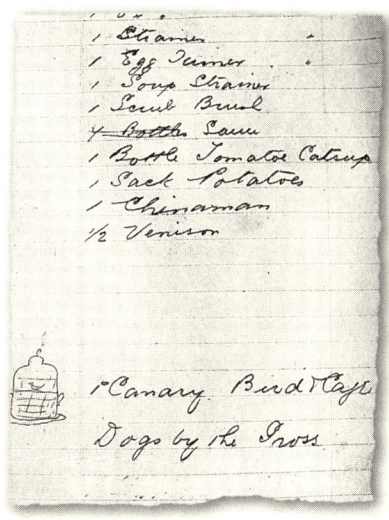

Dated September 28, 1898, the detailed inventory for the new hotel on Stockham island even included the kitchen help.

This second hotel was bigger and fancier than their original one on Stockham Island. An inventory from the Stubbs Island hotel reveals no fewer than sixteen bedrooms, several with both carpets and mirrors. Carpets adorned the stairs and hallways, and the side tables all had potted plants. A Ladies' Sitting Room, again with carpet, provided dignified comfort with its rocking chairs, highback chairs and lounge, with no fewer than four pictures on the wall, and as many as seven ladies could dine in peace in the seclusion of the Ladies' Dining Room, behind the privacy of two portieres. The Gentlemen's Sitting Room was less genteel. Its furnishings included "1 sofa old (no value)" and "2 damaged tables," seating for about twenty men, four cuspidors, but no pictures or potted plants. The tone improved in the Main Dining Room, which featured a clock, pictures on the walls, curtains at the windows and seating for twenty-six people at the seven tables. At this hotel, the Chinese helpers did not live in; they stayed in small cabins nearby, for which they paid rent.

Wing On and his counterpart Wah Yun, another Chinese merchant and employment broker, were happy enough to send Chinese workers to Clayoquot if the price was right and if they had the manpower, but they could not always oblige. Writing in 1905, Wah Yun politely expressed the hope that his shipment of rice arrived safely at Clayoquot and added, "We beg to reply we are very sorry we cannot get a Chinese boy to sent up to you because those boys all working." Wing On concurred in a similar letter written two years later: "I cannot get a Chinese boy to help the cook at $20.00 the least wages I can get one is $30.00 a month as they are scarce having all gone to the canneries." In subsequent correspondence, Wing On consistently refused to send a boy unless his price was met. "I can't get a China boy at $20.00," he reiterated firmly. "The boy wants $25.00 a month and board and lodging. If you will send the fare down I will send him up. On account of the $500.00 head duty it is very hard to get a boy."

The head duty, or head tax, on Chinese immigrants was first introduced in 1885, but in 1905 the tax jumped to the enormous sum of $500 for each Chinese male entering Canada. This punitive tax was a measure of the growing mistrust and

Inventory Clayoquot Hotel October 22nd 1900

Decorated with potted plants and pictures on the walls, the Clayoquot Hotel dining room could seat up to twenty-six people. The stuffed pelican originally graced the dining room at the hotel on Stockham Island, but here it is pictured in its new setting at the larger hotel on Stubbs Island.

resentment of the increasingly visible Chinese presence in the job market. From the late 1850s, when the Chinese first arrived in British Columbia to join the gold rush to the Fraser River, the employment of Chinese workers increased rapidly. Here was a ready source of labour, uncomplaining workers who could be, and who were, given the dirtiest and most dangerous jobs on the railway and in the coal mines, as well as in the domestic labour market. Generally speaking, these men kept to themselves in their Chinatowns, sent their money home and accepted lower wages and worse working conditions than white men would tolerate. By the first decade of the twentieth century, despite all obstacles, Chinese workers were firmly integrated in the economy of British Columbia and were in demand in the most unlikely places. Even the higher head tax did not change this.

Only scraps of information about Dawley's Chinese employees survive, and the names are almost all lost. One exceptional letter has surfaced, written in January 1905 by a Chinese worker. On cheap paper, laboriously composed, the letter is signed "Your Truly, Chinacook Wong Tuck." The upshot is that Wong Tuck had left Clayoquot but wished to return. "I got no work at present I wish you recall me back," he wrote. "I have pay more attention to do your work and give me some wages I will be much content."

Another Chinese employee named Wong, perhaps the same man, appears in a letter dated August 1911. William Simpson, the assistant at the Clayoquot store, wrote to Dawley in Victoria, explaining that Wong had had an accident: "Wong is to have a trip to Vict this boat having hurt his chest whilst assisting to fall a stump—he got knocked head over heals—and was rather badly shaken. I paid him up to the 10 August—from July 3—$50—he says he is coming back again only he—'heap scared'—wants to see Chinese doctor."

In ledgers detailing Dawley's business transactions, the Chinese help is usually listed only as "Chinaman," with debits and credits duly noted. Unusually, in February 1907, one "Lim Lee (Chinaman)" is named and credited for a month of his cabin's rental, $2.50. In the same month, "Wong (Cook)" is named, along with "Foo (China helper)," all of them apparently living in and paying rent for a cabin or cabins on Stubbs Island.

Quite apart from these few who worked at the hotel, a continually shifting number of Chinese workers came through the Clayoquot area on other business. Chinese prospectors made their way to and from the gold workings at Bear River and Wreck Bay, some Chinese worked in the Clayoquot Cannery and some worked on the coastal steamers, usually in the kitchens. The passage of Chinese workers up and down the coast often attracted comment in the Victoria newspaper. "Willapa sailed for Cape Scott and West Coast ports yesterday morning laden to the hatches with freight. She also had a large crowd of Siwash sealers and their 'ictas' [possessions] some Chinamen and a number of saloon passengers," the *Colonist* commented on October 24, 1900, a typical description of a trip up the coast. Occasionally the newspaper provided numbers, especially after the sawmill at Mosquito Harbour opened in 1906 and many Chinese arrived to work there. On October 6, 1907, it reported that "Tees arrived last night from West Coast points, bringing 28 white passengers and 40 Chinese." These Chinese, like the Indians, travelled "deck class," either on the outer decks or in the cargo area. The dining saloon and sleeping cabins were not available to them.

After the unsuccessful gold rush at Wreck Bay in 1900–1, a band of hopeful Chinese prospectors stubbornly continued to sluice the sands there, and in August 1903, a shipment of gold dust from Wreck Bay attracted comment in the newspaper: "The purser brought 53 ounces of dust which was shipped to Victoria by Sing Lee, the Clayoquot Chinese who has leased the mines at Wreck bay and is working them with a few Chinese." There was an update on November 19, 1903: "Among the arrivals from the West Coast by Queen City was Sing Lee, the Chinaman, who has been operating at Wreck Bay during the season just past. Sing has been working the Wreck Bay mine on something like a 50% lay, and his last clean-up on the beach is said to have been $500."

Sing Lee was a significant presence in the Clayoquot area as early as 1891, establishing himself as a trader on the end of Esowista Peninsula, where the townsite of Tofino eventually emerged. Curtly referred to in Dawley's correspondence as "the Chinaman," Sing Lee bought furs, sold a range of merchandise and traded with Chinese miners and workers in the area, as well as with Indians and some white settlers. He turned his hand to any opportunity that came his way. Occasionally he worked as a cook on the sealing vessels, and through his Chinese contacts he kept himself informed of any reports of gold being sluiced from the sandy river beds in the area.

In June 1901, the newspaper noted that "a shipment of 38 seal skins was sent down, consigned to local Chinese, by Sing Lee, a Chinese storekeeper who has bought the skins in trade with the Indians, the price paid being $14 a skin." At a time when most of his compatriots were dismissed merely as "Chinaman," the newspaper named Sing Lee on several occasions. His name also appeared in the newspaper on passenger lists of the coastal steamers, the only Chinese to be so honoured at the time.

Predictably outraged when his customers or his suppliers traded with Sing Lee, Walter Dawley kept a baleful eye on "the Chinaman." Dawley's old sparring partner, the wholesaler Simon Leiser, refused to be intimidated by Dawley's accusations that he was selling pilot bread to Sing Lee at a favourable price. In a letter of May 14, 1901, Leiser retorted, "This is nonsense…You are getting the goods cheaper than the chinaman or anybody else, and why you should kick I do not know…We have been friends for a long time, and would be very sorry to have any falling out. If we should fall out, it would be disastrous for both, because the writer is just as stubborn as you are."

Another of Dawley's regular suppliers, Turner, Beeton & Company, was more easily cowed. In response to a salvo from Dawley, a cringing letter arrived in December 1902 disclaiming all knowledge of how Sing Lee happened to be selling their shawls, suggesting it was a "batch of old samples" and protesting to Dawley: "You can rest assured we fully appreciate your business and is it likely we would jeopardize our relations with you for a few dollars we could pick up from a Chinaman?"

The itinerant Chinese workers who found themselves in and around Clayoquot Sound generally worked within reasonable range of Sing Lee's store—up at Bear River, at Wreck Bay, or later at Mosquito Harbour. But if one of Walter Dawley's Chinese employees were sent up to Nootka or Ahousat, the scene was entirely different. At these remote villages, the worker was entirely adrift from his fellows, culturally isolated in an Indian village alongside a white storekeeper. To make matters worse, some of these white storekeepers were dubious company. When William Netherby requested that a "Chinaman" be sent up to Ahousat in the winter of 1900, that particular worker would have arrived to find Ahousat in complete turmoil, thanks to Netherby. No records survive to say how this luckless Chinese worker fared, but perhaps, given all the uproar, he made good his escape. To be even remotely associated with Netherby at that time was bad news.

After leaving his original job at the Nootka store in January 1900, Netherby resurfaced at Ahousat in April of the same year. He replaced Fred Thornberg, who no longer worked for Stockham and Dawley, his erratic behaviour having led to a parting of the ways. The disgruntled Thornberg remained in Ahousat, angrily determined to establish another store and to undercut his former employers' business. William Netherby took over Fred's old job and enjoyed reporting Thornberg's actions and comments to Dawley. "Old Fred has a stock [of pilot bread] and is trading in his house…He seems to have a better assortment of fruit than I have as the indians are buying it. He says he is goeing to build a store on that island opposite to where the str stops," Netherby wrote in May

1900. In a later letter he commented, "He says he thinks he can make you loose money in Trading here but he gets up too late in the morning."

At first Netherby seemed fine at Ahousat, and he was decidedly pleased with himself: "I am getting all the seal in the country by the looks of things I have away over 200 now & am out of cash," he wrote on June 8, 1900. He kept close track of merchandise, in one letter complaining that the oranges were rotten and that neither the paint he ordered nor the small boys' pants had arrived. He continued reprovingly: "Now you must do different when I order a thing you can be sure I want it...I need a good stock now as they will soon be buying big. If you have not ordered more biscuit order some at once about 100 bxs & quite a lot Boston Pilot." Netherby frequently took issue with his employers: "You people make me tired," he wrote in July, "when I order flour you send Rice. Are you crazy. I can't sell that rice in ten years." Such predictable bickering continued to dominate his letters until October 10, 1900, when he wrote a sober letter addressed to both Dawley and Stockham.

> I do not know whether or not you have heard of the racket I have got in, anyway here goes. The Indians accuse me and my brother (who came down to make me a visit last str) of robbing an indian grave. I can only say that I am innocent also my brother of such a charge. Anyway they have got out summonses for us both & we are to appear next Saturday at Earl's Hotel.

Grave robbing. Netherby could not have been accused of anything worse. The village of Ahousat was in complete disarray, with several men threatening to kill Netherby and his brother. He continued:

> Now if one of you have not come on this str you had better take a boat & come up here at once so that I can get up some kind of a defence in time & I suppose you will not want me to trade here after this as the indians would no doubt all be down on me & it would be right in Old Fred's hands as it is I think he had something to do with having the charge laid to me...I am feeling pretty bad over it as you can suppose & as I know what Indians evidence is like I would not be surprised if they swore to anything.

In short order both Frederick Stanley Spain, the provincial police constable from Clayoquot, and Indian Agent Harry Guillod entered the fray, each of them keenly aware of the seriousness of the situation. Heightened sensitivities about death and burial, and about white men intervening in such matters, were already evident up and down the coast, for only a few days earlier little Mike from Kyuquot had died at Christie School, and the nervous priests had requested considerable backup from the white community at his funeral. Now here was Netherby, embroiled in an appalling scandal at Ahousat. Stanley Spain wanted to deal with it fairly and firmly. He later wrote a detailed account of events to the Attorney General:

> The body some weeks previously was tied up in a tree in a wooden box. It is an old custom to place whatever money the man had with him. In this instance, they say it was $42.00. They destroyed everything else.
>
> The Indians saw the two defendants going along the beach towards the grave…they afterwards went to it, found the ropes cut, the box broken open, the body hanging out, and no trace of the $42.00. They saw footprints, which were measured, and were the marks of white men.
>
> I may state that, at the time, there were almost no Indians on the Reserve except the old and infirm; and the Indians of this tribe when at home invariably go about barefoot.

Stanley Spain also commented in this letter that "the desecration of their graves is about the greatest crime in the eyes of the Indians, and the escape of anyone from being brought to justice is a serious matter as between them and their respect for the law." As for Harry Guillod, he knew Netherby from before and had no love for him: two years earlier he had convicted Netherby at Clo-oose, fining him fifty dollars for selling alcohol to the Indians there.

The chaotic legal proceedings took place at Earle's hotel at Clayoquot in mid-October 1900, greatly complicated by bad weather and the late arrival of the Indians from Ahousat, who were unable to reach Clayoquot until three days after the summons. According to Stanley Spain, "the weather was most unusually stormy; the ocean covered with foam, rendering it entirely impossible for a canoe to arrive by sea." He asked the two Justices of the Peace who were presiding, Dr. William Rolston and John Grice, for an adjournment or for more time, but they refused his request. This meant the Ahousat Indians had no opportunity to air their grievances in court. The two justices hurriedly dismissed the case, and Netherby was not convicted.

When the Ahousats finally arrived at Clayoquot, they were "greatly excited," in Stanley Spain's words, that the case had been dismissed, and they renewed their death threats against the Netherby brothers. Head Chief Nokamis of

Ahousat later wrote a letter of protest to the Attorney General, demanding that Netherby be removed from the Ahousat reserve and enclosing a petition from the Ahousat Indians to this effect. William Netherby left Ahousat in January 1901. He had been there only nine months.

Clearly unhappy with the outcome of the Netherby incident, Stanley Spain explained to the Attorney General the complexities revealed by this case: "I urged all I could, when brought before this court, that the matter was so serious that the Indians should have an opportunity of being heard, but…local influences carried the day." These local influences were, in Stanley Spain's view, the Justices of the Peace at Clayoquot, and he was most unhappy with how they worked.

In his letter of November 22, 1900, Stanley Spain criticized the conduct of each and every Justice of the Peace from Clo-oose to Quatsino, reserving his most serious allegations for the four JPs of Clayoquot: William Rolston, George Maltby, John Grice and Walter Dawley. Stanley Spain had been stationed at Clayoquot for six years, and, he wrote, "during that time the administration of the law has been most glaringly miscarried on many occasions, business interests being the first consideration." He provided details of how each Clayoquot JP worked: Dr. William Rolston "finds [the role] prejudicial to his practise"; George Maltby "lives at Long Bay, from 12 or 14 miles off…practically it [takes] him a day each way travelling"; John Grice was described as "the oldest and most unfit…known even by the Indians as 'dirty Grice'…and also under the thumb of Mr Dawley." As for Mr. Dawley, he "absolutely refuses to sit on cases except as cannot even in the remotest degree prejudice his trading interests. I have asked him in writing several times to sit on cases, and he has taken no notice of the request."

Dawley's correspondence files reveal little about his role as Justice of the Peace, but a letter from George Munro does confirm that Dawley's "trading interests" could direct the course of justice. Munro was a commission merchant for the owners of various sealing schooners, responsible for paying a number of native hunters at the end of the season. Disputes about payment often arose, some of them coming before the local JPs for resolution. Early in 1899, George Munro received a summons to appear before the JPs at Clayoquot in a matter concerning payments. "Just received a summons to appear at Clayoquot on 4 inst In re: 'Indian George,'" he wrote to Dawley. "Please give judgement against me in this case and send me amount cost…You will please not issue any more summons as one is quite enough…Am not asking you this as a JP but as a friend of the JP…Thanking you for any [advantage] you may give in my favour."

The conscientious policeman Frederick Stanley Spain persevered in his efforts to uphold the law despite the frequent non-cooperation of the JPs. Having no decent boat of his own, he patrolled his vast jurisdiction however he could: by steamer, sealing schooner, canoe, rowboat. Unusually, a complaint was lodged against him in the winter of 1901–2 because he failed to arrest the whiskey-selling owners of a sloop anchored off the Ahousat reserve. He wrote a dignified letter of explanation to the Attorney General in his own defence, pointing out that this was a "sloop driven with naptha," and "upon my approaching in an Indian canoe, which would be the only means of transportation, they would immediately get up steam and move on…they are quite aware of my helplessness in such cases." He concluded: "You, I think, sir, will see how very difficult it is for me to act without any means of quick transportation. I have got 100 miles of very rough coast to look after with only a small row boat to do it in."

Stanley Spain knew the coast well, spoke the local Indian language fluently and managed to carry out his nearly impossible job from Clayoquot for almost a decade, uncomplainingly and diligently. In the Netherby case he felt defeated, and he believed that justice had not been served. But he had tried, and he felt impelled to write formal letters to attempt to set the record straight. Without his letters, this particular tale of the desecration of an Indian grave and the debacle of the legal proceedings would never have been told. Walter Dawley's papers say nothing more about it, and the *Colonist* does not even mention it.

Before his ignominious departure from Ahousat, William Netherby was an entertaining letter writer, clearly on easy terms with both Dawley and Stockham. In July 1900 he came up with a provocative suggestion for Thomas Stockham:

> Tell Mr Stockham to come up & see me. I have a fine young ladie up here waiting to get married & he is the man for her she is the new teacher. She is not pretty nor young but she would just suit Tom. I got a letter from Jack Goss [formerly the Nootka storekeeper, now at Rivers Inlet] last Str & he says there are several young ladies up where he is who are anxious to get married & he thinks it would benefit either of you to take a trip up there & get spliced especially Stockham he says it would cure his rheumatism to get married.

Although he did not follow Netherby's advice to come up to Ahousat to meet the "fine young ladie" there, Thomas Stockham was indeed on the lookout for a wife. Three years later he surprised everyone. In April 1903, at the age of forty-five, without informing any of the boys, without even telling Walter Dawley of his plans, he married Agnes McKenna in Victoria—an event that immediately drew attention up and down the coast. Stuart Stone at Clo-oose remarked soon afterward in a letter to Dawley, "I saw in the Victoria Times last boat that Mr Stockham was married." A week later, in another of his chatty notes to Dawley, Stuart asked, "Is Mr Stockham there yet? Or is he on his honeymoon. I suppose he enjoyed his wedding cake better when he knew that you were ignorant of what he was doing. He ought to come here for his honeymoon, fishing and trapping. I was trapping this last winter, and got 2 coons. Don't you think I was lucky?"

Months later, Stockham's nuptials still attracted comment. "I presume friend Stockham has so tasted the sweets of connubial bliss that he could never relinquish even for a spell," wrote the Reverend William Stone. "But when he gets as old at it as I am I wonder how much nectar there will be. May his cup always overflow."

A polite letter from the newlywed Agnes M. Stockham in Victoria thanks Walter Dawley most punctiliously for the table cover he sent as a wedding gift. "I hope to spend next summer in Clayoquot," Agnes wrote, "and to have the pleasure of meeting my husband's friends." By the following summer, however, Thomas Stockham and Walter Dawley were in no mood for socializing. They were bitter foes.

The Stockham and Dawley partnership came to an acrimonious end in the winter of 1903–4. Throughout the following spring and summer, Dawley's correspondence files bristle with letters from lawyers about the dissolution of the partnership. Ill feeling abounds in letters crammed with references to various disputes and disagreements. When the dust eventually settled, Dawley was left in sole command of the store and hotel on Stubbs Island. Newly printed letterhead expunged Stockham's name entirely from the business, but his reputation lingered for a long time. Three years later, the *Victoria Daily Colonist* still referred to "Stockham and Dawley's" store at Clayoquot, identifying Mr. Stockham as a long-time trader on the west coast.

Stockham had no intention of abandoning his Clayoquot business interests. Much to Dawley's chagrin, his former partner continued to buy furs and, adding insult to injury, began to do his trading through Sing Lee's store over at the Tofino townsite. Father Charles Moser briefly noted this state of affairs in his diary:

May 27, 1905: Last week the Indians caught many seals. The price was good $10.00–$16.00 according to size. This is due to competition between W Dawley of Clayoquot Store and Chinese store at Tofino which buys skins for Tom Stockham, ex partner of W Dawley.

Everything Stockham did infuriated Dawley. He purchased two sealing schooners, first the *Ella G* and later the *Thomas F Bayard*. Dawley had tried to buy the *Bayard* himself, on the recommendation of the sealing captain Fred Hackett. "Now Mr Dawley the 'Baird' is a vessel of 90 tons solid white oak and a beauty for sealing," Hackett wrote in December 1905, adding, "Now Charley Dawley answer this by return mail for the 'Baird' will bring you more money than all…[the Victoria Sealing Company's] fleet." In 1906, with another sealing captain, Hans Blakstad, acting for him, Dawley decided to go ahead with the purchase of the *Bayard*. Blakstad was as enthusiastic about it as Hackett: "I could not find one inch of roten wood," he declared, "inside or outside the boat." But the telegraph lines were down for three days when the deal was to go through, and Dawley missed his opportunity. Shortly after, Dawley heard from Captain George Heater that Thomas Stockham bought the *Bayard* and, furthermore, that Stockham would provision the ship at the "China Store."

Between 1905 and 1910, Thomas Stockham stubbornly continued to send his vessels out hunting during the dying years of the fur seal industry. One of the more conniving opportunists in the business, Stockham was among the first to claim compensation for loss of earnings when the industry closed down in 1911 following the international treaty ending the seal hunt in the Bering Sea. He and his fellow investors in the *Thomas F Bayard* claimed the enormous sum of $164,892 for profits lost due to the imposition of the treaty. In the eventual settlement, the *Bayard's* owners received a mere $7,000. What Walter Dawley thought of his former partner suffering such a financial blow can only be imagined. He probably did not grieve unduly.

The exact reasons for the split between Dawley and Stockham are never specified in the surviving correspondence, but the hard feelings are abundantly clear. Harry Guillod wrote, "I heard from Mr Grice of the changes at Clayoquot and that you and Tom are bitter enemies. It is a pity after being together so long." A few months later, Guillod returned to the subject: "Is Tom simmering down or still rampant? I was surprised he must know he would have never had made the money he has in Clayoquot not without you."

Matters became even worse between the two men following the unexpected death of the storekeeper Sing Lee—a death noted in the *Colonist* on June 20, 1906, after Sing Lee made his final solemn journey down the coast:

> Steamer was well filled with passengers, both in the saloon and tween decks, having brought a large number of Indians en route to the Fraser river. Steamer brought the remains of Sing Lee, a well known Chinese trader, who has kept a store at Clayoquot for the past 15 years…He was brought to Victoria for shipment to China. Included in the cargo of steamer was 50 tons of fertilizer from the whaling station at Sechart, a number of harpoons brought to be repaired, 31 sealskins taken by coast Indians off shore, some ore specimens, a shipment of butter from Alberni and some general freight.

Dawley soon caught wind of a rumour that the Chinese store at Tofino would be for sale, and he asked the merchant James Thomson in Victoria to make enquiries. Although Sing Lee had operated the store, the owner was Dan Yuk Ling, so Thomson approached him on Dawley's behalf. Unfortunately, Mr. Ling "did not seem very anxious about selling the business, stating that the sawmill people would shortly be employing about one hundred Chinamen most of whom would no doubt be dealing at the store…I did not mention for whom I was enquiring but he has evidently got some information from your Chinese cook who is a friend of his. Privately, and strictly confidential, he mentioned that another party here had approached him on this same subject."

Captain George Heater was less circumspect than James Thomson on this subject. On December 20, 1906, he wrote to Dawley sharing bits and pieces of coastal gossip, commenting on Thomas Stockham's interest in the *Thomas F Bayard* and adding robustly, "I hear he is goen to get the China Store so if that is the case we will have lots of fun." The fun, from Heater's maverick point of view, would be seeing Stockham and Dawley squaring off as rival storekeepers.

Dawley did not succeed in buying the Chinese store at Tofino. In an embittering business defeat, he was outmanoeuvred by Thomas Stockham and by his former employee James Sloman. Stockham's brother-in-law John McKenna, supported by Stockham, formed a partnership with Sloman, and together they purchased the store, which became known as Sloman and McKenna's.

By setting up shop with McKenna in Sing Lee's old store, James Sloman fatally soured whatever regard Dawley may have had for him. He had become a competitor. Yet Sloman had been an excellent and, so it seemed at the time, faithful employee during the four years he worked for Dawley as the storekeeper up at Nootka. He was there from August 1901 until April 1905, except for a brief period at the Ahousat store in 1903. The store at Nootka had burned down, but within months it was rebuilt and Sloman was back in business there. Of all Dawley's storekeepers, he was the most able and, evidently, the most ambitious.

When Sloman first arrived at Nootka in 1901 with his wife and young son, he was entirely new to the west coast. He knew nothing of the native people or their language and little about fur trading. He came originally from England, where he had been both a policeman and a soldier before heading to the United States, where he worked as a cowboy, as a sheriff and on the railways of Montana and Texas before heading up to Canada. An articulate and intelligent man, Sloman was confidently in charge of the Nootka store within a year of his arrival. Years later, in an interview with the *Victoria Daily Times*, he recalled his early days as storekeeper and fur buyer:

> "I did not know a rat from a beaver," Mr Sloman says in telling of his early experiences. "I did not know what the Indians wanted to buy but we managed to trade. They would come into the store and point to something—'So-chuck' singling it out on the shelves. I would hand them a bar of soap and register one more learned word of the Indian dialect. They would come in with a skin, put it on the counter and say 'Attch-so,' How much?—and in two months I was talking the Nootka jargon."

Sloman described how skins were traded for goods during his early years at Nootka: "Two plugs of tobacco, two cans of peaches or two boxes of soda crackers was about the average price for a mink skin." As a fur trader, Sloman was a quick study. When faced with no fewer than four sea otter pelts, having never seen one before but knowing they were rare and valuable, he kept a cool head, as he described in a letter to Dawley:

> I could not get them to put a price on the whole lot but from what I could find out it will [be] in the neighbourhood of $1,200 or $1,300. They offered me one for $325 but I did not commit myself regarding the buying of same, of course I handled them and examined them the same as if I had bought hundreds of them, and that I knew a sea otter when I saw one.

Letters from Sloman are always lively and colourful; more than any of Dawley's storekeepers, he painted a vivid picture of his daily life. He was at his graphic best when describing the arrival of a large load of freight—twenty-seven tons—on an October night of pelting rain at Nootka:

> I assure you, it did not stop raining until I had got all the stuff inside and then it let up just to show me that it could stop sometimes… There happened to come down from the arm a couple of Indians with their Klootches [wives]on the morning the steamer arrived or else I should have been in a right fix with 27 tons Frt to handle with a heavy sea running. The Klootches worked 5 or 6 hours & quit, and the men quit me just after midnight, but I managed to get in all the perishable stuff before then. I say that steamer is a peach I never had to receive a lot of Frt in such a broken and dirty condition before everything that was possible was knawed by rats, and they even started in on the onions but their tears choked them so they had to quit them and start dry goods boxes and hardware.

Sloman quickly became savvy about ordering goods. Knowing that the Indians used cheap white blankets for burials, he took to ordering them in bulk, two dozen at a time. "And how about pants," he wrote, "it seems to me that I could do a better pants trade if I took their measure and sent for them… These Indians are so short leg'd and big-waisted and it is hard to fit them, and also the pants are too small in the legs… I am positive if I had a pattern or sample book from some Victoria firm I could sell more pants."

Sloman showed his true colours in the deal-mongering that occurred after the Nootka store was rebuilt following the fire of 1903. Neither he nor Dawley wanted any structure to be near the new store, ostensibly because of the danger of another fire, and Sloman was ready to consider any kind of stratagem to get what he wanted:

> Mr. Neill [the Indian Agent] also requested me to inform [Chief] Napoleon that he expected him to use his influence and stop any new building going up too near the store but I cannot get any satisfaction out of him… could you not draw up a paper stating how much land belonged to you, the location and so forth with an agreement that no one should build within 50 ft of the store and have old Maquinna's signature or his mark together with witnesses that would make the whole thing binding. Old Maquinna is dead, Mr. Guillod [the former Indian Agent] is gone and I should think… that you could easily have an iron bound agreement especially as Napoleon has just received $100 worth of stuff.

This letter is a loaded document. Here Sloman calmly suggests that Dawley draw up a paper favouring their own position, forge the former Chief Maquinna's signature or mark, forge some witnesses, presumably forge the date, and thereby create an "iron bound agreement" from a previous era. The idea appears to be that this will slide past without the current chief, Napoleon, protesting, because he has just received "$100 worth of stuff," and no one else would know or protest, because "Old Maquinna is dead, Mr Guillod is gone."

No record survives among Dawley's papers to indicate that he did draw up such a document, but given this level of guile, it is no wonder Sloman felt able to go into business for himself. He was certainly hard-headed enough. He also had able assistance from his wife, who worked alongside him in the store. "[Mrs. Sloman] may be coming down and she will be able to pick out some dress goods, notions, laces trimmings etc. as she knows as well as myself what would sell here," he wrote to Dawley in July 1904. Bearing a cash deposit for Dawley of $1,940, Mrs. Sloman went to Clayoquot shortly afterward and returned replete with all the appropriate goods and trimmings for the ladies of Nootka.

Once he relocated to Tofino in 1906, Sloman remained there for many years. Letters to Dawley from his suppliers mention Sloman's store from time to time. The McClary Manufacturing Company wrote on February 13, 1911: "You only have the assurance of one of your customers that James Sloman has one of our stoves, and not that we sold it to him...we repeat again to you that we did not do so." In January 1911, Turner, Beeton & Company replied to Dawley: "You state 'I find that you are supplying James Sloman of Tofino'...we are unable to find that such is the case, and think you must surely be mistaken." This was pure prevarication on Turner, Beeton's part, for Dawley knew perfectly well what James Sloman was selling, probably down to the last bit of lace trimming and the number of tin dippers. He was not to be fooled by his suppliers.

Although Walter Dawley continued browbeating his customers and suppliers into dealing solely with him, he faced a losing battle. As Tofino grew, Sloman and McKenna's store went from strength to strength, and in 1909 it even acquired the first "Tofino" post office. With every new development, the situation became increasingly clear: whether or not Walter Dawley liked it, Tofino was set to become the dominant community in Clayoquot Sound.

Wedding photograph of an unidentified couple, taken by one of the priests around 1906.

Vital Events

June 26, 1906: Rose at 3:30 AM and went home [to Opitsat] to prepare for an another wedding. Eustace Andrew the chief of the Hesquiat tribe and Alice Yaksouse of Clayoquot, both ex-pupils of Christie School were the happy couple. The Ceremony took place at 10 AM before a large congregation of Hesquiats and Clayoquot Indians. Almost whole Christie School attended and the following white people: Constable McDougall and wife; the two Mrs. Dawley from Clayoquot; Mr. J. Grice from Tofino; Dr. McKinley and Rev. Mr. Gibson of the Methodist Mission; the Captains of the 2 sealing schooners i.e. Capt. McKiel and Capt. Geo. Heater with his wife. Rev. P. Maurus principal of Christie school played the organ and his pupils sang a 2 voice high Mass. After Mass the newly wed couple with their nearest relatives were served a breakfast in my school room which the Sisters had prepared.

THE MARRIAGE OF Eustace Andrews and Alice Yaksouse stands out in Father Charles's diary as the most harmonious social event he ever described. This wedding brought together Indians and white settlers, Methodists and Catholics, the local policeman, two sealing captains, and all the Christie school students for a grand celebration at the church and schoolhouse in Opitsat. The only note of discord admitted by the priest was the reaction of the bride's parents: "Father and mother of the bride, however, did not take part either in the Church Service or breakfast owing to much talking of the old Indians who wanted to have a 'Siwash Marriage'; and Yaksouse was an old fashioned Indian."

Father Charles mentioned Harry Yaksouse, Alice's father, in earlier diary entries. "Went fishing with Harry Yaksouse with his halibut line," he wrote on March 6, 1902. "We caught 2 halibut, 10 codfish and about a dozen dogfish which latter as soon as they were unhooked were thrown back into the ocean." Later the same month, on March 25, a disturbed and angry Harry came to see Father Charles:

> Harry Yaksouse comes to me this evening accusing me that I had killed his baby which died last Sunday. For the last seven weeks the child was covered with sores. I had baptized it in January and Harry now claims that I with the Baptism was the cause of its death. When the Indians were home from sealing he would call all the Indians together and charge the priest for having killed his baby through Baptism.

Harry's name appears only once more in the diary, when he refused to darken the door of the church for his daughter's wedding.

Apparently untroubled by Harry's actions, Father Charles was in good spirits, highly gratified that the young people chose to be married in church rather than following their traditional ways. Furthermore, this was his second wedding in two days. "Pauline, an ex-pupil of Christie School becomes the wife of Joseph Jackson," he wrote on June 25, 1906. The wedding of Pauline and Joseph was the first time Father Charles had married former pupils, but his diary provides no details. Typically, weddings merited only a few words.

The following day, though, the marriage of the Hesquiat chief Eustace Andrews and Alice Yaksouse was different. The only wedding Father Charles ever recounted in any detail, this ceremony clearly meant a great deal to him. Here was a native chief, a former student, choosing to be married in church, outfacing opposition from his bride's family and attracting widespread local attention. Just why such a notable collection of influential white people from the area came to pay their respects to the young couple, who invited them, what any of them said or did, no one knows, for no other account of this wedding survives. Clearly, though, the wedding marked a personal triumph for Father Charles. He would not forget this day.

The list of white people attending the wedding contains a reference to two women never before mentioned in Father Charles's diary: "the two Mrs. Dawley from Clayoquot." By the time Eustace Andrews and Alice Yaksouse were married in June 1906, these two women had been resident in the area for over a year. Their presence marked an extraordinary change in the lives of both Clarence and Walter Dawley: the two Mr. Dawleys were now married men.

On February 8, 1905, Walter Dawley married Rose Angela Dennan in Victoria. The circumstances were unusual, not only because Rose was a twenty-one-year-old showgirl from California and Dawley was a portly, forty-five-year-old merchant from Clayoquot, but also because on the same day, at the same time, in a double marriage ceremony, Clarence Dawley also married, and his chosen bride was Mamie Dennan, Rose's older sister. The Dennan sisters were the most unlikely partners the Dawley brothers could have hoped to find.

Just how the Dawleys met the Misses Dennan is unclear, but given the profession of the two sisters, they could well have met at a theatre in Victoria. The Dennans were both in show business; they were two of five sisters—Nellie, Inez, Mamie, Rose and Marie—all of whom worked in the theatre, according to family lore. Their family came from San Francisco, and their mother, May Lydia Dennan, had also been an actress. The Dennan girls likely travelled with various theatrical productions through the Pacific Northwest. At least four of the five girls ended up in Victoria in late 1904 and early 1905, and three of them were married there: Inez led the way, marrying William Reid in November 1904; Mamie and Rose followed suit several months later.

The Dennans' names do not appear on playbills or in newspaper coverage of any theatrical productions in Victoria in the year preceding their marriages. Not for them the glories heaped on Miss Florence Pringle, the star of the comedy *My Sweetheart* at the Crystal Theatre, who received lavish attention in the *Victoria Daily Colonist* in November 1904. Yet companies like the one featuring Miss Pringle needed more than just their star actress; they required a reliable supporting cast, for their output was prodigious.

The Pringle Company was a stock theatre company "from the Sound," according to the *Colonist*, meaning Puget Sound and the Seattle area. Providing affordable family theatre—the cost per seat was a mere ten cents in Victoria—to cities and towns all over the Pacific Northwest, the company had a large repertoire of plays. During a six-week run in Victoria, the Pringles staged *East Lynne*, *Only a Farmer's Daughter*, *A Bashful Lover* and *My Sweetheart*, summarized in the newspaper as "a list of high class comedies and dramas, several of which have never before been presented on the Western Coast." The company also played more robust pieces, including *Eccles Girls*, "a whirlwind of fun that blows the blues away," according to the *Colonist*. This romp of a play featured two British soldiers, a ballet dancer, a drunken father and the gasman, altogether "a screaming farce comedy" from which hundreds were turned away nightly. The Pringles were excellent self-publicists, distributing engravings of their actresses and actors at each production and routinely engaging in sentimental acts of generosity. In late November 1904, for instance, the "newsboys of Victoria" enjoyed free seats at the front of the house.

Given that other theatrical offerings in Victoria in 1904 included George Bernard Shaw's new play *Candida*, a highbrow effort to stage *Everyman*, and the vaudeville acts of "Bigney the Deep Sea Diver" and "Musical Thor"—none of which seem appropriate productions for the singing and dancing talents of the Dennans—the possibility is strong that the Dennan girls were part of the Pringle Company or one very like it. Certainly the timing is right, for the Pringles were in Victoria in the autumn of 1904.

Irresistibly, images come to mind of Clarence and Walter Dawley at the Crystal Theatre, enjoying the farce and the pretty actresses, perhaps jostling for elbow room with the newsboys of Victoria on one of those special nights in November. The atmosphere of ribaldry and laughter may have allowed even Walter to forget, for a moment, his usual preoccupations with debts, suppliers and coastal transport. The brothers would have been dressed immaculately for the theatre, for despite years of living on the wild edge of Vancouver Island, these two men were always impeccably turned out, "dressed to the nines" according to Joan Nicholson, Walter's granddaughter, who remembers the two brothers always in white shirts and ties. Clarence was small, dapper and neat; Walter was large, dominant and expansive, always sporting a gold watch fob, its chain adorning his impressive belly.

The first mention of a "Mrs. Dawley" in the *Colonist* comes in a passenger list from the *Queen City* southbound to Victoria on April 12, 1905, two months after the double wedding. This could have been either Rose or Mamie, for they both took up residence at Clayoquot following their marriages. Laughing audiences, backstage hubbub and the constant challenges of life with a theatrical company must have seemed like a distant dream when the Dennan sisters found themselves facing the daunting realities of life on Stubbs Island. They no doubt were glad of each other's company when they reached their remote new home, after the enormity of their marital decisions had sunk in. They welcomed their youngest sister, Marie, as a frequent visitor. Indeed, Marie appears to have lived full-time at Clayoquot during much of 1906.

From the long sandy beach on Stubbs Island, the sisters could watch small canoes and rowboats heading out to Lennard Island or over to Opitsat, or heading eagerly towards the Clayoquot dock when the steamer arrived. Like everyone else, they fell into a rhythm dictated by the schedule of the coastal steamers, and they too looked forward to the regular arrivals of people and goods and mail on the *Queen City*. For entertainment they could walk down the dock and meet the steamer or visit with customers at the store, offering assistance if needed by measuring out lengths of print fabric and lamp wick and hair ribbon, weighing bags of Royal Mix candy and Scotch peppermints, sorting boxes of fruit and vegetables. The variety of people coming and going at the hotel also provided interesting diversions, and the sisters soon became familiar with the regulars.

On Stubbs Island, the Mrs. Dawleys' neighbours included Lawrence Carter, who worked in the store, and his wife, as well as Constable McDougall of the provincial police, his wife Mary and their young children. Because the McDougalls were Catholic, Father Charles mentioned them frequently in his diary. He would occasionally say Mass at their house and sometimes overnighted there in stormy weather. "Baptized McDougalls baby born yesterday," he noted in August 1906.

Mrs. McDougall took an interest in gardening, becoming one of Walter Dawley's best customers for plants and bulbs; one transaction alone shows that she purchased eight houseplants (50 cents), 3 cacti (60 cents), four dahlias (one dollar) and one dozen gladioli (25 cents) in May 1907. The Mrs. Dawleys may have shared this horticultural flair, for, following his marriage, Walter Dawley's records show him ordering more nursery stock than ever before. In 1906, Dawley corresponded with Jay and Company in Victoria, "Nurserymen, seedmen and florists," and John Grice of Tofino wrote to recommend a source of good, strong apple trees—ten dwarf for five dollars—adding that he could send more if required. Another source for plants was the eccentric settler Henry Varney up in Quatsino Sound. Renowned for his claim to be a titled lord from England, Varney periodically sent Dawley lists of available nursery stock, along with shipments of eggs for sale. "I cannot understand why those Eggs should have moulded, as they left me perfectly dry and fresh," he asserted on November 24, 1905. On one occasion he sent, unsolicited, five-pound pails of jam for sale in the store—black currant, lemon marmalade, raspberry, ginger preserve, gooseberry and apricot for sixty cents per pail. "I have also sent you a young red climbing Rose bush for one of your verandah pillars if you will accept it," he wrote. "It will climb 20 or 30 feet high and cover a large space in a very short while…Now I want you to give me an order for other climbing flowers and flowering shrubs and herbaceous border plants as I have quite a collection of them."

No one knows if Varney's roses ever took root around the verandah pillars on Stubbs Island, but plants from his garden would have been of excellent quality; however dubious his claim to a British title may have been, Varney was an outstanding gardener. He settled at Quatsino in the mid-1890s, and by 1898 his vegetables were noted at an exhibition in Victoria as "products that would be hard to surpass in a much better known agricultural district. There are samples of cabbage, squash, corn, beans, tobacco leaf, cucumbers, onions, apples and tomatoes." If he managed to grow tobacco at Quatsino, Varney ranked as a true master gardener.

Mamie and Clarence Dawley in later years.

From the outset, Mamie Dawley had a better chance of living happily at Clayoquot than her sister Rose, and in the long term she spent far more time there than her sister. Mamie was several years older than Rose, and her husband, Clarence, was a full sixteen years younger than Walter, so Mamie and Clarence were close in age, whereas twenty-four years separated Rose and Walter. In Clarence, Mamie found an entirely convivial partner, for he was a cheerful, affable soul, fondly remembered by his great-niece Joan Nicholson as a kindly man who dandled her on his knee when she was a child, talked to her and showed gentle affection for her—this being notable in her young mind because her far-less-loving grandfather, Walter, never so much as patted her on the head, let alone hugged her. In later years, Mamie called Clarence "her baby." Theirs was a very happy marriage, continually enlivened by Mamie, who in the memory of her great-niece was always merry, always smiling. Mamie adored dressing up, having parties and playing the piano, and she would happily spend hours entertaining other people's children, who always loved to visit her. She and Clarence had no children of their own.

Several years of married life passed on Stubbs Island for the Mrs. Dawleys before rumours of family life surfaced. The first hint of any such thing in Dawley's correspondence files comes in a letter from the sealing captain George

Heater, dated November 20, 1909. "I am sending a pair of slippers for Baby," Heater wrote. Walter and Rose Dawley's first child, Madeline, had been born in Victoria on August 3, 1909.

Others writing to Dawley also noted Madeline's birth. James Thomson ended one of his businesslike letters by saying, "With kind regards to Mistress Dawley and yourself, and I was surprised to hear the other day that there was a little family. Is it a boy or a girl?" In a subsequent letter he commented, "I am glad to hear you have a wee girl, and as you say next time may be the Boy."

Mr. Thomson was correct. Before the end of 1909, Rose Dawley was expecting another child, and her first son, George, was born the following summer. He too was greeted by Dawley's correspondents, including Lawrence Carter, now running a store in Alberni. "I congratulate you on the birth of the son and heir and hope he will have a successful career. Hope Mrs. Dawley is getting along nicely." And John Chesterman remarked, "Remember me to your estimable wife and tell her I feel proud of her as she is certainly doing her duty to her country."

Rose Dawley continued to do her duty. She presented her husband with no fewer than five children during the sixth decade of his life. Madeline in 1909, George in 1910 and Lydia two years later—her arrival was heralded by Mr. Carter from Alberni with a note: "How is the wife (has it arrived yet)." Walter Junior arrived in 1914, and finally there was Clarence, known as Bud, in 1917. With the exception of Walter Junior, all the children were born in Victoria.

Rose and Walter Dawley in 1914 or 1915 with, left to right, Walter Junior, George, Madeline and Lydia.

"I saw Mr Dawley's children it was over a year since I had seen them I could hardly believe my eyes," wrote one of the sisters in an undated and unsigned letter to Father Maurus following a trip over to the Clayoquot store. "How they have grown, they are so sweet the dear little ones. Also met Mrs McLeod and Mrs Dawley she is soon expecting a visit from the Stork!"

When the stork finally stopped arriving, Rose Dawley had had enough of living at Clayoquot. Lydia, who was born with a malformed leg, needed constant medical attention, the schools in Victoria suited a wealthy merchant's family better than the little school at Tofino, and the idea of settling into a comfortable city home took hold of the Dawleys. In 1918 Dawley purchased a house on McClure Street in Victoria, and from then on, Rose and the children spent a great deal of their time in town, while Walter divided his time between Clayoquot Sound and Victoria. On January 21, 1919, he wrote to his store manager at Clayoquot from the new house on McClure Street:

> Dear Mr Johnson:
> Mr. Gardhouse sent me 13 Bear I sold them for $250.00 Cost $81.00
> Good No 1 Bear are worth $18 to $20.00 poor ones in proportion...
> We are pretty nearly fixed up and we like the place well...I find the benefit of hot water heating most comfortable.

Formal family portraits taken in Victoria show the Dawleys grouped solemnly together, the children and Rose watchful and well dressed; Walter Dawley,

The Dawleys in the early 1920s. Left to right, Walter Junior, Rose, Clarence, Lydia, Madeline, Walter and George.

prosperous and large. His bulk increased with his prosperity, although even around the time of his marriage, Walter's waistline measured forty-six inches. His clothes were made to measure, and he patronized tailors from Vancouver to New York to Glasgow, suffering many trials to obtain a good fit at an appropriate price. The patient letters from his much-maligned tailors reveal how, at various times, Dawley accused them of overcharging, lying and incompetence.

"We regret exceedingly that the pants and vests made for yourself are not a satisfactory fit," one supplier apologized in 1907, having evidently received a letter from Dawley claiming the clothes he ordered were too small. "We cannot of course do more than carry out the instructions we receive and cut the goods according to the measurements furnished us. This we did." The writer bravely continued, saying that even if a professional had properly measured Dawley, difficulties might have arisen because "the measurements are somewhat out of proportion and consequently you are a little harder to fit than some others." In June 1911, a clerk from Stewart and McDonald's head office in Glasgow wrote Dawley to state courteously but firmly that the three suits they sent were indeed handmade, not ready-to-wear as Dawley alleged. Again, he was not pleased with the fit and blamed the tailor.

Similar problems persisted year after year, and when the ever-larger Dawley rejected two made-to-measure khaki coats—"Chest 47" Waist 50" length of coat 33" with brass buttons"—his supplier soothingly wrote: "Will you be good enough to check the coats you have and see if these measurements bear out. In addition to this will you have Mrs. Dawley put the tape measure around you, and also take the length of the sleeves, and I will see if I can get two coats made for you which will not fit like a sausage skin. I can quite readily understand that you do not like to be bound up like that."

His girth vexed Dawley, not least because his clothing cost more than the norm. "You ordered the goods in Pope's sizes," the polite correspondent at Stewart and McDonald pointed out, responding to a protest about the high cost of the garments Dawley had ordered, "…consequently costing a little over the men's in price." Even some of Dawley's undergarments were custom made, including the three "Extra Large Adonis Supporters, with absorbent linen sack," ordered from Carl C. Lantz Company in New York, makers of "Athletic Creations for Men's Wear." Such marvels of personal tailoring did not come cheap.

On occasion, Walter Dawley attempted to rein in his increasing waistline. A few years after his marriage, he and Rose travelled to Victoria, and he continued on to Harrison Hot Springs. Rose wrote to Mr. Carter, who was still the assistant storekeeper at Clayoquot at the time, with news of her husband:

Victoria July 12, 1909

Friend Mr. Carter
We arrived safely and we had a very nice trip…Walter is at the springs he is feeling fine he said that he takes one bath a day and looses one and a half pounds after every bath he intends staying another week he told me to ask you to kindly send us some eggs send the fresh one about 10 doz if you have them…Believe me as ever

Your Friend
Mrs WT Dawley

From time to time, the more sociable and chatty of Dawley's correspondents remembered to acknowledge politely the Dawley ladies, strange though their presence must have seemed at Clayoquot, particularly in their early days of marriage. "Remember me most kindly to the Mrs. Dawleys and Miss Denning [Dennan]…also McCurdy and all the boys Hoping to hear soon." This comment came from the long-absent James Jones. After months of silence following his surgery in the autumn of 1905, he re-emerges in Dawley's correspondence in 1906, writing from the Empress Mine at Britannia Beach north of Vancouver.

"Kindly keep me posted about the mining at Trout River and elsewhere and let me know when the snow goes," he asked, a request repeated several times that spring. He told Dawley that he would love to return to Sydney Inlet to work for Edgar Dewdney, now in charge of developments there, but "Mr. Dewdney's man has not arrived from San Francisco and I fear the Earthquake has upset his plans." In the end, Jones did not return to the west coast that summer, and by September he was back in Victoria, again writing to Dawley about his mining claims, not forgetting to end the letter with a punctilious salute to the ladies: "Remember me most kindly to your wife Mrs. Clarent [Clarence] Dawley, Mrs. Carter and Mrs McDougal now I have included the bunch I believe. Sincerely yours, James W. Jones."

James Jones continued to come and go on the coast, and traces of his movements drift erratically through Dawley's records and letters. He returned to Clayoquot in the winter of 1906–7, his name appearing in a sales ledger at the store when he purchased two cakes of soap, twenty cents apiece, in January 1907. In 1907 and 1908 his name was on the voters' list for Clayoquot, but in February 1908 Jones declared to Dawley that he was leaving for California. Later he sent a letter from Los Angeles, "the land of sun and flowers," as he phrased it, asking, "How is the West Coast dead I will bet is Sidney Inlet working?"

Back in Victoria in June 1908, he reverted again to his most cherished subject: "So, Sidney Inlet is to go in to the hands of the Crofton Smelter I heard as much before leaving Victoria last Spring." This letter concludes sadly, "You know I am still and allways will be interested in the West Coast and my friends there only I think it wise to give it a rest for the present." He asked Dawley to get rid of the possessions he had left behind at Clayoquot: gumboots, blankets, gun. In October 1908 he wrote from Port Angeles, saying he planned to return permanently to Vancouver Island and again—inevitably—asking, "How is Sidney Inlet, please give me all the news."

The following year Jones wrote to Dawley from the Balmoral Hotel in Victoria to ask if any timber cruisers were working at Tranquil Creek. After this he is difficult to trace until his name appears in a passenger list in the *Colonist* on November 9, 1910: "JW Jones who is working a copper property at Sydney Inlet." Jones had evidently made it back to Sydney Inlet. In April 1911 his name crops up in a letter from Lawrence Carter in Alberni. Carter enjoyed writing long and gossipy letters, filled with information about merchandise, suppliers and people:

> How is the egg question you can send down two or three cases if you have them to spare. I will send you payment for account on next boat...I see a lot of lumber on the wharf tonight for John Grice is he...building an annex or is it his annual new fence...Jim Clark and family arrived here on last boat...he was telling me that James Jones is sick at your place, he was not looking very well when he went up, hope he is better now.

James Jones was not better. Far from it. Two months later, in an article dated June 7, 1911, the *Victoria Daily Colonist* revealed his fate:

> Apparently in a fit of despondency and temporary mental relapse, James Warren Jones, for several years a well-known mining man and timber cruiser, familiarly known as "'Black" Jones, ended his existence June 6, by shooting himself through the body in Beacon Hill Park, near Heywood Av.

Jones took his life on a small grassy plot of land on the edge of the park, "in full view of the residents on Heywood Avenue," according to the disapproving newspaper. He placed his Winchester rifle against his chest, and the bullet, presumably aimed at his heart, went right through his body. He died in the patrol wagon on the way to hospital.

As Jones set out from the Balmoral Hotel with his Winchester rifle on June 6, 1911, the *Tees* steamed south from Clayoquot on her regular run down to Victoria. All the usual coastal cargo was on board: whale oil from the whaling stations at Sechart and Cachalot, fertilizer from the fish plants, china clay from Kyuquot Sound, "salt salmon for shipment to the Orient," and a good number of passengers. On this particular run, two totem poles were also on board for Dr. C.F. Newcombe, "the well known ethnological authority who has been securing totems and other Indian relics at Nootka." The *Tees* docked in Victoria Harbour the following day, and the bustle of unloading attracted onlookers and passersby, more so on this day than usual as the two totem poles were winched high in the air and lowered carefully onto the wharf.

Many people on board the *Tees* had known James Jones for years; certainly long-serving crew members like Captain Edward Gillam knew him well. They heard soon enough about the shot that shattered the calm of an early summer day in Beacon Hill Park. Walter Dawley, too, soon heard the news, perhaps in the newspaper that the *Tees* delivered on her next northbound trip. Word spread up the coast.

Although the *Colonist* did not care for the public nature of Jones's death, reporting huffily that "the suicide did not take the trouble to enter the thick underbrush which at this point covers the park grounds," the newspaper discovered some detail about his recent state of mind.

> Jones had been a resident of Victoria off and on for several years...
> Of late he had been staying at the Balmoral Hotel, where his strange actions have attracted the attention of the guests. Yesterday morning he called upon a legal friend and expressed his intention of making his will in favor of his sister, who resides in Seattle. Later he returned to the hotel, but no one saw him leave with the rifle in his possession...
> An inquest will be held this afternoon.

James Jones left everything he owned to his sister Emily. He had little enough to leave, but Emily received one object of great personal value: a gold watch, ornate and impressive, owned by Jones since his twenty-first birthday in 1889. Many sets of initials and dates engraved on the back of the watch mark when various owners took possession of this family heirloom, always on their twenty-first birthdays. Originally a gift for James's grandfather on his twenty-first, "JWJ 1829" is the earliest engraving on the watch. It passed to his eldest son Richard—"RHJ 1857"—and then to James W. Jones, "JWJ 1889." Through his sister Emily's marriage, the watch passed into the Byington family, and the tradition continued, generation after generation. The latest engraving on the watch is "HHB 1979," marking the twenty-first birthday of its current owner, Hank Byington, James Jones's great-great-nephew.

On June 8, 1911, Jones was buried in Ross Bay Cemetery in Victoria. Near the western edge of the cemetery, just out of sight of the sea, his six pallbearers, all of whom had been fellow adventurers in the first Canadian contingent sent to the Boer War, lowered his remains into the earth. No gravestone has ever marked the place, no passerby would ever know or guess this to be the resting place of James Warren Jones, that cheerful letter writer who travelled so hopefully up and down the west coast at the turn of the twentieth century, ever-optimistic in his search for minerals, the very man who discovered some of the "prettiest peacock copper" on Vancouver Island, the man described in the newspaper as "'Black Jones', than whom there is no better prospector in the district." In his unmarked grave, James W. Jones lay silenced, along with all his hopes.

In early June, the extreme greens of new forest growth are reflected, shimmering and intense, in the dark waters of Sydney Inlet. The mountains rise straight out of the sea, and massive cedars grow right down to the water's edge, the sharp line of their lower branches lapping their own reflections at high tide. At the time of James Jones's death, Sydney Inlet was silent; the site of his original mining claim up on the steep northern slope lay abandoned and forlorn. But in the previous few years, many changes had occurred here, and for a while this had been an active and bustling place. No longer a mere scratch on the face of the rock, barely visible from the water, James Jones's mining claim had been developed.

In 1907 the Tyee Copper Company established a small copper mine here; wharves and a number of buildings appeared along the shore, and an aerial tramway extended up the side of the mountain toward the mine. Throughout 1907 and 1908, hundreds of tons of ore travelled down the coast from this mine, and a number of men lived and worked in Sydney Inlet. Father Charles Moser travelled there frequently on priestly duties:

> *November 3, 1907:* My first Mass at Sidney Inlet, a copper mining camp, where quite a few Indians are employed. The trip yesterday to this place was a very rough one. Rounding Catface Mountain I had to

take the Steamer Channel and besides made my life preservers ready for emergency.

The Victoria newspapers repeatedly commented on activity at Sydney Inlet during the following year. On August 6, 1908: "News was brought from Sydney Inlet that about 25 miners are at work on the Tyee Copper Co property there, and 600 tons of ore is on the dump ready for shipment." By 1909, according to the *Directory of Vancouver Island*, thirty-seven men lived and worked at Sydney Inlet, described as "a mining camp on the west coast, 20 miles north of Clayoquot, which is the nearest post office. The Indian Chief Copper Mine, operated by the Tyee Copper Co. is situated here. The residents are all employees of that Company." But this population boom, along with the mine, did not endure. Silence fell again on Sydney Inlet, at least for a while.

By 1916, Walter Dawley was shipping considerable quantities of goods up to Sydney Inlet, including explosives, because the mine was back in action, this time under the name Tidewater Copper. Father Charles mentioned the mine in his diary in April 1917, delighted to have sold the mine owners 208 pounds of beef from his cattle at Hesquiat. He later commented on a strike at the mine in May 1918: "We found the whole plant seized by the miners and other employees for wages due," he wrote, but the mine was soon back in production. Following this, Father Charles frequently took note of the mine, usually because his voyages up and down the coast were often seriously delayed as the steamer crew unloaded large amounts of cargo at Sydney Inlet and loaded even larger amounts of copper concentrate. In December 1923, after several years of such productivity, Father Charles commented on the end days of the Tidewater mine: "At Sidney Inlet over 60 miners joined the boat, the mine being shut down." On May 6, 1924, he made one final comment: "Spend last night at Sidney Inlet. In the morning at 8 AM they began to load the 12 ton diesel engine which the steamer had delivered here just a year ago. The mining co failed and had never paid a cent on this engine."

Even this was not the end for Sydney Inlet. In the mid-1930s the mine was again revitalized, remaining active until 1939. In the end, Sydney Inlet became recognized as one of the few locations in Clayoquot Sound where a truly viable mine could be located. In its various incarnations it certainly was the single biggest operation, and the most enduring, in the entire area.

James W. Jones had been right all along.

– 9 –

Liquid Dominion

Tidal Wave Ranch, Long Bay, BC
February 7, 1909

W. Dawley Esq., Clayoquot

Dear Sir:
Kindly accept herewith best thanks for Christmas matter sent by you may add that not having any particular personal use for same handed it over to Mr. Coomb's family who seemed quite pleased, notwithstanding my thanks are equally sincere to you not so much on account of the value of the offering as the thoughtfullness included in the action. May your health continue in the most supreme degree of satisfaction. I may possibly be coming down shortly to review once more the liquid dominion of Clayoquot.

Yours Faithfully,
FG Tibbs

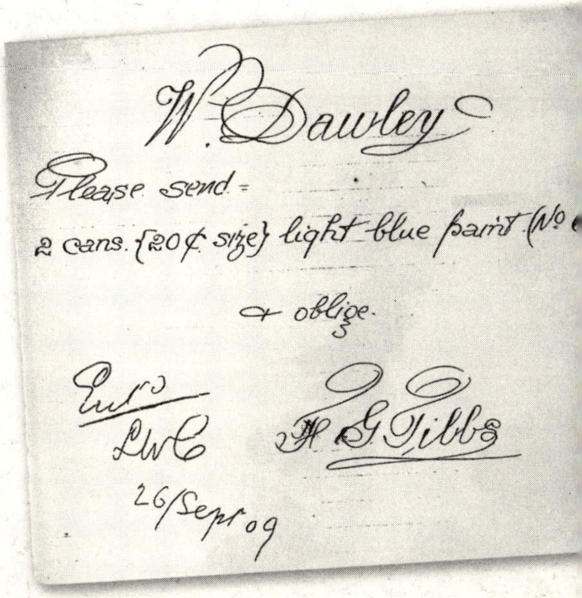

WRITING FROM LONG BAY, now named Long Beach, Fred Tibbs's letter ends with his usual signature, a happy flourish of curlicues. Destined to become one of Tofino's most memorable citizens, Tibbs emigrated from England and pre-empted land at Long Beach in 1908. At the time, the number of adult male settlers in the Clayoquot Sound area was well over one hundred;

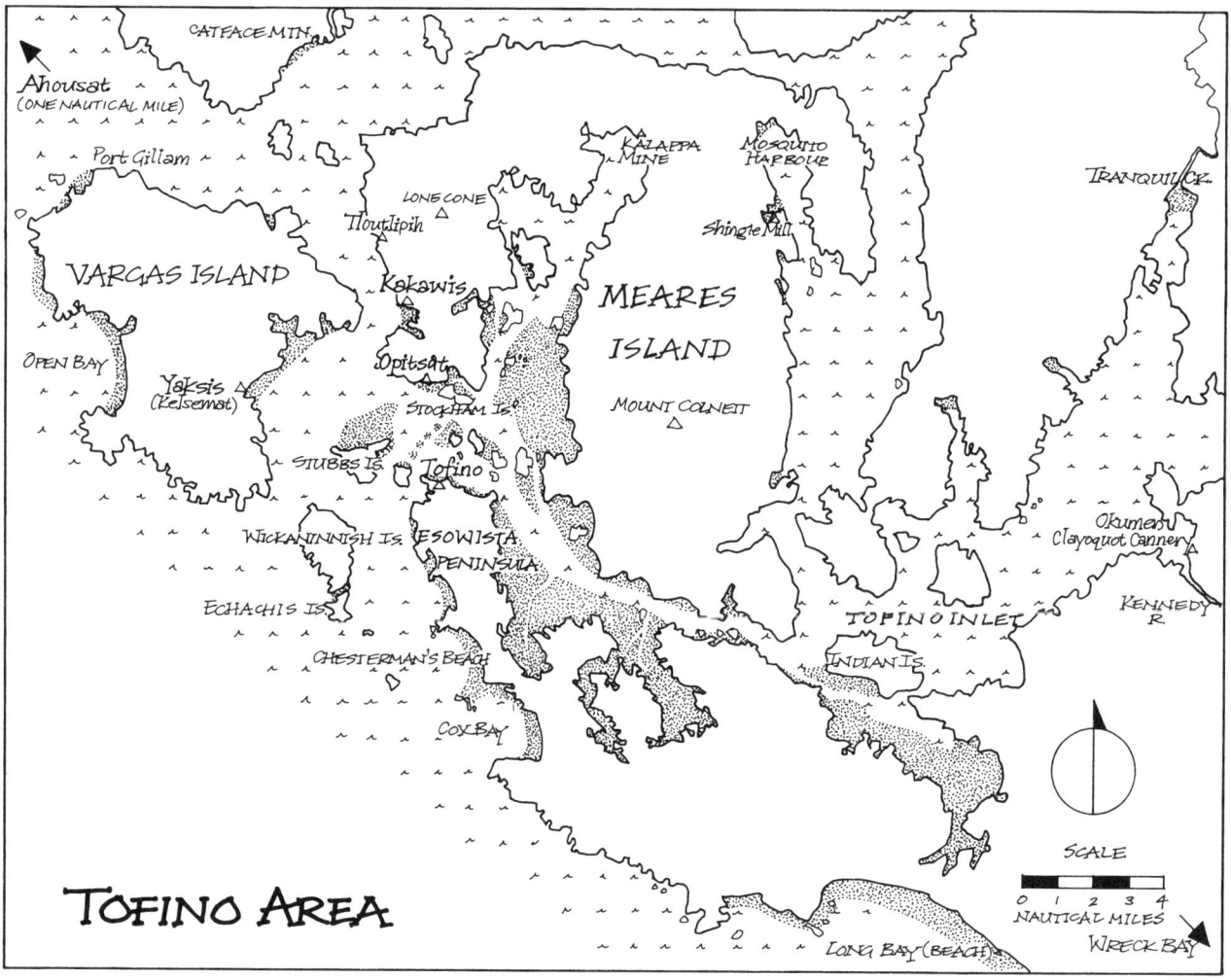

with women and children factored in, this meant a population of some two hundred settlers, most of them of English, Scottish or Norwegian descent.

To be receiving "Christmas matter" from Walter Dawley within a few months of his arrival in the area meant Fred Tibbs was highly favoured. Generally, Dawley graced only his old friends with gifts of game and fish at Christmas time, but Tibbs was new to the area and, given his prosperous middle-class English background, probably not at all wise to the ways of coastal living. Yet he appears to have had sufficient know-how and funds to get by, certainly enough to indulge personal whims, and he cheerfully set out to create a niche for himself in this challenging new setting. A disarming character, benignly good-natured in his letters, Tibbs engaged the goodwill even of Dawley from the very outset.

Just what drew Tibbs, then in his early twenties, to the west coast, no one knows. Disfigured by a childhood accident, he bore an unsightly scar that burrowed deeply into the left side of his face, not improved at all by various operations, and he was painfully self-conscious about this. In later years his niece speculated that perhaps Tibbs simply wanted to "get right away where he wasn't known." During his first year on the coast he busied himself at his Long Bay property, clearing land and building a home, and when he reached the finishing stages, he requested that Dawley send a gallon of pink paint to match a sample of lavishly rose-strewn wallpaper, which he attached to the letter.

Tibbs's precise, finicky, shopping orders pop up regularly in Dawley's papers: one dozen lemons, a dozen cans of St. Charles Milk, two twenty-cent cans of roast beef, "beans pink" and a pound of tea appear on one list; another modestly requests two thimbles, one small and one large. On one occasion he returns the "fancy vest" and asks for a blue sweater and "one bottle of limewater glycerine for hair." Requests for nails, mousetraps, vinegar and Popham biscuits also arrived, and in short order Tibbs became a faithful and regular customer.

His Conservative leanings soon became known in the locality, and this probably ensured his favourable connection with Dawley, who had no time for anyone inclining towards the Liberals. In 1904, Dawley's ex-partner, Thomas Stockham, had courted the Liberal cause, even trying to set up a Liberal association in Clayoquot, no doubt with the hope of furthering his sealing compensation claims. Dawley remained staunchly Conservative, a supporter of provincial premier Richard McBride's government, pleased to see men of his own persuasion, like Tibbs, settle in the area.

In all his letters to Walter Dawley, Fred Tibbs never once ordered liquor of any kind. Perhaps he was too intoxicated by his dreams and too busy in his new rosy-hued home to need any further stimulant, but he knew very well that in the "liquid dominion" of Clayoquot, as he grandiloquently described it, alcohol was readily available. Stories about drinking in the hotel saloon made for lively local gossip—for instance, how the boys from the Mosquito Harbour sawmill would sometimes come down, pin their paycheques to the wall and drink till the money was gone. But most settlers on their scattered homesteads had no time for such goings-on, though they might order a bottle or two from Clayoquot now and then.

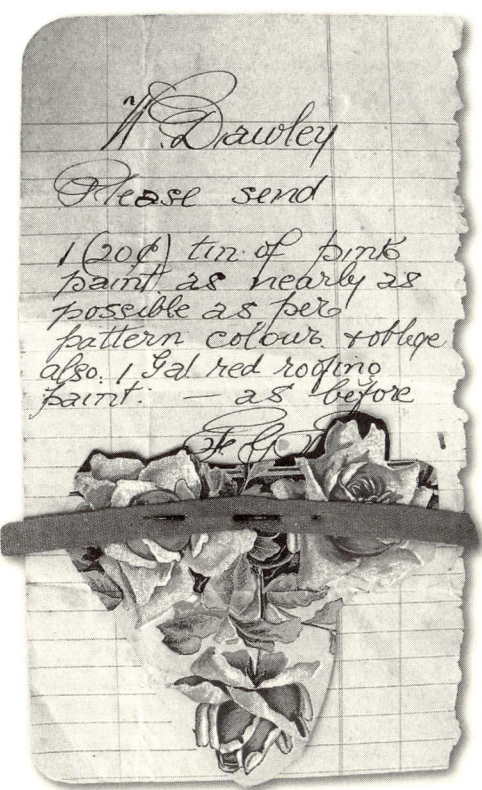

Fred Tibbs's neighbour at Long Bay, Mr. F. C. Coomes, was not shy about ordering liquor from Dawley, though he was not always pleased with the quality:

July 7, 1910

Dear Sir:

The bottle of liquor you sent me was whiskey or ment for that. Will you send by my son a bottle of Jamaca Rum, I prefer Hudson Bay if you have it. I wish part of it to make the medicine Caskara Lagrada the rest to refresh the inner man as the occasion may require.

Respectfully,
FC Coomes

Mr. Coomes's preference for the Hudson's Bay brands of liquor over the "whiskey or ment for that" provided by Dawley may or may not have been justified. In a letter dated May 14, 1907, the Hudson's Bay Company was on the defensive about its products: "In reference to liquors, we do not adulterate them in any shape or form but sell them exactly as received. Should you wish a highly colored whisky we could procure some coloring for you and you could then color it to suit."

References to the sale of various forms of alcohol often came in scribbled notes to Dawley, his correspondents demanding everything from "Irish Wky 2 cases" to "10 Gals of Claret Bulk" to "10 gals Rum." More modest requests are sometimes hidden in oblique terms at the end of longer shopping lists. In October 1909, Robert Pollock wrote from the lighthouse on Lennard Island with a diverse list requesting a box mattress, eggs ("fresh eggs if you have them...only got 11 good ones out of the last 2 doz"), coffee, cloves and cinnamon, adding at the bottom of the note: "get bottle special from Clarance and 1 Seagram and ask him to put some milk in Jar. N.B. If the molasses has not arrived send small can we must have gingerbread and beans Put the special in a package to conceal it." Clarence Dawley was by this time in charge of the Clayoquot Hotel and saloon, and he was no doubt adept at concealing "special" orders for shipment to men in remote places.

Writing to Dawley from Estevan Point, where he was working on the construction of the lighthouse and ordering supplies, John Chesterman submitted a sober, technical shopping list in April 1910, concluding with "Jimmy Murphy is here with me and he has the 'Grippe' and he wants Clarence to send him a Gallon of Rye, send me the bill." James Murphy was a faithful customer at the hotel saloon whenever he was at Clayoquot. Before heading to Estevan, he worked for a while on the telegraph line between Carmanah and Clo-oose. "Mr Daley Der Sir," he wrote from Clo-oose in February 1909. "...Well Mr Daley how are you getting along I will be Up in April for to drink some of that Rum...for I will Be dry." His letter concluded: "Find enclosed too dollars."

For a brief, dire period in 1908, men with dry throats in Clayoquot Sound suffered great deprivation. The Clayoquot Hotel was the only licensed premises for many dismally long miles; its saloon was even popular with the Roman Catholic priests, who occasionally dropped in for a glass or two of beer. But when fire raced through the hotel on June 9, 1908, this invaluable locale was destroyed. Despite the valiant efforts of every available person, many of whom rushed over from Opitsat and Tofino to help, the fire triumphed. Father Charles Moser was there. "Clayoquot Hotel on fire," he recorded in his diary. "Burnt to the ground; but store and other buildings were safed by the help of the Indians. I, too, carried water from the sea, luckily it was high tide."

The *Victoria Daily Colonist* reported on the event, adding that "the store adjoining and other buildings caught fire from the burning hotel, but there was little wind and settlers managed to save them. There was no insurance on the hotel." Undaunted, Walter Dawley immediately set about rebuilding, soon embroiling himself in several invigorating arguments with the Cameron Lumber Company in Victoria about shipments of lumber for the new hotel. He disputed freight charges and quantities of material shipped, eventually provoking three pages of painstaking explanation from the company's president. Mr. Cameron politely pointed out that he could not ship the lumber as Dawley wished, in one economical load, because the *Tees* and other vessels on the coast were so busy with freight that they would not take more than twenty thousand board feet at any one time to Clayoquot. Of the forty-seven–thousand board feet of lumber shipped on July 28, 1908, only twenty thousand went to Dawley's hotel. The rest was "for the mines," including the Tyee Copper Company's mine at Sydney Inlet.

Walter Dawley brooked such frustrations with ill will. These were bustling and prosperous days at Clayoquot, and he did not want to lose a day's more business at the hotel than was absolutely necessary. With all possible speed he had both the hotel and saloon up and running again, no doubt to the relief of his clientele.

In its description of Clayoquot for 1909, the *Directory of Vancouver Island* discreetly omits any mention of the hotel saloon, but every other detail is there:

> An important settlement on Stubbs Island, southeast of Mears Island, on West coast of Vancouver Island. It is about 150 miles northwest of Victoria, with which it has regular steamer connections. The Mining Recording Office and Provincial Police Station for the West Coast are situated here. There is a postoffice, hotel, courthouse and telegraph station; also a steam and a water power sawmill. There is considerable activity in mining and development work in the vicinity and this is also the supply centre for whaling and sealing schooners.

As the sealing industry declined during the first decade of the century, commercial whaling picked up some of the economic slack. From 1905 onward, the Pacific Whaling Company operated a shore-based whaling industry, first at Sechart in Barkley Sound, and from 1907 also at Cachalot in Kyuquot Sound. The industry was determined and purposeful, using specially built, fast-moving steamboats equipped with exploding harpoons to go after the whales.

"The bomb on the harpoon," explained the *Victoria Daily Colonist*, "explodes as it penetrates the carcass of the whale, usually with fatal results; but if the whale is not killed, there is a strong line of Russian hemp 400 fathoms long attached to the harpoon, and the whale is hauled nearer by the windlass until a second harpoon finishes the killing." The whales did not stand a chance; tens of thousands died off the coast of British Columbia in the ensuing twenty years.

The *Colonist* followed the whaling industry with mathematical precision, keeping close track of the number of whales killed month after month and year after year, always commenting on bumper kills. The Sechart whaling station recorded a catch of fifty-seven whales in three weeks during the spring of 1907. Another record followed during one week in July when, according to the *Colonist*, "18 whales were brought to the Sechart station. Tees spent 16 hours there loading cargo, 600 barrels of oil and 1,000 bags of fertilizer, the delay occasioned considerable protest."

When the new whaling station at Cachalot opened in mid-July 1907, the volume of the catch almost overwhelmed the employees; in less than a month, thirty-six whales were taken, and the new plant, still finding its feet, could barely cope with all the work of flensing and rendering so many carcasses. That season, shipments of up to eleven hundred barrels of whale oil at a time arrived in Victoria on board the *Tees*. The industry continued to expand, and by 1911 the Pacific Whaling Company had four whaling stations: two on the west coast of Vancouver Island, two in the Queen Charlotte Islands. The total number of whales taken by all four stations that year was 1,624.

Once brought into the whaling stations, the enormous beasts were quickly processed on site; the end products were always oil and fertilizer, sometimes bones or baleen. In later years, Cachalot processed canned whale meat, and at peak production times, up to two thousand cases of meat came out of the plant each day. The output of all whale products was prodigious: a large sperm whale could yield up to eighty barrels of oil; an average-sized whale, between thirty-five and forty barrels.

Shortly after the Sechart whaling station opened in 1905, the *Colonist* reported an average of two whales a day being processed. Early in January 1906, "372 barrels and 102 drums of whale oil" arrived in Victoria, "142 tons of oil in all, valued at about $17,000 for shipment to Glasgow." This was only the beginning. For years to come, vast quantities of whale oil and fertilizer made their way to destinations as diverse as Glasgow, San Francisco, Honolulu, Japan and India. Whale products increasingly made up the bulk of the cargo travelling down the coast on the various steamers, and the sheer volume of this cargo led to increasingly shrill demands for a larger and better steamer to serve the route.

The two whaling stations became macabre tourist attractions; passengers and crew from the coastal steamers would disembark for a quick tour, keen to be photographed alongside the large dead creatures on the docks. However, as an attraction, a whaling station had one powerful drawback. Mr. H. Brodie of the Canadian Pacific Railway, on an inspection tour of the coastal steamship route, did not mince his words. "The most indescribable stench prevails at the whaling station. There is no stench that is known the world over that equals that which permeates the whaling station and makes a large number of people very ill."

Father Charles Moser was undeterred by this smell. Over the years he visited both whaling stations at regular intervals, taking Mass to the Catholic workers there.

His first visit to Sechart was on June 12, 1906, to greet the "9 Catholic men from Newfoundland...employed and engaged to instruct westerners [in] the whaling business." He enjoyed his visit, remaining there for four days. "My services were well appreciated, the manager was very kind and did not charge me for board and lodging. 2 sulphur bottom

Two views of Kyuquot whaling station, 1919. The lower one shows steamer passengers in the background, looking on; this became a popular, if smelly, tourist stop along the west coast route.

[blue] whales were brought into the station…during my stay and were manufactured into oil and fertilizer."

The ease and the speed of dispatching these whales were in striking contrast to Father Charles's descriptions elsewhere in his diary of traditional whaling methods. On several occasions he observed Indians going whaling, commenting on the rituals, the preparation and the heightened atmosphere:

> *May 13, 1902:* 6 Canoes with 8 men in each went out whaling. The houses of the whale hunters are all darkened by placing mats or blankets in front of doors and windows. There exists a superstitious belief among the Indians that if the houses of the whalers have no light the hunters will see and catch the whale. At 8 PM the whalers return not having sighted a whale all day long.

Whale baleen at Kyuquot. Flexible and strong, baleen was used to stiffen corsets and to make umbrellas, carriage springs, horse whips and other products.

The hunters often came back empty-handed; Father Charles only once chronicled a successful whale hunt. "Indians caught a whale, a big monster of a humpback," he wrote on April 21, 1904. Several times, though, he noted the keen delight when a dead whale washed ashore; this was always cause for rejoicing and sharing:

December 17, 1913: News was brought into the camp by two Indians who had been hunting wild ducks along outside beach, that a dead whale had drifted on shore about 10–12 miles from here. This causes great excitement and all men are preparing to go and fetch whale blubber tomorrow.

December 18: Weather nice and sea calm. So the Indians go by canoes to the dead whale.

December 19: 7:30 AM Indians return with canoe loads of putrified, stinking whale blubber. It seems not to be fit for any other use but manure. But Indians think different. They will boil it out mix the rendered oil with dog fish oil to kill the strong taste and enjoy it with their dried fish.

These two different worlds of whaling—traditional and commercial—coexisted on the coast for a number of years. The contrasts between the two could not have been more extreme. Father Charles never remarked on this, placidly and uncritically continuing to enjoy his periodic visits to the whaling stations. On one occasion at Sechart, he received a singularly odd gift: "One of the engineers at the plant (from Zurich in Switzerland) gave me a baby whale—about 4' long—preserved in alcohol, for the Museum in Mt. Angel." This pickled whale travelled down to Mount Angel and took up residence in the abbey's museum, but Father Charles regretfully noted its destruction in a fire there in 1926.

Humpback whale ashore at Echachis, date unknown.

"Tees reached port yesterday from Quatsino and way ports of the West Coast with a cargo of whale oil, marble, sealskins, etc, and about 35 passengers," the *Colonist* reported on April 16, 1909, going on to name some of the passengers on board, including Fred Tibbs and the sealing captain Delouchrey, "who went to ship Indian hunters." As always, the cargo and passengers on the coastal steamers faithfully reflected both social and economic activity on the coast.

By the beginning of 1909, slabs of marble from Nootka Sound often joined the mixture of cargo on the steamers. Comments about the promising finds of coloured marble near Nootka appeared in the *Colonist* as early as 1894, and toward the end of that year an unspecified amount of marble was shipped out to Victoria. Apart from a few scattered references, little more is heard of this marble deposit until 1907, when it came under serious scrutiny. In early November that year, "a trial shipment of marble from a new quarry at Nootka Sound" travelled to Victoria on board the *Tees*. After a flurry of construction and preparation in 1908, the quarry began serious production. Periodic reports of marble shipments continued for the next three years.

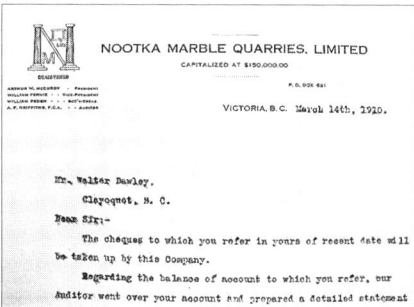

By this time, the storekeeper at Nootka was Mr. H. Smith, who took the job in February 1908 following the very short stay of his predecessor, Mr. Alfred Vaughan. Like Vaughan, Smith was interviewed for the job in Victoria, on Walter Dawley's behalf, by James Thomson of the Hudson's Bay Company. Unlike Vaughan, Smith could handle the job. The unfortunate Alfred Vaughan was a young Englishman with no experience of storekeeping, and he lasted less than two horror-stricken weeks at Nootka before fleeing back to Victoria. Judging from James Thomson's comments in a letter to Dawley dated January 10, 1908, Vaughan's only qualification for the position was that "his general physique indicates that he would be quite equal to doing a hard day's work." Strong he may have been, but Vaughan proved himself a timid creature. On February 1, 1908, Mr. Thomson wrote to Dawley in baffled amazement following Vaughan's precipitate flight back to civilization:

> I was sorry to learn from your letter of 25th that Mr Vaughan has not seen fit to remain at Nootka. I indicated to him that it was an Indian village and that he would have a large proportion of natives to deal with but this didn't seem to cause him any anxiety. For a young man who has seen so much of the world I didn't think he would have got scared by a few Indians dancing.

Next in line for the job, Smith was made of sterner stuff, having worked at Simon Leiser's branch store in Ladysmith for some time. Smith shared Dawley's keen interest in deal-making and made sure to inform him of key events. When the Nootka marble quarry changed hands in February 1910, Smith wrote, "I saw a copy of Balance sheet & the notes of meeting they tried hard to raise the funds but could not so the only alternative was to sell." The quarry closed shortly afterward.

In the same letter, Smith informed Dawley that Chief Napoleon "has bought a Marble Headstone for the Young Chief & that cost $140 dollars." The "Young Chief," the son of Chief Napoleon Maquinna, great-nephew of the old Chief Maquinna, had died in infancy. Erecting a headstone of local marble for the little boy was a non-traditional gesture, a display of wealth and a powerful expression of the importance of the boy and his family. Chief Napoleon here again demonstrated his ability to make strong social and ceremonial statements. He had done so before, a few years earlier and in happier circumstances, at his own wedding.

According to Father Maurus Snyder, Napoleon's lavish and splendid wedding in May 1908 was the first Christian marriage at Nootka, and it created a sensation up and down the coast. Father Maurus wrote about the wedding years afterward:

> Chief Napoleon gave a striking example of the fearlessness inherited from his ancestors at the time of his own wedding. Defying all Indian traditions and the violent opposition of the chiefs and councilmen

Led by a flag-bearer and the brass band from Christie School, the processional march along the beach at Friendly Cove marked the wedding of Chief Napoleon Maquinna in May 1908. Attended by a great crowd of guests, this was the first Christian wedding at Nootka.

Chief Napoleon Maquinna and his bride.

of his tribe he wanted and had a perfectly Christian and civilized marriage ceremony… The sumptious banquet served by the chief in the largest old-time Indian houses of the camp, built of immense cedar logs and hand-hewn planking to every member of the tribe helped much to smooth over the opposition.

The wedding party included a processional march to the church, with a cross leading the way and a flag-bearer following. Flanked by robed priests and nuns, the bride and groom made their way along the beach, accompanied by many guests and the full brass band from Kakawis. The band travelled up to Nootka with Father Maurus on board the *Tees*, a departure noted by Father Charles in his diary: "*May 23, 1908:* Steamer day. Fr Maurus with his band boarded steamer for Nootka to take part in the Christian marriage of Napoleon, chief of the Nootka tribe."

Keenly aware of the significance of this wedding, Christian weddings being so unusual, Father Maurus travelled with his camera at the ready. His photographs of the event show Chief Napoleon wearing a straw boater and his bride in a fashionable white wedding dress, their faces composed and proud. Their procession along the beach and even the wedding feast inside the longhouse are recorded for posterity, rare images of an outstanding event.

Capitalizing on his connections with the native villages up and down the coast, and always keen to develop new enterprises, Walter Dawley became a middleman in the expanding trade in Indian artefacts and handicrafts. One of the

Chief Napoleon Maquinna's wedding feast in the longhouse at Friendly Cove, May 1908.

earliest hints of his involvement in this trade dates from 1902, when a customer in Nelson, BC, requested "a good Hydah hat or similar kind made by your Indians," and "anything nice in basket work." In 1905, the surveyor Mr. H. A. Browne ordered several of "those cedar bark Indian hats of yours," and the same year, James Thomson in Victoria commented: "We will keep you in mind if we have a chance to sell another Totem Pole." But the most popular items of trade were always handwoven Indian baskets, and a few years into the twentieth century, this trade was brisk.

The baskets Dawley purchased from Indians generally went to dealers in Victoria. From 1904 to 1907, Mr. and Mrs. A. A. Aaronson purchased Indian baskets and crafts from Dawley, particularly small, finely worked baskets that could cost as little as fifteen or twenty-five cents wholesale. The Aaronsons were always on the lookout for "table mats of Indian work and any old curios." The wordy banner on Mrs. Aaronson's letterhead declared her business to be "Indian Curio Bazaar, 52 Government Street, Victoria, B. C.," with smaller letters announcing that this was "The cheapest place on the Pacific Coast to buy all kinds of Indian Baskets, Pow-Wow Bags, Wood and Stone Totems, Pipes, Carved Horn and Silver Spoons, Rattles, Souvenirs, Novelties, Etc., Old English Brass Candlesticks, Colored Post Cards 2 for 5¢."

When Mr. Aaronson made the mistake of buying "Indian curios" directly from Fred Thornberg, now operating as an independent, rival storekeeper at Ahousat, Dawley quickly intervened. "I wrote to Thornberg at Ahouset," Mr. Aaronson declared, "but did not know that it would conflict with you as I was under the impression that it was quite a long distance from your district…I would not have written to him if I thought you were buying from Ahouset." Within a short time the enterprising Chief Billy August of Ahousat also took the initiative and started selling handicrafts directly to the dealers. "Chief Billy is going to Victoria with some women to sell Baskets, mats, &c.," reported Thomas Gardhouse, Dawley's Ahousat storekeeper, on September 9, 1907.

Meanwhile, in Victoria, the Aaronsons became increasingly critical. They did not like the basketwork-covered bottles Dawley purchased for them: "Do not send any large beer or whisky bottles as I have lots of them, but I want flasks and small bottles of fine work. Table mats and picture frames." Shortly afterward, they became even more dissatisfied: "I notice you did not send me any fine baskets all summer and I certainly cannot use rubbish." Correspondence with the Aaronsons ceased at this point.

In 1909, Henry Varney of Quatsino recommended another dealer in "Indian curios" to Dawley: "As promised I have written to my friend Mr. Clubb at the Empress hotel," Varney wrote, "and I have no doubt that he will be able to take all your stock of baskets, as well as any other Indian curios you happen to have. In the season that man has an unlimited demand for baskets." Ever hopeful, Varney continued, "I could not see your man the other day as the steamer left the wharf, but I am going to ask you to send me a sample lot of some of your cheaper grades [of baskets]…I occasionally come across a few tourists up here now, and could dispose of quite a number of articles myself." Varney did not mention selling Indian baskets again; in 1909, tourists in Quatsino may have been more imaginary than real, although interest in all manner of Indian crafts was on the increase everywhere. In 1909, Dawley's papers contain references to carved silver bracelets, and also to stone totem poles from the Queen Charlotte Islands.

At various times Dawley sold native goods to several different dealers in Victoria, including Mr. H. Stadthagen of Johnson Street, whose advertisements claimed "he sold in the year 1903 over 14,800 Indian baskets all over the world";

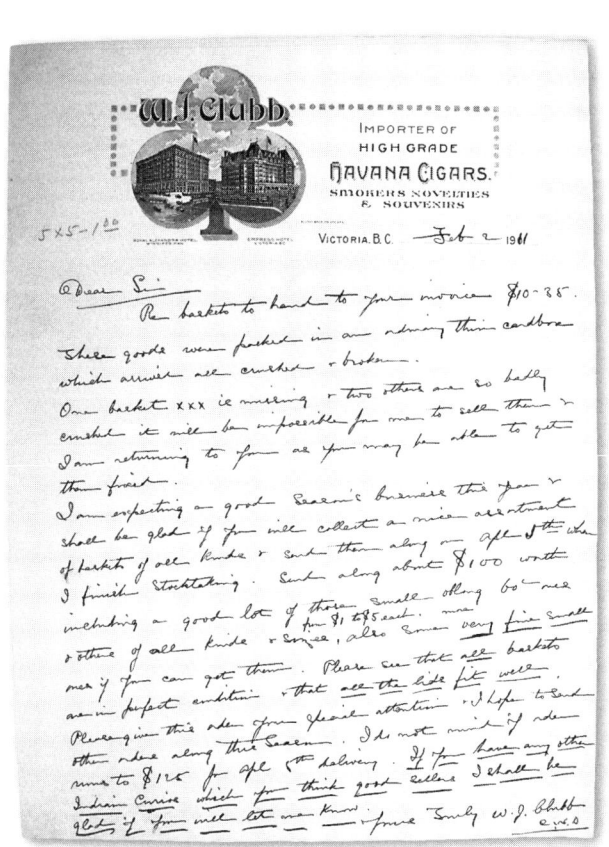

but it was Mr. Clubb at the Empress Hotel who became Dawley's most consistent outlet for Indian handicrafts. Mr. Clubb's letters arrived at Clayoquot on stationery declaring him to be "Importer of High Grade Havana Cigars Smokers Novelties & Souvenirs," and the man emerges in his letters as a peppery character, emphatically underlining whole rows of words with sharp jabs of the pen. His small, spiky handwriting, always in black ink, exudes nervous energy, giving the impression of a wiry little man, cigar in hand, gesticulating furiously at the large and impassive Dawley, intent on making himself heard all the way from Victoria.

"Please see that all baskets are in perfect condition & that all the lids fit well," he demanded on February 2, 1911. "If you have any other Indian curios which you think good sellers I shall be glad if you will let me know." Like Mrs. Aaronson, Clubb wanted the best— "Do your best to get me some of the very finely worked small ones"—and he was always a discerning buyer: "I do not think the totem poles you mention will interest me as I can only sell cheap wooden ones & also black stone poles which I get from Queen Charlotte Islands." Clubb repeatedly and testily protested that he did not want any more bottles covered in basketwork, and he insisted on obtaining the very finely woven small baskets, having in mind a price between sixty cents and $1.50 for these particular curios. Dawley continued to trade with Mr. Clubb as late as 1917, and Clubb never ceased stabbing at his paper with staccato pen strokes: "For extra fine large baskets I will pay up to $5 each. If you have none in stock put some in hand if possible… See that all lids fit well."

Details of a more ambitious transaction concerning Indian handicrafts appear in Dawley's correspondence in 1914. That year he shipped two small totem poles, each about four feet high, to a purchaser in New York who paid thirty dollars for the pair and expressed interest in obtaining a larger pole, between twelve and fifteen feet in height. P.L. Lyford of Vancouver brokered the deal for the smaller poles, and he asked: "Are these genuine totem poles or are they made especially for the trade in selling?" Dawley must have replied that they were genuine poles, for later on Lyford asked about the identity of the carvers, adding, "Can you give me some idea of what [the totems] stand for and when they have been used?" He also asked where the "Hydah" Indians lived, so it appears Dawley had somehow acquired these totem poles from the Queen Charlotte Islands.

This "trade in selling" Indian artefacts to eastern collectors was nothing new. Ever since noting, back in 1875, that an enormous canoe "made by Maquinna, chief of the Nootka Sound Indians," was about to be shipped to Philadelphia, the *Victoria Daily Colonist* had occasionally reported when valuable native artefacts were shipped off to collectors in the United States and elsewhere. On November 4, 1900, the steamer *Willapa* arrived in Victoria with "two large cases of Indian curios and small totems, which have been collected on the Coast for eastern US museums." Four months later, on March 2, 1901, the newspaper commented that "Willapa, on her down trip, is expected to bring a large consignment of Indian curios and archeological effects, which G. Hunt, of Alert Bay has been collecting for some time past for Dr Francis Boaz, who is acting on behalf of a New York museum." Protests began to arise about this trade in artefacts, and on November 1, 1903, the newspaper published an article deploring the "despoiling process which has been in progress for many years past" and the removal from the province of so many native relics and works of art: "The people of BC as a whole… should atone for their past neglect and urge upon the government of the day the great need of protecting its wealth of native relics and curiosities from the depredations of foreign collectors."

Walter Dawley did not deal with serious collectors of old, valuable native artefacts—perhaps it was more trouble than it was worth, or perhaps he lacked the necessary contacts. Instead, he purchased small handcrafted items from his Indian customers to sell to dealers in Victoria, a technique that assured him a tidy little business and attracted more Indians into his commercial web. And tucked away within his files are a number of letters hinting at other ways he turned the skills and know-how of native people into a profitable trade. For a while he employed native people to collect cascara bark for one Mr. Pollak, a buyer in Seattle. In September 1912, Dawley sent out an invoice for 1,417 pounds of the bark, and the reply from Mr. Pollak came swiftly, revealing a typical Dawley transaction. Pollak claimed that he received only 1,271 pounds of bark. "The scales of the public weigher in Seattle are very correct," he wrote, "and... I am inclined to think that you must have made a mistake in figuring up your weights... In the meantime I am enclosing check for $57.19 being for 1271 lbs of bark @ four and a half cents per pound."

This cascara bark, which the Indians had long known for its medicinal qualities, found ready customers in pharmaceutical companies in the eastern United States, who used it to manufacture the tonic laxative cascara sagrada. In Oregon and Washington, a commercial harvest of the bark continued for several decades, and by the time Dawley entered the cascara trade, these northwestern states were running low on supplies of the bark. Dawley's interest in the trade was sporadic, but it resurfaced in the autumn of 1915, when J. Howshall and Company, billing themselves "Co-operative growers of medicinal plants etc.," sent a polite request to Dawley: "We are buyers of wild native medicinal plants, roots and barks and are given to understand that you trade in same."

No records survive that detail the types of medicinal plants Dawley could provide, or how he bought and sold them, but he was always open to any ideas that could expand and diversify his trade. He even proved himself willing to cooperate with Chinese purchasers in Victoria, shipping them quantities of seaweed on occasion. Writing through an interpreter, a Chinese man named Yet Wo Lung asked, in the spring of 1908, why his order for 280 pounds of seaweed had not yet arrived. Presumably, when it did arrive, Yet Wo Lung checked the weight.

Triangle Island March 15, 1910

Dear Mr Dawley:
After a week and two days we affected a landing on this mountain top, surrounded by ocean. Talk about wind! Not a tree, not a bush.

Lighthouse 680 feet up…Will be obliged if you send up by the next boat coming here 1 pair tennis shoes size 9, and if you have one, good deep toned mouth harp.

Hoping that the winds may descend on you with slightly less violence than hereabouts.

Yours truly,
FG Tibbs

Early in 1910, Fred Tibbs abandoned the pink interior of his house at Long Bay and took a construction job at the new lighthouse going up on Triangle Island, a dramatically exposed rock out in the Pacific some two hundred miles north of Clayoquot. The gales were ferocious, the work gruellingly difficult and the isolation extreme. Tibbs remained there for several months, taking in his new experiences with unflappable good-nature. On June 15 he remarked in a letter to Dawley: "The birds have arrived here & egg hunting is the principal amusement out of working hours for everybody, catching young sea lions offers another pastime. Just now we are expecting the Leebro up here in 2 or 3 days a much looked forward to event in these parts."

Having survived Triangle Island, Tibbs travelled home to England at the end of 1910, writing to Dawley from his home at Sanderstead in Surrey: "I hope you got that cheque for November all right also that you are not suffering with Rheumatism." Meanwhile, Lawrence Carter of Alberni wrote to Dawley, enclosing a money order for $2.80 for dogfish oil and commenting enviously, "I saw Tibbs on last down trip, but had very little time to talk to him. It does not take the fellows on Government work long to save enough for a trip to England." These "fellows on Government work"—steady, well-paid, sought-after jobs—were often expatriate Brits; they tended to attract such resentment.

Back at his Tidal Wave Ranch a few months later, Tibbs resumed his local interests and by the end of the year became president of the area's Conservative association (annual subscription $1.00). "You might order some suitable headed writing paper and envelopes for the Clayoquot Conservative Association," he suggested to Dawley on November 6, 1911. The Clayoquot Liberal Association, headed by William Stone, must have found another source for letterhead: to order such an item from Dawley would have been politically inflammatory. After the federal election of 1911 brought the Conservative government of Robert Borden to power, defeating the longstanding Liberal regime of Sir Wilfrid Laurier, Dawley received a cryptic letter from Mr. R. J. Burde, editor of the *Alberni Pioneer News*, dated November 21, 1911: "You can rest assured that

Liberal patronage on the west coast will no longer be tolerated... As far as the Conservative patronage goes it is all in your own hands."

In 1912, Fred Tibbs took a position at the government-run salmon hatchery at Kennedy Lake, a job he held for several years. About the same time, he sold his ranch at Long Bay, reportedly for the huge sum of $5,000, and embarked on the quixotic scheme that would bring him lasting fame in the Tofino area.

Fred Tibbs bought an island, and he decided to build a castle.

His island is now called Tibbs Island or Arnet Island, though in his time people called it Dream Isle or even Castle Island. There, in full view of fascinated onlookers at Tofino, Tibbs went about pursuing his extraordinary dream. First, he decided, to have a castle on an island, he must clearcut the entire island—but he chose to leave one tree standing, an enormous spruce, which he topped at one hundred feet. Over time, he cut all the limbs off the tree trunk, leaving a huge standing spar, and he constructed a sturdy kind of ladder, almost a small scaffolding, that mounted up the tree, step by step. Eventually he could ascend right to the top, where he built a narrow platform with a glorious view of Clayoquot Sound. According to some local sources, he took his cornet up there every morning at 8 AM to play "Come to the Cookhouse Door, Boys."

He also constructed the castle itself, a four-storey wooden building, complete with a tower and crenellated battlements. Painted white, red and blue, the castle eventually featured a garden with trellises and roses, a love seat and a sunken well. Tibbs brought a piano and a phonograph to the castle, and friends would come over to hear music, drink cocoa and marvel at his achievements. He painted the words "Dream Isle" in large letters on a rock face, and he tirelessly worked to rid the island of stumps, usually by dynamiting them. He told friends he planned to build a bicycle track around the island.

"I'd row over and we'd talk about, oh gosh, clearing land," remarked Tofino settler Bill Sharp. "That's about all you did in those days is talk about what you're going to clear and how you're going to do it and how you're going to take this stump out or that other thing. Then I'd row back."

"He was so determined," Alma Arnet recalled. "My father said to him that he should leave some trees for protection against the storms, but he just went ahead."

Tibbs fell in love with a local girl. In fact, he fell in love with—or at least he was attracted to—two local girls: Alma Arnet and Olive Garrard. They

The "tree rig" built by Fred Tibbs on his Dream Isle.
From the platform on top, about 100 feet in the air,
he had a splendid view of Clayoquot Sound.

both knew him, although not well, and he never openly declared his attachment or asked either of them to marry him. But after several years of hard work on his island, he did draw up his will, leaving the island "and everything thereon, excepting the house and ten feet of land on either side of the house site," to Alma Arnet, "because she's the nicest girl I ever met and another reason she knows." He left the house and contents, except for the gramophone, to Olive Garrard, "because it was built for her," with the caveat that if Olive Garrard married, the house should go to Alma Arnet, "if she still is single."

"Alma and I were friends and we were both underage," Olive commented many years later. Both were blonde. Neither knew a thing about Fred Tibbs's will until after his death, and they were completely taken aback, not least because many people in Tofino believed that Tibbs had a soft spot for Winnie Dixson, the doctor's daughter. "Oh he tried all of us, all the different girls," Winnie said later. "I didn't have much interest. I didn't have time. I had about 300 chickens."

Tibbs's castle on Dream Isle was never fully finished. In May 1917 he enlisted, joining the Canadian Forestry Corps as a private and heading overseas, where he worked on railway construction at the front lines and as a bugler. He boarded up the windows in his castle, and on one of them, up in the tower, he painted a picture of a beautiful princess. Some say she looked just like Olive Garrard. But he gave a photograph of himself, "his soldier picture" as she called it, to Alma Arnet. "It was taken from the side," she commented matter-of-factly, "because of his disfigurement."

Little is known of Tibbs's experiences during the First World War. Perhaps images of Dream Isle and memories of his happy castle sustained him through the challenges and the horrors of life at the front, just as James Jones had dreamed of the green silences of Sydney Inlet when he was serving in the Boer War. Perhaps as Tibbs played his bugle in war-torn landscapes, he imagined how his horn would sound from the top of his tree in the clear air of the liquid dominion of Clayoquot. Perhaps. Meanwhile his castle and his island awaited him. His legacy was yet to unravel.

St. Antonine Church at Hesquiat around 1910. The original church, built by Father Brabant in 1875, burned down, to be replaced by this elaborate Gothic-style building in 1891. Although damaged again by fire in 1897, it endured until the 1920s, when the tall bell tower was replaced with a domed structure.

— 10 —

Hesquiat Days

February 22, 1911: News arrived per wireless that my predecessor Fr. A.J. Brabant was on board SS Tees bound for Hesquiat. This caused general rejoicing in the village. Canoes were got ready at high tide and anchored out, as steamer might come tonight.

FATHER AUGUSTIN BRABANT came to Hesquiat for the last time in 1911, disembarking from the *Tees* on February 23 and bringing Father Charles a dog for company. In the weeks that followed, both men relished the time to talk, to work together, to remember the old days. "Cold wind from the West. In the house lots of smoke from our pipes and long and useful conversations between Fr. Brabant and myself," Father Charles reported with satisfaction. He was also pleased to be asked to assist Father Brabant with his English/Indian dictionary, a project Brabant had worked on for many years.

During this visit, Father Charles's spirits were high, not only because he had stimulating company, but also because he had received word that he would be allowed to travel to Switzerland on a four-month leave to visit his elderly father and his family. He planned to leave in early June and return in October. Father Charles's diary for the month of Brabant's visit reveals him at his happiest; full of energy and tackling many projects. A new organ for the church arrived on the steamer, and within a day or two it was triumphantly installed. "*February 26, 1911:* After High Mass at 10 AM Fr. Brabant preached. Evening services as usual. William Aloysius played the organ."

In the following weeks, Father Charles's diary describes housework and land clearing, making firewood and hearing confession, singing High Mass, castrating bulls and baking hosts, one unlikely detail leading directly and amiably to another. Throughout this month, his tone is entirely positive, with none of the vague unhappiness, no complaints about his fellow priests and none of the repetitive comments on the wrongdoings of the Indians that so often characterize the diary.

> *March 1, 1911:* Ash Wednesday. Fr. Brabant said the first Mass and I had the people's Mass with blessing and distribution of ashes. Nearly all people participated. After dinner till 4 PM Ignace and myself cleared away young spruce trees and piled them up for burning.
>
> *March 2:* In the forenoon split wood and did general housework. From 2 till 4 PM worked hard cutting down trees behind the church. Confessions in the evening.
>
> *March 3:* First Friday. People's Mass with 12 Communions. After dinner worked outside again and made fire. Had two bull calves castrated, age 4 and a half and 3 weeks. Stations of the Cross in the evening.

During this month, Father Charles wrote of reviving a "fainting old woman" with a glass of rum and water, of Constant Charleson coming several times to

The beach at Hesquiat, date unknown.

help with the English/Indian dictionary, of many visitors: Gussie Luckovitch from the lighthouse, Mr. Collins the wireless operator, and Mr. Jensen from the lighthouse, who kindly brought a "fresh piece of butter." Perhaps Father Charles used this valuable butter with the potatoes he purchased from "Jeannie" in the village, forty-eight pounds for one dollar, or perhaps he saved it to use with the welcome batch of fresh bread from Kakawis that arrived on the *Tees*. He remarked with approval that the *Tees* would now be making two "long trips" per month, passing by Hesquiat twice monthly during the coming season.

> *March 4, 1911:* Saturday. Ignace cleared land and burnt several piles. East wind. At 2 PM singing practise in the church with organ. Let calves run free with their mothers.

> *March 5:* Sunday. Fr Brabant said early Mass at 7:30 and I sang High Mass at 10 o'clock. Band practise at 1:30 PM. Rosary and benediction at 5 PM.

Bleak weather prevailed throughout March, rain and more rain, some snow, plenty of wind. Undeterred, Father Charles mustered the men of the village to re-shingle the church roof, a project carried out efficiently and quickly despite the weather, and Father Brabant remained contentedly indoors.

> *March 11, 1911:* Snow storms today, sometimes rain. Cold wind, but snow did not stay on ground. Father Brabant cooked dinner today, plenty of slapjacks, baked herrings and potatoes.

> *March 12:* Sunday services same as last Sunday. Steamer stopped here on her return trip at 8 AM. Jimmy Codfish from Nootka disembarked, went to Confession and received Holy Communion immediately before High Mass. Gussie and his father at Mass, had dinner with us, which consisted of corned beef, potatoes, and canned fruit for desert. After supper Nootka Jimmy came to tell me that he came to get me for his very sick mother.

Nootka Jimmy, also called Jimmy Codfish, and Father Charles headed out by canoe for Nootka on the morning of March 13. After a very seasick voyage of several hours, they arrived at Friendly Cove, and Father Charles settled into the cold, unoccupied, priest's house, made coffee and ate some hard tack biscuits with butter before going to visit Jimmy's mother. She agreed to be baptized on the spot but died the following day.

Back at Hesquiat with Father Brabant, Father Charles enjoyed another couple of days of good cooking, hearing stories of Brabant's early days, including "a nice story about Bishop Segher's visit to Hesquiat and Kyuquot in 1886 for which official visit the Bishop had forgotten to bring his episcopal paraphernalia along," evidently an in-house kind of story, better appreciated by those in the business.

Father Brabant's visit to Hesquiat, peppered with ecclesiastical shoptalk of this kind, undoubtedly raised his own spirits, as well as those of Father Charles. For a long while now, Brabant had been bitterly convinced that he was being put out to grass by the church authorities. In 1907 the bishop requested that he leave Hesquiat and move to Victoria and, most unwillingly, Brabant made the move. He worked for some time as diocesan administrator in Victoria and latterly as chaplain at St. Ann's Convent, in each position feeling overlooked and unappreciated. "The next you will hear is that I am again an altar boy!" he wrote to Father Maurus in disgust. In 1909 he begged the bishop to allow him to return to Hesquiat; the answer, recorded in a letter, was clear. "No! Father, you are too old—and if I am too old now, I cannot expect to be younger next year—and so my condemnation was pronounced."

By January 1910, Brabant was in despair. "My position is simply unbearable and I am certainly having my purgatory on earth," he declared to Father Maurus. A few months later he wrote again: "You would now hardly know me; in fact I hardly realise myself that I am the same individual who at one time held the fort at Hesquiat and cast bombs and explosives amongst the Indian Doctors, administered blistering plasters, doses of castor oil and other items...the

The church and priest's house at Friendly Cove, probably around 1912.

same who presided at the ceremonies of altering calves and many other unmentionable performances! Quantum mutatus!"

Unhappily removed from the missions on the coast, in his darkest moments Father Brabant feared these missions would prove unsustainable. Yet for a number of years he had realized—albeit unwillingly—that the hold of the church was loosening, even amongst the people he believed to be staunch Catholics. Back in 1904, Brabant wrote with horror of a traditional Indian marriage at Hesquiat between a Kelsemat man and a Hesquiat girl:

> The matter has given me great grief; and to a number of the Hesquiats has given great scandal…Before I went to Nootka everything was fine in Hesquiat—the church every day full of Indians at Mass—confessions, communions, everything in fact beyond anything I ever expected to see in my lifetime…This is only the second time in more than twenty years that a marriage has been contracted outside of the Church.

Brabant roundly condemned all who were involved in the wedding, refusing to allow them to be confirmed in the church, requesting the intervention of the bishop and demanding shrilly that the newly married Kelsemat man leave Hesquiat.

By that time, Brabant had been on the coast for nearly thirty years, and the Hesquiat people over whom he had exerted such iron control were beginning to defy his stern authority. For many years they had been part of the cash economy on the coast, through sealing and through seasonal work in the canneries on the Fraser River and hop-picking in Puget Sound. Increasingly exposed to new pressures, new social influences and many conflicting forms of authority, the entire social fabric of their lives was changing due to economic pressures, drink, disease and disenfranchisement. Small wonder the authority of the old priest on the coast was crumbling.

It was all too much for Brabant. His greatest fear, clearly stated in a letter to Father Maurus dated November 29, 1909, was for the Catholic mission at Hesquiat: "But, Father, what is going to become of our Mission at Hesquiat—Can you not prevail on the Abbot to let a father join you at Kakawis and have Hesquiat attended from there—it is no credit to the church to abandon the only Catholic tribe on the coast!!"

For years to come, the fate of the Catholic missions around Clayoquot Sound was a debating point amongst church authorities. Were it not for Father Charles, who proved himself almost as stubborn as Father Brabant, the Roman

Seated beside the Hesquiat church, a young woman poses for the camera with two children. The girl in the hat is dressed as if ready to return to Christie School. Schoolgirls often wore their best clothes when they travelled back to school by steamer.

Catholic mission at Hesquiat may well have folded sooner than it did. Although Father Charles was initially taken aback at being sent to this isolated mission in 1910, judging by his diary, this is where he spent his most peaceful and content years on the coast.

On March 17, 1911, shortly after returning from Nootka, Father Charles decided to go to Kakawis by canoe. He prepared firewood for Father Brabant's use during his absence, checked on his cattle—"seven calves born this year"—and arranged for three Hesquiat men to travel with him. In the early evening, one of the men decided not to go. "Now with my coal oil lantern I had to go to look for another man to take his place," Father Charles wrote testily. "Indian reliability!"

The following day, Father Charles and three men headed down the coast, calling at Refuge Cove to land one of their passengers. It was a hard pull, taking them nine and a half hours to reach Kakawis. Father Charles spent three days there, and on March 22 he boarded the steamer *Tees* to return to Hesquiat. Because of the strong southeast wind and rain, "what the sailors call dirty weather," he landed inside Hesquiat Harbour at Anton's Point and walked the mile-long trail to Hesquiat in the rain and the dark. "Fr. Brabant had supper ready for me," he recorded in his diary. "About 8:30 a wireless operator also a passenger on the steamer but whom I had not met on board, came to my house to stay overnight as it was too dark and nasty to walk to Estevan Pt. Made a supper for him and gave him a pair of my pants as he was all wet."

Children at Hesquiat around 1912.

Over the next couple of days, as Father Charles sorted mail and Father Brabant smoked his incessant pipes of tobacco, they had many visitors, including some Clayoquot Indians who were on board the sealing schooner *Jessie*. George Heater, captain of the *Jessie*, had anchored at Hesquiat while recruiting crew members for a season of offshore sealing. He eventually found eight Hesquiat hunters, and Father Charles, who was not only postmaster of Hesquiat but also shipping master, arranged that they sign on to the *Jessie* for the season.

Later the same day, visitors from the lighthouse dropped by with news that the southbound steamer was en route, having left Kyuquot at 10 AM. Father

Brabant was due to take this steamer back to Victoria. He and Father Charles took a walk to look for the survey post marking the mission land on the northeast side, but they failed to find it. In the evening, while Father Charles heard confessions, the steamer sounded its whistle, and Father Brabant went aboard. The priest's house was empty when Father Charles returned. Life resumed its normal pattern.

> *April 2, 1911:* All services both forenoon and evening at the usual time. Quite a number of Indians called on me during the afternoon. West wind and cold all day.
>
> *April 3:* Monday. About an inch of snow on the ground. Instruction for first communicants. After dinner sawed fifteen blocks of wood in halves. Then cut down limbs from many young spruce and hemlock trees that grow like grass around church and house; they are so thick together that even the cattle could not get through.
>
> *April 4:* Tuesday. Fine day. Instruction as yesterday. After dinner I burned limbs and cut down more of them. Two canoes had gone out hunting seals for the first time this season but they returned without any skins. One canoe, however had come across a dead whale and brought a big load of whale meat home.
>
> *April 5:* Wednesday. Beautiful day again. At 9:30 AM had singing practise in the church. Practiced the Regina coeli. Afterwards about a dozen men mended the church roof on Epistle side. Old shakes were found to be in good condition. Meanwhile I chopped down limbs and kept fire going. But at 3 PM I felt exhausted, quit work and went into the house to get dinner ready.

Unidentified family around 1912.

The next news of Father Brabant comes in a letter from Fred Thornberg to Father Maurus Snyder. Thornberg had visited Brabant in Victoria in mid-November 1911: "He is pretty bad now & I dont think he can hold out much longer," wrote Thornberg, going on to relate their lengthy conversation concerning the history of the Roman Catholics at Ahousat. Thornberg had visited Brabant in Victoria before, in July 1909, when he "callet in & had quite a long powow about old times etc with Father Braband."

In June 1912, over a year after Brabant's visit to Hesquiat, Father Charles saw the older priest for the last time: "Arrived in Victoria at noon. At St. Joseph's Hospital I found Fr. Brabant very sick." On July 4, 1912, Father Charles received

Doing housework for the priest. On April 21, 1916, Father Charles wrote: "After the service five girls scrubbed my sitting room and kitchen and baked two pies."

the following telegram at Hesquiat: "Father Brabant died this morning. Funeral next Tuesday morning. Please communicate Nootka, Kakawis." His diary takes due note: "At once I went to toll the church bell and hoisted flag at half mast." In the next couple of days, Father Charles held two Requiem Masses at Hesquiat for his mentor and friend.

Augustin Brabant was buried in Victoria, at Ross Bay Cemetery. He was sixty-seven years old.

June 1, 1912: Saturday. Instruction for two engaged couples. Two men working all day on new porch. Mickie one of the new bridegrooms came asking me to lend him a pair of shoes for tomorrow and for his marriage day which was set for next Tuesday. With pleasure I gave him my only pair of Sunday shoes, to be returned tomorrow after Mass and that he could get them again for his marriage. I needed them myself on Sunday after Mass. Poor boy, I wish I could give him a pair of new shoes for his marriage!

At Hesquiat, Father Charles continued his mission work, generally following traditions and methods initiated many years earlier by Father Brabant. Just as Brabant had done, the younger priest did his best to assert his authority over the village's temporal affairs, as well as church affairs. He assumed direction over the village "policemen," a group of local leaders appointed by Father Brabant many years earlier. Father Charles had no hesitation in demanding their support when he needed it.

January 16, 1912: Had two Indians clearing land, about five canoes went to Anton's Pt to get pipes. I commissioned today an Indian policeman to shoot all the dogs that chase the cattle, his own dog being the worst in the matter.

January 17: Four Indians working on clearing land for paying beef. One of them finished today at 6 PM. I had all the eleven Indian policemen in my house, laying before them my plan to reduce the number of dogs…I suggested a yearly license of $2.00 per dog, all the dogs to be shot that are found on church ground during services as of late they had caused a lot of disturbance during devotions; again all dogs to be shot that chase the cattle.

No one wanted to shoot the dogs except Father Charles. He decided to lead by example:

January 22, 1912: I took my dog to the end of the church land, administered him a poisoned morsel and after awhile shot him. I did this so the Indians could not blame me for having a dog when I demanded that their dogs be killed, though there was a vast difference between my trained dog and their wild, uncared for animals.

The dog killed by Father Charles was Spitz, who made several appearances in the priest's diary, from the very day of his arrival at Hesquiat: "*February 23, 1911:* Steamer arrived at 9 AM and Fr. Brabant disembarked bringing a dog along for my company." Later that year, when Father Charles went on his trip to Switzerland, he was pleased to report in a letter to Father Maurus that he had heard from Constant of Hesquiat. "He…wrote that my dog was ok. I was very glad to hear that as I was afraid he might go astray and die." Once back at Hesquiat, Father Charles noted with concern that the dog was not well. In an entry dated November 10, 1911, a day so cold that "water in cruet frozen during Mass," Father Charles worried about his canine companion: "My dog Spitz sick; lying down, when I call him moving very lazely. At dinner he ate pretty much, though."

The dog recovered, and more than once that winter Father Charles mentioned walking "in the company of my dog" to Anton's Point. But however good a companion Spitz was, Father Charles killed him in January 1912 on a point of principle. The diary admits no personal comment, no emotion.

Father Charles and his dog at Hesquiat, around 1911.

The tempest Father Charles stirred up about dogs temporarily subsided. Later that year he once again found company for his lonely house at Hesquiat. "Cooked all the fresh meat for my own use," he wrote in November, "and a fish for cat and dog... The whole day never spoke a word except to cat and dog and myself, in fact never saw a human being except two attending Mass."

The replacement dog was also named Spitz, and he remained a companion for several years, periodically mentioned in the diary. The fate of the second Spitz is unknown, but Father Charles's implacable hostility toward the village dogs who chased his cattle continued to surface, leading to ugly scenes and confrontations. This culminated in 1923 when he coldly eradicated all dogs from the village. "*July 2, 1923:* With the help of an Indian and approved by the others present poisoned 5 dogs. There is none left at Hesquiat now."

Father Charles's animosity toward the dogs of Hesquiat sprang from a desire to protect his cattle. From 1910 onward, he was in charge of the local cattle belonging to the church, and he took his duties most seriously. Christie School relied on him to provide meat, and the needs of the school were great.

The number of cattle at Hesquiat had increased gradually over many years, starting with the very first mission cattle that arrived with Father Brabant in 1875. Brabant disembarked from the sailing sloop *Thornton* with three calves, "one bull and two heifers, which were destined to become the pioneer cattle in this part of the country." They ran happily along the beach on that first day, "like dogs" according to Father Brabant, "sometimes forgetting themselves when amidst good pasture, and then running up to us with the utmost speed."

These pioneer calves founded a remarkable bovine dynasty. Their independent offspring scorned fences and enclosures and wandered away to revel in the "good pasture" of the forest. Some never returned to the village, instead establishing a renowned herd of wild cattle on Hesquiat Peninsula. New stock was brought in from time to time, and some of these newcomers, in their turn, were wooed away to live wild and free in the forest. By the time Father Charles came to live at Hesquiat, two different types of cattle were under his scrutiny: the fierce wild ones, whom he regarded from a wary distance, and "his" cattle, the domesticated or semi-domesticated ones he struggled to keep near the village and in a more biddable frame of mind.

In his unofficial role as provider to the school, Father Charles was in his element. Continually busy tending his large garden, he raised tons of potatoes and hay, and he paid close attention to the cattle, building enclosures for them, searching for them when they strayed and, when the time was right, killing them. He spent many long hours butchering his cows, salting beef, making sausages, putting meat in brine and in glass jars. Over the years he sent countless tons of beef down to Christie School, some from his own cattle and some from wild cattle. He also sold or gave meat away to a number of other outlets: to Dawley's hotel at Clayoquot, to Sloman's store in Tofino, to a hotel up in Quatsino Sound, to the Indians at Hesquiat, to the stewards on the coastal steamers, to the lighthouse keepers at Estevan and to random settlers along the coast if they requested it. Some years he butchered up to twelve head of cattle.

With characteristic precision, Father Charles recorded in his diary the weight and measure of each and every beast he slaughtered, as well as details of who received the meat and exactly how much he shipped. "Killed bull," he wrote on September 9, 1912. "In the evening loaded a canoe with 700 lbs beef and anchored canoe out, ready to be shipped to Quatsino." Four years later, on September 10, 1916, "SS Tees here at 12:30 AM. Shipped 540 lbs meat @ 12 cents per lb. to Chief Steward." On April 5, 1917, "soon after 8 AM two Indians left with 208 lbs of beef for Sidney Inlet mine," and on August 25, 1918, "steamer came shortly before midnight. Chief Steward took 185 lbs hindquarter for which I received 24 cts per lb. Shipped 200 lbs Fr Quarter to St. Joseph's Hospital in Victoria, gratis; and a whole side, 450 lbs, to P. Burns Meat Co., Victoria."

Speedy butchering and rapid dispatch of the meat to its destination was always Father Charles's aim. Faced with a large dead beast, he and his native helpers worked extremely fast, never faster than in April 1919: "Killed a wild bull at 5 PM and shipped at 8 PM by steamer 500 lbs of meat to Kakawis." Butchering and wrapping the meat in burlap was hard and heavy work, but Father Charles seemed to relish the job. Not so Father Brabant. He became fed up with butchering meat for Kakawis during his final years at Hesquiat and made this known to Father Maurus on November 11, 1903:

> This supplying of beef to your school—although done with a good heart is, for a man crawling fast towards his sixtieth year, a task both too hard and too exhausting. Besides there is no merit in it and it seems to be a source of scandal. I have a letter in my possession, written by a priest in good standing, in which he uses these words addressed to me: "From Monday till Saturday you are wasting your time in running after the cows." This is not very complimentary and it shows the value which well meaning men attach to my endeavours to supply your institution with beef!

Keeping cattle at Kakawis was problematic because the location offered no decent meadow or pasture land, hence the school's dependence on the meat from

Hesquiat. But despite this, the priests and brothers at Kakawis did their utmost to raise cattle there. Having livestock of any kind—and particularly cows—was hugely important to them. Stolid and familiar, cows somehow symbolized the values of a more rational world elsewhere; their bovine presence was strangely comforting. The reassuring sound of cowbells perhaps reminded these European priests, brothers and sisters of civilized green fields and the orderly neat farms in their home countries, a world away from the vast wilderness around them. "Please send by bearer two cow bells with straps," wrote one of the sisters to Walter Dawley in an unsigned and undated note, specifying "bells of different time and charge. Let boy select the bells."

The few cows stationed at Kakawis were doomed to travel far to find good pasturage. Prodded into freight scows, they were towed several miles from Kakawis up to the open grassy areas at the mouth of Bear River. There they grazed for several months in the summer, later returning to Kakawis, again by freight scow. Some never made the return journey, having been killed and butchered at Bear River. The priests also cultivated hay at Bear River, laboriously harvesting and transporting it back to Kakawis to feed the livestock in the winter.

Although Father Charles frequently helped out with this awkward cattle transport, he was fortunate in having limited contact with the Kakawis cows. They caused ceaseless wrangling, particularly between Father Maurus and Father Brabant in the early years of the school. Brabant had tried his best to introduce cattle to Kakawis during a brief period when he was in charge of Christie School in the winter of 1901–2, while Father Maurus was away. Sister Mary Placide, reporting on the school's progress that year, thanked Brabant "for providing the school with a milk cow and calf, and for a neat picket fence which now adorns the front part of the grounds."

This favourable report was one of the only positive comments about keeping cows at Kakawis. In November 1902, Father Brabant wrote an embittered seven-page letter to Father Maurus, discussing nothing but cattle in the most acrimonious terms. Brabant declared he no longer wanted to share "his" cattle from Hesquiat with the priests or children at Kakawis, mostly because they had entirely disregarded his advice concerning cattle husbandry, pasturage and fence building.

Brabant could not bear to be gainsaid on any subject, but particularly on the sensitive subject of cattle. Even Walter Dawley managed to offend him on this topic. Brabant resentfully commented on Dawley's refusal to sell his thoroughbred stock: "Meeting Mr Dawley I spoke to him about buying a bull-calf from him. But the mean fellow refused." The "mean fellow" naturally kept his quality animals for himself; why sell a valuable bull calf when the creature's services could be hired out repeatedly, with a far better return? By 1901, Dawley was the proud owner of a newly arrived pedigree bull calf named Aristotle, shipped up from Victoria and costing seventy dollars. Dawley was not about to part with Aristotle or any other of his pedigree bulls; over the years he owned several.

These bulls profitably serviced the cattle of Clayoquot Sound for many years. The mission cows from Kakawis were particularly good customers; loaded onto freight scows, they frequently made their way down to Clayoquot for productive encounters with Aristotle or one of the other bulls. "My dear Mr Dawley," declared a letter from Christie School in June 1910, "I take the liberty to impose the acquaintance of two of our cows upon your Bovine Gentleman." Such bovine traffic became commonplace, even though transport was predictably awkward. "We towed the Christie School's freight boat with a cow in it to Clayoquot," commented Father Charles in his diary. "We almost reached the

A load of hay arriving for the livestock at Kakawis, probably from Bear River, early 1900s.

sand spit at Clayoquot when the cow got loose and jumped overboard, swimming towards Opitsat, a distance of about half a mile...We left her there."

Many settlers shared the priests' ambition to own cattle, never reckoning the practicalities or the problems. Tethered unhappily in enclosures on the outside decks of the steamers, these cattle often endured grave indignities before reaching their destinations. On one particularly rough trip, the *Tees* had on board no fewer than six unhappy cows and three dogs when a huge wave struck her. She bucked and rolled sickeningly, lifting one passenger into the air and hurling him down the companionway to the lower deck. He found himself staring up into the surprised face of a cow that was wedged firmly into the stairwell entrance. Two of the dogs had gone overboard and were hanging by their chains. "However, this was merely routine for the deckhands and order was swiftly restored," the passenger placidly commented.

Loading and unloading cattle at remote locations without docks was always fraught with difficulty. "It may amuse you to learn how the cow was landed," Father Maurus wrote from Kakawis. "From the steamer anchored in the bay before the school, deckhands pushed the cow with long rope attached around the horns overboard. Boys in a canoe led the swimming animal by the rope to the beach." If no canoe were nearby with a rope at the ready to tow a cow by the horns, the beast would swim all the way and collapse on shore in the surf, too exhausted to move farther.

Forcing a large, frightened cow into the water from the height of the cargo deck could also be achieved by a simple teeter-totter. The crew would sometimes position a long, wide board horizontally, extending from the freight door over the water. Prodded onto it, the cow was forced to walk the plank. Its weight quickly bore the board down, the cow fell awkwardly into the water, the board was retracted and the terrified beast thrashed its way toward shore.

Sometimes calves were spared a ducking. Girded in canvas slings and winched into the air, they were lowered into waiting canoes or freight scows, legs tethered. On several occasions, Father Charles had to carry out the reverse manoeuvre, loading calves onto the steamer from a disadvantageous position in a dugout canoe. One particularly hazardous adventure occurred at Hesquiat in November 1916.

> After dinner we got the six month old bull calf ready for shipment to Kakawis. We had it boxed up in the barn and wheeled and carried the box to the beach into a canoe. Three Indians helped besides Mr. Fraser and Anton Luckowitch. The canoe proved to be too small;

we got a bigger one and transferred the calf. The tide was going out meanwhile—now we had to pull and push the loaded canoe into the water. When the canoe floated the calf pushed the box sideways and capsized the canoe. In the water the calf kicked the box to pieces and freed itself…We put the calf into the canoe with feet tied to the cross pieces and anchored her in deep water. Steamer came in an hour and a half. Three more passengers arrived from Estevan. So we had a full load going out to steamer viz. calf, four white and one Indian passenger, three Indians handling the canoe, myself and Mr. Cole. Though S East wind was coming up everything went alright and I paid $10.00 freight for calf. [Mr. Fraser] did the hardest work and suggested the right thing at the proper time. He also put the canvass sling around the calf for hauling it aboard.

The cows that survived the perils of transport were generally well-cherished creatures. Frank Garrard wrote fondly of taking a cow over to Lennard Island, observing how well the creature took to life on the island, eating the "wild wheat" growing there. And when Walter Dawley purchased four cows in May 1919, their travels up to Clayoquot attracted genuine concern. They awaited transport for days, repeatedly failing to gain passage on the heavily loaded coastal steamer. When the cows at last made it on board, their owner sent Dawley an anxious telegram. "Kindly wire on arrival," he said, explaining that these highly valued cattle were "Heavy Milkers very gentle if treated kindly, never used a switch always been pets." He even provided the names of the gentle travellers—Maquinna, Prince, Bell and Dutch—and gave their birthdates.

Ill-tempered disputes about ownership of the wild cattle at Hesquiat erupted continually. As late as 1950, when Father Charles was in his eighties and living back at Mount Angel, the bishop in Victoria requested that he provide the history of these cows to determine whether or not they could be counted as church property. Father Charles attested that when he left the coast in 1930 there were about fifteen head of tame or half-tame cattle around the village. The wild cattle were a different bunch, unnumbered and unaccountable, roaming "around the beaches from Pachista Bay (3 miles N. of Estevan) to opposite Nootka, and also in the interior country." Even after two decades' absence from the west coast, the elderly priest believed that many wild cattle must still be at Hesquiat. In his view, they were nearly indestructible, often stubbornly escaping even when they

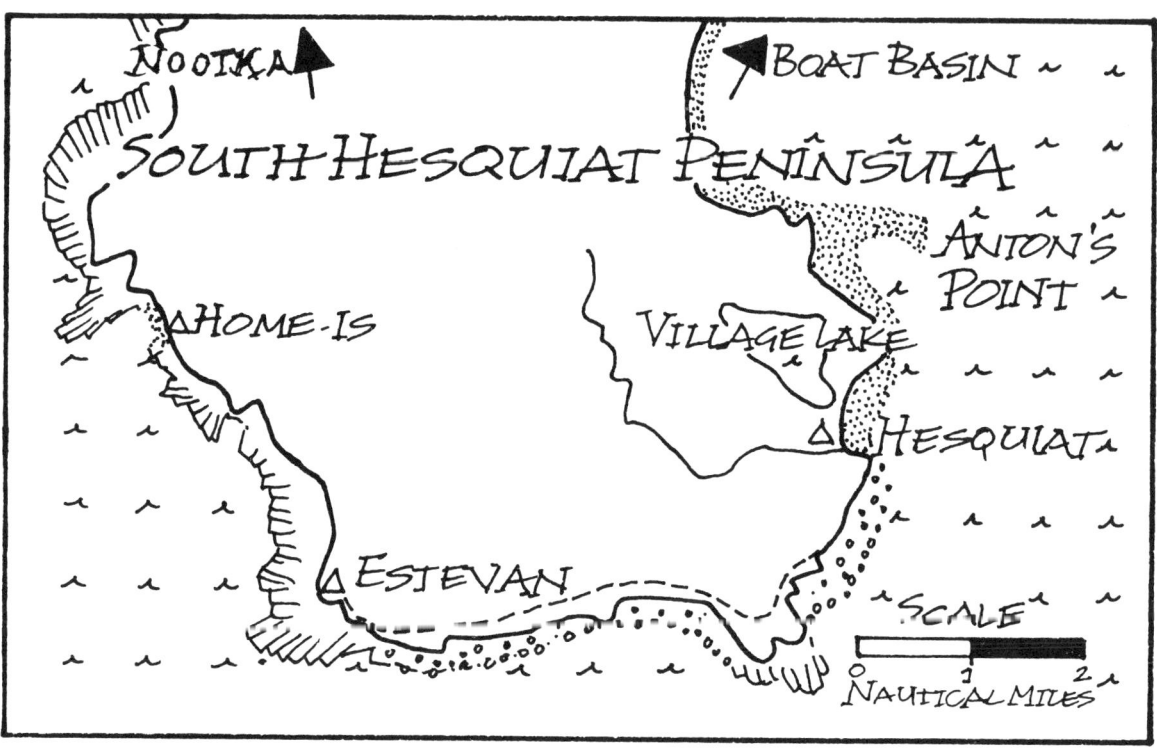

had been shot. He recalled that one wild animal he shot and butchered already had a load of gunshot in its flesh, and another one had a "big rifle bullet in a hind quarter. The Estevan people did that."

The "Estevan people" were forever in the wrong about the cattle, according to Father Charles. Their regrettable tendency to shoot "his" wild cows or, worse still, his wandering domestic cattle caused years of rancorous disagreement while he was at Hesquiat. Even when he tried to sort matters out, nothing was ever resolved. "In one year I sold by contract to a Mr. Wilson all wild cattle for $1.00 a head. He had 5 yrs to come and get them. He never came and had pd me $100.00 for the bargain. Later on J. P. Jensen paid me $75 for beef he could get out of wild cattle. But he moved away soon. So. The wild cattle are wild and though coming of the stock of Fr. Brabant's I doubt we could claim as church property."

Disputes about the cattle at Estevan and Hesquiat even made it into the newspaper. In 1909, Captain Otto Bucholz, a well-known sealing captain, was working at the newly finished Estevan Point lighthouse. Out hunting, he shot what he mistakenly believed to be a wild cow, and trouble erupted almost immediately. The wife of Anton Luckovitch, who had lived for many years at

Hesquiat and Estevan, accused Bucholz of killing a cow belonging to her family. According to the *Colonist* of August 8, 1909, Mrs. Luckovitch "hurried to the superintendent of provincial police and asked that the law be brought into place at once and that the body and person of Capt Buckholtz be seized forthwith." The reporter facetiously concluded that "the law waits while further investigation is made of the fate of the West Coast cow."

That particular West Coast cow was merely a domestic animal on the loose, and killing it was little more than an infraction of an unwritten code. Killing a wild beast, on the other hand, inspired more respect than outrage, for everyone knew that hunting wild cows required nerves of steel and a sure aim. These cattle were huge and ferocious, mean-tempered and massively horned. They outfaced many a hunter when they loomed out of the forest onto the beach, where they would snort menacingly at any danger and charge headlong if threatened. Anyone hunting them was, at least in Father Brabant's estimation, to be congratulated for his hunting prowess. When Father Maurus was at Hesquiat for a visit in August 1901, he managed this feat, although undoubtedly with the help of some native hunters. Father Brabant, who was up in Nootka Sound, wrote to him at once:

Unidentified men with the carcass of a wild bull, date unknown.

> Rev'd dear Father:
> I have just now received your letter of 15 august. I am glad you shot an ox: you have experienced that it is not so easy to get at those old fellows, yet the Indian who brought your letter, told me that there were lots of them on the beach, this side of Estevan Point, as they passed there this morning. I suppose the cool breeze from the East tempted them to come out of the bush and have a look at the sea.

Shooting a wild ox on the beach when it emerged from the forest to sniff the sea breeze was, Brabant implied, relatively easy. To track it through the bush was another matter altogether. "It was no simple task," recalled Mike Hamilton, "to shoot one of those [wild] animals several miles away and probably in dense bush and carry the meat back to civilization. On one, and only one occasion, I helped to do it." This happened when Hamilton worked on the installation of the telegraph line at Hesquiat in 1914. He never forgot meeting wild cattle in the bush while working on the line, describing to his daughters in later years how the cattle could hear the slightest sound, and once alerted they would run off at extraordinary speed, an amazing performance to witness, especially if it was "a monster bull with hooves fully a foot long. Having not had hard ground to walk on they would grow like long slippers—hard to believe, but true."

Father Charles always feared encountering such huge bulls on his walks to Estevan Point, and if he ever hunted wild cattle, he only tackled the smaller ones, and never on his own. Whenever possible he stayed home and had native hunters do the job for him.

June 9, 1914: Two Indians went out at 5 AM to hunt a wild cattle for me. Soon after six o'clock one of the men returned with the news that they shot one but was still living after having 11 bullets in him. I gave him last two cartridges I had and told him to get two more Indians to help carry out the meat… The first load reached here at 1 PM. All the meat came to 900 to 1000 lbs.

Stories of the wild cattle lose nothing in the retelling. Throughout the twentieth century, long after the mission at Hesquiat fell into disrepair, long after the church there was abandoned, long after regular steamship travel on the coast ended, these wild creatures of Hesquiat Peninsula endured, and their near-legendary reputation continued to grow. As late as the 1980s they still wended their mysterious ways through the forest and along the beach, seldom glimpsed, much discussed and greatly feared. Some locals believe—and why not?—the cattle are still there, invisible, defiant and powerful, running triumphantly amok in the wilderness.

– 11 –

A Winter's Tale

November 23, 1911: Very strong S East wind. Still expecting steamer. I finished my Office for today and did a lot of little chores…At 4:30 steamer in sight. Took lantern and walked towards Anton's Point where Indians had already gone. But after I had gone a short distance I changed my mind and returned. Sea must be running big back there…It is now 6 PM and steamer has not yet steamed out, perhaps the wooden pipes the Ind. Dept. is furnishing for waterworks for Hesquiat village, are on board. At 6:45 PM Tees passed out of the harbor. Mail was brought to me at 8 PM; had 20 letters and cards. Indians report that pipes are on board but owing to bad sea could not be unloaded.

A LATE NOVEMBER DAY at Hesquiat, blustery and dark. Father Charles went about his business as usual, keeping an eye on the steamer *Tees* as it bypassed Hesquiat village, heading to a safer anchorage over at Anton's Point. Having discharged only part of the expected cargo, the vessel steamed away again, heading out into the rough weather. Father Charles regretted that the wooden pipes could not be unloaded. He had been waiting for them for quite a while and planned to use them to create a water system, bringing water down to the village from the small, shallow lake nearby.

The steamer *Tees* was a familiar sight along Vancouver Island's west coast. Sometimes she shared the route with other steamers; sometimes she was absent for long periods working on other routes, but on and off she served the west coast for over twenty years. Known as the "Holy Roller," she was an uncomfortable ship in heavy weather.

But the *Tees* steamed northward, bearing the pipes away from Hesquiat. All being well, they would return within a few days when the steamer came south once again, stopping at Hesquiat. Little did Father Charles know how long he would wait before those pipes finally arrived.

> *November 27, 1911:* Strong S. East wind springing up. Indians brought canoes to Anton's Pt. to wait there for steamer. At 3 PM I walked also to Anton's Pt. but steamer having not yet come we all started to walk back to Hesquiat at 5 PM.

Trudging the mile-long trail between Hesquiat village and Anton's Point in expectation of the steamer arriving was a predictable, if tedious, feature of living at Hesquiat, especially during the heavy storms of winter. The steamer frequently could not anchor safely in the exposed waters in front of the village, so it would head into the harbour, making for the lee side of the long, sandy bar known as Anton's Point. There it was safe to unload cargo and passengers and take on freight from the loaded canoes that were paddled over to Anton's Point—ahead of time if possible, or hurriedly if the steamer arrived early.

In extreme weather, the steamer might not appear in Hesquiat Harbour at all, for even Anton's Point could be too hazardous. On such days, all the cargo and passengers destined for Hesquiat were forced to take a prolonged rough-weather tour of the coast in the hope that a landing would be possible on the next trip past Hesquiat. Overshooting one's destination was a common hazard of winter travel on the west coast, and sometimes passengers and cargo would pass their destination more than once—once on the way north, and again on the return journey south if the weather was still heavy.

Those were the really bad days, though. Most of the time the steamer did manage to make its usual calls, and no one on the coast expected a perfect schedule, so the delayed arrival of the *Tees* in late November 1911 was not too worrying at first. Certainly it was no worse than when the steamer played its other unpopular trick of arriving considerably ahead of schedule. Just a few weeks earlier, Father Maurus, visiting from Kakawis, had a terrible scramble to be ready when the *Tees* arrived several hours before it was expected at Hesquiat. "P. Maurus had to pack up in a hurry," recounted Father Charles, "and he left with hardly having time to say goodbye." Those sudden departures on vessels that arrived early always left Father Charles feeling unsettled. But so did inexplicably delayed ships.

> *November 28, 1911:* Gale of wind shook my house all night long. Gale continued till noon; rain from 8 AM till noon. Indians in the early

morning had gone to Anton's Pt to look after their canoes...Most of the Indians stopped at Anton's Pt to waite for steamer, but no steamer came. In the evning all wind died out. At 4 PM an Indian coming from Estevan brought news that steamer had been at Kyuquot this morning. Hence she should be here any time.

"...she should be here any time." Everyone shared that hope, but tension began to mount. November 28 passed, and November 29. This was no longer a normal delay. A few hours late, half a day, a day—such delays were unremarkable, especially at this time of year, but the *Tees* was now seriously overdue: she should have steamed around Estevan Point into Hesquiat Harbour nearly three days ago.

Father Charles's unease grew. Over at Anton's Point, the canoes loaded with cargo awaiting the steamer remained at anchor, some of them full of valuable meat that Father Charles intended to send down the coast to Christie School. They had to be watched day and night in expectation of the boat's arrival and could not be left much longer. Already one of them had broken loose from its moorings in the high wind. Retrieving it had taken many hours. Only a fool could still believe that the *Tees* was about to arrive. Something was wrong. On November 29, Father Charles wrote: "All Indians at Anton's Pt. returned to the village to sleep. They are getting tired to watch for steamer, so today they stayed and worked at home. After my Mass I alone went to Anton's Pt. but returned after 12 o'clock noon, and cooked a good dinner, the first decent meal since Sunday on acct of expecting steamer any minute."

November 30 came, and still no sign of the steamer, still no definite news. Father Charles took action:

> Two Indians started out at 9 AM with a letter from me to the Wireless Operator at Estevan to find out the SS Tees. At 3 PM the two Indians returned with the following note: "SS Tees ashore somewhere in Kyuquot Sound, after leaving whaling station. No news can not hear Tees. BC steamer Salvor and Wm Joliffe near Entrance Sound too foggy to enter. US Revenue cutter Takama 4 miles SW of Nootka Island in thick fog waiting chance to look for Tees." Indians were again at Anton's Pt. pulling up all canoes and hanging up the meat. Baked Hosts today. Had good luck with it.

What had happened to the *Tees?* Following the first wireless message from Captain Gillam, which said the *Tees* was ashore in Kyuquot Sound, silence fell. No further wireless communication came from the vessel. In Victoria, the

Colonist made the matter public on November 30: "There was much anxiety regarding Tees since early yesterday. The Northwestern en route to Seattle from Alaska, caught a wireless message from Tees. It was brief, stating only: 'Tees stuck rock Kyuquot Sound.'... Throughout the day every operator in the coast wireless service listened for further messages, but nothing was learned. It was anticipated that the accident had resulted in the engine room being flooded." Search vessels set out to look for the stricken ship, but weather conditions were terrible, and Father Charles recorded in his diary that "steamers looking for Tees have not yet found her owing to thick fog." The silence lengthened.

Images of shipwreck rose, stark and terrible, in the imagination of anyone who knew the *Tees* was in trouble. Not again, surely not again. Lurid and tragic stories of previous shipwrecks haunted everyone on the coast. Worst of all were the stories of the *Valencia*. Only five years earlier, at Pachena Point, over a hundred people had perished in that most piteous of shipwrecks. Father Charles, now waiting at Hesquiat, had been at Opitsat then, and he well remembered receiving a note from the telegraph operator at Tofino on the afternoon of January 22, 1906: "Large steamer just gone down between Cape Beal and Clo-oose...100 drowned, 9 saved; no particulars yet." Many of the victims had stayed with the *Valencia*, clinging to the rigging for desperate hours, only to be pitched into the churning water as the ship split up in full view of horrified onlookers on the cliffs, less than half a mile distant. Worse, no other ships had come to the aid of the *Valencia* in time, though several had been nearby. The *Queen City*, the *Czar* and the *Salvor* hovered some distance away but failed to provide aid; troubling accusations of cowardice and dishonour reverberated to this day. The *Valencia* was a shipwreck with few survivors and fewer heroes, setting new standards for dread and horror on the coast.

And now the *Tees* had fallen silent, lost somewhere in Kyuquot Sound. Surely not again.

"In many homes in Victoria," intoned the *Colonist*, "relatives and friends of those on board feared the worst. Many imagined that the failure of Tees to send further messages indicated that she had probably struck somewhere on the dread Barrier reef, a long stretch of partially submerged rocks which run for many miles along the coast, and with the prevailing gales no vessel could have lived long in such a position."

On December 1, Father Charles shook his head and decided to dispose of his perishable cargo awaiting the *Tees*. About a week earlier he had butchered a wild cow, and three quarters of beef awaited steamer transport down to Kakawis. The meat could wait no longer. Already removed from the canoes, it hung in the meat sheds at Hesquiat, and Father Charles now offered it to the Indians for seven dollars per quarter. "When I told them that they need not pay in money but could work, clearing land, for that amount it did not take long before I was rid of the beef. Indian who had gone to Estevan for more news re SS Tees came back just before dark with no further news."

The *Colonist* intently reported on the vessels attempting to aid the *Tees*. "The fleet of [rescue] vessels sent to the scene lay last night hove-to in thick weather with a SE gale blowing off the coast, and none had received any tidings of Tees…Tug William Jolliffe was 1st vessel to arrive, Salvor and Tahoma have also arrived…All the operators had to report, however, was that their vessels rolled in the sea during the blow, and the weather was too thick to attempt to run into Kyuquot."

Dogged and courageous, these small steamers, including a tug and a salvage vessel, repeatedly attempted to approach the location where they believed the *Tees* to be, but to no avail. As the *Colonist* reported later, "the steamers Salvor and William Jolliffe rolled with heavy seas breaking over them in thick fog and more than once were in most dangerous positions. Twice they were almost wrecked on outlying reefs during a gale blowing 70 mph. Inside the breakers of the dread Barrier reef they swung from beam to beam, shipping big seas when the mist lifted and disclosed their position."

Superlative piled upon superlative in the excited newspaper coverage of the ensuing events. The *Colonist* quoted the intrepid Captain Logan of the *Salvor*: "Fog and spindrift made it hard to see anything in a gale with a big topping sea which broke over the Salvor…The Jolliffe reported she had been in the breakers and had encountered a howling gale all night…At no time was land visible…Had the steamers gone ashore heavy loss of life could not have been avoided…We went at full speed through thick fog, spindrift and hurricane, and suddenly the Jolliffe made the breakers off Solander Island dead ahead…That was one of the wildest scenes I have seen in a long life at sea."

Thankfully, given the grim circumstances, not many people were on board the lost and ominously silent *Tees*—fewer than fifty all told, including crew and "seven Chinamen," as always counted as a separate species. The ship was heavily loaded, though. Just before the accident, *Tees* took on over five hundred barrels of whale oil at the Kyuquot whaling station and 150 tons of china clay from the workings at Easy Creek. The vessel also carried odds and ends of freight for delivery down the coast, including the water pipes and empty oil barrels that should have been delivered to Father Charles at Hesquiat on the way up the coast.

The year 1911 had been relentlessly busy for the *Tees*. She regularly sailed with over a hundred people on board, and on one trip in late October she was bursting at the seams with 147 passengers. She broke all records for the amount of freight carried, particularly whale oil. In a ten-day period in July, the whalers at the Kyuquot whaling station brought in seven sperm whales, thirty-one humpbacks, two finbacks and one sulphur bottom (blue) whale; then, in the next four days, they caught a further eleven whales. In the same period at Sechart whaling station, twenty-five whales were taken. This translated into huge shipments of whale products, particularly whale oil, and that at a time when the fish canneries were also going full steam. It was not unusual for the *Tees* to arrive in Victoria with three or four thousand cases of canned salmon from the canneries at Clayoquot and Uchuckleset, along with several hundred barrels of whale oil.

By the end of 1911, this volume of freight and passengers was clearly becoming far too much for the aging *Tees*. In the offices and meeting rooms of Canadian Pacific, both in Victoria and at the headquarters in Montreal, plans were afoot to replace this old workhorse with a larger, more lavish ship, but in the meantime, the *Tees* soldiered on with no respite, although she was now equipped with a primitive form of wireless to ensure her continued service and efficiency.

In early December 1911, the well-known problems and shortcomings of the *Tees* received no mention in the newspapers. The *Victoria Colonist* knew only too well from past experience covering shipwrecks that any ship missing at sea was, by definition, heroic and must be recalled with the loftiest of sentiments and in the most lavish language, guaranteed to wrench the hearts of all readers. This was no time to recall how uncomfortable *Tees* was, a "wet ship," mostly underwater in a high sea according to her critical crew, and a "blunt-nosed ugly duckling" to boot. More of a plodder than a heroine on the high seas, she was capable of doing, at best, nine knots. The *Colonist* ignored such details, dwelling on the dramatic possibility of doom and disaster, putting into words the haunting fears of local residents, imagining their distress and their tormented anxiety: "Many saw a wrecked ship, her decks awash with breaking seas, death and disaster, and for fear that the seas might be battering the steel sides of the staunch coaster, the rescue steamers struggled in the gale."

The rescue steamers indeed struggled in the gale, and they were not alone in doing so. Shortly after the *Tees* ran into trouble, Captain Edward Gillam realized that the messages he was sending from the ship were not getting through by wireless, and he sent five men off in a lifeboat to seek help. Chief Officer Alex Thompson and four seamen, in an open boat, undertook to reach Estevan Point, sixty miles distant, through foul wind and weather and terrifying seas. "It was a brave task," reported the *Colonist*. "For six days the five men struggled against wind and heavy sea, fog shutting in on them, and, lost and weather beaten, they spent 3 trying days without food, struggling hopelessly on."

On December 3 the rescue vessels *William Jolliffe* and *Salvor* were at last able to enter Kyuquot Sound after repeated and risky attempts. They sighted the lifeboat containing Chief Officer Thompson and his crew, and the *Jolliffe* took the bedraggled and exhausted men on board, learning from them the whereabouts of the *Tees*. The rescuers hastened to the aid of the afflicted ship, fearing the worst.

Their rescue was entirely anticlimactic. The *Tees* was perfectly safe. Indeed, she had never been seriously endangered at all. The *Colonist*, so poised for a disaster, sounded almost chagrined at this insipid ending to the story: "The complement on board suffered nothing more than the missing of one meal of the usual three, and they sang and laughed, and enjoyed the amusements the ship's officers provided for them, while thousands imagined pictures that differed immensely from this condition of affairs."

What had happened? In west coast terms, the most mundane of incidents. The *Tees* had struck a rock. "Backing from the wharf at the clay pits at Easy Creek Tees ran on a submerged rock on Sunday last…The propeller blades were broken off and the rudder jammed, rendering the vessel helpless. She came off easily and went to an anchorage in the sheltered harbor. Owing to the topographical conditions efforts to send news of her predicament by wireless failed."

Arriving at Easy Creek, "in a snug cove…in waters as calm as those of James Bay," as the *Colonist* disgustedly reported, the rescue vessels discovered the *Tees* and all aboard her to be in fine form. Although the rudder had jammed on the rocks and the propeller was stripped, the ship was not holed, and the passengers seemed in almost indecently good spirits. The chief steward had done all he could to make the passengers happy and comfortable: "We…fortunately had some good musical talent, so we arranged concerts, mock trials, etc…Mr Ramsay had a piccolo and with his solos some songs and other entertainment we passed the time. We did not know how long we might have to wait for assistance, so it was decided to make the provisions spin out by serving only two meals per day." The passengers on the *Tees* even managed to obtain fresh meat when two of the men went ashore and killed a wild bullock, butchering it with "an axe and an old bread knife."

Given that few images are less pitiable than stranded passengers cheerfully eating roast beef dinner to the accompaniment of a piccolo, the *Colonist* turned elsewhere for a stirring story: "It is the story of the brave effort of Chief

Officer Thompson and Quartermaster Robson and Seamen Gallagher, Boyce and Sparks, to make their way to Estevan in a ship's boat from Tees, and the experiences of the Salvor and William Jolliffe that is the most interesting." The newspaper carried on at considerable length and with breathless relish, describing how the men on the lifeboat nearly sacrificed their lives to obey the call of duty and the instructions of their captain as they sought aid. Chief Officer Thompson described how they tried to row against the howling wind and heavy seas:

> One [wave] half-filled the boat, broke an oar and rowlock. One hit me full in the back, lifting us along. One of the sailors collapsed about this time, and we had a hard job to keep clear of the break of the seas. We baled continuously. The drenching we got almost froze us. It was very cold. In seven hours we had made little headway. The gale increased, and a southwest swell against the southeast wind made the sea very rough. We took water right along in this cross sea. It was no use. One fellow was down, collapsed, and the seas began to fill the boat.

Hesquiat church and the priest's house.

As for the rescue vessels, the newspaper spared no hyperbole reporting how they "twice...were almost wrecked on outlying reefs during a gale blowing 70 miles per hour" as heavy seas broke over them in thick fog. Captain Logan explained that "the Salvor and Jolliffe were several times near the disaster. They were five times in the breakers and while those on Tees held mock trials, concerts, etc, we were in a hurricane. The steamers and all on board were risked again and again in effort to get into Kyuquot...and how the vessels escaped wreck is a marvel." Finding the *Tees* unharmed, Logan commented caustically that "it was a small affair for the amount of risk taken."

The passengers of the *Tees* transferred to the *Salvor* and resumed their journey down the coast. The *Salvor* also obligingly picked up extra freight en route, taking "45 cases of gill bone and 65 drums of whale oil" on board at Sechart. They arrived in Victoria on December 5, none the worse for wear and a mere seven or eight days late.

The *Tees* was towed into Victoria Harbour for repairs, and the faithful *Queen City* took her place. Now creaky and elderly, contemptuously referred to as a "tub" by most who knew her, the *Queen City* was even less popular than the *Tees*. During the winter of 1911, Father Charles had equally bad luck with both vessels.

> *December 2, 1911:* Indians returning from Nootka brought news obtained at Estevan that SS Queen City had left Victoria for West Coast Points in place of disabled Tees.
>
> *December 3:* First Sunday of Advent. Around 7 PM Constant came to me telling me that a vessel's light was approaching. It might be the Queen City. We watched the light; it moved to the inner harbor and blew the whistle when approaching Anton's Pt. So we dressed up and with lanterns in hand proceeded with half a dozen Indians in rain and SE wind on foot to Anton's Pt. On the way we heard a second whistle. Coming out of the woods to the beach we saw the steamer moving out of the harbor but swung our lanterns but to no use, she moved on and up the Coast. It was 20 minutes to nine when I reached my house.

Father Charles never expressed disappointment or irritation about the actions of any steamer, but this experience of seeing the *Queen City* steaming out of Hesquiat Harbour would have been enough to make a saint swear. Nearly two weeks earlier the *Tees* had been unable to deliver cargo on her northbound voyage, and now the *Queen City* was passing them by. The priest and his companions stood on shore, clad in clumsy oilskins, fruitlessly swinging their lanterns through the dark night and the rain. They had trudged more than halfway to Anton's Point, hoping for mail and supplies, but the steamer did not stay for them, perhaps did not even see them, and once again they were left behind, the lights of the steamer diminishing, leaving the harbour dark and wide and empty, and they had nothing whatsoever to show for their chilly, wet hike.

In the following days, Father Charles busied himself sawing wood and giving choral instruction. Some Hesquiats were learning the *Missa de Angelis* for Christmas, and rehearsals continued throughout Advent. On December 6 in the evening, just as Father Charles was at choir practice and the singers were "stuck" in the *Gloria*, the welcome sound of the *Queen City*'s whistle was heard. She was now on her southbound trip, heading back to Victoria.

> At 8 PM Queen City whistled in front of village, she did not anchor though there was quite a little freight for the Indians. Three canoes went out, I was in one of them. Incoming mail was very light.

Father Charles sent off his Christmas mail on the *Queen City*, no doubt relieved that a steamer had finally appeared at Hesquiat after a gap of over two weeks, even though the bulk of the cargo had not been unloaded. Life resumed its daily round.

> *December 7, 1911:* After the instruction prepared sermon for tomorrow. At 3:45 in the afternoon went to church where already half a dozen people were assembled for Confession. First, however, I prepared the altar, and then sat in the [confession] box till 8:15. Took lunch, had a smoke, said Vespers and Compline, looked over my sermon at 11 PM, same as yesterday, went to bed.

> *December 8:* Ave Maria Immaculata! Three different calls for Confession before Mass, each time for one person; the first call came when I was still in bed. 31 Communions during Mass. After Benediction towards evening about half a dozen more Confessions.

Father Charles slashed brush, baked more hosts, washed the corporals and purificators, sawed wood, heard confessions. He would have liked to get on with installing his water system, but the pipes were still on their coastal travels. After many years on the coast, he did not waste energy fretting about them; the pipes were sure to make an appearance sometime soon.

Trudging along the trail to Anton's Point to meet the steamship on a dark, rainy night.

December 18, 1911: During Mass Queen City whistled altogether unexpected. She came from up the Coast and brought mail and pipes. Strong S East wind. Steamer stopped at Anton's Pt. After Mass I went with the last canoe leaving the village for the steamer. All Indians helping getting the pipes. Chief Steward Brown gave me breakfast on the boat—no pay—I was home again at 11 AM having walked home with the mail bag on my shoulders. Very much rain all day.

The pipes that finally arrived on December 18 had many adventures. They were on board the *Tees* when she could not land at Hesquiat on November 23, and they endured minor shipwreck at Kyuquot Sound. They lay in the cargo hold for many days while the *Tees* was fogbound without a propeller, while Mr. Ramsay entertained passengers with his piccolo and they all awaited rescue. Back the pipes went to Victoria aboard the injured *Tees* as she was towed into harbour. On December 10 they swung onto the *Queen City* as she headed up the coast, but this was another ill-fated voyage. The pipes experienced another minor shipwreck, for on December 12 it was *Queen City*'s turn to run aground about five miles from Alberni, at Dunsmuir Point in the Alberni Canal.

Captain Gillam was in charge of the vessel at the time, having transferred from the disabled *Tees* to take charge of *Queen City*. He was unaccustomed to such a run of bad luck; this was his second accident in two weeks. A marine inquiry held in January 1912 heard that Gillam had just fallen asleep in his bunk at the time of the accident. He explained that there were very few chances on the route for the master of the vessel to sleep, and the longest period of rest between Victoria and Alberni was four hours. He was exonerated of responsibility for the incident.

The steamer *Leebro* went to assist *Queen City* when she was aground in the Alberni Canal. According to the *Colonist*, she "was floated by Leebro after lightening about 40 tons of cargo. The damage was not great, only a portion of the forefoot and keel being broken, and the cargo was reloaded and the vessel proceeded." Presumably this cargo, so unceremoniously heaved off the *Queen City* and back on again once she was afloat, included the pipes, now northbound for Hesquiat a second time. But their travels were not yet over because "Queen City encountered a heavy gale when off Hesquoit, and was unable to enter across the breaking bar, the freight for that port being landed on the return trip." This return southbound trip on December 18 is the one recorded by Father Charles as the day the pipes finally arrived. To ensure maximum inconvenience, they went ashore at Anton's Point and later made their final mile-long trip to Hesquiat by canoe. So having been on board two different ships and experiencing two different accidents, having overshot Hesquiat twice heading north and once heading south, having been loaded once onto the *Tees*, once off the *Tees*, twice onto the *Queen City* and twice off the *Queen City*, at least once and possibly more than that into and out of canoes, the wooden pipes for the proposed waterworks system finally came to rest at Hesquiat.

The *Tees* was back on the route before Christmas 1911, with Captain Gillam at the helm, and the *Colonist* kept up its gossipy coverage of her travels, informing readers that the *Tees* spent Christmas at Quatsino, eventually arriving in Victoria on December 30 with twenty passengers, 150 barrels of whale oil, and a hundred tons of clay from Kyuquot. "Tees had stormy weather throughout the voyage, and when rounding Cape Cook on December 26 on her way south a heavy gale prevailed and the steamer labored in a high sea...Tees will sail again for Clayoquot and way ports January 1."

At Hesquiat, Father Charles passed a peaceful Christmas, the few days of excitement and anxiety concerning the *Tees* quickly forgotten in the bustle of preparations. The choir practised the *Gloria*, the women of the village made wreaths of cedar to decorate the church, and some of the women obliged Father Charles by cleaning and scrubbing his house for the festive season. They also prepared for their own celebrations; the winter potlatch and wolf dance would soon begin. Father Charles was content: visitors from Estevan Point came and went, a spirit of harmony reigned, and the pervasive sense of unease that came to plague him in later years remained at bay for now.

"A rainy day in the superlative," he wrote on December 21. "Rain rain and constant rain. Agatha came at noon to blacken my kitchen stove. As I had a cold for the last three days and was hoarse I did not go to the singing practise but retired at 8 PM." Two days later, the *Tees* arrived at Hesquiat, just before Christmas and in time for a potlatch.

> *December 23, 1911:* Saturday. Jensen from Lighthouse came to my house about 11 AM saying SS Tees had arrived this morning at 4 o'clock at Clayoquot. He came to meet his wife who is on board. Tees came at 2 PM bringing lots of freight for the Indians. Some Clayoquot Indians came on shore here with 20 boxes of apples for a potlatch. As it was too late for Mrs. Jensen to walk to the lighthouse, Jensen, his wife and the 2 little girls had supper with me and stayed over night.

December 24: Sunday. At 8 AM I had breakfast ready for my visitors. High Mass at 9 AM after which Constant, Jackson and Dan brought the Jensen family and their freight to the lighthouse per canoe. Beautiful, but cold day. Fed the cattle...

December 25: Christmas ushered in with High Mass and Sermon at midnight. At 8:30 second Mass followed by High Mass with Communions, 45 received. Afternoon Indians visited me. After Benedictions five more Confessions. At 6 PM fireworks on the beach.

Two days later, at 3 AM, Father Charles awoke to hear the whistle of the *Tees* outside, southbound to Victoria. He did not go out to meet the ship—perhaps that night no one did, but the *Tees* obligingly called at Hesquiat nonetheless. Father Charles passed a restless night; there were many comings and goings outside. "In a dream afterwards I jumped out of bed, litt the candle, but hearing no noise I went back to bed again. In dream I had seen the light of a lantern pass my window and heard two people talking. At 5:30 AM Fr. Sobry from Kyuquot arrived at my house. The Nootkas also had arrived for a potlatch."

Father Sobry, normally based at Nootka, and Father Charles spent the last days of 1911 together at Hesquiat.

December 31, 1911: Sunday. Freezing cold. Fr. Sobry sang the High Mass and I preached. Introduced the Angelus prayer after High Mass. Heard some Confessions in the afternoon and again for about one hour after Benediction. From 7–8 Fr. Sobry heard Confessions at my request. At 9 PM we two celebrated the end of the year with a hot toddy.

On January 1, 1912, the two priests shared a celebratory meal of sausage, ox tongue and, for dessert, canned peaches with fruit cake. They each enjoyed a glass of wine. Father Charles did his customary year-end accounting, not of money but of his priestly duties: "Had in all 359 Communions this year at Hesquiat."

Meanwhile, at the other end of the village, music and drumming sounded night after night as the Hesquiats welcomed their coastal neighbours for the potlatch and the wolf dance. The dancers, their shadows huge in the firelight inside the lodge, followed the familiar patterns of their timeless winter ritual, and the celebrations and feasting carried on for many nights.

— 12 —

Next Boat

Victoria May 30, 1907

Dear Mr Dawley

I understand that there are a number of men leaving Clayoquot by next boat.

We are wanting a few men to work in the mill at Ucluelet. Possibly you might be able to pick out a couple of good men for us and have them stop off at Ucluelet.

We are paying $2.50 per day for mill work and later may give them a good job getting out shingle bolts by contract.

Wm Sutton

The *Princess Maquinna* at Tofino dock around 1917.

WILLIAM SUTTON had no need to discuss dates in this note to Walter Dawley. He wanted men at his Ucluelet sawmill by next boat: Dawley would understand. No measure of time meant more than the movements of the coastal steamers, and everyone knew the coded terminology of "next boat," "last boat," "return boat." In mid-1907, when Sutton dashed off this request, the steamer *Tees* made four runs up the coast every month, leaving Victoria northbound on the 1st, 7th, 14th and 21st of every month. When her schedule changed, as it often did, everyone on the coast adjusted their inner clocks accordingly: "next boat" could mean something subtly different each season.

Although the schedule of the steamers shifted and changed through the early 1900s—sometimes two trips a month, sometimes three or four a month; some voyages going to the northern reaches of western Vancouver Island, up to Quatsino or even Holberg, and others going only as far as Clayoquot or perhaps to Nootka—by 1911 a pattern emerged that would endure for decades. The steamer left Victoria at 11 PM on the 1st, 10th and 20th of every month, and although the dates altered in later years, broadly speaking the every-ten-day pattern and the 11 PM departure remained constant. So when Father Charles wrote to Father Maurus in June 1917, "I shall go there [to Hesquiat], 1st boat next month, and remain over for one boat," anyone with a grain of west coast knowledge would know he intended to spend ten days at Hesquiat, or as near to ten days as "next boat" permitted.

Well-intentioned timetables were fine and dandy, but a caveat on all printed schedules warned, understandably, that the steamers were "subject to Tidal and Weather Conditions and Change without notice." Such "change without notice" occurred far too often for the liking of regular travellers. "The CPR seem to have adopted this winter schedule very suddenly without giving notice even to the Merchants," snapped James Thomson of the Hudson's Bay Company in the autumn of 1906. Father Charles Moser frequently remarked on unheralded schedule changes. "Took steamer for Hesquiat, intending to return on Oct 12 but on Oct 12th no steamer came," he wrote in September 1910. "Without previous notification the CPR Co changed the sailing dates of SS Tees...Nolens volens I had to waite at Hesquiat till the 27 Oct." A mere fifteen-day layover: why would anyone fret about that?

Father Charles's diary is a goldmine of information about the movements of steamers. Time and again he takes part in the perpetual guessing game, shared by so many on the coast, about the steamer's whereabouts, and he continually records its arrivals and departures. After the telegraph line extended from Clayoquot up to Nootka in 1914, he was better informed about the movements of the steamers, but only if the line was working—and in stormy conditions it often failed. So Father Charles made a habit of anticipating and calculating delays, particularly in heavy weather and if he expected cargo. One stormy November night at Kakawis he implored, "St. Joseph, hold the steamer back at Ucluelet!" dreading having to unload a large shipment of hay during the storm. The following day he noted with relief: "Steamer came here at 10 AM. Calm and nice, which favored the unloading of our ton of hay."

Father Charles rarely knew the luxury of loading and unloading at a dock; most of his direct experience with the steamers was at Hesquiat or Kakawis, both "boat landings" where cargo offloaded from the steamer into waiting canoes or onto freight scows, a perilous procedure. On November 23, 1910, the "steamer from Victoria arrived and anchored off the village at 6 PM. SE wind was blowing and sea rather rough. One canoe getting freight from steamer capsized alongside steamer."

Father Charles seems to have passed his days with a watch in his hand, timing his own activities, his voyages and most particularly his religious duties. Perhaps because of his deeply ingrained habit of marking the hours of the day with religious observances, his remarks about the movements of the steamers always include precise times. Even if no other records survived, entire voyages and schedules could probably be reconstructed from this diary, with its steady stream of comments like "Waiting at Clayoquot since 4 PM for SS Queen City. She docked at 9 PM" (October 4, 1905); "At 3 PM SS Tees arrived with freight and mail" (March 9, 1911); and "Steamer called for me at 6 AM just when I was ready to leave by canoe. Landed at Kakawis 11 AM" (October 11, 1909).

On the occasions when the steamer arrived early, dramatic hustle and bustle ensued. "I could not even say Mass today," Father Charles wrote agitatedly on July 22, 1916. "Steamer came unexpectedly to Kakawis at 6:15 AM and I had to go. Reached Hesquiat by common time just before noon hour. At Hesquiat we have daylight saving time."

Early arrivals annoyed everyone, especially the storekeepers, who had to prepare the outgoing mail and line up helpers to assist with cargo. "I was sorry not to be able to write you last boat but the old Tees is good on surprise visits," reported Nootka storekeeper H. Smith in a letter to Walter Dawley on January 14, 1910. "She must have made [a] record that trip."

Steamer schedule for spring 1917.

Everyone learned to accept these uncertainties as part of their daily lives, though some found this easier than others. Quick-tempered Mike Hamilton often cursed the steamer's schedule when he operated his machine shop in Tofino in the early 1920s:

> The blamed steamer is expected tonight. On her way up from Victoria she got in here at 5 AM. Say I could have pulled Capt Gillam's wool off because that hasn't happened for nearly a year and it happened when I least expected or wanted it. I had an engine to be shipped to Nootka and of course I missed the boat. She was pulling away from the wharf before I knew she had been in at all... At other times they would have been one or two days late. I guess they will get back here again at some unearthly hour when everyone is in bed.

Long-time residents learned through experience. They became resigned to getting out of bed in the dead of night at the sound of the steamer whistle; they became accustomed to waiting on dark docks and shores in all manner of foul weather, to rowing tiredly across cold, rough waters to meet a boat that might have passed by hours earlier. Such were the realities along the coast, particularly in the earlier years of the century and in more remote locations without telegraph connections.

Father Augustin Brabant, throughout his many years in Clayoquot Sound, considered all coastal steamers as wilfully unaccountable beasts; he expected nothing better from them. Even if they should arrive more or less on time, he knew he could not be sure of boarding them at remote locations where there were no docks. Thus in March 1901, when, yet again, he failed to connect with a steamer at Hesquiat, his tone is one of familiar resignation. "The steamer arrived here Wednesday morning just after I was through with my Mass," he wrote, "and although I had everything ready and packed up I could not go on board owing to the severe gale of wind and rain, so that I am here yet at Hesquiat... I will try to go to Nootka per canoe when the weather becomes favorable."

In a similar spirit, the teenaged Stuart Stone seems unperturbed by the erratic nature of "next boat" at Clo-oose. "I will try to write you a big letter next boat," he wrote to Stockham and Dawley. "I wrote this letter when the steamer went down because she did not call in last time and I am afraid of the steamer passing again when she goes up."

Stuart's father, the Reverend William Stone, had been working at Clo-oose for

The faithful and unpopular *Tees*, with Christie School in the background.

A native family travelling "deck class" aboard the *Tees* around 1912. On the left, children shelter underneath the stairs.

several years by the time Stuart was writing his friendly letters to the Clayoquot storekeepers in the late 1890s. Living at the most notoriously exposed boat landing on the run, the Stone family learned to shake off whatever disappointment they might feel when the boat failed to stop. "I will be along next steamer unless she should fail to call, which I hope will not be the case as I am very anxious to see the people," wrote William Stone in early January 1899. Even with the steamer so frequently bypassing Clo-oose in bad weather, there is no hint of irritation in letters from the Stones. Stuart wrote his long, chatty letters in the serene expectation that the boat would eventually come, one day, and meanwhile he had plenty to interest him and to report to his friends at the store. He was teaching himself telegraphy, setting up primitive telephone lines with cords and tin cans, and he was very keen on his dogs. "Have you heard of [dog biscuits] yet?" he wrote, explaining, "They are square and mixed with all kinds of meat and tallow." Stuart also shared his delight in his new baby sister. "We are going to call baby Hoopkwistuk an Indian name it means the rising of the moon at night they say it is the best Indian name." On her birth certificate, the name appears in full: Gwendolyn Hoop-Kwis-Tuck Stone.

Regular steamship runs on Vancouver Island's west coast started when the Canadian Pacific Navigation Company began sending the steamer *Maude* from Victoria to Nootka three times each month. *Maude*'s first trip on this new schedule was in August 1897. On her return from Nootka, her cargo included one ton of ore from a claim on Nootka Sound, sent for assay in Victoria, as well as four mules and one horse from Alberni, animals destined to be shipped to the Yukon gold fields, where pack animals were at a premium. The *Maude* retired from service in 1903 and was sold as a coal barge. By this time the steamers *Tees* and *Queen City* were sharing the route, with occasional help from other vessels.

Of all these ships, *Tees* served the longest. Her steam whistle was the first ever heard on the west coast, a raucous blast announcing her arrival in Alberni on her inaugural trip in August 1896. Deflected from this route during the Klondike gold rush, for a while *Tees* ran up to Skagway from Vancouver, but from 1903 onward she was a regular on the west coast. The *Victoria Daily Colonist* described her as "a steel screw steamer of 679 tons gross register, 441 tons net, built in 1893 at Stockton-on-Tees... She is 165 feet long, 26 feet beam, and 10.8 feet deep." The ship was sturdy, reliable and by all accounts impressively ugly. Before being converted to passenger use in British Columbia's coastal waters, she was an iron-ore carrier in Britain and Spain.

In 1901 the Canadian Pacific Railway purchased all the steamers belonging to the Canadian Pacific Navigation Company and took control of their routes, establishing the British Columbia Coastal Steamship Service. Captain J.W. Troup became manager in 1901, remaining in charge until 1928. Intensely proud of his steamship service, the stern and autocratic Troup commanded great respect. He oversaw a complex operation with numerous vessels running on many different routes, including Vancouver to Victoria and Nanaimo, Vancouver and Victoria to Seattle, up the inside passage to Alaska, and, of course, along Vancouver Island's west coast. Of all the routes plied by his ships, the last one caused Captain Troup the most headaches during his many years in charge—hardly surprising given the nature of the exposed, storm-lashed coast and the persistent lack of road development. Most other areas served by the steamship fleet developed broader options for transport or alternative means of access during Troup's years in charge, but on the west coast, apart from the railway reaching Port Alberni in 1911, not much changed in terms of transport. Almost without exception, everyone and everything relied on the service provided by the CPR steamships.

As the population expanded and the west coast developed in the early years of the century, the demand for improved cargo and passenger transport grew. The cargo capacity of the ships on the route was clearly inadequate for the freight generated by new industries including sawmills and whaling stations. "I will ship your rustic and shiplap...next boat 1st prox," wrote George Bird from New Alberni on September 22, 1905. "I have 3000 feet waiting on the wharf now and I don't know whether the boat can take it as they are loaded down with

Captain Edward Gillam with native passengers aboard the *Tees*.

stuff for the Whalery every trip." Four years later, Bird still had trouble finding deck space for the goods he wanted to ship to Clayoquot. "The Tees has more lumber for the two whaling stations than she can take," he informed Dawley on July 7, 1909. Walter Dawley's papers indicate how often cargo was left behind on various docks, the steamers being filled to capacity. In addition to this perpetual problem, the dangers of the route and the repeated accidents meant that the service came in for much attention and criticism.

Even at the distant CPR head office in Montreal, the dangers of the west coast route caused a good deal of head-shaking. In a letter of November 5, 1908, to Sir Thomas Shaughnessy, head of the CPR, Captain Troup was on the defensive. "Some of the waters which our vessels traverse regularly are unsurveyed, unchartered, and the men are merely depending upon their own observation and by word of mouth for the information they have about the various channels and harbors used," Troup wrote, adding, "I think it is unnecessary for me to point out the very dangerous nature of the West Coast of Vancouver Island, and the extreme good luck we have had there to date."

In Troup's view, it was foolhardy to rely on good luck for the successful operation of the route. "The Tees is a seaworthy little vessel, is well manned, and so long as nothing goes wrong she will, no doubt, turn up all right, but there is no denying the fact that it is a risky route. She is obliged to enter numerous harbors etc, which, in stormy or thick weather is a precarious business…I think, however, that it is time we were looking for a better vessel than the Tees."

The poor *Tees*. As she continued to plod stoically up and down the west coast, she was regularly and roundly abused. "It was popularly conceded that the wallowing old tub never sheared the water, she pushed it ahead of her," Mike Hamilton wrote bitterly in his memoirs. On another occasion he declared, "Boy, that blinking old tub could roll and take a nose dive at the same time so much so that hardened sailors got seasick on her." The *Tees* became known as the "Holy Roller," legendary for the seasickness she caused as she pitched and rolled her way up the coast. "I was sick thirteen times on one voyage on the *Tees*," marvelled Nan Beere, the youngest daughter of Harlan Brewster, owner of the Clayoquot Cannery. "Into a white hat, I remember."

And yet the *Tees* proved to have remarkable staying power. Despite all expectations, she continued on the run long, long after the initial rumours of her replacement. Sharing the route with other vessels, she carried on until 1917, dismally unpopular with passengers and much harangued till the very end.

> The steel steamer being built by British Columbia Marine Railway Co. at Esquimalt for C.P.R. service on West Coast of Vancouver Island will be christened Princess Maquinna, according to announcement made yesterday by Captain J. W. Troup. (*Victoria Daily Colonist*, September 4, 1912)

Princess Maquinna became one of the best-loved ships in the coastal history of British Columbia. At the time of her launch in 1913, anticipation rippled up and down the coast. Everyone awaited her eagerly. The excitement even reached Father Maurus Snyder, by then living back at Mount Angel Abbey in Oregon, in a letter dated June 1, 1913, from Sister Mary Frances at Kakawis:

> At the potlatch lately Jimmy Jimm made a speech that the white men are coming up the coast now and that they must send the children to school. The Indians are waking up to see that the white men are coming building every place, a new copper mine was discovered at the Bear River just a few weeks ago and 11 men working there already… The new steamer Maquinna will come the 20th of this month and bring people and lots of excitement.

Descriptions of the *Princess Maquinna* abound in the correspondence and memoranda of the CPR. Some of these read like loving incantations in the long-lost language of steam, proudly detailing all her merits and features in a stream of happy technicalities:

> 3 cylinder Triple Expansion. Single Screw. 1500 Horse Power, 2 Scotch Marine Single Ended boilers. Speed in knots 12.5. Working pressure 180 lbs. 6 Furnaces, Fuel Capacity 1,705 barrels…Overall length 244' Length between perpendiculars 232' Breadth 38' Gross tonnage 1777, 50 rooms, 100 beds or berths. 70 crew members (Deck 29 Purser 3 Engine 12 Stewards Dept 26.)

Paeans of praise poured forth in the Victoria newspapers as the about-to-be-launched *Princess Maquinna* was introduced to her public. No detail escaped the *Colonist* on June 20, 1913:

> This magnificent steel craft is intended for the service on the West Coast of Vancouver Island, and she has been specially designed for this somewhat rough service, all the decks, with the exception of the boat deck, being enclosed by the steel sides of the vessel, and the usual housing above the awning deck has been eliminated.

Princess Maquinna is built of steel throughout to Lloyd's highest class. There is a double bottom, and she is fitted with 5 tanks, the third, situated under the cross bunker, being reserved for the storage of oil fuel. There is passenger accommodation for 104 first and a large number of second class, the first class staterooms all being located on the awning deck. On the main deck aft is the dining saloon, with accommodation for 90 passengers.

The walls are panelled in mahogany, with cornices and pilaster finishing. The smoking room is located on the boat deck, aft and is finished in hardwood.

By the time the ship reached Victoria Harbour, with last-minute teams of "furnishers, decorators and others…feverishly putting the interior fittings of the new Coast steamship in shape for the reception of the large number of passengers who will make the first trip," the *Colonist*'s cup was running over: "The arrival of Maquinna on the West Coast of Vancouver Island will prove an eye-opener to the towns on the Vancouver Island coast, as no vessel approaching the design and lines of the new craft has ever plied those waters."

Father Charles was more laconic. By chance, he travelled on the *Maquinna* on her first voyage in July 1913. "Came back to Hesquiat on board SS Princess Maquinna. This is the maiden trip of the Princess, a fine boat, built in Victoria especially for the West Coast run." Later that year, Father Joseph Schindler was more descriptive in a postcard to Father Maurus: "Sept 4, 1913 Dear Father: Princess Maquinna is a fine boat up to date in every regard. The Tees looks like a wash tub along side of her and small."

Several years passed before the *Maquinna* truly dedicated herself to the west coast, at least in part because the wharves along the route had not been upgraded to accommodate such a big ship. Even the official CPR report of her maiden voyage commented brusquely on the "inadequacy of the wharves," many of which were only half long enough for the *Maquinna* and were "worm eaten and practically ready to fall down" to boot. Other CPR steamer routes frequently claimed the *Maquinna* during her early years, and the loyal *Tees* continued to do the job on the west coast. Choruses of complaint continued, damning the *Tees* as "totally inadequate to meet the requirements in handling the large quantities of supplies needed at the various mining, lumber, pulp and fishing ports, and in shipping products of the West Coast to Victoria and Vancouver." Finally, on May 30, 1917, the *Colonist* delightedly announced that the days of the *Tees* were over. The *Maquinna* was officially, and permanently, back on the run. She would make three "long runs" every month up to Quatsino, and once each month would go as far as Nootka Cannery. The newspaper listed her ports of call: "Port Renfrew, Carmanah, Clo-oose, Banfield [Bamfield], Uchucklesit, Alberni, Sechart, Ucluelet, Tofino, Clayoquot, Christie's School, Port Gillam, Ahousat, Sydney Inlet, Hesquiot, Friendly Cove, Nootka Cannery, Ehatesat, Centre Island, Kyuquot Whaling Station, Kyuquot Village, Winter Harbour, Quatsino Cannery, Quiet Cove, Quatsino, Jeune Landing and Colonial [Quatsino]."

In later years, the *Maquinna* made even more stops, as many as forty, on her voyage up the coast. She became famed for her appearances at the smallest and most remote logging camps and fish reduction plants, which began to spring up like mushrooms at countless locations along the coast. In the loneliest of inlets she might be greeted by one solitary person in a canoe, looking for the mail or a delivery of groceries; at others she would deliver countless tons of machinery or lumber to bustling communities. She would host dances at her major stops, and people would crowd into her famous dining saloon for first-rate dinners, while children scrambled on board to buy comic books and candy at her commissariat.

The *Maquinna* effectively put the west coast on the map for the rest of British Columbia. The biggest ship built in the province to that time, she set the standard for speed, reliability and faithful service. She served the coast for nearly forty years, continuing right through till 1952. Known as the "Good Ship Maquinna," she was at the heart of all coastal activity, providing the stage on which much of it took place.

Memories of the *Maquinna* have remained as fresh as paint in the minds of people who travelled on her. "I loved that blessed thing," Ray Jones recalled with a smile, nearly eighty years after his first voyage aboard the ship. He was seven years old at that time, in the early 1920s, living at Port Alice with his family. His face glowed when he remembered one particular storm, water churning over the tip-tilting decks, nothing but green water visible through the portholes, and everyone directed to stay in the staterooms. For a child, it was remarkable to see a steward with arms and legs wrapped around a pole, trying to stay upright, and even more remarkable to see his mother holding the teapot up at the dining table in the saloon as all the crockery crashed onto the floor. "Oh son, we're going to drown," she cried. But they didn't. The *Maquinna* was more than equal to such storms. She was the stuff of legends.

Known as a happy ship and beloved by her crew, for her first sixteen years the *Maquinna* was under the command of Captain Edward Gillam. A big, companionable man, kindly and firm, with great dignity and presence, he was entirely the master on his ship, renowned for his remarkable seamanship and his intricate knowledge of the coast. Originally from Newfoundland, he came to Victoria to participate in the sealing industry, later joining the Canadian Pacific Navigation Company as a deckhand. He worked his way up, eventually obtaining his papers and serving as a ship's officer on the *Willapa* and the *Queen City*, and later as captain on both *Queen City* and *Tees*. When Captain Troup needed advice about the design of the new steamer for the west coast, he turned to Gillam, whose main recommendation was that the ship be double-bottomed.

Captain Gillam's calm authority and good nature were as famous as his seamanship. He could control a group of drunken loggers with a glance. "My darling Betty," he wrote in a letter to his wife in Victoria, "…a great crowd of passengers on this time…mostly loggers, but they are keeping very quiet, they are the most sober crowd of loggers I have seen for some time." According to Mike Hamilton, the prospectors were even worse than the loggers. "Seldom did the coast steamer sail north or south without having aboard a number of miners and prospectors either coming or going. They were usually a rough tough bunch frequently hard drinkers with a vocabulary, when in their cups, capable of making anyone's hair curl." Even Father Charles was provoked to an outburst in Latin about "Aqua Fortis in abundantia" aboard a particularly well-liquored steamer trip. But Captain Gillam could be counted on to keep the atmosphere on his ship amiable, and he always ensured the well-being of the ladies and children on board. Ray Jones sometimes had the thrill of being invited to sit at the captain's table, a special treat for well-mannered children.

Gillam played the violin for the frequent dances on the ship, and every year he played the part of Santa Claus for children in remote communities, cramming the wheelhouse and his own sleeping quarters with parcels, to the point that he had almost no space to lie down. Continually at sea, he saw little of his own children—three daughters and a son—as they were growing up, and an evening out with his wife was a rare event. When the famous stage show *Chu Chin Chow* was playing in Victoria, the *Maquinna* had to sail at midnight rather than at 11 PM, just that once, so Captain Gillam and his wife could attend the performance.

"I feel sure that you will have a memory of her terrible whistle," Mike Hamilton mused, remembering the *Princess Maquinna* in a recorded conversation with his daughters. "…It was ear splitting and nerve shattering and I have seen you run, screaming, to your Mother and myself when Captain Gillam pulled that whistle cord." According to Hamilton, the whistle could be heard miles away, reverberating from mountain to mountain, purposely designed to wake up entire settlements at unearthly hours. "That whistle was History all in itself because of the untold thousands who swore at it and at Captain Gillam. The sound of the whistle would begin with a sort of squeal of a one- or two-second duration before the shattering blast commenced which...gave you time to steel yourself against the shock and to clap your hands over both ears."

On all the coastal steamers, the whistle was one of the most important pieces of equipment on board, an essential navigation tool. The captains relied entirely on the whistle and its echo from shore to gauge their location as they guided their boats through dense fog. Mrs. Rolston, wife of Dr. William Rolston, witnessed this on her first voyage up the coast on the *Tees* in 1898: "Amid constant fog horns and stoppages we pursued our journey. There is always a feeling of discomfort and misgiving when the engines stop, the pumping noise of the propellor stops, the ship rolls like a cradle on the bosom of the deep. This is frequently the case in these waters where the echo of the steam whistle is anxiously waited for to decide the distance from land."

Experienced navigators knew the nature of the echoes intimately—a long sandy spit gives an echo with a distinct hiss, a rocky cliff gives a clear echo, thick forest produces a muffled echo—and they knew how to calculate the distance to shore by timing these echoes. According to Captain W. J. Boyce in an article for the *Canadian Merchant Service Guild Annual* of 1923, "a six second echo means that there is land within half a mile, as it takes three seconds to go and three seconds to come back. A one second echo means the shore is one cable's length away." Boyce conceded that the primary requirement for navigating in the fog was "a thorough mental photograph of the coast on the course the ship is taking. As the vessel proceeds the navigator must picture the shore as it slips by. Perhaps he cannot see further than the bows with his eyes. But with his ears he is seeing everything necessary within a couple of miles. At his hand he has the steam siren." Boyce described how the echoes change as the land around changes, that "a two-second echo return from abaft the beam" means that the channel is open ahead and he has passed the nearest point of land; when the echoes become "splendidly equalized," he is right in the middle of a narrow channel. Yet echoes are sometimes misleading; the shores can send back unwelcome and unexpected sounds, especially in narrow inlets, where sound bounces back and forth confusingly. And worse even than fog is thick blinding snow, for it muffles sound, preventing the echoes from speaking at all.

Local knowledge of the coastline and all its features was essential. Captain Gillam routinely picked up sounds from the shore to help identify his location. One foggy day after he slowly and silently nosed the *Maquinna* into Refuge

Cove, a tricky and narrow entrance, a passenger remarked to him at dinner, "My, we went into that place very quietly." The captain agreed, saying, "I was waiting for those dogs to bark in order to get my bearings." A good captain would know all the sounds to expect: roosters, chickens, dogs, as well as whistle buoys and sounds from creeks and gravel beaches. Captain Gillam's ability to navigate in fog was legendary, not only on the west coast but elsewhere as well. Once when the *Maquinna* was on the Victoria-to-Vancouver run, Vancouver's English Bay was enveloped in thick fog and crowded with vessels at anchor. None of them dared to move, not even the large *Empress* ships with local pilots on board, but Gillam and the *Maquinna* arrived precisely on time, untroubled by the fog. One of the pilots wryly asked him afterward, "Did you have to do that to us?"

Captain Edward Gillam and his wife, Betty.

In November 1915, the *Maquinna* and Captain Gillam gained widespread recognition and respect following a valiant attempt to rescue the shipwrecked Chilean schooner *Carelmapu*. The vessel foundered on Gowlland Rocks, off Schooner Cove, in extremely high seas and winds. Gillam brought the *Maquinna* as close as he dared in the towering waves; at one point he was within 150 yards of the doomed ship, able to witness a desperate attempt of those aboard to launch a lifeboat, but the danger proved too extreme. It was impossible to maintain *Maquinna*'s position without risking the entire ship, and the heroic rescue attempt failed. Five men survived the wreck of the *Carelmapu*; eighteen perished.

Edward Gillam served as captain of the *Maquinna* with dedication and unflappable calm throughout the 1910s and 1920s. Combined with his earlier service on board other vessels, he navigated the west coast for some thirty years, witnessing at close quarters the changes in all the settlements: the growth of Tofino, the slow eclipse of Clayoquot and the rise and fall of many enterprises. He saw the end of sealing, the heyday of the region's whaling industry and, by the mid-1920s, its demise. He saw small mines open and close and sawmills flourish and fade. He saw the end of the hand-logging era and the coming of mechanization, the early years of the massive pilchard fishery, the beginning of the pulp and paper industry as mills opened at Port Alice, Alberni and Tahsis. His ship served fish canneries at Clayoquot, Kildonan, Nitinat and Nootka, and he saw the scheduled stops along the route increase year by year to serve the ever-changing industries and settlements. Through their cargo, he knew every single development on the coast and all the individuals involved: the powerful Gibson family at their successful shingle mill at Ahousat, the struggling Rae-Arthur family trying to operate a nursery garden at their remote Boat Basin homestead, the sick children from Kakawis occasionally travelling down to Victoria with one of the sisters for treatment at the hospital. He knew the storekeepers, the teachers, and all the Indians travelling to and from their seasonal work in the canneries and hop fields, as well as those selling baskets and carvings to *Maquinna* passengers disembarking at the docks at Tofino, Nootka and Kyuquot. And Gillam also knew the priests.

Given that Edward Gillam was a Protestant, his amicable friendship with Father Charles—a great distruster of Protestants—is noteworthy. The two men saw each other frequently. Father Charles relished his occasional meals with the captain on board ship, and they shared many good conversations and memorable experiences. When Father Charles succeeded in convincing the postal authorities that Hesquiat must have its own post office and that he should become postmaster, he had to swear an oath before Captain Gillam, who was a Justice of the Peace, at the earliest opportunity. Unluckily, this fell in the middle of the night. "*March 27, 1912:* SS Tees arrived at 2 AM. I went out to take Post Master's oath before Capt. Gillam. At 3:30 I went to bed again." When the priest needed the captain's cooperation to carry out his religious duties, Captain Gillam always obliged. "*December 4, 1924:* Steamer here at 11 AM. I am leaving for Port Alice. Arriving at Nootka 6:30 PM heard of Mrs. A Murphy's critical condition. Went to see her, she can not last long. Heard her Confession and gave her Extreme Unction. Capt. Gillam was kind enough to wait until I was through."

In 1929 a new steamer, the *Princess Norah*, came to the west coast. Her declared role was to accommodate the increasing tourist traffic on the route, and Captain Gillam agreed to cross over to the *Norah*, leaving the *Maquinna*, to become her captain. In early April, *Norah* made her triumphant inaugural voyage up the coast, complete with the Governor General, Lord Willingdon, and his wife on board, as well as Lieutenant Governor Bruce and throngs of dignitaries. The *Norah* attracted crowds of well-wishers and onlookers at every stop along the way; welcoming ceremonies awaited her at all major stops. Greeted by native dancers, Girl Guides and eccentric settlers alike, she wended her way northward, while those on board enjoyed luxurious meals and special entertainments. A CPR publication noted at the time that the *Norah* travelled a total of 492 miles between Victoria and Port Alice, calling at a multitude of small places.

Father Charles was visiting Port Alice when the *Norah* arrived, and he had the satisfaction of joining the illustrious crowd on board and sharing the celebratory mood on the southbound journey as he travelled to Nootka. History

Father Charles aboard the new *Princess Norah*, 1929.

repeated itself, for just as Father Charles was on board for the *Maquinna*'s maiden voyage, so he was for the *Norah*'s, again with Captain Gillam in charge.

This was the last time the two men saw each other. Three weeks later, on May 3, 1929, Father Charles was at Kakawis, sorrowfully writing in his diary: "The sad news was told us that our good Captain Gillam had passed into eternity about an hour or two ago, [having] fallen when going up to his room, just when the steamer pulled out of Ucluelet."

Edward Gillam fell down a short flight of steps on the *Princess Norah* while on duty. No one witnessed the incident. At Tofino, Dr. Douglas Dixson examined his body, and John Grice, as coroner, signed the death certificate. Gillam was sixty-five years old. According to Dr. Dixson, the expression on his face was tranquil. Gillam was buried in Ross Bay Cemetery in Victoria.

"RIP," Father Charles wrote in his diary. Rest in peace. "He was a good friend of mine."

The coming of the *Princess Norah* in 1929 marked a significant shift of perspective on the coast. From then on, tourism became an accepted reality. The idea had been around for many years, but it had only gradually gained momentum. As early as 1886, the *Colonist* advertised that "excursionists" could travel to Clayoquot on the little steamer *Maude*. "This excursion offers a most favorable opportunity for tourists and others to view the fine scenery of the west coast of the island…the round trip has been placed at a very low figure." As steamer traffic improved, passengers who travelled up the coast came back inspired by its tourist potential, as the newspaper revealed on October 9, 1898. "The grand and beautiful scenery along the coast," one passenger exclaimed, "will make the trip a favorite one for tourists when the knowledge of its attractions becomes better known."

The appeal slowly spread. On July 23, 1899, the *Colonist*, waxing lyrical on the theme of coastal development, added tourism to the mix:

> The scenic attractions of the West Coast of this island have remained till now unheralded…the men who…visit the West Coast are more interested in quartz indications, fishery possibilities, farming land or the securing of seal hunters…With the new wagon road now building from Ucluelet to Clayoquot, these beaches will be brought into direct touch with the calling places for Victoria steamers, and it is greatly to be wondered at if some enterprising syndicate does not in the very near

future take advantage of the opportunity…and provide a seaside hotel for British Columbians.

A seaside hotel? Such a frivolous notion could not have been further from the minds of Walter Dawley and Thomas Stockham when they built their original hotel on Stockham Island one year earlier. They catered chiefly to sealers and prospectors, and their notion of good service amounted to strategically placing the spittoons. Although the stuffed pelican and a potted plant adorned the dining room, perhaps with the intention of adding a genteel tone to the place, and despite the fact that one of the bedrooms even boasted a piece of carpeting, this hotel was not, nor was it remotely intended to be, a pleasure resort for tourists.

Undeterred, and carried away on a cloud of its own purple prose, the *Colonist* continued, praising the "infinite variety in sea and cloud, in mountain and forest cataract, in giant peak and undulating valley still undesecrated by the woodsman's axe." Yet even the *Colonist* had to admit to being ahead of itself. "Some time," this article concluded with a sigh, "perhaps a century hence—tourists will learn of the wonders of nature that the West Coast has to present to their admiring eyes."

Musings about the region's tourist potential continued intermittently, often focusing on Long Beach. On August 4, 1908, the newspaper stated, "There is little doubt that, when the railway reaches Alberni, a summer hotel at Long Beach would attract…hundreds of people…if for no other purpose than to see the ocean breaking upon a long stretch of sand." When Vargas Island opened up to British settlers just before the First World War, the Department of Lands report of 1914, in the course of encouraging further settlement, emphasized the beauty of the island's far-flung beaches, declaring that "these beaches are…comparable with those of any pleasure resort on the Pacific Coast. No more enjoyable sport can be imagined than surf-riding at any one of these delightful stretches of clean sand, free from rocks." Whether this enthusiast had in mind body surfing, surfboards or surfing through the waves in a canoe to land on the beach, he was ahead of the wave. Many decades would pass before surfers discovered the west coast of Vancouver Island.

Another local attraction inspired Mr. H. Brodie, the CPR inspector sent to sniff out the area's tourist potential in 1918. While the *Maquinna* busily loaded cargo at Nootka Cannery, Brodie travelled with a group of passengers two miles across the sound to Friendly Cove. Landing on the gravel beach, they made their way to the row of Indian houses about a hundred yards above the shoreline. "In front of the village they have two of the finest totem poles on the Pacific

Coast," enthused Brodie. "One is crowned by a figure of Capt. Vancouver in a grotesquely painted black silk hat." But the site that truly captured Brodie's attention at Friendly Cove was the graveyard. "One of the most interesting places on the Pacific Coast," he declared, describing in detail the small spirit houses built above the graves, and the offerings left for the dead:

> One grave is of particular interest... A monument in the centre informs you that this is the son of Chief Napoleon Maquinna... the Chief has placed on each side of the grave two very fine dugouts. At the back of the grave in the centre of the fence, is a small model of a ship which the boy once played with, and on each side are the ends of an iron bed stead, with some wash basins and some other trinkets. On another grave of an Indian woman is a sewing machine, wash basins and baskets, together with several other small effects. One man who died has over his grave a bicycle pump, a lantern, and old gas tank, lunch basket and some wash basins. Another has a gramophone. Sewing machines and bed steads seem to be quite popular.

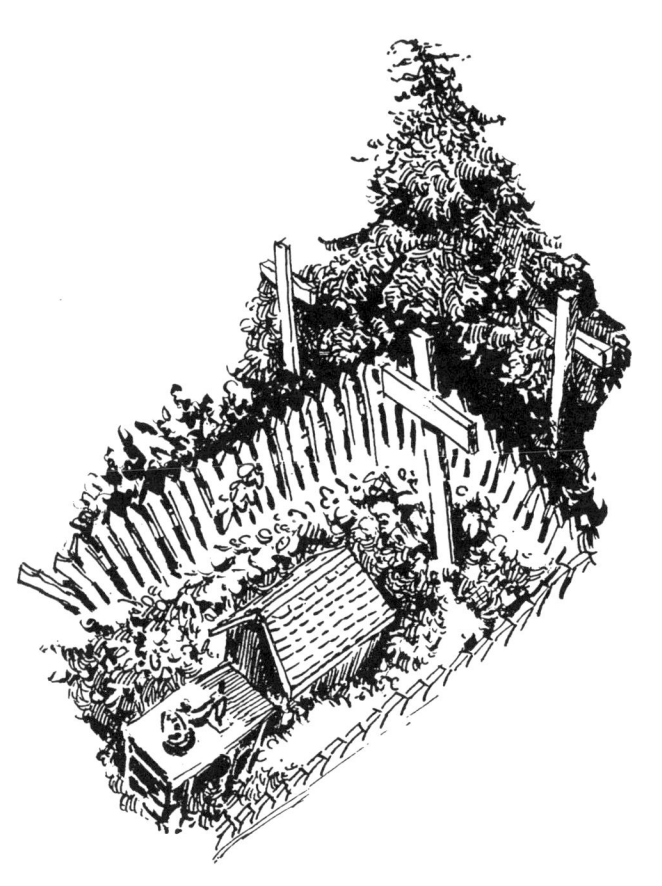

Although Brodie calculated it would be easy to bring groups of visitors over to Friendly Cove on each steamer trip up the coast, especially to see this graveyard, he had qualms about promoting the idea: "I am afraid if many tourists visited it they would steal some of the baskets and other articles as souvenirs... it would cause a great row among the Indians."

Brodie's report set the tone for later tourist publications by the CPR. These emphasized two kinds of attraction on the steamer route: bluntly, these were the scenery and the Indians. During the 1920s and 1930s, as the company expanded its tourist trade on the route, brochures for the *Princess Maquinna* consistently featured totem poles and dugout canoes, sketches of Indian handicrafts and sketches of native people. Publicity leaflets informed tourists about the Indians in glowing terms. "The coast is rich in Indian color and the aborigines do much to brighten the way," declares one undated publication. Another, from 1936, states:

> Although the influence of civilization has had much to do with changing the mode of living of these aborigines, much remains to show that in earlier days they were a highly cultured race, enjoying a normal and happy existence, and making the best use of the means of living which nature had put into their hands…On the whole a jovial and carefree people, these Indians offer an interesting study.

And yet, while their images and their handicrafts might be useful for selling tickets, members of this "highly cultured race" could only travel deck class on the CPR coastal steamers; they did not mingle with white passengers, share their class of accommodation or eat with them in the dining saloon.

Wildlife along the coast received no attention whatsoever in any literature to do with the emerging tourist trade. No one had yet dreamed up the notion of whale watching or bear spotting. Whales were merely known to be fair—if rather oversized—prey, and bears were valued chiefly for their potential as hearthrugs.

Even without whales and bears as its mascots, by the late 1920s the tourist trade was an established phenomenon. In many locations it was truly welcome because some of the tourists might be young single ladies, glad to pass the time of day with local men at dances or meals, either on board ship or ashore. The Gibson boys up at their Ahousat shingle mill wholeheartedly enjoyed such visitors. In his book *Bull of the Woods*, Gordon Gibson recalled: "In the summertime the *Maquinna* would bring groups of tourists up the coast, arriving at our place about six in the afternoon. All of us young bucks were tickled to death to take the tourists for a walk to the outside beaches, often building a campfire for a singsong. Naturally, we were most anxious to escort any of the attractive young ladies. After the walk we took everyone back to our home for coffee and a dance."

Although he was generally uninterested in the tourists on the steamers, Father Charles first noted their presence on August 3, 1923, on a trip from Kakawis to Hesquiat, when he counted forty-seven of these creatures on board. By 1929, when the newly launched *Princess Norah* attracted ever more of these travellers, Father Charles took note only if their number was large. On one trip in July 1929, he counted ninety-two tourists, expressing relief that even with such a crowd on board he could reserve a bunk.

Mike Hamilton had a low opinion of all this. "Usually on trips up the coast from Victoria, almost everyone knew each other so [the *Maquinna*] was a gathering place to converse and gossip," he recalled. "This was so except in the tourist season…It was a continual nuisance to the coastal residents to find every single cabin and bunk booked up. So that usually meant a sitting up session. Although complaints were made the company never held sleeping quarters for such passengers [coastal residents]—which wasn't fair as they were the mainstay for the service when there were no tourists."

A 1922 CPR brochure candidly admits the problem of seasonal overbooking, and even more frankly raises another touchy subject: "The steamer is quite often, and sometimes for several hours at a time, in the open Pacific, and even in pleasant weather the ground swell…results in attacks of seasickness with those who are poor sailors. The majority of passengers, however, are not affected, and most of the small minority look upon it as an experience to be talked about on their return home."

"The sea is never really calm, in my opinion," pronounced Dorothy Abraham with magisterial authority in her book *Lone Cone*, following yet another green-faced encounter with "great oily rollers." Nonetheless, she gamely accustomed herself to the realities around her when she and her husband settled in Tofino: "I even got used to being sea-sick," she declared, "although I can't say I ever liked it."

Despite this experience, and despite the persistent lack of a road to the west coast, Mrs. Abraham had no hesitation in predicting what lay ahead for the area. "One day all the West Coast territory will be opened up," she wrote, "there is so much of it yet unknown, so much beauty unimagined, so much unexplored… one day it will be the greatest playground of the Pacific: people will swarm in and the silence will be broken."

– 13 –

Dear Father

Christie Ind School
Kakawis, BC

January 24, 1912

Dear Father
I must tell you first about myself that I am sorry to say that I am spitting blood for three days but now I feel better again. I can walk around inside the house any way. I never work because I feel very weak, someday I think I will get well again. I used to be very happy before but I am feeling very sick now. Please pray for me dear Father.

I have some news to tell you about the Clayoquot people. They had great potlatch and hee hee with Ehattisat people they came to Clayoquot. They went home by this boat. Oscar and his sister Lucy went home. They are coming back next month. The boys and girls are all well and happy. Next time I will write a longer letter.

I am your thankful child,
Cosmos Damian William

IN HIS PERFECT copperplate handwriting, Cosmos Damian William, one of the older boys at Christie School, wrote to Father Maurus Snyder several times at the beginning of 1912. Father Maurus had left Kakawis a few weeks earlier to return permanently to Mount Angel Abbey in Oregon.

Cosmos was not well, nor was he happy about Father Maurus leaving. "I have to tell you that all the west coast Indian are very sorry for you dear Father," he wrote on January 4, 1912, "they are wishing for you to come back to Kakawis… we had always lots of fun when you were here dear Father. I am very sorry that you are not with us." Signing off as "your grateful spiritual child," Cosmos added, "I will say some prayers for you at the holy sacrifice of the mass I often think of you and how very good you were to me and also to my friends at Kakawis."

Cosmos never mentioned the problems at Christie School in any of his letters, but several of the older boys decided they must do so. They joined forces to write a lengthy letter to Father Maurus, providing details of how everything seemed to be going awry at the school. Dated January 20, 1912, their five-page letter is an outpouring of grievances, signed simply "from your poor Indian boys of Kakawis." No names are appended. Written in great agitation of spirit, in rambling and repetitive language, this letter stresses how much the children miss Father Maurus and reveals a fractious, miserable atmosphere at the school.

> Dear Father:
> I am sorry to say that our school master is pretty mean to the boys. He gives the fireman no breakfast when the radiators are not heated before mass. He does not allow the fireman to use the coals. Mr. Cosmos and Mickie are discharged from fireman by using coals there is no fireman any more accept two boys but they are not quite good. Now I must say that Rev Father Frowin give no food to the boys they are about 25 boys that got no breakfast, dinner and supper pretty near every day… The Sisters are the same way they never get happy from Rev Father Frowin.

The nuns also wrote Father Maurus, and their letters generally confirm everything in the boys' letter. Not only were the sisters unhappy with the situation; they were almost beside themselves after Father Maurus left, not knowing what to think or do now that a new principal was in charge of the school. Father Maurus's replacement was Father Frowin Epper, also called Father Froben or, amongst the sisters, "FF." The sisters wrote detailed accounts of disturbing incidents at the school, begging Father Maurus to intervene, pleading for him to return to set matters to rights.

Sister Mary Elizabeth wrote almost immediately after Father Maurus left, on January 12, 1912: "Father F had trouble lately with some boys, they asked to go to the village & he refused them, but they went anyhow, so when they came back, got no supper & locked them up three together in sickroom, Cosmos, Micci & Felix. They were like furios, but came out the next day… went on their knees

In 1912, following his departure from Christie School, Father Maurus received a number of letters from children at the school. The older boys expressed great unhappiness in a group letter.

& asked pardon & got of smoothly." Sister Mary Scholastica's version of events was that "Cosmos…went on strike the 5 of Jan. He refused to play the organ for Benediction because P. Frowin punished him." In her turn, Sister Mary Clara confided to Father Maurus that "FF has had a hard time latly with the boys just as you foresaw. Cosmos, Mikie and Toby are the worst. At the time of writing it is a little better, Cosmos had a hemorage and that settled them a little." She provided further information about what she termed the "troubles":

> What I meant by troubles was mostly in regard to the boys. Soon after you left Cosmos revolted, he must have had something before with FF. Then one morning I was late waking him to make the fire. FF came into the Chapel scolding him terrible, telling me he could not have breakfast. I then went and told him it was my fault and he allowed breakfast. Wherever they did something, no supper. It made the boys wild. Then they asked to go to Opitsat for Potlage [potlatch], F said no, the boys went anyhow…I then went to F and told him it can not go this way…can not make any impression on him, so I say not much, although I feel sometimes I am not doing my duty.

Father Maurus's departure from Kakawis came suddenly and unexpectedly. No one wanted him to go, and in his personal papers he left no chronicle of his own reaction. On his return to Mount Angel, he immediately wrote to Walter Dawley, largely concerning a piano he wished to sell, but also mentioning his new circumstances. In this letter, he seems unsettled and at a loss:

> It seems to me an age since I left Clayoquot and I haven't received a line from anybody since. This more than anything else makes the time drag along so slowly…In the eleven years I was away the country around here has developed wonderfully. The big farms have been parceled off into small homes, gardenspots, and values have increased 1000%. Who knows but such a windfall may come to you…if you live long enough.

Father Maurus's departure marked the end of an era at Christie School. After he left, life at the school became more difficult for students and staff alike.

Once settled back at Mount Angel, Father Maurus had no reason to complain about a lack of letters from the west coast. During the months following his return, the letters came thick and fast. Taken as a whole, they are a dismal litany relating how things had changed at the school and how badly everyone was feeling. If the general tone of these letters can be believed, Father Maurus had run the school smoothly, he was loved and respected, and in his time he employed little or no physical punishment. When he left, things simply fell apart. His successor, Father Frowin, seems to have used more force with the children and meted out more punishment. He was also extremely tactless with the sisters. None of them liked him.

The sisters were unrestrained in their distress at losing Father Maurus, and some of their letters reveal a pitiable, naked grief at his departure. Shortly after his departure, Sister Mary Elizabeth wrote to thank him for candy he sent: "At times it is just like I hear you cough somewhere, I look for you, but not to be found anywhere." Later in the letter she mourned, "As long as you were here, I had you, now I have nobody." Similarly, Sister Mary Clara wrote of her immense joy at receiving the candy and described how she missed him: "I don't know what to call it but I think I feel your absence more than the others in a certain way…I have to hold up FF and look pleasant when I would rather cry." Sister Mary Sophie wrote: "I long to throw myself at your feet and tell you all my heartache and sorrows." These emotional outpourings kept coming. Several months after his departure, Sister Mary Clara wrote that she still yearned for Father Maurus: "When will you write me once something nice for myself, I am really starving and all cold and disheartened." When she did receive a letter addressed to her privately, she was overwhelmed, telling him how she cried and laughed for joy.

The letters Father Maurus received following his departure from Kakawis are preserved amongst his papers at Mount Angel—a remarkable clutch of inbound mail, much of it written in 1912–13, outlining the changes occurring at Christie School. None of his responses to these letters survive. A significant handful of the letters are from children at Kakawis. Unnervingly perfect in their handwriting, these are usually written in pencil on cheap, lined notepaper. Letters also came to him, in slightly greater numbers and over a longer period, from the sisters at Kakawis. All of these letters tell Father Maurus how he is missed, recalling picnics they took together, outings to the various beaches and happier times. Among the children who wrote to him were Cosmos Damian William, Maggie Stevens, Emily Jacob, Mamie Sam, Mary Alphonse Swan and the unnamed "poor Indian boys of Kakawis."

The letter from these unidentified boys stands out from the other letters and is one of the lengthiest. "Every day Father Frowin [is] vexed and scolding the boys," the writers declared, "and when the boys don't mind him…he always say no breakfast dinner or supper…you did nothing bad to us and you never had giving us no meal." The letter contains a lengthy explanation telling why a boy named Mickie was punished for failing to "make the fire." As a fireman at the school, he was responsible for preparing wood and lighting the school's furnace and stoves, but on one particular day, Mickie had no time to prepare the wood because he was working hard unloading the freight boat. Father Frowin said that, as punishment, Mickie would have no meals that day.

> Mickie he does not care for no meal and Father Frowin punched him and he stopped him and the boys were watching at him Mickie did not to [do] anything to him. Many times Rev Father Frowin fight against the boys, but the boys never mind him. Rev. Father Frowin called the firemen rotten and rotten and apples and potatoes and lazy fellows… Dear Father Maurus We should like to tell you one more news it is that Father Frowin does not like any Indians to come to visit their children at school. Believe us, dear Father.

The girls who wrote to Father Maurus were younger than the boys, and they never commented on any problems at the school. Their letters strike an entirely different note:

> January 9, 1912
>
> Dearly Beloved Father
> As New Year has past already and your names day is at hand I wish you a Very Happy Feast and many blessings. I will offer up Holy Communion for you and I will pray hard that we may meet here again. I can not thank you enough for what you have done for us all but all I can do is I will try not to give up my religion and will try to be a good girl to the sisters and my pastor.
>
> When you left us all we felt very bad I thought of those days when we all together spent our picnics and holidays with you and I had to cry so much to think that we were losing you dear Father.

I made a lace for a surplice for here it was nearly 3 yards and sister Mary Clare give me a nice ribbon for it. My father came down last boat for a visit and now he is going back this boat.

I will tell you what I got for Christmas. I got a box with nice coloured thread and needles in it, side combs, handkerchiefs and soap. I did not expect such nice things as that.

Now I will close wishing you once more a Very Happy Feast.

I am your little friend,
Mamie Sam

Mamie Sam wrote again to Father Maurus in April 1912, thanking him "with great joy" for a postcard he sent. In this letter, Mamie described going to Opitsat with one of the sisters to decorate the church there for Easter, shared her pleasure in the newly hatched chicks and stressed how much she missed him. "Alice seems getting better every day," she added at the end, along with the reassurance: "I am just the same as I always was, talkative and mischievous."

In her single letter to Father Maurus, Emily Jacob thanked him for the card he sent to her. "I nearly cried for joy when Rev Father Frowin handed it to me," she declared, adding, "I have a sore on my neck both sides. Please remember me in your holy prayers...I pray for you every day. I was not feeling well for some time. But I am getting better again."

Maggie Stevens contented herself with sending a postcard to Father Maurus. "I thank you very much for the post card which you sent me. I am sorry to tell you that I am sick yet. Please pray for me. I always pray for you. I am your little girl, Maggie Stevens."

The health of the children is often the subject of these letters, and the sisters occasionally provided details. "Alice is not improving, Maggie [illegible] has also bad consumptive cough," Sister Mary Clara wrote on January 24, 1912, and in another letter a few weeks later she said, "Alice is lively, full of mischief, but looks pale. Cosmos and Jos. Alex are down with sore throats again." Within two months she shared another concern: "I am so troubled about Maggie Stevens. Her consumptive cough is like that of Mariam of Opitset who died many years ago. In the afternoon her face is flushed."

Maggie wrote to Father Maurus again on May 15, 1912: "I wish to tell you that I am going hom on this boat because I am sick yet I always pray for you Please pray for me so I can get well...I liked to be at school but I am always sick. We had boat rides with the sisters on Sunday and had a good time. Please never forget me in your prayers. Now good bye Rev. Father Maurus I am your little Indian girl."

The sisters sent Father Maurus detailed news from the coast: how his ex-pupils were, who had married or had babies or died. "We lost dear little Barnabas," wrote Sister Mary Frances. "He was well when he went home, got very wet on the way the day they left and after 2 weeks died. The children said he was very good and patient, had a crucifix always in his hand and repeated Jesus, Mary & Joseph etc. His father takes it very hard."

Father Frowin Epper at Ahousat around 1913 with an unidentified group.

Several letters from the sisters hint obliquely at changes at the school, giving few explicit details. Writing in February 1912, Sister Mary Sophie declared brokenly, "I could tell you many things about how thing are going on here but… I have not the heart to do…it is heartbreaking to see what we do see at times I cannot believe that the good God will let this place go to ruin that has cost so many sacrifice and tear and trials." She continued:

> Oh how the children miss you now we can see how much they must have loved you what you realy were to them the boys are the ones that miss you the most as you were with them most the big boys are the worse as they do not like Father Froben and he has made a few mistake in handling them I am afraid it is finish with him the boys have little respect and love…I never dream they could be and act the way they have been.

"Chief Joseph and Mary were over Saturday," she reported in another letter. "…I treated them as nice as I could remembering your injunctions on such occasions. Queen Mary got quite confidential in the [illegible] while Joseph was out and said 'Joseph always want to help, to get children, but Clayoquot people say no. Father Maurus not there, don't like FF.' The same thing we heard from Nootka."

As Father Frowin's tenure at the school continued, the sisters came to regard him with dispassionate malice. One of them wrote to Father Maurus about a memorable boat trip. She cannot be identified and the letter cannot be dated because only part of it has survived, composed in richly broken English:

> In the afternoon Father Froben took the Sisters and girls out for a ride. Sr M Clare and I stayed home with the sick ones, he is getting quite fatherly now ha ha. He and one of the boys carried them all out

from the boat, I think he had enough of it. Last week Sr M. Clare and I went over to do some shoping…and we got swamp we had to come back. I went up to change…he did not want change but empty his boots wringing out his socks on the beach, next day he was sick. I told him that what he got for not changing his cloths. I am having my times in training him I don't see any improvement yet.

Father Charles Moser's diary provides no information about the developments at Christie School following Father Maurus's departure. Safely ensconced at Hesquiat, he kept his distance, and Sister Mary Sophie indicated in a letter to Father Maurus that she believed Father Charles was staying away deliberately: "Father Charles was here on a visit came 18th left on steamer 22nd we were glad to see him too he did not come to see us very much as he used to do he said he afraid of Frowin."

No hint of any such fear surfaces directly in Father Charles's diary. The only personal comment he allowed himself about Father Frowin followed a visit Father Frowin made to Hesquiat in August 1913. Together, the two priests killed and butchered a bull; after dinner, "Fr Frowin with two Indians and the meat left per canoe for Kakawis," Father Charles remarked, adding dryly, "Deo Gratias alone again."

In March 1912, Sister Mary Clara wrote, "The boys are doing fairly well now, the hope of soon leaving I suppose keeps them up," and in another letter that month she added, "Now for some time it is better during [March] the boys often went to holy Communion." With the end of the school year coming, the bigger boys knew they would soon be going home. Uneasy peace prevailed.

Cosmos Damian William's final, and longest, letter to Father Maurus is dated March 20, 1912. In six and a half pages he made no further reference to his illness, to spitting blood, to the angry confrontations with Father Frowin. Instead, the letter is full of details of the daily life at the school, describing how he is building a fence as well as the side altars in the school chapel: "They are very nice and beautiful. If they are guilded they would be very beautiful." The letter tells how the boys are fixing the bedsteads and scrubbing the kitchen walls: "It is very clean now. We are not yet finished scrubbing. I think we will finish soon." Ending with the reassurance "I am getting well all now," Cosmos continued to lament Father Maurus's absence:

> We are all sorry that you had to leave us and go away from us…I wish you were here at Kakawis so we would be very happy with you. We

never play football anymore because Rev Father Frowin told us that the football is too costly to buy. I think we will never play any kind of games anymore.

I think he will never buy for us anything. You were always buying things for us when you were here at Kakawis so we were very happy with you.

We are not happy anymore because you are far away from us. The boys are starting to spade in the gardens already. Our front yard looks white with flowers. It looks very nice now. I wish you were here yet so you could enjoy Kakawis…

I am sorry to say that Didac is dead. He died on the 8 of February. He got sick when he came here he took cold coming on the steamer and he went home but he was very sick. He lived only four days after he left here. When we heard that he was dead we all were sorry because he was very good to us when he used to visit this school at Kakawis.

Well dear Father I hope you will have a very enjoyable time at Easter.

I will say some prayers for you. Please remember me in your holy prayers…

I am your thankful big Indian boy
Cosmos Damian William

Cosmos presumably left Christie School later in 1912, and with great relief, but after that—silence. He wrote no more letters to Father Maurus, and official records reveal nothing about him: no marriage certificate, no death certificate. Given that he was spitting blood, he may have died young of tuberculosis, like so many other young natives on the coast.

Deaths of Indians were not recorded in any systematic fashion until 1917, when record keeping improved somewhat with the introduction of an official form entitled "Return of Death of an Indian." Father Joseph Schindler, who took over Opitsat mission in 1910 and later worked at both Kakawis and Hesquiat, recalled bluntly, in an article about his years on the coast, that when he first arrived he "never reported any births, deaths or marriages to the Indian Department or elsewhere, because they were not wanted. The missionaries' books were the only records kept then." But no book, diary or other source has yet emerged with any further mention of Cosmos Damian William.

Exactly what occurred at Christie School following the departure of Father Maurus is unclear, but judging by letters from the sisters and children, Father Frowin would hit the boys, frequently disallow meals and sometimes lock the boys in the sickroom for days on end for various perceived wrongdoings. Such punishments shocked the sisters, and the children, for under Father Maurus the school had been run very differently. The official reports to the Department of Indian Affairs, written by successive principals of the school, yield no information. In 1913, Father Frowin reported briskly that "the pupils are continually taught the advantages and necessity of purity of mind and body." What this means is anyone's guess, and his reports become even briefer and less informative in later years.

Father Frowin Epper's tenure as Christie School principal lasted until the end of 1916. No letters from the sisters or the children describe his last few years as principal, but that autumn, Father Charles's diary suddenly begins to provide more information about events at the school.

> *September 22, 1916:* Delivered to SS Tees 494 lbs meat, having sold to the two settlers in the harbor 25 lbs. Steamer came at 3:30 PM...Letters from Fr. Frowin and Joseph [Father Joseph Schindler] tell me of the terrible conditions at Kakawis, boys and girls running away, stealing and getting drunk from stolen Mass wine etc, girls going in the night to boys dormitory and vice versa etc. When punished for it they run away...The devil seems to be loose. Sursum Corda!

Within a few weeks of this, the abbot at Mount Angel decided to remove Father Frowin from Christie School, and Father Joseph took over as principal in the autumn of 1916. The abbot first offered the position to Father Charles, but he wrote in his diary: "Finding the children still in a rebellious mood I was not anxious for the Principalship of Kakawis." Yet Father Charles was no longer able to distance himself from the affairs of Kakawis; from now on he would be more closely involved, for better or worse.

Father Joseph wrote several letters to Father Maurus at Mount Angel, sharing his early experiences at Kakawis and occasionally asking for advice. Some of his revelations are harsh, as in this letter from March 1917:

> Since Christmas I have punished a boy four times for serious offences: the first penance was the rosary four days in chapel—2nd 3 days in darkroom adjoining dormitory—3rd 2 weeks in bath room adjoining boys sick room and hard work on nice days—and the 4th and I hope

last, was two weeks in jail fed on two pieces of bread and water three
times a day.

Father Joseph elaborated in a postscript to this letter that the old blacksmith shop had been turned into a school jail, and he added further explanation:

> The same boy was put in [school jail] again but this time stood it only
> three days and refused to stay there longer saying he has enough of
> it now. He is behaving himself now. The others whom I considered
> incorrigable were his companions in jail. They know now that I have
> the policeman to back me up and that the provincial jail or reformatory
> is open to them.

According to Father Joseph, the relatives of the boy whom he locked up for two weeks told the boy he deserved it. Opposition to this punishment came from other boys at the school, who were greatly angered and, Father Joseph wrote, "told me that F. Frowin was better than I because he did not lock up the boys for two weeks like I do."

Father Joseph made it clear in this letter that he believed the sisters to be partly responsible for the problems at the school. In August 1916, Sister Mary Clara and Sister Mary Clotilde left Kakawis. Sister Mary Clotilde was one of the three sisters who arrived at the school in 1900, and Sister Mary Clara had arrived at Kakawis a year later. Between them, they had a wealth of experience, far more than the new sisters or priests they left in charge at Kakawis. "Much of the trouble during the past year has been occasioned or at least increased by changing the sisters," declared Father Joseph. "None of the new sisters have handled Indian children before and they had the wrong idea of Indians when they came here and do not know them yet." He mentioned one sister in particular who "came here with an aversion to her charge and is not reconciled to her mission yet. No matter how good she is and how hard she trys to do her work right; she betrays her feelings in dealing with the children who say that Sister does not like them, and they are mean to her." This particular sister lasted less than one year at the school.

In the spring of 1917, Father Joseph faced a major outbreak of hostility from the children at the school. "They broke out at the time in a kind of revolution…" he wrote on April 2, 1917. "I could hear curses every day from the boys esp when I corrected them. S.B and G.d.s.b. were the usual expressions and the children used the full words—you know what it means. The girls used these curses as much as the boys." Father Joseph called the policeman in from Tofino to help control the situation. He "gave the ring leaders severe reprimand and promised them the jail or reform school if they cause any more trouble."

By May 1917, the abbot decided to intervene once again at Christie School. He instructed Father Charles to leave Hesquiat and go to the school to assist Father Joseph. "I know it will be a sacrifice on my part to move there," Father Charles wrote to Father Maurus on May 11, 1917, "as Kakawis as it is at present has no attraction for me."

Knowing of the problems at the school, Father Charles probably foresaw this move. In January 1917 he wrote to Father Maurus from Hesquiat, ostensibly a newsy letter about coastal developments: "I suppose you know that a Seattle firm is erecting a large cannery at Nootka, a few miles from Friendly Cove… The Dewdney mine at Sidney Inlet is also being worked again. The Tees took last month a shipment of 450 tons of ore to Tacoma." Although seeming pleased to report all this industry, he continued sombrely, "The Indians are going down, backward i.e. getting slowly worse through their contact with whites during the summer season…I wish I could talk over with you some Indian problems."

Christie School around 1913.

For several years following his move to Kakawis, Father Charles was only able to make monthly visits to Hesquiat. He would have far preferred to return to Mount Angel, and he requested this of the abbot, but to no avail. His instructions from his superior were to stay, stretching himself between Kakawis and Hesquiat.

This shift marked a significant change for Father Charles on the coast; from this point on, his world became fractured, and a sense of unease becomes increasingly evident in his diary. In his estimation, everything took a turn for the worse following this move to Kakawis. The post office he had enjoyed running at Hesquiat had to be closed; his house there, once so busy with visitors, stood empty; his garden could not be properly tended; and the church at Hesquiat went into decline. His years at Hesquiat mission had been, for him, peaceful and, on the whole, happy. That period had ended.

Father Charles found little to please him at Kakawis. He complained to Father Maurus that "here [at Kakawis] the attention at Mass is far below Hesquiat. Moreover, the high Mass and Benediction at Hesquiat is beautiful whilst here it is very bad." Yet such complaints were trivial given the real trouble erupting at the school. In a letter to Father Maurus on June 25, 1917, Father Charles bitterly recounted what had been happening. "Sit down, brace yourself against the shock you will get," he wrote, going on to describe, in a four-page letter, how some of the children had repeatedly tried to burn down the school. This reflected incendiary activity at other schools; children had also set fires at residential schools in Ahousat and Alberni. "The Ahousat school burnt down on May 5th this year. 3 Ahousat girls did it... The Alberni Indian school was also burnt down on June 3rd this year," Father Charles wrote in his letter, while in his diary he noted that an Indian school at Sechelt, on the mainland north of Vancouver, had also been torched.

Following these attempts to burn down the school at Kakawis, Father Joseph wired for Indian Agent Cox to come and investigate. Both Cox and School Inspector Kearen came and closely interrogated the children to discover the details of the story. They learned that on June 9 and 10 the children lit fires in the attic, but the fires had gone out by themselves. Father Charles was not there on those dates; he returned just in time for the more successful attempt of June 13, when part of the school roof caught fire. And after June 13, even with the fathers and sisters and various outraged authorities bustling around, investigating the fire, the children did not give up. They remained determined to burn down Christie School, systematically stashing bundles of kindling wood under their beds and inside their pillows, awaiting their next chance. The kindling was discovered.

"Result:" wrote Father Charles, "2 big boys from Hesquiat, Joseph Ignace and Placide, and 4 smaller boys from Clayoquot were brought before Dawley and Grice, JP, where they pleaded guilty to the charge of attempting to burn down our school. The 2 big boys gave the smaller ones the matches, the smaller ones made and brought the kindling upstairs and did the actual firing. The six will be brought this return boat to Nanaimo or Victoria for trial before a judge, and as all are under 16 years of age, are liable to be sent to reform school."

At no point in his letter to Father Maurus, nor in his diary, did Father Charles ever question why the children should want to burn down the school, why they were so angry and unhappy. He wrote of their rebellious spirit, of how hard it was to be a priest at such a time, of how angry and insulting the parents of the boys were toward the authorities, yet as to the motives of the children, he understood only that Christie School had been spared. "So many times the boys tried to burn the school, but no success. The finger of God! Deus etiam providebit."

> *June 21, 1917:* After dinner we went again to court... Then Indian agent Cox had a speech to the Opitsat Indians who were in great numbers present saying they should not blame us nor the court, as the children alone were to blame; the guilty children would be taken to Victoria to a higher court, where they would either be dismissed or

sent to the Reform School... After the court, Mr. Cox, Fr. Joseph and myself were subjected by the infuriated Indians to the most insulting language and threats. Fr. Joseph got the most because he tried to argue with them in spite of my warning to move on and go home.

After their appearance before the two JPs of Clayoquot, all six boys from Christie School were kept in the lockup at Clayoquot in the care of the provincial policeman. The boys had company, for the two girls accused of burning down their school at Ahousat were also in the jail. They all faced further legal proceedings at Victoria. The local native communities were outraged, as Father Charles explained in his letter of June 25:

> After the investigations court at Clayoquot on June 20th and 21 we, Fr. Jos. & myself and Cox (the Clayoquot Indians were greatly excited...) were subjected to all kinds of insults. Cox and I walked away and were left alone then, but Fr. Jos...tried to sooth them and talked over an hour with them to no use. We were bad priests, drunkerts and thiefs and I don't know what. They were going to take all the children home for good and even hinted that we made the children burn the school. They would never go to church anymore. They were finished Catholics.

Within a couple of days, the *Tees* took the apprehended children down to Victoria. Father Charles then dropped the subject, not mentioning it again in his diary until July 15: "Report has it that the two big boys were sentenced to two years in the Reform School, the four smaller ones were pardoned after a good warning."

Life at the school went back to normal, but "normal" was becoming increasingly difficult. Unwillingly headquartered at Kakawis, Father Charles made no pretence of enjoying his work at the school, acknowledging that "the rebellious spirit of the children is far from subdued." Conflict became part of everyday life. The boys frequently had their hair "clipped" for bad behaviour; sometimes the girls refused to answer the priests; occasionally children ran away. The atmosphere at the school was perpetually stormy and at times violent.

> *August 15, 1917:* After Benediction at 7 o'clock Fr. Joseph, his brother Ted and myself sat down in my room for a game of cards. The boys being rather boisterous around the house were told to go to the beach... At 9 o'clock the bell rang for them to go to bed, but as soon as Fr. Joseph left the dormitory to continue our game they started to talk

aloud and run around. After some time Fr. Joseph went upstairs to get them quiet but they would not obey. So Ted and I went to help and then a regular battle took place in which we almost lost out. A stool or two figured in the case. Finally we got them subdued and took the ringleader along and locked him in jail. After that we went to finish our game.

On May 1, 1918, near the end of his first year at Kakawis, Father Charles wrote to Father Maurus during one of his brief retreats to Hesquiat, complaining that everything was falling apart there, too. "Spiritual life is not anymore as it used to be few years ago…People do not go to the Sacraments anymore…The best instructed, and those living nearest to Church never go anymore…When I come here on my monthly visits I am always glad when I can go back to Kakawis again." Given how difficult matters were becoming at Kakawis, this was a strong statement.

Father Charles faced increasing challenges at Kakawis in the ensuing years. In July 1919, Father Joseph returned to Mount Angel, relinquishing his position as school principal, and the abbot appointed Father Charles to take over. His diary gives no hint at all of his reaction to this appointment; he doggedly shouldered the task and said little, serving as principal until 1922.

Towards the end of 1921, Sister Mary Elizabeth wrote to Father Maurus at Mount Angel to report that the school now had sixty-two students and that four had recently left for "Reformed School to Vancouver last boat." The students at the school displeased her during a recent visit of the abbot because "he would treat them with candy & in return they would steal his cigars & the like because he never locked his room." She clearly expected the worst of the students. "Every once in a while they get a bad mean ugly spell," she complained. Meanwhile, she wanted to know more about a rumour that Father Maurus might return to work at Kakawis, although she worried on his behalf. "I'm only afraid you will not like it any more," she wrote. "The children are not so bad if they would only have some Religion pounded into them but there is something lacking, something missing in them, they have no Fear & Love of God."

This is one of the last letters Father Maurus received from Kakawis. From this point on, his papers reveal little about day-to-day events at Christie School. If he received other, later letters, he did not keep them.

He never returned to work at Kakawis.

A Go-Ahead Little Settlement

It was during this period that I left Tofino for the first time since I had arrived in the district on taking up the work at Lennard Island [in 1904]; since doing so material alterations had taken place in Port-Alberni and while there for the first time I saw & had a drive in an automobile, also I saw for the first time a Cinema or Movie, which was then of course the silent movie; also since we had left the railway had arrived at Port-Alberni, and the daily train service, except on Sunday, been established.

Tofino waterfront, 1913. The newly constructed St. Columba's Anglican church is on the far left.

LIFE WAS GOOD for Frank Garrard in Tofino in 1913. He would never have dreamed of taking time away from his work to marvel at the modern technologies of Alberni unless everything was going well. Garrard recalled

the prosperous and optimistic years leading up to the First World War in his memoirs, which are filled with the hustle and bustle of development on the west coast. As Tofino postmaster and employee of the telegraph service, Garrard knew pretty much everything that was happening in and around the growing town. He was also president of the Clayoquot Development League, an offshoot of the Vancouver Island Development League, formed back in 1909 with the express aim of encouraging all forms of development on the island. According to Garrard, the League was, in some mysterious fashion, "of great service in preventing the overthrow of Tofino as a townsite," defeating shadowy plots against Tofino, perhaps initiated by the storekeeper at Clayoquot.

By 1913, Tofino was in no danger of overthrow. Described in the *Victoria Daily Colonist* as "a go-ahead little settlement," Tofino had "a large public hall, 60' × 40', built by co-operation of its residents, and this is used so freely for dances, social entertainments and other meetings that it already has begun to pay dividends." The area of Tofino township had been surveyed into lots and streets for future development, and the town now had a decent wharf, a customs office, a school, a post office and, at least for a while, a hotel, elegantly named the White Wing Hotel—just a few rooms, admittedly—adjacent to the White Wing Cafe and run by a Chinese entrepreneur known locally as Wing.

Most impressively of all, in the view of some, the town now featured an Anglican church. Frank Garrard, along with John Chesterman and several others, had campaigned to build this church, and the attractive little building dedicated to St. Columba opened its doors in 1913. In his memoirs, Garrard described the construction of a special post office and telegraph building, the establishment of the permanent lifeboat crew and the growth of the school, which "was gaining in numbers, most of the house-holders in Tofino having families from which children went to school." New social and political organizations were forming in the town, including a Women's Auxiliary, the Settlers' Association and the Overseas Club, as well as the perennially warring Conservative and Liberal associations.

Norwegian, Scottish and English newcomers continued to arrive, making the community their own, some of them acquiring large tracts of land in the surrounding area. These settlers, often people with young families, came intending to "take up" land and to stay. In a pamphlet dated 1912, the Clayoquot Development League declared: "The Government surveyed land in this district is nearly all pre-empted or purchased already, but there are varying areas of good land still to be had, both waterfront and inland...for from $5.00 to $10.00 per acre." Frank Garrard had recently purchased eighty acres of land "adjoining the Tofino townsite" as an investment and was clearing it with his new stump-puller.

Although it was little more than a rooming house built on an old scow, the White Wing Hotel had impressive letterhead. The small print declares the hotel is "The Tourist Resort of the West Coast of Vancouver Island" and offers "Boating and Launch Parties" as well as a "Splendid Beach Drive for Automobiles." This was in 1913. The first automobile in Tofino arrived in 1921.

He noted the continuing debate about a road that surely one day would connect Tofino to the rest of Vancouver Island, an issue "which already had become a serious question to the community, there being at that time only a trail between Ucluelet and Tofino."

The future looked promising for local industry. Over at Bear River, the Ptarmigan Mine was a hive of activity, with roadways and tramways under construction, a prelude, surely, to extracting huge amounts of valuable ore. The Clayoquot Cannery provided steady employment for a number of people, and John Chesterman and his partners were shipping ore from their workings at the Kalappa mine in Lemmens Inlet. The mill at Mosquito Harbour was working hard, the Sydney Inlet mine was likely to reopen, fishing was prosperous and timber cruisers were going up and down the coast staking ever more speculative claims in Crown timberlands. Best of all, the new coastal steamer—the *Princess Maquinna*—was soon to be launched from the Esquimalt shipyard.

Comfortably established in Tofino, Garrard and his family watched with keen interest and pleasure as settlers arrived, as enterprises thrived and as land was taken up. Although they had been many years on the coast, the Garrards at last felt themselves to be in the right place at the right time. The entire family was fully and profitably employed. By 1913, Garrard's eldest son, Burdett, was in charge of the fisheries patrol boat; his son Noel was working with the government telegraph service, extending the line northwards from Clayoquot toward Nootka; and his wife, Annie, and daughters Olive and Ethel were helping to run the telegraph and post office at Tofino. Garrard held the job of telegraph lineman, continually patrolling and repairing the thin line that looped precariously from tree to tree "over the trail between [Long Beach] and Tofino, also over the trail between Long-bay & Wreck-bay," as he wrote in his memoirs. "I also had the line at Stubbs Is to the store, this being connected to the peninsula at Tofino by a cable; besides this line there was a line to Mosquito-harbour which was kept in order by me." Garrard sometimes helped repair the line to Clayoquot Cannery, and when the line was extended to the Ptarmigan Mine and the Kalappa Mine, he was also on hand. His salary as a lineman was $80 per month; for operating the post office, he and his family received $300 per year.

Such steady employment in the town was a great relief to Garrard. Despite the rigours of monitoring the telegraph line, plodding for ceaseless miles in all weather to check for breaks—"old hikes over the road which never was," as Murdo MacLeod described the trail in a letter to Garrard—and despite the hard labour involved in replacing vast lengths of line, even miles at a time, after it was downed by a storm, this work based in Tofino was far preferable to the

Garrard family's previous life at the lighthouse on Lennard Island. Garrard had worked alongside John Chesterman, George Fraser of Ucluelet and John Grice to build the light station back in 1904. The crew camped in tents during the construction, sometimes making trips over to Chesterman's beach at his property on Esowista Peninsula, where they played baseball. When the Lennard light was complete, Garrard became the first lightkeeper there, remaining for four years.

At first this job seemed a grand adventure for the whole Garrard family, and a fine opportunity. Annie Garrard and the children travelled from their home in Alberni to Clayoquot on board the *Queen City*, complete with a cow, a dog—"I forget if we had a cat," mused Garrard—a sewing machine, "which had already been hauled across the mountains from Nanaimo," and all their household effects. With this and five children, they loaded up a freight scow and set out from Clayoquot to Lennard Island. "During the trip," wrote Garrard, "Lilly [his daughter] was quite intrigued with the pieces of Kelp & the attached bulbs and remarked what a lot of onions had been upset into the sea, she had not seen kelp before."

The reality of living at the light with a growing family proved harsh. The hazards of rowing considerable distances back and forth between Lennard Island, Clayoquot and Tofino, often in hostile wind and weather, and with young children, troubled Garrard: "There was always the element of danger…" Years afterward, he was still haunted by the memory of seeing his children's canoe capsize far from shore when they were paddling from Lennard Island to Clayoquot, knowing that his daughter Ethel could not swim at all and Olive and Noel just barely. He and his son Burdett rowed desperately towards them, arriving in time to rescue them along with three frantic cats who had also, inexplicably, been in the canoe. Garrard could never forget the "vision before [his] eyes, of the upturned canoe & the splashing in the water."

On the Tofino waterfront around 1914.

On another trip by rowboat to collect the mail at Clayoquot, he, Ethel and Burdett lost both oarlocks when trying frantically to avoid a huge breaker. "It broke about eight feet above the bow of the boat which for the second was almost perpendicular," wrote Garrard. "I thought she would capsize end over end, the sea thundered down into the stern of the boat where poor Ethel was." By some miracle, Ethel was knocked into the bottom of the boat rather than washed overboard, and when the boat righted itself, the Garrards were shaken but unscathed and "there was not more than a couple of buckets full in the boat when she was on a level keel again; for some time after this Ethel didn't like the look of these breakers."

Schooling was also a problem. To ensure his children had an education, Garrard helped build the first school in Tofino in 1906 and arranged for his children to stay in town during the week, returning to the lighthouse on weekends. The Garrards, along with the children of the Chesterman and Arnet families, made up a sufficient number for the school to qualify for a government grant in its early years, and despite the perils of commuting back and forth to the lighthouse on the weekend, the arrangement proved workable, although awkward.

It was the tragic death of their youngest son, Edward, that marked the end of the Garrards' time on Lennard Island. The little boy, only fourteen months old, ate a piece of lye, possibly mistaking it for sugar. Despite the dangerously rough weather, the Garrards launched their boat and took the agonized child to Dr. Raynor at the Methodist hospital on Mission Island—formerly Stockham Island—but it was too late. Edward lingered several days but died on January 17, 1908.

The Garrards left Lennard Island shortly after this, eventually settling in Tofino, where they built a house on one of the two waterfront lots they owned. Before becoming town-dwellers, the family lived for a period on Vargas Island, where they homesteaded on land Garrard acquired in partnership with Pierre Hovelaque, with whom he had worked on Lennard Island. There the Garrards cleared land, built cottages and planted a garden and fruit trees. Writing from Vargas on July 20, 1909, Garrard assured Walter Dawley, in reply to a reminder about his outstanding account of $123.55, "[I] hope to make the payment on the account shortly [and] will see you personally on the first opportunity." Garrard was already finding, as others would later discover, that attempting to farm on Vargas, or even to cultivate a market garden, was a daunting prospect.

Clayoquot Cannery, probably 1913–14.

Determined to overlook such gloomy practicalities, Garrard and Hovelaque had great plans for Vargas Island. Together they pre-empted and leased 1,280 acres of land and cooked up a scheme to attract settlers to the island. The two men became, in effect, the first large-scale property promoters in the Tofino area. They advertised in England for settlers to come to Vargas and managed to convince some thirty unsuspecting people that this was an ideal place to live. What these new arrivals thought when they finally landed by skiff on the empty beaches of Vargas can only be imagined, but they set out to do their best. Some of them came with their wives, but many were single men. "Mr Greiss told me that every inch of land on Vargas Island has been taken up," Father Frowin Epper wrote to Father Maurus on February 13, 1913, "and the land adjoining ours to the south has also been sold to an Englishman."

The settlers on Vargas cleared land, built houses and began trying to raise produce in the boggy, acidic soil. Hopes ran high, encouraged by comments in the lands inspector's report of 1914. Submitted to the Surveyor General, this report supposedly gave a realistic assessment of the area for the information of potential settlers. With suitable drainage, the inspector insisted, much of Vargas Island could be "brought under cultivation," for "the soil is rich and will grow almost anything." Concluding that "the island is very suitable for mixed farming on a small scale," the inspector went on to mention that there was a good trail across the island and that a wagon trail would soon be completed.

The part about the trail was true. Eventually, with the help of oxen to clear the way, a rough corduroy trail crossed Vargas Island, connecting Malon's Bay on the southeast side of the island with Open Bay on the west. An even rougher trail led to the homesteads on the north end of the island. Jacob Eby owned two of the Vargas oxen; he and these beasts make a brief, cameo appearance in Dawley's correspondence files, at the centre of a financial dispute. Writing from Port Alberni in April 1913, Mrs. F.M. Barnes, unfortunately entangled with Eby, appealed to Dawley for help:

> There is a man down your way named Jacob Eby. He undertook to stake some land for me on Vargas Island & whether intentionally or not he gave the wrong numbers & so the Govt have turned down my application. On the strength of this staking & promises to clear my land, he got me to lend him $200, for which I hold a mortgage on the pair of oxen. I have since heard some tales of him, not to his credit & as he has also since sent me two begging letters, I begin to feel a bit uneasy about my $200. I am a widow with three small children, & find money pretty hard to get. Please treat this as very confidential. I should

hate anyone to know that I had been such a fool as to part with cash so easily. I thought perhaps you would be able to prevent him selling the oxen & clearing out.

Dawley replied, advising Mrs. Barnes to register the mortgage. She wrote again in October, the matter still unresolved, asking if there were a constable at Clayoquot as she wanted Eby arrested. Dawley eventually negotiated to take over the mortgage on these two debt-ridden oxen; the fate of the elusive Eby remains a mystery.

At the northern end of Vargas Island, a settlement of sorts came into being on a small bay. This was Port Gillam, named in honour of Captain Edward Gillam who skippered both the *Tees* and the *Princess Maquinna*. Its appearance on the map was short-lived, the lifespan of its wharf even shorter. A number of Vargas settlers optimistically built this wharf in the winter of 1914; Father Charles noted the event in his diary. "Left Kakawis at midnight," he wrote on December 3, 1914. "Steamer had 15,000 ft of lumber on board for a new wharf on Vargas Isld. I reached Hesquiat at 6 PM." Although the wharf only lasted one season before a winter storm dashed it to pieces, the steamer called at Port Gillam for several years, and it was sufficiently important to be a scheduled stop. Its name appeared on printed steamer schedules in 1917 and 1918, the one port of call between Christie School and Ahousat. After 1918, Port Gillam disappeared from the maps and from the steamer schedules. By then, Vargas Island had changed greatly.

References to various Vargas Island settlers appear sporadically in Walter Dawley's correspondence: in a hurried note headlined "Vargas Island," Henry Hilton asked Dawley to "send by Don Forsythe a can of gasoline." Freeman Hopkins described working on the wharf at Port Gillam early in 1915. His wife later wrote to the Clayoquot store, giving her return address as "Port Gillam" and anxiously discussing her account. Several of these settlers did business with Dawley, and their accounts turn up regularly in his correspondence. Nonetheless, the Vargas people were a distinct and, in many ways, private group, set apart from the Tofino and Clayoquot scene by distance and by the nature of their settlement. "These settlers were definitely not of the moneyed class, possessing expensive power boats," commented Mike Hamilton in his memoirs. "Their only means of transportation was by lowly dugout canoe."

Some exploits of Vargas Islanders gained local renown. Fletcher Cleland and his wife managed to transport a horse and buggy to the west side of the island, to their home at Open Bay, where they went for genteel carriage rides up and down the long, sandy beach. And one dark morning, tall, strong Syd Price swam over a mile through the icy water, against the "adverse currents and whirl pools which tended to suck him under," after his canoe capsized in a whirlpool on an outgoing tide when he was en route to Clayoquot from Vargas. Mike Hamilton, who had just disembarked from the steamer on his very first trip up the coast to Clayoquot, walked up the long beach on Stubbs Island to recover from his seasickness and was just in time to witness Price emerging from the water like a bizarre vision. Hamilton watched him staggering up the beach towards the hotel. "[I was a] stranger in a strange land all alone on a vacant and uninhabited beach in the eerie predawn darkness, with a wet and bedraggled human form coming toward me… The man, as a man it was, staggered past me, mumbling to himself." A few days later, after being cared for at the hotel and provided with "hot blankets and… stimulants," Price was as fit as a fiddle.

By the time the Vargas settlers arrived in 1913, Frank Garrard was well established in Tofino with his family. There he continued, in his own words, "taking up land and by holding it for sale making some profitable transactions." Like many others in the district at that time and ever since, Garrard had a keen eye for property value, and his memoirs are punctuated by cryptic and at times unintelligible references to potential deals:

> We… cruised over some land which was, as we thought, open for purchase on the peninsula, but found on application that two of the plots were already taken up, but that one having been pre-empted had lapsed, owing to the party having left, and that on paying the valuation of the improvements, assessed at $100.00, the plot would be open to purchase.

The vocabulary and the logic of land tenure in the early twentieth century can seem bizarre today. Tracts of Crown land of up to 160 acres could be staked and pre-empted by people prepared to settle there and work on or "improve" the land. If improvements—generally meaning clearing part of the land, erecting buildings and fences, and trying to farm—met the approval of the lands inspectors who regularly visited the area, the land could be purchased cheaply by, or even granted to, the hard-working pre-emptor after a certain time had elapsed. Yet all too often, pre-emptions in remote locations lay unoccupied and abandoned after would-be settlers tried and failed to make a go of it as subsistence farmers or after they simply lost interest. This pattern was not unique to the west coast; the same improbable compulsion to settle and farm hostile tracts of land gripped many hopeful newcomers in many unlikely areas of British Columbia. They arrived with high expectations, sometimes with a cow or two, and almost always with no experience of the climate or terrain.

In the heady and hopeful years just before the Great War, such dreamers and schemers flocked to the frontiers in all parts of British Columbia seeking land. In retrospect, they seem to have been extraordinarily confident that development would follow them. They believed that if they paved the way, spread the word and set the pace, more settlers would surely throng to these remote areas in great numbers—followed by schools, farms, industry and roads. For some, everything worked out well, but others, like the Rae-Arthur family, were doomed to disappointment because they chose to settle in impossibly difficult locations. After living at Boat Basin, near Hesquiat, for six years, hoping all the while for others to join them, Ada Annie Rae-Arthur finally faced facts. In July 1921 she wrote to the Ministry of Education about her children's schooling:

Willie and Ada Annie Rae-Arthur arrived at their remote Boat Basin property in 1915 with three small children. In the following years, Ada Annie bore eight more children. The family cleared five acres of forest and struggled to make a living. Willie, pictured here in 1917, drowned in Hesquiat Harbour in 1936. Ada Annie remained on her isolated homestead, outlived three more husbands, and became known as "Cougar Annie."

I understand your department provides free education to the children of parents resident in isolated districts. My husband and self have for some years past been lone settlers here, and being the parents of six young children have continually hoped that more people with children might settle here so that a school might be established; however, as there appears to be no immediate prospect of this I shall be most thankful if you will arrange a Correspondence Course for my two elder children.

The Rae-Arthurs stubbornly remained at Boat Basin despite their isolation, despite the many problems of schooling. In the end, Ada-Annie outlasted all her family members and no fewer than four husbands, remaining on her property, tending her beloved garden, until she was in her mid-nineties. She gained renown as a grower of dahlias and as a cougar bounty hunter, but her hopes that "more people with children" might settle there proved hollow. No other settlers ever came to Boat Basin, and her life became increasingly solitary as she aged.

Capitalizing on such overwhelming passion for land, however inappropriate the land, developers and speculators enjoyed a heyday throughout the province in the early twentieth century. The politician John Oliver, who was later elected premier of the province, commented caustically on a rash of dubious land deals: "The speculators," he declared in 1912, "with the connivance of the government, sometimes get their land for a dollar and a drink and sometimes for a drink without the dollar."

Walter Dawley was no stranger to this kind of land dealing. He received numerous odd offers and requests from people interested in investing in land, any land at all, no matter where or what. In August 1912 he received a letter from Mr. A. R. Love, whose letterhead declared him to be involved in "Investments, Mining, Timber Etc." with a head office in Liverpool, England. Mr. Love claimed to represent "a considerable amount of English capital" and wished to obtain land rich in natural resources:

> I believe that in your position you are in touch with many people who either own or know of such property…I may say that the magnitude of any proposition is more or less immaterial; whether it be a thousand pounds or several million required for development purposed, providing the property stand inspection, the money will be forthcoming.

Even out at remote Hesquiat, with little or no interest in such worldly matters, Father Charles Moser could not help but notice the prevailing interest in acquiring land. On July 22, 1913, he disembarked from the steamer with "two shareholders of the Hesquiat Land Co. These latter were from Chicago, Ill." The following day he noted that "the Land Lords cruised around inspecting their holdings, till evening." Entirely incurious about these men and their business, Father Charles commented no further, and the "Land Lords" and their "Hesquiat Land Co." drift casually through his narrative, never to be seen again—rather like Mr. A. R. Love, from whom nothing more is heard in Walter Dawley's papers. Whatever the Hesquiat Land Company was, it left no readily discernible proof of its activities or even of its existence.

The hordes of settlers attracted to British Columbia between the mid-1890s and the beginning of the First World War were frequently ill prepared for their new lives. Some had been duped by well-oiled advertising campaigns extolling the thrilling future of many different places in the province. According to the historian Margaret Ormsby, in the years leading up to the war, Fort George (now Prince George) was hyped as the inland hub of no fewer than ten future railway lines; Kamloops was advertised as "the Los Angeles of Canada"; remote Stewart was "the Pacific's Treasure Chest." On Vancouver Island, the Quatsino Land and Improvement Company announced that Quatsino had a sure future as a major railway terminus. Residential lots could be purchased in this hopeful town for as little as fifty dollars, and in the near future "A Great Ocean Terminal" for trans-Pacific trade would be built. None of this ever happened. Similarly, property developers tried to lure settlers up to the dramatic isolation of Cape Scott, an area abandoned not long before by despondent Danish settlers who tried and failed to establish a farming colony there at the turn of the century. Now developers predicted a glittering future for the cape, proclaiming that it would soon be connected by railway to Nanaimo and become the marine "gateway to Alaska." Cape Scott remains the most inaccessible and isolated area of Vancouver Island to this day.

The promises of property developers and the high hopes of property seekers landed many people in awkward and uncomfortable situations. In December 1912, Father Charles Moser encountered two unknown men at Hesquiat, sitting disconsolately on a log, eating their lunch in gloomy silence. "I went up to them and found they had arrived by this morning's steamer looking for land but were disappointed. I invited them to my house. After sometime they came along and made their home with me waiting for the return of the steamer." Three days later, these men left on the southbound steamer. They had not bothered looking any further for land after their first encounter with the area. In similar fashion, Father Charles described one Mr. Wrotnowsky, who also arrived unannounced at Hesquiat, disembarking from the *Tees* at five in the morning on September 10, 1913. "Mr. Wrotnowsky is looking around the Hesquiat Peninsula with the idea or plan to establish a Russian Polish Colony." After a cursory visit, Stanislas Wrotnowsky promptly returned to the Alberni area, where he lived out his days, dying there in 1940. According to his obituary in the *West Coast Advocate*, he was "a deeply respected resident of this district...a gentleman of the old school, tall, dignified, loved and respected." He did briefly try to establish an "estate along the lines of the one he had left in Poland" on some land he acquired near Alberni, but the First World War disrupted this endeavour. His interest in wilderness land out near Hesquiat had been, at best, a brief folly.

> Reports from the West Coast of Vancouver Island are to the effect that Ucluelet is forging ahead. Every day inquiries come to the branch of the Development League regarding land and farming possibilities. Stump pulling is progressing, and the government workmen are clearing a roadway into the Long Beach district. Many survey parties are out. (*Victoria Daily Colonist*, May 17, 1913)

By 1913, work was at last underway on improving the trail between Ucluelet and Tofino. On January 11, the *Colonist* printed a petition sent to the minister of Public Works by citizens of Ucluelet, who claimed that the need for the road was indisputable: "We point out that the right-of-way is now practically impassable, and beg that the work of grading and ditching be proceeded with." The petitioners also asserted that some twenty-seven people made regular use of the existing trail, and they asked that the trail "be made passable for a vehicle" in anticipation of more settlers coming to the area.

An even greater ambition burned in the hearts of some local people, surpassing this desire for a local road connecting the two communities. They wanted a road through the mountains that would link the west coast to Alberni and thus to the rest of the island. The Clayoquot Sound branch of the Vancouver Island Development League supported this ambitious notion and in July 1913 presented a request to the deputy minister of Public Works for a road from Alberni to Long Beach. The horrified reply was that "the government had had the route surveyed and an estimate of cost got out, and that this reached the enormous sum of $732,000." The project was unthinkable.

The dream remained in limbo for decades, surfacing periodically in various campaigns and debates. "Boost for a Road—Yell for a Road!" trumpeted a pamphlet of the Tofino branch of the BC Good Roads League in the early 1920s, under the slogan "We Want Roads, We Want Settlers, We Want Advertising." The pamphlet pointed out Tofino's "need for a means of ingress and egress other than by sea," adding that when the road was finally constructed, people would be able to "drive over it in [their] auto along with the multitudes of nature lovers who will hasten to worship her in this, her last, grandest and most glorious playground of the west."

Such staggering effusions had little effect. The wait for a road went on and on and on. In 1913, no one dreamed that it would be 1959 before a rough gravel road finally linked Tofino and Ucluelet to Alberni. This was a time of limitless, cockeyed optimism about what could be achieved and what the future held. If local residents yelled for a road, the road would surely come, and come quickly.

The most cockeyed optimists of all on the coast—or perhaps the most cynical opportunists—were the creators of the West Coast Development Company. In 1913 this company launched its bizarre advertising campaign to entice people to the coast, where they could buy land at "absurdly easy prices" on the site of a development that was guaranteed to become "Canada's Only Real Pleasure

Resort." The location of this luxurious seaside paradise—which "outstrips in every feature Atlantic City"—was the beach between Carmanah lighthouse and the village of Clo-oose, one of the most forbidding stretches of coastline anywhere on Vancouver Island.

The declared aim was to attract settlers to come and live in bungalows on "beautifully treed lots, with rich deep soil, all of which are waterfront lots." They would work to establish a three-hundred–room resort of astonishing magnificence, linked to the outside world by a "motor road along the West Coast" and, eventually, by rail. The developers assured prospective settlers that a thriving community would quickly develop around the resort and that thousands of eager visitors were sure to pour in. Cargo ships would call regularly at the large steel pier, soon to be constructed, and this destination would become world famous. Purchasing the surveyed parcels of land was, of course, guaranteed to be a brilliant investment.

The promotional literature gushed with superlatives, describing the "long, deep beach of pure white sand sloping gently upwards to a belt of green woods" into which enchanting pathways beckoned. "Natural bowers and Lovers' Lanes invite the stroller from the heat of the sun to the cool fragrant shade of these Palaces of Nature." In these woods, the charmed explorer would be overcome with the scent of "wood violets" and "sweet-briar," while out on the beach, "rank after rank of deep green waves…curl and break with an avalanche of foam." Illustrated brochures described tennis courts and golf links, the elegant promenade, the opportunities for sea bathing and fishing and hunting game. Willowy ladies with parasols and gentlemen in straw boaters strolled along the "amusement pier" in one illustration; another featured a smiling lady in modest bathing dress ready to experience one of the heated medicinal pools; a publicity photograph showed a car on a well-built road hemmed in by huge trees.

There was, of course, no road—no resort, promenade nor pier. There would never be a golf links or tennis court; no Lovers' Lanes penetrated the rain forest, and not a single straw boater was in sight. Not even the weather could live up to the promises of the promoters. Descriptions of the "brightest warm suns, the bluest of blue skies; a blue and green sea tumbling, with acres of frothy foam, on a golden beach" with "just enough rain to keep things green and pleasant" were at best grossly misleading, as anyone knew who later stood in the grey unending deluges of rain, surrounded by the dismal tent city that scrambled into existence as the first unwary settlers arrived.

Settlers did arrive. The West Coast Development Company did sell parcels of land, mostly sight unseen, to optimistic and hopeful folk from near and far. These people came up the coast on the steamer from Victoria to be greeted by a flotilla of canoes. They watched in horror-struck amazement as everything they owned swung off the heaving steamer into the canoes. From the decks, straining to glimpse what awaited them, the newcomers could see—nothing. Some people turned tail and departed on the return boat. Others remained, bringing ashore their improbable possessions and hoping for the best. Grandfather clocks, pianos and damask linen eventually came to rest in the rough wooden cabins that were soon under construction, and one Royal Worcester tea set took up a position on shelves constructed within a tent frame. At its height, this settlement burgeoned to nearly two hundred people, a gallant band of families eking out a living as best they could, resolved to make the best of it.

The company folded, giving way to the equally dubious Canada Ocean Beach Resort Company. The resort idea, in one form or another, survived until about 1920, when a promoter of yet another development scheme offered to buy the settlers out. All the cheques bounced. Eventually the community dwindled to about twenty people, reduced as much by the First World War as by the death of the dream. During the war, thirty-one men from Clo-oose enlisted and went overseas; eleven were killed.

On Vargas Island, the effect of the First World War was equally dramatic. After it was all over, after the years of bloodshed and death in Europe allowed survivors to return and reclaim their lives, most Vargas Island homesteads lay deserted. In 1919, when Dorothy Abraham arrived from England and settled on Vargas with her husband, Ted, the isolation overwhelmed her.

> Before the war there had been as many as thirty people living on the island, but none came back except my husband, and it was very pathetic to come across little clearings and houses with desolate gardens, which had been laid out with such care and hard labour… There were no other people on the island except the Indians and… one white man, and, although I am not vain, no one to see all my nice English trousseau, unless we went over to Tofino or Clayoquot.

Such a deserted landscape was more than Dorothy Abraham bargained for: "No fields! No grass! No people! No anything!" she exclaimed with horror, recalling those early days in her book *Lone Cone*.

> The awful loneliness of it all frightened me. I am not a very timid sort of person… but this was a loneliness unknown and unheard of. My heart sank… The only sign of life to be seen from the house was the

Beach picnic, Vargas Island, 1911.

Roman Catholic Mission on Mears Island, three or four miles across the water, and at night their light seemed such a friendly sign. I used to watch for it, and wonder if all my life...I would only have that light to look at.

Had Dorothy Abraham been on Vargas before the war, she would have known other homesteaders, the sense of a community building itself up, working towards a common purpose. The war changed all that completely and forever.

In Frank Garrard's memoirs, when he recalled the busy, halcyon days before the war, he described one golden September afternoon in 1913. The occasion was a community picnic at Garrards Beach (now called Mackenzie Beach) near Tofino:

> On the 1st of September which being Monday this year, was a holiday, Labour day...a cricket match was played on the beach and a picnic held, the people of Tofino, Clayoquot & Vargas taking part; I saw then for the first time, Charlie Dixson, also Arthur Park, both of whom I next saw after their return from the war; although there were many at that picnic who went overseas and some who never returned.

At this carefree picnic, energetic young men played cricket on the beach while the ladies served tea, and the Union Jack, mounted on a drift log, fluttered overhead.

Less than a year later, war was declared. A long shadow fell over the entire world. The west coast of Vancouver Island did not escape the shadow.

— 15 —

Writing Under Difficulties

September 19, 1916

WT Dawley Esq
Clayoquot BC

Dear Friends:
The parcel received a few days ago and very thankful for the same. Every article came in very handy especially tobacco pipe and Mr Johnston's safety razors…Please give him my thanks for same…We're having a great time of it at presant driving the Huns back to where they belong. Our Batt has been kept busy but we dont growl as long as everything is going in our favour as it is in the meantime. Well we will be all glad when it's all over & back to God's Country again.

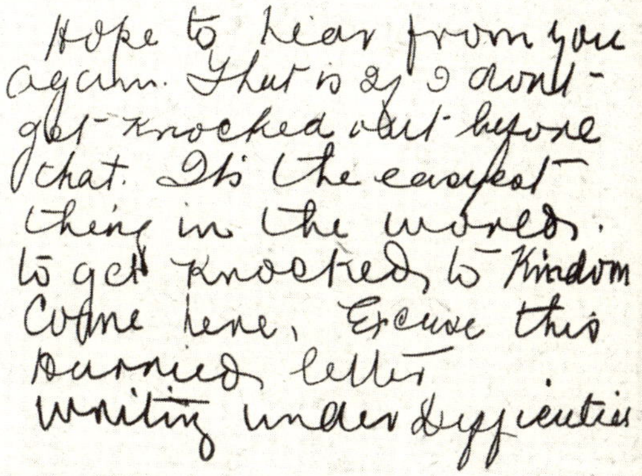

WRITING FROM AN unspecified location in France, Murdo MacLeod's letter is barely legible, written hurriedly in pencil on small sheets of paper. It concludes soberly:

No use in me saying any more about it as you can see by the papers more than I can tell. Anyhow I hope to live to see you & have a yarn about some of my experience since I left…Hope to hear from you again. That is if I dont get knocked out before that. It's the easyest

259

thing in the world to get knocked to Kindom [Kingdom] Come here. Excuse this hurried letter. Writing under difficulties. Best wishes to all on the Old Island.

I remain as ever yrs sincerely
Corp M MacLeod
154471 A Corp
1st Can Pioneers
1st Can Division
Army PO, France

"It will be no good trying to relate the effects of the war on us," Frank Garrard commented woodenly in his memoirs. He wrote of the war years in a disjointed, almost forced manner, markedly different from his fluent descriptions of happier, earlier activities—of rowing to Lennard Island or fixing the telegraph line or grounding his boat in the mud flats on a falling tide. The war did not allow such unshadowed recollection.

From the outset, the town of Tofino was on edge. Garrard noted that "at the beginning of the war, there seemed to be a considerable amount of distrust as between the Norwegians & the British element at Tofino, but later on after hearing of the sinking of many Norwegian vessels by the Germans, the former seemed to view matters more from the Canadian point of view."

The Garrard family solidly supported the war effort. Lilly Garrard went overseas as a nurse, and both Burdett and Noel Garrard signed up. Scattered through Garrard's memoirs of this time are the names of various other young men who enlisted:

> There were the two Abraham brothers, Arthur & Ted...there also was Cleland, Hopkins brothers, Price, who never should have been accepted as he was terribly short sighted, in fact nearly all the population of Vargas either joined up or were represented by one or more of the family. As regards Tofino, those of British blood who were single and eligible all enlisted before conscription was instituted.

The young men who enlisted from Tofino, Vargas Island and the Clayoquot Sound area included Harold Monks, who in his attestation papers described himself as a rancher, resident of Port Gillam. Charlie Dixson, the doctor's son, enlisted, as did Harold Sloman, Joseph Grice, Thomas Howard Evans, Arthur Park, Frederick Tibbs, Murdo MacLeod, John MacLeod and police constable Robert A. Beavan. Freeman Hopkins and his brother Frank Elliott Hopkins

Censor and field post office stamps on letters from Ray Brewster to his family.

from Vargas Island both enlisted, leaving behind their young wives, Esther and Lillian. Fletcher Cleland's wife also stayed behind on Vargas when he enlisted, along with Helen Carolan, whose son Allan enlisted, and Helen Malon, mother of Ted and Arthur Abraham. According to Harold Monks, recalling events in later years, as many as thirteen men enlisted from Vargas, including Frederic Sydney Price.

From Ahousat, Jack Ross, son of the Presbyterian minister, enlisted, as did John and Andy Thornberg and young Freddie Thornberg too, when he was only sixteen. From Tofino there were the Garrard boys, Burdett and Noel, and Harry Harris, Clarence Drader, Gerald Lane and Arvo Haikala. Donald Forsythe enlisted, and his brother William, who worked at Clayoquot Cannery and in his attestation papers described his occupation as "Gentleman."

Raymond Brewster signed up. He was the son of the Clayoquot Cannery owner and politician Harlan Brewster, who became the first Liberal premier of British Columbia in 1916. Harlan Brewster died in office after only fifteen months, and Raymond heard of his father's death while he was at training camp in England. He wrote to his two little sisters on receiving this news, trying to lift their spirits. The letter, written on notepaper headed "Salvation Army Recreation and Reading Room for his Majesty's Troops," came from an indecipherable location in Surrey.

April 8, 1918

Dear Marjorie and Nan:
How are Ray's two little sweethearts to-night. Hope you are both feeling well and strong…Well dears I expect to be away to France before very long now, probably about a week. I'll try and catch a nice little Kaiser for you…

Tel Auntie that if she is sending a parcel sometime, that I would like to have some date cookies or cakes, a fruit cake, and some sugar.

I must close for to-night dears, as I have to be up at 5:30 in the morning. With heaps of love.

Your brother, Ray xx oo

The fate of most of these soldiers can be traced in the official records of the First World War. The names and statistics can be amassed, scraps of information pieced together and a roll call created. Killed in action: Arthur Abraham, Raymond Brewster, Donald Forsythe, Joseph Grice, Arvo Haikala, John MacLeod, Frederic Sydney Price. Burdett Garrard's papers state that he was "invalided back to Canada for further medical treatment"; Murdo MacLeod, Fletcher Cleland and William Forsythe were wounded in action. The list carries on, names tolling like a bell. Every community in Canada can produce comparable lists, names enshrined on cenotaphs that would later accommodate yet more names from the war of 1939–45. Every name represents a world of personal experience, an individual wealth of story, much of which has been almost obliterated by the passing of time. And yet, in a handful of surviving documents, a few strands of a few of the stories of these men from Clayoquot can be traced. The information in these documents may be partial and fragmented, but it is unquestionably powerful.

"How does the war affect you over there?" wrote Mr. D. W. Gardiner to Walter Dawley from his home in Kalama, Washington, on August 21, 1914. "It is fierce [isn't] it and altogether wrong, hope the US does not get mixed up in it…It seems to me a terrible thing for one man to send thousands to certain slaughter which is the case when attacking a fort like Liege Belgium." Some months later, Gardiner again wrote to Dawley, asking, "Has anyone enlisted in the war from Clayoquot?"

Young men who had optimistically invested in land or prospecting gear or motor launches wrote to Dawley wondering what to do. "Dear Mr Dawley," wrote Arthur Park from Friendly Cove in September 1914. "What do you think of the present crisis. I am thinking seriously of offering my services for the front." A year earlier, Park had been seeking work, offering to carry freight for the Nootka store in his motor launch. The storekeeper there, Thomas Gardhouse, scotched the idea. "I don't think he would care for the job," he wrote to Dawley, adding darkly, "Park likes the liquor when he gets a chance." But now Park was heading overseas and asking Dawley's advice on practical matters. "Its kind of puzzling me what to do with the launch…What do you think yourself?"

In a similar vein, a letter arrived from Clarence Drader, signing himself C. Wilbert A. Drader, in May 1915. "Are you buying any land now," he wrote, "and if so can you make an offer on my place out there?…if I could get it off my hands right away I think I would go to the war." Drader, who was secretary of the Clayoquot Development League, went to the war shortly afterward.

Arvo Haikala, once employed at the Clayoquot Cannery, had already been killed in action by this time. One of the six thousand Canadian casualties at Ypres, he died in April 1915. Eino Haikala, Arvo's father or brother, left Clayoquot and wrote to Dawley a few times from other locations, discussing the

Harold Monks of Vargas Island, writing a letter from overseas.

mortgage Dawley held on his land. The following spring the Haikala family, back on the west coast, was destitute and receiving relief grocery vouchers at Walter Dawley's store.

In January 1916, without settling his outstanding bill at Walter Dawley's store, Gerald Lane enlisted. Lane had been working at the Clayoquot Cannery and cheerfully living on credit. Dawley angrily demanded payment of his account, but to no effect: "When you came to me pleading for permission to obtain goods…" he wrote to Lane, "you stated that money was on its way to you from the Old Country and that you would not fail to pay immediately on receipt. Why have you not kept your word for as a man of honour…"

Arthur Park wrote to Walter Dawley only once from overseas, a remarkably detailed letter, undated and written in pencil:

> Dear Mr Dawley
> No doubt you will have noticed in the papers of our arrival in France. We have been out here about five weeks and have received our baptism of fire. You will remember young Burden the surveyor who was in Clayoquot a nephew of Burden of Preen Bros and Burden, he received a compound fracture below the knee, it is rather a bad fracture, & is liable to keep him hors de combat for the rest of the war. So we rather think he is fortunate in a way. Woodward the fellow who was in the same part of the trench as Burden received wounds from the same shot (shrapnell) from which he died the following day. Our Sargent Major Jack Marshall was the first in our Squadron to get killed he received a bullet wound through the heart.

In this vivid letter, Park described life in the trenches: the cold, the exhaustion, the dark, the rats, the mud, the deaths—and the thirst:

> Water is very scarce in this part of the country where we are. A water bottle in two weeks is all I have been able to rustle & it isn't much good at that. The tea they dose with chloride of lime & the first time I had a drink of it I thought the Germans had been there before me. Well things are quiet around here just now Mr Dawley but rumor says there's going to be something doing soon. Nootka would look good to me right now.

Park closed with polite regards to the Dawley family, added that he had heard from "Anderson of Vargas," who was in hospital in England, and asked Dawley to give Cleland his kind regards.

Fletcher Cleland had been home for some time, having been wounded in action in the summer of 1915. The *Victoria Daily Colonist* noted his return with approving comments about Cleland's undampened military ardour: "He has no complaint to make except that it should be his luck to have been a victim of the enemy's fire within a few weeks of the time he made his 1st visit to the advanced trenches. Like the majority of Canada's volunteer soldiers now serving their Empire, Sgt Cleland looks on the brightest side of the situation."

Freeman Hopkins also wrote to Walter Dawley from overseas. His letters focused almost exclusively on his account with Dawley and various financial arrangements. Small matter that Hopkins had gone marching off to war in another country—back home, Dawley wanted to make sure his outstanding bills were paid, and he determinedly held Hopkins, and his wife, accountable.

Immediately after her husband departed, the unfortunate Esther Hopkins, left behind on Vargas Island, had to deal directly with Walter Dawley. Until then her husband had been the business correspondent, and Freeman Hopkins was untroubled by Dawley's abrasive manner. He left for training camp in England, blithely promising Dawley that his wife would do all her business at his store and that Dawley would receive regular payments from her toward their bill.

Unidentified soldiers. Ray Brewster sent this photograph to his sisters. He never returned home.

> Port Vargas, Vargas Island
> May 9, 1916
>
> Dear Sir:
> In view of my husband Mr Freeman Hopkins joining the Canadian Expeditionary Forces I desire to confirm the arrangement he has made with you viz: That I pay to you the sum of $20.00 per month out of my Husband's pay until I shall receive the allowance due to wives and families of married men in service when I shall pay cash for all goods had by me and still continue to pay the $20.00 per month in addition until the debt owing is liquidated.
>
> Yours Truly,
> Mrs Freeman Hopkins

Dawley was soon in conflict with the young Mrs. Hopkins. Even though she was isolated and without a boat over on the north end of Vargas Island, he insisted that their arrangement obliged her to deal exclusively at his store. Esther, in need of groceries, courageously pleaded her case in a letter dated August 11, 1916, this time giving her address as Port Gillam rather than Port Vargas—the Vargas settlers may have used the terms interchangeably during the brief life of the community. Esther pointed out that to reach Dawley's store she would have to hire a motor launch, and she indicated she found his demands unreasonable. "While I don't blame you, Mr Dawley, for making an effort to hold all my future cash trade," she concluded, "I hope you will see the matter from my point of view in securing my groceries in a more convenient manner. I trust you will pardon me."

This letter did nothing to appease Dawley. He immediately wrote to Freeman Hopkins in England, and a hastily written note came back in response. "A few hurried lines to ask you not to bother Mrs Hopkins, about how (now that I am transferred to the Imperial Army) you are to be paid the $20.00 per mo. as I am making arrangements & you will be settled in due course."

On September 10, 1916, Hopkins replied more fully, this time on YMCA letterhead, impressively decorated with sketches of wheeled cannons, bearing the declaration "H.M. Forces on Active Service" and the slogan "For God, For King, and For Empire" at the top of the page. Hopkins reassured Dawley, "I have written Mrs Hopkins that it is my wish that she should continue to deal with you," and added that his wife may have been "induced by others in this respect." Hopkins added news of men from Clayoquot:

> Jerry Lane & Harry Harris are now over in France in the thick of it I expect by this time. John McLeod, Beaven & also a fellow who used to be purser on the Tees is still in camp here…tomorrow my bro. & self leave this camp for London en route for Messopatamia sailing about the 21st inst. We were examined by the Imperial Doctors this morning… & passed as fit to go forward.

Back on Vargas Island, Esther Hopkins was not entirely alone in her struggles with Walter Dawley. The spirited Helen Carolan drew his ire by attempting to set up a small store on the island to serve her fellow settlers. Dawley heard of this through his supplier Kelly Douglas, in a letter dated December 8, 1915: "We have further inquiry from Mrs H. Carolan…who proposes to open up a Grocery business on Vargas Island. We are under the impression that this is in your district and will be pleased to hear from you regarding the proposed venture."

Helen Carolan persisted with this notion, at least for a while, and in February 1916 Dawley heard again from one of his suppliers that "the idea of the Vargas store still seems in the air." Meanwhile, Mrs. Carolan coolly disputed her bill with Dawley. A copy of his angry reply survives amongst his papers, dated June 20, 1916. In his opening salvo, Dawley pointed out that Mrs. Carolan failed to place a two-cent war stamp on her latest cheque, which meant she had broken the law. He continued:

> Re balance of Store bill. Your request is not a very reasonable one seeing how long I have waited for a settlement... Re: Oars and oarlocks in boat returned. You say "Do you wish me to pay for them and then give them back to you?" You probably consider this smart repartee but it is beside the question and such as I hardly expected from a lady of your refinement and education. You know quite well I never asked you to give me back anything you have paid for... I feel sure on reflection you will regret the tone of your letter.

The dispute between the two carried on over a two-year period, during which time Helen Carolan left Vargas for Victoria. She kept up payments on the mortgage held by Dawley on the Hopkins brothers' property, eventually offering to buy out the entire mortgage. Dawley continued to demand payment of her overdue account and finally threatened to involve his solicitors. In her final letter to him, written in August 1917, both the mortgage and the bill remained unresolved. Maintaining that some items on the bill were not hers but belonged to "the boys," probably the Hopkins brothers, Mrs. Carolan then lashed out at Dawley for the tone of his comments about the boys: "I have just got your letter about the boys account and I would express a hope that the time when they will be home will not be 'indefinite'. They <u>will</u> be home if they are spared and they will pay your bill." She offered to settle up part of the bill on behalf of her son Allan, adding, "It is only a trifle anyway and not worth all the talk but it is not right for me to pay it as you must know."

Another woman targeted by Dawley to settle her debt was Bertha Beavan, the wife of Robert Arthur Beavan, the provincial constable who worked at Clayoquot before the outbreak of war. Beavan and his brother Walter both enlisted early in 1916, leaving their wives, Bertha and Annie Louise, living together at the same address in Victoria. The improvident Robert Beavan instructed his wife to handle a debt he incurred much earlier at Dawley's store, but she had health problems and wrote to Dawley to explain her predicament. His reply has survived.

June 14, 1916

> Dear Madam: I was sorry to hear you have been so unwell as to necessitate your going into the hospital but I hope you will soon be well again. I have received a letter...from which I gather you propose to pay the hospital expenses before you pay anything to me. If my surmise is correct I hope you will see the injustice of such a proposal. I have waited patiently for nearly three years...I certainly feel I ought to impress upon you that I expect to be paid first.

Ten dollars came with Mrs. Beavan's next letter, and more explanation and apology. Dawley wrote again on July 16, 1916. "I should have considered it a great favour if when you were aware the account had been started you had then told me I should not continue to give your husband credit. However I am pleased you have made a beginning and trust you will continue to pay regularly." Over a year later, in November 1917, the account was still unpaid. Mrs. Beavan wrote once more, again enclosing ten dollars, "which is the best I can do," she explained, continuing:

> There is much I would like to say in connection with this. But is useless. Except to let you know that I did not approve of our running a bill with you & much prefer paying ready money at any time & I consider you did a very unwise thing to do knowing my Husband as you did. I had no voice in the matter. Mrs Dawly will tell you as I used to speak to her about it & tell her how badly I felt about it.

Murdo MacLeod's war correspondence with Dawley is untainted by the aggravation of unpaid bills. The MacLeod brothers, Murdo, Alex and Ewan, were all familiar with Dawley; they had been on good terms with him ever since their arrival in Tofino. Along with an unrelated John MacLeod and a cousin John MacLeod, a good number of MacLeod boys lived in Tofino prior to the war. In 1913, when Ewan moved to Hope, east of Vancouver, in search of work on the railroad, he wrote excitedly to Dawley, advising him to buy land and to invest in a mine near Hope, and concluding, "Have they started the Telegraph line to Nootka yet. Do you still have Conserv meetings and how is business in general looking there. When are you going to send me my title for my Clayoquot lot?...I trust you will keep the MacLeod boys in order there and dont let them drink too much boose. Regards to all and yourself and family."

Fond memories of the MacLeod boys drinking a good deal of "boose" emerged in Murdo's first letter to Dawley from overseas:

> Hounslow Heath Brks
> January 8, 1916
>
> Dear Friend:
> Just a note to let you know that I'm living & in good health wishing you & family are the same also that you enjoyed Xmas & N Year per usual. Was thinking Christmas Night of the good old time we had the last two Xmas. Good many miles from there this year, might be further next year…couldn't say how long we are going to be here, not very long by the looks of things…you will understand we can't say nothing about matters even if we new…How is times up at Clayoquot, did old John Grice visit you at Christmas & N Year. How all the boys doing. Give my wishes to Clarence & wife. Tell him I'll write him next. I haven't much news but would like to hear some. Remember me to Mrs Dawley and the family…
>
> Yours sincerely
> Murdo MacLeod

On October 8, 1916, Murdo MacLeod was wounded in action at Courcelette during the protracted agony of the Battle of the Somme. The *Colonist* picked up his story in an article dated November 23, by which time he was in hospital in England. "In a letter to his brother, Mr. Ewan MacLeod, of Lytton, BC, he gives particulars as to the nature of his wounds and states that he is getting first class treatment and consideration from the British Red Cross. He was wounded in the face at Courcelette. Parts of his nose and upper lip are shot away and his lower lip and chin are badly split. Corporal MacLeod left with the First Canadian Pioneers Battalion and had been in the trenches about seven months when he was wounded in action."

Nearly a year later, Murdo MacLeod wrote to Frank Garrard from a hospital in Orpington, England, where he was having what he termed a "plastic" operation. He had just seen Lilly Garrard, working as a nursing sister there, and he had also seen Noel Garrard, who was visiting his sister while on leave:

> What a surprise I got when I met Lilly, didn't know she was over on this side of the water, was awful glad to meet them, Noel stayed one night and we compared notes on various subjects, you may be sure, some of them very thrilling at least it seems that way now as we have

time to reflect over the past couple of years…met another Clayoquot-sound man here wounded for the 3rd time (slightly) Bill Forsythe, late of the Hatchery, heard Price from Vargas Is and Joe Lomp were killed some time ago.

Frederic Sydney Price died at Vimy Ridge in the bright air of April 1917, one of the nearly 3,600 soldiers from Canada killed at the same place and time. According to Mike Hamilton, Price had "hardly got to…France when he was killed by an enemy bullet." Joseph Lomp, a one-time sealer, had been mate on Captain Peppett's sealing schooner, the *Umbrina*. When he went to war in 1916, he left most of his personal effects in Walter Dawley's care and gave Dawley power of attorney over his affairs, agreeing that his wages from the lifeboat crew would go to Dawley to pay off his outstanding bill. Joe Lomp never returned to Clayoquot.

Although seriously injured, Murdo MacLeod survived. Douglas Dixson, the Tofino doctor, noted the fate of another of the MacLeod boys in his diary in September 1917: "John McLeod drowned in Tigris." Dixson's diary is a messy collection of jottings, mostly about his work, but the war intrudes repeatedly. He mentions the names of men who have enlisted and indicates when he received letters from, or sent parcels to, his son Charlie, fighting in Belgium, and when he received in the mail a "map of war area." In May 1916, Dixson commented in his diary that a recruiting officer had been visiting the area and that he left on the *Tees* with new recruits. "Recruiting officer—2 Hopkins, Cleland, J Martin, Todd left by boat."

Word of this visit also appears in Walter Dawley's papers. On May 5, 1916, Dawley received a telegram from Captain B. J. Scharschmidt announcing that a recruiting officer would shortly arrive on board the *Tees*. In response, the captain received a telegram from Dawley, dated May 6: "About six possible recruits but doubtful if worth while recruiting officers time and expense in coming." This discouraging communiqué is signed merely "Postmaster."

Viewed from the blinkered perspective of Walter Dawley's correspondence, the First World War was a decided irritant. He was displeased that he could not obtain any khaki overalls, although his supplier, James Thomson, explained that "owing to the present demand for goods of this nature by the Militia it is impossible to get anything in Khaki colour." Soon even wool socks and underwear became rarities. "Dear Dawley," Mr. Thomson wrote. "You possibly have little idea of how merchandise is, we are now forced to buy wool hose, underwear etc in USA working socks would scare you the prices asked."

One after the other, such letters arrived from suppliers, showing the effects of war. Some even took the trouble to inform Dawley of impending problems. The sales representative for the Remington Arms company warned, in February 1915, that "there will be an advance in the factory cost on all makes of loaded shot shells in Canada and have no doubt the wholesaler will advance their price accordingly." Even more seriously, from Dawley's point of view, the fur market was totally disrupted. Buyer Alfred Fraser in New York replied to Dawley's query about sealskin prices on October 2, 1915: "In reply to your enquiry as to the market price, I would state that as the market in London is so disorganized by the War, I regret I am unable to make any quotations whatever."

In Clayoquot Sound, the Kalappa mine went into liquidation, as did the Rose Marie. Bad debts became ever more difficult to collect. Take the Ptarmigan mine account—what could be done when virtually everyone concerned had enlisted? Recalling the mine in his memoirs, Mike Hamilton described how the outbreak of war "caused a complete halt to all activities; all the valuable material, stores and equipment were abandoned. No one was left to prevent theft of the material so everyone helped themselves and in a short time there was nothing left but great spools of steel cable." Dawley received a despairing letter from Mr. H.A. Round, on Ptarmigan Mines letterhead, dated October 28, 1915:

> The position is extraordinary, all the directors from the Chairman down, the engineers and in fact many of the shareholders, are with the Army at the "front." The Secretary writes me that it is impossible to get any authority for any action so matters are at a stand still. I should be only too pleased to assist you if in my power but when I tell you that I have received no salary for seven months you will readily understand the situation.
>
> As you say everyone feels the effects of this terrible war, but I feel sure that all the obligations of my company will be met at the earliest possible opportunity.

Following the flurry of letters about his wife's shopping rights, Freeman Hopkins wrote only once more to Dawley, a letter dated June 3, 1917, with his location given simply as "Persia." The paper is shredded and stained on one side, and the writing, in faded purple pencil, is difficult to decipher. Hopkins asked about his account at the store, hoping it was now paid off, and reported that "in spite of the damnable hot weather" he felt fit, adding:

> Can you give me any news of the boys that have left Tofino & Clayoquot for the Front? Hear Monks is thinking of joining up, if not already gone?…When is this war going to finish, as I am ready for home-sweet-home (not the only one, eh?) If I return safely would like to get a job as Homestead Inspector. Hear old McIntosh has joined up, how does he look in uniform? should judge he would look out of place.

Hopkins was referring to Donald Mackintosh, another Vargas Island pre-emptor, and a man well known to both Dawley and Hopkins. He was the uncle of the Forsythe boys, Donald and William, both of whom had signed up. In September 1917, Dawley received the following letter from Mackintosh:

> Dear Mr Dawley:
> No money yet. If you are in Victoria next month I will call and I think I will be able to satisfy you that the thing will be all right eventually…
>
> Yours Faithfully,
> D Mackintosh.
>
> P.S. My poor nephew Don was killed and Willie badly wounded the second time.

Such brief, bleak glimpses of the reality of war recur throughout Dawley's correspondence. The comments are usually terse, the full stories left untold, but they combine to reveal how the small, self-absorbed world of Clayoquot was drawn into the teeming tragedy of the Great War.

"I suppose you are looking for a German ship to land in Clayoquot any time," wrote Clarence Dawley to his brother at the beginning of the war, "what do you think of it?" No one can say what Walter Dawley thought. He never said. He filed his letters neatly away while a handful of boys from the west coast of Vancouver Island struggled through the appalling realities facing them overseas. None would have argued with Arthur Park's comment that "Nootka would look good to me right now," or with Murdo MacLeod's "Well we will be all glad when it's all over & back to God's Country again." They all knew, as MacLeod put it, "It's the easyest thing in the world to get knocked to Kindom Come here." Any one of them could have appeared, could still appear, in a brief comment in a letter addressed to Walter Dawley telling of yet another local boy who would not come home.

Father Charles Moser almost completely ignored the First World War in his diary. His only detailed comment, throughout the war years, came on August 7, 1914: "News reached me today by telephone of the sinking of 19 German battleships and six Brittish ones." While the world geared up for war that month, Father Charles tranquilly took note of the death of Pope Pius X, commented that he was alone at Hesquiat when everyone else was at the canneries, butchered a big cow, started major repairs on the church and recorded small personal triumphs. "I am 40 years old today," he wrote on August 25. "I discovered on a small tree a great big apple, the first fruit since planting the trees in spring 1911. Oh how I was glad to look at this apple."

Such lack of comment about the war in no way reflects the reaction within the Indian communities Father Charles supposedly knew so well. According to the *Daily Colonist* of August 16, 1914, native leaders' response to the outbreak of war was swift and interested: "Mr CA Cox, Indian Agent for West Coast of Vancouver Island, stated yesterday that the leading men of a number of West Coast tribes, at present in Victoria, have expressed their desire to be allowed to serve the Empire at this crisis, and offer to send numbers of their younger men if called upon. The tribes represented are the Kyuquots, Nootka, Ahousats and Ehattisahts."

According to Fred Gaffen in his book *Forgotten Soldiers*, some 3,500 native men from across Canada enlisted for active service in the First World War. Other estimates put the figure over 4,000, but given the imperfect nature of the records, Gaffen and other sources all acknowledge that such statistics, along with details of the enlisted men, are impossible to ascertain, at least in part because when these men signed up, their ancestry was not specified—they were described simply as "Canadian." While most of these native soldiers came from Ontario and the prairie provinces, Gaffen estimates that several hundred came from British Columbia. Records indicate that individual soldiers enlisted from various coastal villages, specifically Alert Bay, Port Simpson and Metlakatla; villages on the west coast of Vancouver Island are not in evidence.

As the war continued, however, the *Colonist* reported that west coast Indians showed support for this distant conflict by fundraising, if not by enlisting. Indian Agents across Canada encouraged fundraising efforts on reserves for the

Canadian Patriotic Fund. According to a publicity leaflet in Dawley's papers, this fund was "to provide assistance for wives and families of [those] who have volunteered for active service at the front."

Early in 1917, a publicity campaign for the fund was launched on Indian reserves. Posters distributed across the country featured a hawk-faced Indian chief sternly displaying a letter written by Chief Moo-chew-eines from Onion Lake, Saskatchewan. This elderly chief had donated $150 of his own money to the Patriotic Fund, and in his letter, reproduced on the poster both in Cree syllabics and in English, the chief wrote, "I heard there was a big war going on over there; I feel like I want to help." The banner headline on the poster said, "Pale Face, My Skin is Dark but My Heart is White, for I also give to the Canadian Patriotic Fund." The response to this campaign came mostly from the prairie provinces, but the natives of Clayoquot Sound also responded. On the Ucluelet reserve, a concert at the Indian school raised $68.55 in March 1917, and "Indians and white settlers attended in large numbers," according to the newspaper. Not to be outdone, the Clayoquot band "collected and forwarded to Patriotic Fund headquarters the sum of $121.75" in December 1917. On some reserves in Canada, many hundreds and even thousands of dollars were raised, and across the country, natives contributed a total of $44,000 to the fund.

As the war continued, Father Charles persisted in taking no notice. During most of the war years he was at Hesquiat, preoccupied with affairs in the village, until he unwillingly left to go to Christie School in 1917. In the summer of 1918 he enjoyed a brief respite from the escalating troubles at the school, for this proved to be an unusually mellow period at Kakawis. The days passed peacefully, marked by mild excitements such as the arrival of the first case of canned whale meat from the Kyuquot whaling station, the butchering of a fat cow at Bear River and by the news that the sisters would stay at Kakawis, despite earlier talk that they would all return to Mount Angel.

In early August 1918, Father Charles travelled to Comox to relieve the resident priest, remaining there for two weeks and in his spare time copying out Father Brabant's English/Indian dictionary—"from I to N inclusive," he declared with some pride. After a few days in Victoria, Father Charles headed up the coast once again. Among his hundred or more fellow travellers on board the *Princess Maquinna* were Mr. Ruck from the whaling station at Kyuquot, many Indians returning to Ahousat from the canneries, and Mr. H. Brodie. Employed by the CPR, Brodie was an inspector, making the round trip from Victoria to

Port Alice to assess the commercial efficiency and the tourist potential of the route. His report on this particular trip leaves no detail unobserved:

> The ship was scheduled to leave Victoria at 11:00 PM. She carried a full cargo, which included a partial deck load of lumber and machinery, also considerable iron piping and oil drums. There were about fifty Indians returning from the…canneries to their homes on the West Coast. They carry a large assortment of baggage, including blankets, mats, pots, pans and other cooking utensils. The entire family moves, including the smallest infant and the youngest dog. They take their position between decks and proceed to squat down amongst their effects, making themselves as comfortable as possible, and, Indian fashion, taking everything as it comes. The fact that half a dozen cows are in a pen close by makes little or no difference. A heavy mail delayed the departure and we did not cast off until midnight.

Brodie and Father Charles likely exchanged few, if any, words on this trip. Father Charles rarely expressed interest in his fellow passengers unless they had matters of mutual interest or a good card game to share, and Brodie was far too busy for any social distractions: he bustled around the ship, taking notes, recording details, verifying data with the captain and timing every arrival and departure on his pocket watch.

At Tofino, Brodie commented on the "large fleet of small gasoline fishing boats," and at Clayoquot he noted the "old hotel and general store" without much enthusiasm. Farther along the steamer route, he watched a boat landing at Kakawis, and here Brodie was even less enthusiastic. "This is an Indian school, and we landed nails and provisions," he wrote in his report. "The work among the Indians is not, so far as we can learn, very successful. They very soon fall back into their old ways once the children return to their parents."

That an outsider should comment so dismissively on the shortcomings of Christie School would have been a bitter pill for Father Charles to swallow. Word was spreading about difficulties at the school, but even in the privacy of his own diary, Father Charles barely articulated these problems. Still, his brief comments continue to bear witness to the distressing events that had become commonplace at the school. Earlier in 1918 there had been a spate of runaways.

> *February 7, 1918:* Policeman brought Sennen (from Opitsat) back to school.

> *February 8:* Sennen ran away again after 4 PM.

February 14: Policeman brought back Sennen for the second time, also Dan. In the evening around 8 o'clock Policeman brought a third boy back to school.

"Trouble again," Father Charles wrote on March 3, giving no details. "The whole house unruly." In April, he commented more fully on a disturbance.

April 17, 1918: A big boy got into trouble…Ted [Schindler, brother of Father Joseph] was supposed to give him a whipping but the boy refused to take it and attacked Ted. A fight issued and the boy no doubt got enough of it. This happened just before supper, during which but especially afterwards the rest of the big boys were very excited, unruly and warlike.

Unloading freight from the *Maquinna* at Ahousat, 1919.

Mr. Brodie probably knew none of this disturbing detail; he simply dismissed the entire notion of having such a school as "not...very successful" and swept on up the coast aboard the *Princess Maquinna* without giving the school a second thought. From his viewpoint, the place had no potential, either commercially or as a tourist destination.

Father Charles also continued northbound: his destination was Hesquiat. First, though, came the stop at Ahousat, which Mr. Brodie found most enjoyable.

> This is a very beautiful spot, the village being on a curved beach. The majority of our Indians disembarked at this point. It is very interesting disembarking them, as they are all handled in dugouts. These come along side of the ship, which anchors in the bay. The Indians pile into the dugouts, baggage, men, women, children, dogs, pots, pans, etc etc. Among other things there were small cook stoves, stove pipe, hats, strips of oil cloth and all sorts of paraphernalia. It took about an hour to disembark all the Indians, and we weighed anchor at 4:09 PM.

After Ahousat, the *Maquinna* steamed into Sydney Inlet, arriving "at 6:47 PM." Here Brodie reported a population of about forty white people at the thriving Tidewater Copper mine. After that they "ran out of Sidney Inlet into the open sea. The fog was very thick and there was a heavy swell running." Brodie focused disapprovingly on the thick weather and the persistent seasickness of the passengers, and he had little to say at the next stop.

> We arrived at Hesquiat at 8:47 PM. This is a boat landing. We put ashore a few Indians and Father Charles, who is an Indian missionary in the North. We weighed anchor again at 9:00 PM. There is a population of about 50 Indians at this point.

According to Brodie, this landing at Hesquiat was remarkably efficient; thirteen minutes from the time of arrival to the time of weighing anchor. Then, having left Hesquiat behind, with no time wasted, the *Princess Maquinna* disappeared on her northbound journey. The repeated sounding of the steamer's whistle faded away, and Father Charles returned to his empty house in the dense fogbound silence of Hesquiat.

Canoe alongside the *Princess Maquinna*, 1919.

– 16 –

Affliction

Hesquiat, BC, March 5, 1916

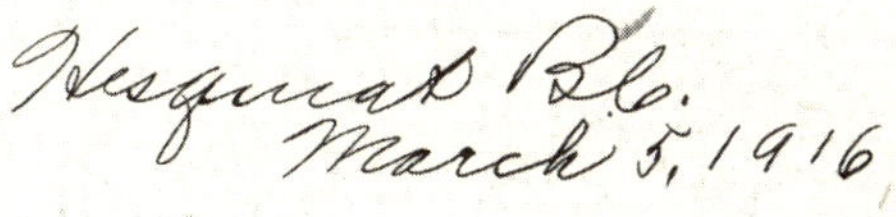

Dear Sir:

Please send by next boat two bottles of Castoria for baby use also send the prices of each bottle so I can pay for them & send the money on return boat. Please also pay on diliverey charges & let me know what it will cost you to ship them here so I can pay up all square.

Respectfully yours,
William Aloysius.

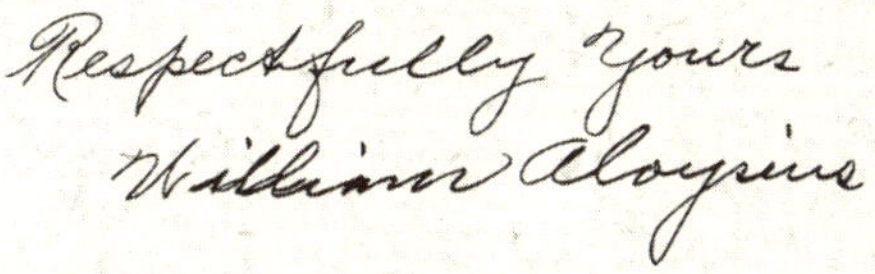

Clayoquot, BC, March 22, 1916

Dear Father Charles:

I have received a letter from William Aloysius asking me to send him by this boat two bottles of castoria. My rule is to first obtain cash but as he states it is for his baby I do not like to disappoint, and therefore send through you and I would be obliged if you would get him to pay you the amount due viz 2 bottles each 35¢ = 70¢ and portage 10¢ Total 80¢ and you could forward to me by Postal note. Trusting I am not trespassing too much on your kindness.

Walter Dawley

FATHER CHARLES knew William Aloysius, his wife, Josephine, and their family situation well. William had been a pupil at Kakawis, and after leaving school he sometimes did odd jobs to help the priest. Along with the young Hesquiat chief Eustace Andrews, he laid pipe for Father Charles's water system in the village in 1912. William played the organ at the Hesquiat church, and he and Josephine had been married in church. An undated wedding photograph of the young couple survives amongst Father Maurus Snyder's papers.

In the summer of 1913, William and Josephine's two-year-old daughter Maggie died while her parents were working at Quatsino Cannery. They went there from Hesquiat in the usual wave of summer migration from the villages to various canneries along the coast. Father Charles saw them off in mid-June, but only a month later he briefly noted the return of a number of people from Quatsino: "Last night SS Oronte brought from Quatsino cannery some Hesquiat Indians with the body of Wm Aloysius' two year old Maggie, who was burried at noon." Her death attracted no further comment, and no official record marked the end of her short life.

Three years later, in the spring of 1916, William Aloysius and Josephine faced another crisis: their baby was sick. They did their utmost to help the child, even ordering medicine from the Clayoquot store. Fletcher's Castoria was a widely touted patent medicine, popular across North America for curing all manner of children's ills, including stomach pain, tapeworms and constipation. "Children cry for Chas H Fletcher's Castoria" was one of the best-known advertising slogans for any medicine, appearing on billboards from New York City to California. Although far from ideal for babies (it contained senna, wintergreen and sodium bicarbonate), Castoria was the best Dawley's store had to offer.

William Aloysius as a young boy, with his family.

A year later, in April 1917, fifteen-month-old Sophie Aloysius died at Hesquiat, perhaps the same child who had been ill the previous spring. She died in the year a new government document, "Return of Death of an Indian," came into circulation, so there is an official record of her death, signed by Father Charles. He stated the cause of death—"Cholera Infantus, as I judge"— and commented on the form that Sophie had been sick three weeks.

The following year, her mother, Josephine, fell gravely ill. Father Charles was at Kakawis for most of January and February 1918, and by the time he came to Hesquiat in late February, four people had died in under a month. Josephine was the next; she died on March 7, 1918. Father Charles prepared her "Return of Death" certificate, giving the cause of death as "Hectic consumption since beginning of January." He did not provide her surname on the form, so in the public archives she is catalogued as "Unknown Josephine." She was twenty-nine years old. Father Charles had nothing more to say about her death, and in his diary he did not even mention little Sophie's death.

The death of a small child was a common-enough event. Whether in his early years at Opitsat or later at Hesquiat, Father Charles's main concern was always whether the child had been baptized. "Not having succeeded in persuading Jimmy Jim to have his sick baby boy baptized, Sr. M. Placida visits the family and baptized the baby secretly," he wrote on July 12, 1906, at Opitsat. That baby died the following day. "I heard death-cries in a neighboring house," he commented in March 1907. "A baby was sick for the last two days but they would not let me administer Baptism. Now I went again to see if I could safe the child's soul." In this instance, the Indian doctor allowed him to baptize the baby, who died a few minutes later.

Father Charles's accounts of sick and dying babies are generally taciturn. "Sick call for a baby 10:30 PM," he commented on Christmas Day 1910, and in July 1912, "This afternoon burried a baby of one week." Such entries are relentlessly repetitive:

> *February 10, 1912:* After breakfast prepared my Sunday sermon. General cleaning up and baking hosts. At 5:30 PM received word that Sabbas' boy 2 yrs old had died. He had been sick for the last 2 or 3 weeks. Their baby, one month old, is also sick and probably will die too. At 8:30 word came that this baby died also. Poor mother!

"After Mass, funeral of the two children," he wrote the following day. He generally conducted funerals as soon after the death as possible, and burials also if he was permitted. "I read part of the funeral service in the house," he noted following another death, "and later on went to the graveyard but when I arrived they had the box already up on a tree." Traditionally, bodies were placed in boxes in a tree, a method preferred by many families despite years of priestly influence. By burying people as quickly as possible, Father Charles did his utmost to counteract this tradition.

On the back of this picture, Father Maurus Snyder wrote "Wm Aloysius and Josephine." The wedding probably took place around 1910.

In his diary, Father Charles never recorded the names of the babies who died, nor did he mention the cause of death. Often infant deaths went unremarked. Although he completed and signed a death certificate for baby Jimmy Michael at Hesquiat, who died at the age of three days on March 29, 1919, the baby's death does not appear in his diary. On the death certificate he wrote: "Was sick one night. Unable to diagnose it."

To diagnose and treat illness, or at least to make an attempt, was part of Father Charles's missionary role. Most missionaries of the period had, or quickly developed, some rudimentary medical skills when they worked in remote areas. Several times during his early years on the coast, Father Brabant responded to outbreaks of smallpox, vaccinating against the disease and burying its victims. Although the incidence of smallpox lessened over the years, it still reappeared periodically. As late as March 1909, Father Charles wrote of assisting with a vaccination campaign among the Clayoquot and Kelsemat people after an outbreak of smallpox on the east coast of Vancouver Island.

The Indian Affairs Department officially sanctioned the medical help missionaries provided by equipping them with basic medical supplies. In April 1911, Father Charles recorded that he "unpacked a case of drugs which had recently arrived from the Indian Department. Put all the medicines in good order on shelves, throwing away old stuff that was not marked."

The "Return of Death of an Indian" form came into use in 1917.

Requests for medical help appear frequently in Father Charles's diary throughout his years on the west coast. Often he could do little, if anything, to help because the requests tended to come when death was imminent. In such cases, he was usually more preoccupied with saving the soul of the dying person than with administering medical aid.

> *May 4, 1904:* Boston Bob having been sick the last few days sent his sister to me for Medicine…I looked in to see how he was getting along. He was a pretty sick man. When I returned a few hours later I saw him again. Signs of death. I spoke about Baptism and Salvation. First he did not want but explaining more he said "go ahead". I rushed to my house, dressed and with the sick call outfit was soon in his house again. He received Baptism, Extreme Unction and Indulgenia in articulo mortis in a most edifying way and thanked me very much…We said the prayers and litany for the dying, he praying in all earnest along. When I came to a stop once he prayed aloud in Chinook: "Tlosh mika haul-neika, Saghali Taye." (Lord God take me to thee)…These were his last words.

The next day, Father Charles buried Boston Bob.

> At 8 o'clock I shouldered my shovel and left for the place of burial… Before we lowered the coffin we said some prayers in the Indian language and I gave a little speech to those present (about 8 men). I went home and the Indians covered the grave and built a little house over it according to their fashion. Boston Bob was an Indian that very seldom visited the Catholic Church. He inclined more towards the Methodist church—a Mr. Stone man—he could, however, not be called a Methodist, he was still a pagan.

"How sad about Boston Bob," commented the Methodist missionary, William Stone, a month later in a letter to Dawley. "Poor fellow he was not too bad for an Indian."

Relentlessly determined to save souls at the point of death, Father Charles never missed an opportunity and would travel many miles, in all weathers, to be at a deathbed. In his estimation, if the person were "pagan," conversion was always possible, and if the person were Catholic, either lapsed or practising, his duty dictated that he be present to hear confession and to administer the last rites of the church. His diary contains repeated accounts of taking *Viaticum* (the final communion) to dying people, hearing final confessions and arriving with holy oils to dispense extreme unction. Yet even amid his priestly preoccupations, Father Charles sometimes noted symptoms and medical treatment:

> *February 6, 1912:* After Mass brought Viaticum to Didac who suffered great pain on left side of chest with 102 temperature, rapid respiration, fast pulse, rusty expectoration and no sleep. All the signs of pneumonia. At my second visit around 4 PM I gave him Extreme Unction and as he had quite a little money, advised him to make his will which he did…
>
> *February 7:* Wednesday After a stormy night a stormy day with rain. Sea high. Didac has less fever and less pain but still no sleep. Hence I gave him 40 drops of Hydrate of Clorate in three tablespoons of water with ten drops of Essence of Peppermint for the taste with instructions to take one tablespoon, if not followed by sleep in half an hour to take an other spoonful. Steamer here at 5 PM.

Although the "Hydrate of Clorate" (chloral hydrate) could not help Didac much, it was an apt treatment. A mild sedative, it would have encouraged sleep and calmed his laboured breathing to some extent. Didac had been a student at Christie School and only a few days earlier had married a girl called Lucy. Father Charles married them "in a private house owing to the serious sickness of Didac," rather than in the church.

> *February 8, 1912:* Soon after I got up Nonat brought me the news that Didac had died during the night… After 8 PM funeral with Mass. Lucy after being married a few days is now a widow, not yet 16 years old.

Over the years, Father Charles chronicled one death after another of former students from Christie School. The first came in July 1901, only a year after the school opened: "Emma Ucluelet…who had spent a year at Christie School died at her mothers home in Opitsat, well fortified with the last Sacraments."

When records of a death exist, the cause of death, variously worded, is often a form of tuberculosis. This disease ravaged the Indians of North America in the late nineteenth and early twentieth century. Combined with the devastating effect of smallpox and other diseases brought by European contact, tuberculosis seemed to sound a death knell for an entire people. Estimates of the drop in native population of the Pacific Northwest during the first 150 years after contact range as high as 70 and even 90 percent. Exact numbers may never be known, but the overall decline in numbers was, by any standard, dramatic. In Clayoquot Sound, one of the few sources of information about native populations in the late nineteenth century is the annual reports of the Indian Agent Harry Guillod. According to his figures, between 1881 and 1901 the population in Kyuquot Sound declined by more than half, Hesquiat's by nearly one third.

On the west coast of Vancouver Island in the early years of the twentieth century, the death toll continued to mount. Even Fred Thornberg, usually so preoccupied with his own affairs, observed what was happening at Ahousat and wrote soberly to Father Maurus on January 5, 1910: "There have already bean 3 deaths in Ahouset this year and 4 others are pretty bad & the Ind tell me that the dont think that those 4 that are sick will live very long = one is callet Short Charly & his daughter a school girl about 17 is pretty bad, Peters seen her ones lately & he say she is only skin & bone & looks sick."

In British Columbia, most Indians who contracted tuberculosis were under the age of twenty. The disease flourished in crowded conditions; accommodation at the canneries and at residential schools provided excellent settings for contagion. "I sincerely regret to report the loss by death of three of our children during the past year," Father Frowin Epper wrote to the Indian Affairs Department in 1913, "one through tuberculous glands and two through consumption." By then, this was a familiar pattern in residential schools across Canada.

As early as 1907, Dr. Peter Bryce, chief medical officer of the Department of Indian Affairs, publicly voiced concern about the death rates from tuberculosis amongst residential school students. In his controversial and outspoken report on the health conditions in residential schools (chiefly on the prairies), Bryce claimed that 24 percent of the schools' students had died of tuberculosis. He campaigned to improve conditions for native children in the schools and elsewhere. In 1908, the department conducted the first of many surveys to determine how many native people across the country suffered from tuberculosis, but little was done to alleviate the problem. Meanwhile, Bryce claimed that authorities must consider "every residential school pupil to be a potential tuberculosis sufferer and adjust conditions accordingly." No one listened, but for years Bryce persisted, blaming the intransigence of the Department of Indian Affairs for the continued high death rates. His superiors repudiated his comments, and he was eventually forced to resign.

Father Charles stoically accepted the deaths of his former students, most of whom died very young. He expressed neither grief nor surprise at their mortality rate, ministering to them on their deathbeds whether or not he was welcome.

In 1907, Emma Peter lay dying. Back in 1902, her family had strongly resisted sending her to school, and Emma hid under the blankets, fighting "like a wild animal" according to Father Charles's diary, before being forced into the boat and carried off to Kakawis. She had no fight left in her now.

> *October 22, 1907:* At 5 PM I gave Extreme Unction to Emma…During the whole time Mrs. Peter was scolding and even slapped my hand. On a former visit to the sick girl old Tom, the Grand father and a friend of mine, cursed me with "God damn you" and called me a "damned fool."…Emma gave her mother no sign of disapproval or to be quiet.

Three days later, Father Charles visited Emma again:

> She was in her death agony. I made an act of contrition with her and gave her absolution. Her mother still acted mean and scolded; hence I left with the remark I would soon return. About 10 o'clock a woman was sent from Peters house with the message I should come and "make church" for Emma. With surplice and stole I gave her the last blessing with plenary indulgence. An hour later I entered the house again. I found her breathing her last and just had time to call the name of Jesus. Then she was dead…I said the funeral prayers in the house over the trunk in which she had been laid and the Indians took her to a rocky Island.

On several occasions, Father Charles visited the deathbeds of former pupils whom he had married only a few years earlier. Mary Alphonse Swan was one: she and Philip Chester Charlie were married by Father Charles on February 5, 1920, aged eighteen and nineteen respectively, and a wedding feast at Kelsemat followed their nuptial mass. Two years after the wedding, Father Charles made the following entry in his diary:

> *November 9, 1922:* Mr. Wingen took me to Ahousat in his launch. I carried the Blessed Sacrament with me for Alphonse Swan. I found her very low; she was able to confess and receive a small particle of the Host. She died a few hours after I left her.

The death certificate declares that Mary Alphonse Swan was "ill about three months with tuberculosis of the lungs following pneumonia" and that "Doctor Dixon was called and examined this case and pronounced her incurable. Her brothers brought her home from Nootka just three weeks previous to death." She had been working at Nootka Cannery.

As these former pupils lay dying, Father Charles never doubted that he had the right to interfere directly in their lives. "Mamie of Kelsemat one of our ex pupils is reported to me by telegram 'very sick will live only one day,'" he wrote on May 30, 1925. He went at once to visit her, determined that she should renounce the man she was living with outside of marriage and repent her sins. "She is living for the last few years with a married man at Ahousat," he noted disapprovingly.

> I hired an Indian launch for $6.00, take my sick call case and the Holy Sacrament along, I found her deaf. So I had to write down my message, insisting and advising her to declare her man not to be her husband any longer... I showed what I had written to her man with verbal explanations, advising him to help his concubine to save her soul. He told the people present that I wanted them to separate and started to cry. Others began to go against me and... her father told me to leave.

Two days later, Mamie died. Her death certificate states that she was twenty-one years old, the cause of death was tuberculosis of the lungs and she had been ill for about one year. Father Charles did not see her again. "After Mass I went back to Kakawis disgusted," he wrote angrily on June 1. "I heard Mamie died." She died defying his wishes, refusing to renounce her partner and without receiving the last rites. Many years earlier, this same young woman was a little girl at Kakawis—Mamie Sam. In 1912 she penned two chatty letters to Father Maurus, addressing him as "Dearly Beloved Father" and telling him of the Easter decorations in the church and the lace she was making for surplices. "I am just the same as I always was," she wrote cheerfully, "talkative and mischievous."

Another former student, Mamie Napoleon, was more compliant when Father Charles appeared at her deathbed demanding that she repent. Like the other Mamie, she was, in his view, "a sinful woman." He visited her at Nootka Cannery in June 1918.

> Oh how glad she was to see me, a priest. "I am in the last hour of death and the devil wants to take me" she said to me. Promising that she would send the man away with whom she was living, her right husband was still living, I heard her Confession after which she made a most beautiful speech to the many people present telling in plain words that her false husband has to leave her and how sorry she was of the past. That was a true conversion over which the angels in heaven

rejoiced. Afterwards, steamer not coming till afternoon, I went back to Friendly Cove and asked Fr. Sobry to go to Mamie and give her the Sacraments of the dying which he did after dinner. Steamer came at 4 PM and I left, also the false husband with all his baggage boarded the steamer for his home at Clo-oose.

In these deathbed encounters, if relatives angrily turned on Father Charles, demanding that he leave, he was unmoved. He was particularly determined to outface any Indian doctors in attendance. When he heard that Rose of Opitsat was dying on May 31, 1924, he wrote: "I went intending to give her the last Blessing. About 30 women were there. Siwash doctor woman tried to prevent me, hence first quarrel." The following day, Father Charles saw Rose again and "preached against Siwash doctorism" in church that Sunday. Rose died shortly after.

The greatest personal loss for Father Charles was the death of Eustace Andrews in 1922. The priest had known Eustace, chief of the Hesquiats and one of the first students at Christie School, ever since he had arrived on the coast. When Eustace married Alice Yaksouse in 1906, their wedding at the Opitsat church, with Father Charles presiding, attracted widespread attention. After the priest moved to Hesquiat in 1910, he saw Eustace regularly—and from this time usually referred to him as Chief Eustace.

Chief Eustace and his wife did much to smooth Father Charles's way at Hesquiat, welcoming him and at times deferring to him. The chief even asked permission, in January 1912, to hold the annual wolf dance ceremonies. Father Charles reported, "After he promised to eliminate certain objectionable parts I told him to go ahead for this time expressing my hope that this would be the last time, as I regarded the 'Tloukwanna' [wolf dance] as a step backward to the Siwash tomtom."

Father Charles knew full well that Chief Eustace could easily hold the wolf dance without referring to him at all; this traditional ceremony was far too important to be subject to a priestly veto. The chief's visit, and the request, was more a polite gesture than a genuine request for permission. In the same amiable spirit, the chief and his wife invited Father Charles into their home, on one occasion offering hospitality so notable that he recorded it in detail:

December 8, 1912: Forty Communions at High Mass…After Benediction I was invited by Chief Eustace to a meal. I had supper there in the kitchen. The table was covered with a table cloth and had a chair to sit on. I was eating alone, entertained by Mrs. Eustace standing by the kitchen stove. In the adjoining "parlor" was the rest of the family with the chief entertaining a number of Indians; they also took supper but on the floor as usual.

Ten days after this meal, sad news arrived: "Chief Eustace receives message from his wife at Clayoquot that his first born boy, Maurus, is very sick and may not recover. Eustace, therefore leaves per canoe to Clayoquot." By the time the chief reached his son, the boy was dead. Within another day, "Body of Maurus arrived here 6 PM but father and mother remain at Clayoquot," and shortly afterward, "Funeral of Maurus after Mass."

The two men occasionally disagreed. Early in 1916 a dispute arose between the two when Father Charles imposed an obligatory Sunday collection in the church.

> *March 4, 1916:* Arrived home by steamer at 10 A.M. Here I was told that during my absence Chief Eustace had called the whole male population to a meeting on the beach…against the Sunday Collection. Mention was made…of the Priest having much money from Post Office, Telephone and Cattle. All men present at the meeting—three were absent—voted not to contribute.

Chief Eustace and two others arrived at the priest's house to state their objections in person. "After he was finished talking I asked him to send the other two men away…then I had a talk with him, after which he asked me pardon for what he had done." Following this, the chief was obliged to do "public penance in church" for going against his priest, and "from now on he will take up the collection." The nature of Chief Eustace's public penance is not described.

In 1920, Chief Eustace signed up two of his sons, Benedict and Lawrence, to attend Christie School. Following that, apart from remarking on two hundred pounds of "wild beef" that he purchased from Chief Eustace at ten cents a pound, Father Charles did not mention him again until November 11, 1922, two days after the death of Mary Alphonse Swan at Ahousat.

The diary entry is brief: "I brought Viaticum to Eustace at Opitsat." Chief Eustace was dying. On November 14, his father-in-law, Harry Yaksouse, who once accused the priest of poisoning his baby with baptism, arrived at Hesquiat to take Father Charles to Eustace, who "had great joy at my coming and bringing him Holy Communion." This was the last time the two men saw each other. On November 17, "Eustace, the Hesquiat Chief, died at Opitsat 6 AM. R.I.P."

A Requiem Mass took place the next day at Opitsat. It was a sad affair. "When he married in the same church some 15 years ago what a grand celebration!" Father Charles recalled. "Today his body lies in the same church and only five Clayoquot people are present. Sic transit gloria mundi." Within a few days, Father Charles returned to Hesquiat with Mrs. Eustace. She had business to transact.

> *November 25, 1922:* Mrs Eustace in an assembly of the Hesquiat Indians—she treats them with 2 boxes of apples—announces now officially the death of her husband who was their chief, and appoints John Lucas to be chief until her son now about 12 years old would be old enough to act as such. As she is going to live with her parents at Opitsat she also donates their house at Hesquiat to John Lucas.

Mrs. Eustace did not remain living with her parents at Opitsat. The following year she returned to Hesquiat and remarried. On November 24, 1923, Father Charles wrote: "Marriage of Wm Aloysius and Mrs. Eustace Andrews, both widower and widow."

Whether or not Father Charles was able to render appropriate medical help, he received continual requests for such assistance. Even the non-Catholic white settlers near Hesquiat turned to him. When Ada Annie Rae-Arthur—later renowned as Cougar Annie—experienced difficulty in labour, her husband Willie called for Father Charles to come. "I went, taking my doctor book and Ergot along, after having sent at noon already a good Indian midwife." The baby, Isabel, was born safely.

This was Ada Annie Rae-Arthur's fourth child, and the first to be born at Boat Basin, at the head of Hesquiat Harbour, far from medical help. Her husband was sufficiently anxious about the birth to contact not only the priest but also Walter Dawley. Several weeks before the birth he added a worried postscript to a grocery order: "In case of sickness if at any time I wired you to send a gasoline launch here I guess you could manage all right? please let me know." Such a request revealed Willie Rae-Arthur as a naive newcomer on the coast; a more experienced settler would have known that an eleventh-hour rescue in a medical emergency at Boat Basin was highly unlikely.

Ada Annie went on to bear seven more children at Boat Basin; three of the babies died at birth. In time, she became known at Hesquiat village for helping other women in childbirth. Her expertise was undoubtedly welcome, for midwifery was certainly not Father Charles's forte. "In the afternoon visited a woman who since yesterday was in painful labor," he wrote on February 12, 1911. "I found her sitting on the floor. I gave her from the Ritual the blessing for such an occasion. After admonishing her to patience and resignation to the Holy Will of God I left again."

In this case, both mother and child came through the labour in good health, but such a result could not be taken for granted. "After supper received the following wire from Hesquiat," Father Charles noted on December 29, 1917. "'Mrs. Adolph John died at 3 o'clock from child birth. Baby is well.'...May her soul rest in peace. She had been to the Sacraments on Christmas, and was a good girl, an ex-pupil of our school, educated and trained by Father Maurus. R.I.P."

Although on many occasions he was clearly out of his depth, medically speaking, Father Charles often proved he could be useful in an emergency.

> *January 2, 1914:* A fierce gale from the S East...At noon Dan came to get some castor oil for his baby. Hardly had he left when Eustace's wife ran up to my house in great excitement bringing news that a tree had fallen over Constant's house...Mrs. Constant she reported was hurt on the head. I buttoned up my cassock, pocketed some adhesive tape—no other useful remedy came into my mind in the hurry, put on gumboots, raincoat and souwester—ran to the church for Holy Oils and ritual and stole and then proceeded as fast as I could against the wind and rain to the unfortunate house. What a mess!

The ecclesiastical gear and the holy oils proved unnecessary, for no one was dying after all, but the sticking plaster came in handy, as Father Charles patched up various cuts and injuries. He helped to sort out the mess and later visited the family, taking along a box of apples for the children. In addition he "administered Mrs. Constant...a drink of rum; also had brought some food along for the whole family; and rubbed the different bruises with arsenic [arnica]."

Father Charles kept his supply of rum for medical emergencies in a cupboard under lock and key. In earlier years, his predecessor at Opitsat, Father Van Nevel, also relied on the healing powers of strong liquor in special circumstances. Walter Dawley's files contain several letters from Father Van Nevel on this subject. One, dated February 7, 1899, says: "In my opinion the present condition of Jimmy Jim's sickness could well be relieved by the use of some warm stimulant, therefore I consider that you would be justified to give him some whiskey to be taken with sugar and hot water." A month later, another letter in the same vein: "Aleck is not well yet and some whiskey would do him good. It restored Jimmy Jim in a similar complaint…therefore you will be justified if you let him have some whiskey."

In common with the priests, Walter Dawley could find himself medically challenged. He stocked a wide variety of patent medicines, and from time to time his customers would ask his advice, wanting something, anything at all, to alleviate specific symptoms. In May 1903, James Sloman, who was then working for Dawley at Ahousat, wrote for help: "The bearer Chief Billie wishes you to help him all you can in regards to his child who is sick. I think the child is suffering from white-mouth and has been in like condition for over two weeks with no sign of improvement. I have no medicine here which would be of any good for that complaint."

A child suffering "white-mouth" had either diphtheria or scrofula, which is tuberculosis of the lymphatic glands of the neck. For either ailment, the array of patent medicines on the shelves of the Clayoquot store would be utterly useless: none could help a serious illness. However, these medicines were popular, and Dawley ordered them regularly.

In January 1899, when Fred Thornberg sent a lengthy order from Ahousat, including everything from dried prunes to tinned cream to writing paper, he added a postscript, crammed sideways on the page, insisting peevishly, "dont order Milk…am out of cream" and "please dont forget to order the 4 artickles with a x mark." Amongst the urgently required "artickles with a x mark" were three patent medicines: Dr. Thomas' Eclectric Oil, a widely advertised nostrum with amazing properties ("It will positively cure toothache in 5 minutes, earache in two minutes and deafness in two days"); Dr. Williams' Pink Pills for Pale People, sugar-coated pills containing iron oxide and epsom salts that were touted to anyone with digestive problems, blood disorders or emotional disturbance; and Chlorodyne, a mixture of chlorofom and laudanum that was "the true palliative in neuralgia, gout, cancer, toothache, rheumatism," "the great specific for Cholera, Diarrhoea, Dysentry," and a cure for "coughs, colds, asthma and bronchitis." At Clayoquot, Dawley probably also stocked the popular Dr. Wilson's Blue Pills for Blue People, Carter's Little Liver Pills and an array of other medical marvels.

Most frequently mentioned in customers' orders are "pain pills" and "castoria," but some customers had very specific demands. In April 1902, George Stuermer wrote from Bear River: "Will you please send and git ½ dozen bottles of Dr Schoops Restorative." Stuermer sent several orders for this same mysterious medicine during the year, specifying in one instance that he wishes six bottles, "3 Rheumatic 3 nerve." On one occasion, Fred Thornberg requested two dozen bottles of Mrs. Winslow's Soothing Syrup, a teething remedy liberally laced with opium and guaranteed to "allay all pain and spasmodic action and… sure to regulate the bowels." Just how many teething children in Ahousat required this remedy is unknown, but two dozen bottles of this powerful stuff would have done a great deal of soothing, no matter who took it.

Douglas Scott Dixson, for many years the lone doctor in Tofino, was only too familiar with these patent medicines. Sometimes he could offer little more. He rarely dispensed anything stronger than aspirin, Castoria, liniment, Friar's Balsam, Hazeline cream, cough mixture, unspecified "pain pills," or "Bland's Pills" for iron deficiency. Some, if not all, of these items were readily available in the Clayoquot store.

Dixson settled in Tofino in 1912, the same year he emigrated from Scotland. He and his family had arrived in Quebec aboard the *Mauritania*, and after a brief spell in Victoria they came to Tofino, where he remained until his death in 1932. His daughter Winnie recalled that "the government made Father the doctor for all the Indians," although he also served the white settlers in the Tofino area.

Some years ago, a messy, dog-eared notebook emerged by chance amid a jumble of papers in an old house in Tofino. It contains Dixson's diary and account book for 1916–17, hastily pencilled jottings detailing

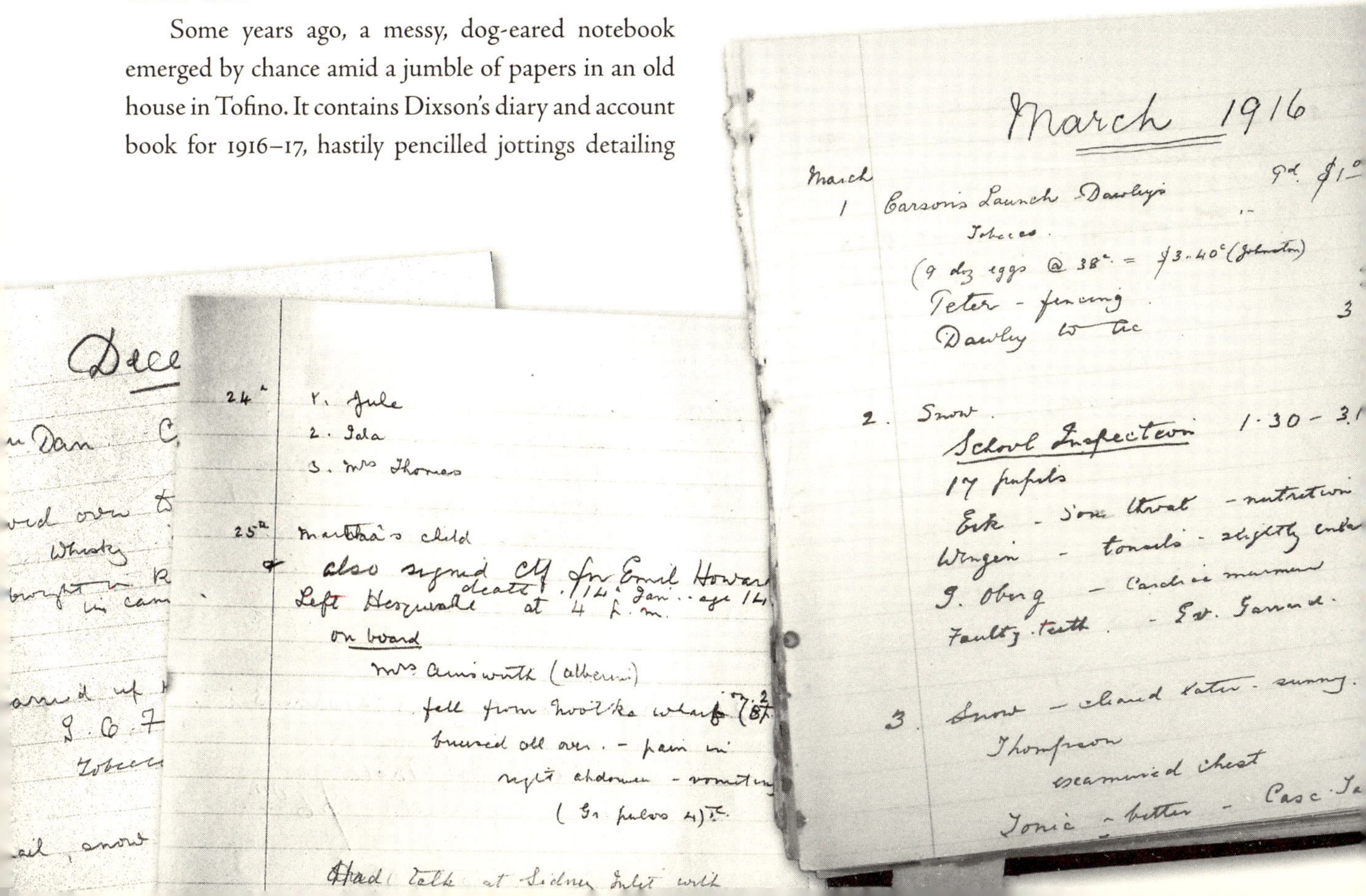

A few pages from Dr. Dixson's diary.

the doctor's daily life: patients visited, medicines prescribed, charges made. Dr. Dixson clearly had an impossible job, tending the ailments of the growing Tofino community and constantly travelling on medical calls to Opitsat, Ahousat, Hesquiat and as far north as Kyuquot. Hampered by distance, he was frequently unable to respond to emergencies. In March 1916, a telegram from Ahousat reported that a child at the Presbyterian school was badly burned; the child died the next day, before Dixson could get there.

The doctor's diary reads like a series of working notes. The entry for November 17, 1916, says: "Rowed over to Mission with Louis. Examined: Edward (Ehatissaht) for entry [to school], Emile—rheumatic endocarditis, Hugo&Mike —convalescent from measles, Amy John—ordered crutches, Alice Sam—improving." The brief notation on June 6, 1917, is "Teleg from Sidney Inlet re case feared appendicitis," and ten days later "Chief Billy's Klooch [wife] Ahousaht improved but spitting blood."

In describing ailments in his diary, Dr. Dixson was always brief, sometimes even unsure. "Whitlow?" he wrote in one instance, "Mumps?" in another. Most commonly he treated rheumatism, chest pains, bronchitis, sore throats and tubercular ailments. The ominous word "phthisis," an outdated medical term for tuberculosis, appears many times. Outbreaks of measles were common: in November 1916, at least a dozen children at Christie School contracted measles. The doctor visited the school four times that month, also travelling once to Ahousat, once to Kelsemat and once to Clayoquot Cannery in the same period.

The doctor's job included medical checkups on all schoolchildren, both white and native. The opening page of his diary declares "School Inspection 1:30–3:15." He examined seventeen students at the Tofino school that day and took cryptic notes: "Eik—sore throat—nutrition, Wingen—tonsils—slightly enlarged, J Oberg—cardiac murmur, Ev Garrard—faulty teeth." As for the native children due to attend Christie School or the Presbyterian school at Ahousat, the doctor had to declare them fit and "sign them" before they could attend residential school; he also treated the children while at school. He compiled regular "Health and Indian reports" and contacted the Indian Agent in Alberni if there was a serious illness. Taking care of the native population was central to his practice and it brought regular remuneration. Every month he received an "Indian cheque," usually around forty dollars. His white patients paid him small and erratic sums for his services, and they did not always pay quickly. "Accounts sent out," he noted in February 1916. "Mrs Wingen $7.00 (2nd time)."

Cases of toothache regularly required Dixson's intervention; he pulled at least one tooth a month on his travels, although by this time a dentist did occasionally come to visit Tofino. In *Lone Cone*, Dorothy Abraham recalled that her toothache was so bad, just after Christmas 1919, she went to see the "travelling dentist [who] had arrived on the boat and put up his 'Chamber of Horrors' at the Clayoquot Hotel... The dentist took out my tooth, nearly taking my head off as well, or so it seemed."

The children at Christie School also had the dubious privilege of seeing a travelling dentist. "Dr. Baker, dentist from Vancouver, arrived at Kakawis to look after the children's teeth by order of the Indian Department," Father Charles wrote on July 28, 1924, adding, "He has to visit all Indian schools in BC." Dr. Baker was a fast worker. Four days later he finished working on the seventy children then at the school. He pulled 210 teeth and filled 300, then boarded a steamer bound for the next batch of native students awaiting his services at the Ahousat school.

Harsh as Dr. Baker's dental treatment seems, Annie Garrard's experience twenty years earlier was infinitely worse. In 1904, when she and her children were about to leave Alberni to join her husband, Frank, at the new Lennard Island light, Annie—then aged thirty-six—took desperate measures. Frank recalled how "Annie visited Dr Watson and had her teeth, which had been giving her a good deal of trouble, all taken out, which although it must have been a very severe ordeal, no anesthetic being used, was the wisest thing she could have done as there was no Doctor and of course no dentist at Clayoquot."

Dr. Dixson spent a great deal of his time in boats, particularly in his own rowboat. He loved rowing: for recreation he rowed his wife from Tofino to the outer beaches on Wickaninnish Island, and together they also rowed to Long Beach and back. One June day in 1916 he "rowed round islands with Mrs D," and on at least one occasion that year she rowed with him to Christie School.

"Rowed over to Dawley's" is a common phrase in Dixson's diary. He rowed to Stubbs Island at least twice a month, often more frequently, to buy meat, sell eggs or pay his bill. Occasionally he jotted down special purchases—Whiskey and Wine $2.50"—and once he had "Dinner at Dawley's $1.00, Rum and Brandy $1.75." Eventually Dixson bowed to the inevitable; for fifty dollars he purchased a machine he called "the Evinrude" in the

Dr. Dixson rowing in Tofino Harbour with two women.

autumn of 1917. He learned to operate it and in mid-October triumphantly declared "Evinrude to Dawley's." But the newfangled motor must have fallen out of favour, for he wrote of it no more and he was soon rowing to Dawley's again.

Although he made many sick calls in his rowboat, ranging as far as Christie School, the doctor had to travel by motor launch when the distances were great, if the weather was ugly or if the call was urgent. He also travelled by steamer, particularly when going greater distances: "May 9 1916—Tees in 6 am. Rowed over to Dawley's & joined boat (9 Nootka people, Jansen, Bishop MacDonald, Father Joseph etc) reached Kyuquot at 4 am."

From time to time, Father Charles asked Dr. Dixson to visit Hesquiat. The month of January 1917 was especially grim. On January 20, Father Charles wrote, "A ten months old baby died," adding, "This is the second baby death in the new year." The following day: "The third baby, born yesterday, is burried today." When a number of Hesquiat people returned from a marriage feast at Nootka, many in the village fell ill. Dr. Dixson's notes show that on January 18 he received a telegram from Father Charles asking for advice about a woman who was in labour prematurely. Dixson did not go to Hesquiat at once but called on the telephone the following day. Father Charles prevailed on him to come, and Dixson arrived on January 23. The doctor put in nearly two full days at Hesquiat visiting "sick and ailing Indians" with Father Charles. He saw fifteen people, treating diseases as varied as dropsy, whooping cough, phthisis, stomach ulcers, eczema, postpartum complications, ulcerated throat and lumbago.

While at Hesquiat, the doctor also "signed ctf. for Emil Howard's death 14 Jan age 14." This death certificate gave the cause of death as "heart disease and dropsy." Emil died at Kakawis, having had rheumatic fever for over two months. Dixson was familiar with Emil's case: this is the same "Emile" he mentioned several times in his diary, suffering from "rheumatic endocarditis." Dixson examined Emil seven times at Kakawis in the last ten weeks of his life, seeing him for the final time only three days before he died.

After Dixson's departure, the weather at Hesquiat turned extremely cold, and the medical alerts kept coming. "The coldest morning I remember for the last 17 years," Father Charles wrote on January 30. "Wine frozen in sacristy and getting thick in the chalice during Mass… In the afternoon Mr. Rae Arthur in Boat Basin sent message to Dr. Dixson at Tofino to come for one of his children who received burns about her arm. Later on Doctor replied: 'Can not come.'"

A month later, Dr. Dixson was up the coast at Nootka. He dressed Chief Napoleon Maquinna's cut hand and saw a case of syphilis, two cases of hip and knee joint disease, and two of phthisis. At Nootka Cannery he treated a woman for tonsillitis, and he tended the "tubercular abscesses" of a patient he called Cosmos—possibly the same Cosmos Damian William who wrote to Father Maurus from Kakawis in 1912 and said that he was spitting blood. Leaving Nootka, Dixson boarded the *Tees* in stormy weather and continued down the coast, disembarking briefly at Hesquiat to tend Chief Eustace Andrews, who had injured his head, before returning to Tofino. Within a few days he set out to Kelsemat where no fewer than twelve children had whooping cough; at the end of March he visited these children again.

In the autumn of 1918, Father Charles enjoyed two peaceful and productive weeks at Hesquiat. On September 24 he "dug up the potatoes and harvested 934 lbs from the 96 lbs seed put in. Deo Gratias." Butchering and selling meat also kept him busy. With apparent indifference to the price, he sold meat from the same animals for fifteen cents per pound to Hesquiat people and to Burns Meats in Victoria, for twenty cents per pound to Kakawis, and to the chief steward on the *Maquinna* for twenty-four cents per pound. The apple harvest was not good; he harvested only three precious apples from the twelve trees he planted with such care in 1911. "The Indians had taken them before my arrival," he wrote without rancour. Given the value placed on apples as special treats and potlatch gifts, he half expected this.

Father Charles returned to Kakawis in early October, little suspecting what lay ahead, though he did note that "Victoria papers are full about Spanish Influentia." For a while the school was spared and all continued normally. "First time househeating today, as we had frosty mornings of late," he wrote on October 16, 1918. "Hence I got up at 5 o'clock and when the children got up the house was warm and comfortable."

Within a day or so, he commented that "boys and girls are getting laid up with the Flu," and on October 19 he summoned the doctor from Tofino. Dr. Dixson was so busy with cases of influenza he could not come. Left to their own devices, the priests and nuns consulted the newspapers: "We are following the instructions of the Health Officer as given in the Victoria papers," wrote Father Charles, but soon almost all the children were too sick to appear at Mass. The hired men were also ill, and one of the sisters.

The favoured treatment for influenza at Kakawis was onion poultices, applied only to the sickest patients. Some children received onion poultices and extreme unction on the same day. The smell of cooking onions must have permeated the school, lingering for several anxious weeks, like a miasma of the illness itself. Father Charles gravely recorded temperatures of 105 degrees in his diary and noted that one of the hired men was "even worse, half dead." The days ticked by. News from elsewhere was not good. On October 28, Father Charles wrote: "Clayoquot Operator told us this evening by phone that up to Friday last eight Indians had died at Uchuktlisat Cannery in Barkly Sd from the Flu."

On November 4, Father Charles boarded the steamer for Hesquiat at 1 AM. There he found a young mother, Amanda, and her three children were very ill. Her husband Jackson died at Nootka on November 7; the same day, Father Charles wrote: "At noon I was told by Estevan phone that the Germans have surrendered." Returning to Kakawis that evening, Father Charles learned that the doctor had finally come to see the patients at the school. On the whole, matters had improved; all the children were up and about except three girls "in serious condition." Two of them recovered, but despite the onion poultices, the third girl, identified only as Monica, died on November 9. Two days later: "Funeral of Monica during rain."

The Spanish influenza claimed only this one student at Christie School, but the children were slow to return to health. On November 13, no High Mass could be held "because children not able to sing yet." Father Joseph went to Opitsat that day to bury a girl who had died the day before at the Clayoquot Cannery.

In his diary, Father Charles made no further reference to the influenza. He was fortunate because, for him, normal life resumed fairly quickly. In early December he was at Hesquiat just in time for a memorable event. "Last night at 1 AM we had a severe earthquake," he wrote on December 6. "I thought the end of the world was here. Both my chimneys were damaged with big holes in them above the roof. Medicine bottles and dishes fell from the shelves." A stormy few days followed, and then, inexplicably, another strange occurrence: "Canned salmon drifting on shore at Hesquiat. Some Indians procured a few cans, others 2 to 4 cases."

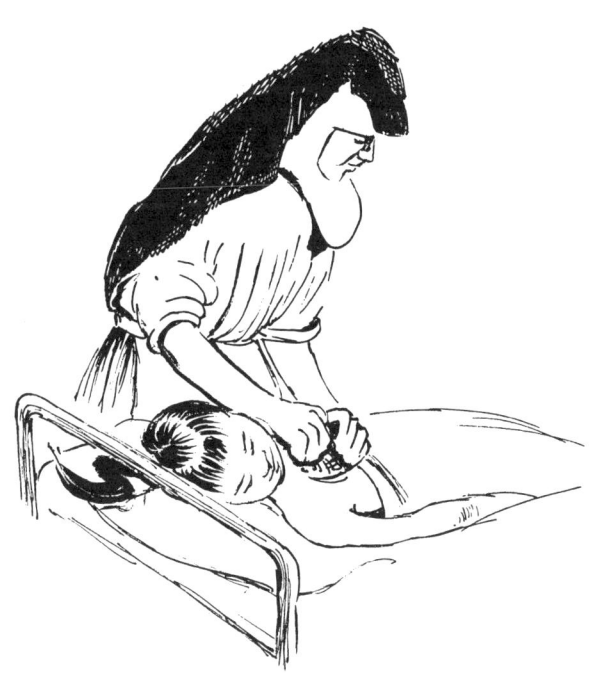

Only those lucky enough to have escaped the influenza could enjoy such novel distractions. For many others, in many different locations, the epidemic continued to dominate their lives well into 1919. Throughout British Columbia, native communities were particularly hard hit; of the 4,000 people estimated to have died of this influenza in the province, some 1,150 were Indian.

— 17 —

Dearest Girl

Wednesday 23rd

Well, Sweetheart, I am here again the Steamer came in late last night—11:30 PM, which means I didn't get my mail till today. I am really sorry I was compelled to miss last mail…I am sure you will be wondering what I have to say about everything. You mention July for our wedding. Please do make it August and then I can take more time.

Mabel Hall in her late teens.

The letters from Mike Hamilton to Mabel Hall are over eighty years old now. Not many have survived: an undated one written before their engagement, two from 1923 and half a dozen from the early months of 1924. The yellowed pages, scored by the lines of the original folds, are dry as wafers, brittle with age.

Pages of impetuous, spiky handwriting flowed from Mike's pen. He often wrote hurriedly from his machine shop in Tofino, racing to finish before "next boat" arrived to take the mail away. Bursting with nervous energy and plans for the future, Mike anxiously reassured Mabel their upcoming marriage would be happy and described how hard he was working to prepare for their life together. He addressed her as "Dearest girl," "My sweetheart," "Mabel dearest," "sweetheart mine" and "girl-of-my-heart." Mike had waited a long time for Mabel: "I am glad that my love and your love proved true. We have both been through the fire, so ours is not an ordinary love affair."

Mike Hamilton came from a farm near Dundalk in the north of Ireland. Born in 1888, the youngest of eight children, he followed the lead of several members of his family when he emigrated to Canada in 1913. His sister Minnie, a trained nurse, left first. She met her future husband, Lou Cole, on board ship, and they initially settled in Nanaimo. Next to leave was Harry, who took up construction work in Ontario before heading west to British Columbia. In 1911, Harry returned briefly to Ireland to help his widowed mother and his brother Addie prepare for their emigration to Canada. They settled on a farm near Langley in British Columbia's Fraser Valley.

Mike was the last to come to Canada. Before emigrating he worked nearly five years in England, laying telegraph cable across Dartmoor and down into Cornwall. During this period, his name changed. Christened Walter Charles Hamilton, in England he became known as Mike because the foreman of his work crew declared that, as he was Irish, he must be either a Pat or a Mike. He was Mike for the rest of his life.

Although he relished gaining experience in the telephone and telegraph services in England, Mike was restless: "Canada called and I could visualize all sorts of wonderful things coming my way." He was good-looking, hard working and optimistic, yet in his wildest dreams Mike could not have foreseen what awaited him. He later told his daughters, "It was on that trip across the ocean in the old *Oceanic* that I had the good fortune to meet your Mother as a very small girl with her Mother and Father and two Uncles. They too were on their way to Langley."

Mabel Hall was only twelve years old when she first set eyes on Mike Hamilton on board ship. He was twenty-five. Their paths diverged upon arrival in Canada; Mike went to work on the telegraph line along the shores of Howe Sound, while Mabel settled into a predictable routine in Langley, living on a farm and attending school—but she did not forget Mike. A few months after their joint arrival in Canada, she wrote to his mother and asked politely for "Mr. Hamilton's address." Sarah Hamilton sent her a brief postcard informing her of Mike's whereabouts. Mabel kept this postcard all her life.

Mike and Mabel began to correspond, and for the next ten years they kept in touch. Mike gravitated towards the west coast of Vancouver Island, working for the government telegraph service for several years and then moving to Tofino, where he established a machine shop. Driven by the ambition to save enough money to marry Mabel, he was continually anxious about winning her hand. "Your dear letter has taken loads & loads off my mind," Mike declared in his earliest surviving letter. "…I will live up to everything you think I should…I love you…I will live for you still & when I make a real headway then I will come

Mike Hamilton.

for you if you are still free." For years, while Mike worked hard to establish himself, Mabel waited. She remained free.

Having signed on to work extending the telegraph line north to Nootka, Mike first arrived at Clayoquot in November 1913. "Now, the Dominion Telegraph Dept had all arrangements made for us to proceed up the West Coast of the Island," he recalled in his memoirs. "We got the information that a line had to be built from Clayoquot to Nootka. As far as I was concerned it could have been from Zanzibar to Tibet, such names meant nothing to me just then." Two teams worked on this line: one coming south from Nootka; one heading north from Tofino.

Installing the line was an ambitious venture involving, as Mike remembered, "the cutting down of many thousands of trees and the stringing of many miles of heavy iron wire carried on 'chosen' trees that had to be trimmed and topped at convenient points along the water's edge, except for certain cross country trails where it was necessary to clear a path through the woods and construct a good walkable trail through the almost impenetrable forests...No cross-cut saw ever entered the woods, all trees were chopped down!" In under a year, the line was complete; the northbound crew met the southbound crew at Estevan in August 1914.

Mabel in Tofino, 1923.

The final stages of the work found the crews camping at Home-is and at Anton's Point in Hesquiat Harbour. Father Charles first remarked on the telegraph workers in April 1914, when he heard confession from some men at the Home-is camp. That same month he also noted loads of construction supplies and telegraph wire arriving on the *Princess Maquinna*. He mentioned the telegraph workers repeatedly in the following months.

Hesquiat was a lively place that spring and summer of 1914. On May 19 the delegates of the "Royal Indian Commission," as Father Charles called the McKenna-McBride Royal Commission on Indian Affairs for the Province of British Columbia, arrived—according to his diary—on the *Tees*. The commissioners were touring the province with the declared aim of settling outstanding concerns about the size and boundaries of Indian reserves. "Only few Indians being here," wrote Father Charles, "word was sent to Home-is for men to come and make suggestions and put in claims in regard to Indian claims for lands. But these did not arrive before 8 PM, which time was too late for a meeting." The following morning, various native leaders met with and talked to the commissioners. Although he was invited, Father Charles did not attend. "The meeting was short" is his only comment on the whole affair. He took more interest in the dinner he enjoyed on board the steamer with the commission delegates, and he commented with satisfaction on the gifts of food they left him: "a box…with apples, oranges, bananas, grapefruit, nuts, cucumbers and a bottle of cognac."

Mike Hamilton's version of events is different. He was at Hesquiat at the time the McKenna-McBride Commission arrived, and he recalled they came on the *Princess Maquinna*: "She was commissioned by the Indian Department to carry a party of Departmental investigators appointed by the then government to inquire into Indian welfare and living conditions on the West Coast of the island. I have no knowledge of who they were and just what they accomplished; not very much by all evidence." Following this, Mike added, "Poor Indians!" He was right. Whoever benefited from the work of the Royal Commission, it was not the native people. The net result of the commission's recommendations was the removal of a great deal of valuable land from reserves across the province, replacing it with land, or with new reserves, of lesser value.

Only two days after the commissioners left, the abbot of Mount Angel arrived for a visit. Father Charles staged a lavish welcome. "On his arrival all Indians come up to my house to greet and welcome him. Flags were up and my porch decorated with a wreath and the sign 'Welcome.'" The abbot sang High Mass the following day and they "had a gala dinner with canned chicken and Plum Pudding. After dinner we took photoes of groups of Indians…Indians were treated by Fr. Abbot with stick candies and by myself with cigarettes, then the women performed some Indian dances, during one of these the steamer whistled and the joyful party broke up."

When the telegraph workers at the Home-is camp moved to Hesquiat in June, they pitched their tents behind the church. The men were in fine spirits; after several months of hard labour out in the bush, they would soon be heading down to the bright lights of Victoria. Father Charles could hear them at their camp, cheerfully singing late into the night; one of them obliged him by helping to butcher and transport the meat and the hide of a large wild bull lying some distance from the village—thirteen bullets had been needed to kill this monster, and 1,000 pounds of meat had to be packed out of the bush.

In mid-June, Father Charles noted: "Telegraph line finished. Now the land line is up from Clayoquot to Nootka, instruments not yet installed and cables not yet laid." On July 5: "At 8 PM a tug passed into the harbor with scow in tow to lay telegraph cable." Before the final connection of the telegraph line, Father

Charles twice had to deliver messages the traditional way, by hand: once to Anton's Point and once when the captain of a whaling ship arrived at his house with a note for him to take to Estevan Point. Having walked for two hours along the beach to deliver the captain's message, Father Charles returned by following the new telegraph line through the forest, which took only an hour and a half.

His days of delivering messages by hand were over. At the end of July the new telegraph operators, who would be permanently based at Estevan Point, came to his house to install the equipment for a telephone connection. These operators were Minnie and Lou Cole, Mike Hamilton's sister and brother-in-law; they became regular visitors at Hesquiat. On August 3, 1914, the Coles were there to make the very first connection on the line. Father Charles marvelled that "at 3 in the afternoon I was able to speak with Nootka and Estevan, from the latter point heard the first war news." Soon he was also able to talk to Ahousat and Clayoquot. The wonders of modern technology were finally at Father Charles's fingertips. In 1912, ten days passed before he heard of the sinking of the *Titanic*, but now news travelled fast. "Heard some more war news, conflicting reports," he wrote on August 6.

With the line now connected between Clayoquot and Nootka, the footslogging maintenance work began. Mile after isolated mile, the fragile wire followed the coast, looping crazily from tree to tree, held in place by wooden brackets. Frequently it cut overland on trails blazed through the forest. Often it spanned streams, and in places it swooped precariously across small inlets and bays. Highly vulnerable to wind and weather, any falling tree or branch could put the entire line out of commission. Mike Hamilton took the job of lineman in charge of forty miles of line between Ahousat and Hesquiat Harbour, a job he held for three years, receiving eighty-five dollars per month for his labours. During this time he often stayed at Riley's Cove, near Sydney Inlet, in an isolated cabin.

After 1916, his isolation lessened when the old sealing schooner *Favorite*, under the optimistic command of Captain George Heater, arrived in Riley's Cove. Heater anchored the schooner and secured a large house float to it, and there he set up a small business salting pilchards. "It was during these years that the waters of the Sound simply teemed with pilchards," wrote Mike Hamilton, "the silvery hordes making it a sight to be remembered when after dark one could stand in the bow of a power boat and watch them in their phosphorescent millions hastening out of the way." Heater's employees lived aboard the *Favorite*, including some twenty young women, reportedly from Aberdeen, Scotland. "A company of girls," Hamilton reported, "…incurred considerable excitement and fun in that far flung outpost." But Captain Heater's enterprise did not last

Telegraph line workers with coils of wire around their necks, 1914.

long. The *Favorite* and the float containing the packing plant fell victim to a big storm in the winter of 1919–20, and the notion of salting pilchards went no further because, according to Hamilton, "pilchards were too fat to be successfully preserved in salt." The *Favorite*, or what remained of her, was later towed to a distant arm of Sydney Inlet. She sank there, and according to Mike Hamilton, writing many years afterward, "the ancient hulk of the schooner can even now be seen beneath the waters on a clear and calm day."

The pilchard fishery, later to become so dominant on the west coast, was just gearing up at this time. On his inspection trip in 1918, Mr. H. Brodie of the CPR noted the vast quantity of pilchards arriving at Nootka Cannery, which at that time employed sixty white people and "40 or more Indians and Orientals," according to Brodie. "In 1917 the cannery put up 45,000 cases of salmon and 10,000 cases canned herring and pilchards. This year they…put up as many as 3,000 cases in one day. They had brought in, the night we arrived, one catch of 25 tons of pilchards, which is a very heavy catch to come in at one time. They have more orders for pilchards than they can fill at the present time."

By the late 1920s, the pilchard fishery was massive. Many purpose-built fish reduction plants worked full tilt to extract oil and to make fertilizer from the thousands of tons of pilchards being caught. These enormous schools of pilchards proved unpredictable, however, and the fish plants opened and closed accordingly, as Father Charles noted in September 1926: "All the Reduction Plants had closed down and their crews were on their way home. The pilchards which had been running in myriads had suddenly ceased to run." The pilchard industry continued, and thrived, for many years, but by the 1940s the pilchards had mysteriously disappeared. They have never reappeared in any number.

During the years he spent on the job, Mike Hamilton found the work of patrolling the telegraph line between Ahousat and Hesquiat both lonely and demanding. "It was nothing unusual," he wrote, "to have miles of line hopelessly wrecked by one big storm." He minded this line in all weather, travelling partly by motor launch, but mostly on foot through the bush, staying at cabins he built along the route.

Farther up the coast, Minnie and Lou Cole also worked to maintain the telegraph line; they were in charge of the stretch of line between Estevan and Anton's Point. Unlike Mike Hamilton, they knew they had a safe haven along their route, for they could always call in at the priest's house at Hesquiat when they were out on the line. Between 1914 and 1917, Father Charles mentioned the Coles frequently and with evident liking. Minnie understood Father Charles's sweet tooth; over the years she made him numerous pies, cakes and other "eatables." They spent many nights at the priest's house, shared many a meal and celebrated Christmas together year after year.

More than once, unofficial family gatherings took place at Father Charles's house; the Coles would be there, and Mike or Harry Hamilton. Harry had been working at the copper mine at Sydney Inlet, but the work did not please him and he decided to try his hand at homesteading farther up the coast. He pre-empted a 160-acre parcel of land near Home-is and stayed on this lonely and exposed stretch of coast for many years.

Father Charles saw more of the Coles than he did of Mike or Harry Hamilton. He well understood the rigours they faced in monitoring the telegraph line strung through the forest and along the shoreline around Hesquiat. He had walked their route many times from Estevan to Hesquiat, or from Home-is to Hesquiat, or from Anton's Point to Hesquiat, walking through the bush, along the beach, through swampy mud and over slippery boulders. He knew what it was like to tramp through the sodden forest in a downpour of rain, or on rough, barely visible trails, or along the rocky beach, skirting the edge of the trees. He understood what it meant to be out there at night, armed with a lantern that could easily blow out in the wind. He knew the exhaustion of clambering around a tangle of windfall trees in the half-light of a winter afternoon, and he also knew the pervasive sense of unease about the wild bulls in the vicinity.

Knowing all this, he was a sympathetic host, as on November 1, 1914: "All Saints day and Sunday. At 6 AM Mr and Mrs Cole arrived having walked all night since 9 PM to repair break in telegraph line. I gave them a hot drink and they left again in search of the break. When I came back from High Mass they had already found and repaired the break so after our dinner they went to bed."

When Minnie and Lou Cole left in 1917 to serve in the war effort overseas, they spent their final night with Father Charles. The *Tees* arrived at three in the morning on March 8, and the Coles roused themselves for the familiar and chilly canoe paddle to the lighted steamer. Once overseas, Lou Cole served as an army officer and Minnie as an ambulance driver and army nurse. Following the war, they both returned to Estevan Point and stayed well into the 1920s. Lou had been poisoned, probably by gas, during the war, and for his remaining years at Estevan Point his health was poor.

The matriarch of the Hamilton clan, Mrs. Sarah Hamilton, met the strangest fate of all the Hamiltons on Vancouver Island. She had settled with her son Addie and his wife on their farm near Langley, but in 1922 when Minnie, no longer a young woman, was expecting her first child, Mrs. Hamilton set out to help her daughter. She made the long journey to Estevan Point, crossing from Vancouver to Victoria by CPR steamer and then boarding the *Princess Maquinna* in Victoria to head up to Hesquiat. An elderly woman entirely unaccustomed to sea travel, she bravely disembarked in the usual perilous manner, descending a rope ladder into a canoe.

She never climbed that rope ladder again, for she did not make the return journey. At Estevan Point she fell ill with a virulent flu, died there and was buried near the lighthouse. Mike Hamilton wrote: "At her own specific request we buried her there on a little level patch high above the shore line where the open ocean comes roaring in…She loved the sea shore. That was her reason for the request to be buried there all alone in unhallowed ground…Harry secured a head stone and erected it over her grave."

For many years Harry Hamilton remained at his homestead at Home-is, tending his livestock and learning many necessary skills like butter making and bread baking. He even built himself a twenty-four-foot motor launch, powered by the engine of a 1916 Model T Ford, which he obtained from his brother (this was the engine from the car Mabel Hall owned before her marriage to Mike). Few traces of Harry's tenure now remain at Home-is, although swathes of naturalized daffodils still bloom in the springtime, and clumps of Michaelmas daisies in the autumn, on the deserted stretch of beach in front of where his cabin stood. These bear witness to Harry's efforts—or the efforts of his wife—to establish a garden there.

Much to everyone's surprise, in 1927 Harry married Mabel Wade, whom he had known years earlier in Ireland. A strong-minded woman, equal to any challenge, Mabel had been a nurse during the war, and now she made it her business to get to know the people around her. She and Harry developed a fondness for the Rae-Arthur children a few miles away in Boat Basin. Realizing how needy the family was, they offered Willie Rae-Arthur some work at their place cutting firewood. Willie did not particularly welcome such employment, occasionally falling asleep behind the woodpile. Having been raised in an upper-class family in Glasgow, he had difficulty accepting that a gentleman of his background should be compelled to do manual labour—not an attitude shared by the capable and practical Hamiltons. Harry and Mabel stayed at Home-is well into the 1930s.

Although his name appears only intermittently in Father Charles's diary, Mike Hamilton's memoirs leave no doubt of his friendship with the priest. The quick-tempered Irish Protestant and the single-minded Benedictine both enjoyed a game of cards, and over the years they shared many convivial evenings at Hesquiat. More than once, Father Charles provided Mike with meals and a roof over his head; most memorably, he came to Mike's rescue following the death of Helen Wheeler at Boat Basin.

Both Mike and Captain George Heater accompanied Arthur Wheeler to Boat Basin on February 2, 1917. Wheeler had been working for Heater at his pilchard saltery in Riley's Cove, and Mike was giving him a ride home. Like the neighbouring Rae-Arthur family, Wheeler had settled at Boat Basin in 1915, pre-empting land and building a cabin. Unlike them, he did not remain long; this was to be his last season on the coast.

On entering his cabin, Wheeler was horrified to discover his wife, Helen, lying dead in the bedroom. He and his companions alerted the Rae-Arthurs and contacted Father Charles. Mike Hamilton anchored offshore, having decided to spend a night there to await developments.

The day after their sad discovery, a strong gale blew up, and Mike's motor launch pulled anchor and drifted away. Although he knew that "Hesquiat Harbour in storm condition is a fearsome place, with its jagged and rocky shoreline, its shallows and its kelp beds," Mike paddled desperately around the shoreline in a canoe, searching for his boat. Hours later he found it, now a heap of wreckage, a great distance across the harbour. He worked frantically, up to his waist in icy water, to salvage the engine, and by the time dark fell he was cold and hungry, miles from any shelter. He heard a loud shout and, to his intense relief, saw a dugout canoe approaching him. The Indians on board had been sent out by Father Charles, who knew that Mike was in trouble somewhere on the harbour.

His rescuers paddled him and Captain George Heater, who was also out looking for the launch, to safety at Hesquiat. Mike was in such bad shape he had to be carried up to the priest's house. Father Charles gave him a measuring glance and then reached into his pocket to bring out a bunch of keys. He unlocked a cupboard, saying, "I think I have something that will fix you up." Mike enjoyed telling the rest of the story:

> [Father Charles] reappeared with a glass containing a brown liquid. "Now, listen Mike," he said, "I don't want you to sip this; I just want you to get it down in one swallow."... I almost blacked out with the jolt I received. My mouth and throat were suddenly afire, I just didn't know what had hit me. When I recovered from the shock I remember him standing in front of me with a knowing grin on his face remarking "That should do the trick," and it did. In not more than ten minutes I was dancing a jig on the kitchen floor of the old mission house, built

many years before by the Rev Father Brabant...I remained at the Priest's residence and enjoyed his hospitality for several days. Father Charles was Swiss, and an expert at making up tasty dishes, and couldn't he prepare sauerkraut!

Years later, Father Charles again came to Mike's rescue. Joan Niblock, Mike's daughter, recalled her father's story of how the priest hauled him out of the water when he had fallen from a dock in Tofino. Weighed down by his oilskins and in terror of drowning, Mike believed Father Charles had saved his life. "Remember, girls," he told his daughters, "I couldn't swim a stroke. Born to be hung, not drowned, eh?" Neither man ever forgot the incident. Still later, when the Hamiltons were living in Alberni, Father Charles telephoned Mike and in the course of the conversation asked him about the state of his soul. "I once saved your life," he said. "Will you now let me save your soul?"

Father Charles had a fearsome reputation for his determination to save souls. Harry Hamilton's wife Mabel once told her niece Joan about visiting Father Charles's classroom at Kakawis. She was taken aback to see the walls lined with large dark sheets of paper on which Father Charles had drawn frightening images of hellfire and souls in torment. This apparently was to warn the children of what he believed awaited the sinners amongst them.

By 1923, Mike Hamilton's machine shop was well established in Tofino, servicing the "large fleet of small gasoline fishing boats" noted by Mr. Brodie several years earlier. Mike spent every moment he could scribbling hopeful letters to Mabel, speaking confidently of marriage. Mabel was in her early twenties by now, and Mike his mid-thirties. In his letters he dreamed that a house might be ready within a year, and he ardently requested that she come up in the spring for a visit. "I am indeed glad that you have decided to try hard to come up in May. It would be just splendid," he wrote, adding a bit more dubiously, "...if you decide to come for good when you have seen Tofino and its inhabitants."

Occasionally Mike indulged in detailed, even comical, descriptions of the daily round of life in Tofino. His observations of his fellow citizens have a biting edge: "There are lots of people, especially in Tofino, who don't want to understand anything or anybody especially if it is beneficial to themselves to misunderstand one." He wrote in veiled terms of Tofino as a backbiting, inward-looking community, with small local wars flaring up from time to time. On one occasion he referred to enemies who would like to see him starve, and he often alluded to small jealousies and outbursts of ill-feeling in the town. As secretary of the Settlers' Association and as a member of the school board, he found himself embroiled in pitched battles about local issues. He commented on these darkly in his letters, always in oblique terms, never specifying the details: "There is a lull in the war in Tofino and everything is very quiet on both fronts. I often wish I was a cartoonist and I could have endless fun out of the situation here. As usual Aunty Dot makes a triumphant victory over her enemies once again."

"Aunty Dot" or "Mrs A.," as Mike called her, was Dorothy Abraham, a powerhouse in the emerging social scene of Tofino. She and her husband Ted moved to Tofino from their home on Vargas Island in 1921. "After Vargas Island it seemed like going to live in the city," she enthused in her book *Lone Cone*, "…at Tofino there was a road, a school, shops, a church and a post office, and about 300 people." They arrived with all their possessions loaded higgledy-piggledy onto a freight scow: stove, furniture and her grandmother's portrait, a dog and a cat and a rooster who crowed the whole way, while the unperturbed chickens calmly laid several eggs en route. "It was so nice to be able to walk to the shop, and not have to cross that horrid piece of water."

After Mabel's visit to Tofino in the spring of 1923, Mike threw himself with even more fervour into his work, trying to establish a photographic business in addition to his other employment. "Work, work is my theme, not only work but plan & scheme & look ahead to see how I can make a dollar." His machine shop on the waterfront serviced all manner of engines; when it came to fixing anything electrical or mechanical, Mike relished all challenges that came his way. According to his daughter Joan, her father had "wheels in his head" and was never happier than when puzzling over some intriguing mechanical problem. The work "comes in spasms," he explained to Mabel. "Some days I make nothing others I make from one to thirty dollars. The thirty dollar mark is rare, though." Nonetheless, Mike knew he was needed and valued, and he behaved accordingly. He meted out his services to his clients as and when he saw fit, and because he hated being interrupted when writing, he frequently ignored his customers for extended periods of time: "Mabel Sweetheart: It is a funny thing that when I just get settled down to get my letters written two boats should pull up at the float and I have been idle more than half my time during the past week. I'll let them wait a bit." Three long pages of handwriting later, he comments, "I see the boat owners have got tired waiting for me and have come to fetch me so I guess I must go."

Mike Hamilton at work, mid-1920s.

Although none of her correspondence survives, Mabel evidently wrote faithfully, every steamer, doing her best to oblige Mike. Obtaining good suits

of woollen underwear was a lively concern for Mike, and when Mabel sent him some on the steamer, he was delighted, adding, "Yes, I sincerely hope that I'll need something lighter for my trousseau! If we are to be married in August as August is usually a fearfully hot month." He asked Mabel's advice about what to wear for his wedding, and she took this question to heart: "I couldn't help laughing at your dream and me turning up in a mackinaw suit. Good heavens—fancy a mackinaw suit to get married in."

Before her marriage to Mike, Mabel Hall was known around the Langley area as "The Heiress," for her family was better-off than most in the area and had only one child to indulge. Mabel owned a car when she was sixteen—a 1916 Model T Ford, which eventually ended up in Tofino, the first car the town had ever seen. She knew absolutely nothing of the west coast other than what Mike had told her, and when she finally came to live there, like so many other young women both before and since, she had no idea what lay in store.

Mike repeatedly told Mabel of the comforts awaiting her—the half-acre lot, well situated, and the house that would emerge on this raw plot of land as her bridal home. "I'll bet it will be, though not elaborate, the only house in Tofino furnished with good taste," he predicted enthusiastically.

> I am jolly glad to get the piece referred to as we will be a little way off from Tofino, just a safe distance from gosspipers and trouble makers. We will be connected to Mrs A by private phone for boat news etc as she has a government phone over which she can get general information. We will have to have an independent lighting plant all on our own…I picture our house, the position is sunny—Tofino faces the north you know—I can see it in a nice little clearing nicely fenced in—not barbed wire—a good gravel walk on either side with flower beds… and rambler roses around the house and porch.

In one of her letters to Mike, Mabel sensibly asked how he ran his business and how he determined who received credit at his shop. Mike provided a lengthy explanation, revealing a great deal about the social and economic realities of Tofino:

> To an Indian we scarcely if ever give credit, they are a poor class of customer anyhow. They are forever grumbling no matter how little your charges may be. They have inferior boats and engines anyhow they don't look after them and only bring them in for repair when they are gone beyond that stage. Therefore they are undesirable as

customers for this reason and because they will never pay a debt... The white people with boats are few and are also poor customers what few there are are usually broke. They are, as a rule, poor fishermen and it is for this reason I don't like giving them credit... Then there are the Japs, our best customer in every way... They usually have splendid boats & engines they keep them in good condition and will not tolerate you doing a poor piece of work. They want the best. They are good payers, always cheerful and ready to lend a hand let it be financial or otherwise. They will subscribe to any good cause to their last cent. In short they are ideal citizens notwithstanding all that has been said against them.

Father Charles also spoke favourably of the Japanese in the area during the mid-1920s, particularly when he relied on them for transportation. In May 1925 he wrote, "I left Kyuquot at 6 PM in a Japanese fish packer, three men in the crew: captain, engineer and cook. They were very kind. Had evening dinner and they gave me the only berth on board." In the summer of 1927 he told of a picnic the Japanese community planned to hold at Echachis. A Japanese spokesman invited everyone at Christie School to attend and offered to provide all boat transport. Sadly, the steamer came early the following day, and "the boys could not go to the Japanese picknick" as they had six tons of freight to unload. The sisters and the girls went without them. A later diary entry, from August 9, 1929, stated: "Arrived in fog at Clayoquot 7 AM. Took breakfast at the Hotel. Then got a Japanese fisherman to bring us to Kakawis. Charges nil. White man would not do that."

According to Walter Dawley's papers, Japanese workers first came to Clayoquot Sound at the turn of the century to cut cordwood on various mining claims, and in 1904 a few Japanese were already fishing on the coast. By the early 1920s some thirty Japanese families had settled permanently in the Tofino area. Some built homes on a six-acre parcel of land in Tofino Inlet; others created a Japanese community on Stubbs Island on a tract of land leased to them by Dawley, a settlement later known locally as "Jap Town."

Around 1922, when Tommy Kimoto was seven years old, his family arrived in the area. "When we got there," Tommy recalled, "the only house available was an old abandoned hotel on Stockham Island. Three families moved in there. That hotel used to leak. We'd put pots and pans all over the place." Life improved once the family moved to the house his father built on Stubbs Island: "I guess you could say the place on Clayoquot was more or less a shack, but it was nice there. We used to grow Japanese vegetables and things. There was an old jail there, and my mother used to lock my kid brother in it when he was bad." As for Mr. Dawley: "He was a nice sort of person, but of course, he got the business too."

From Mabel Hall's photograph album: "Self at Tofino, April 1923" she wrote beneath the picture.

By the time Mike Hamilton and Mabel Hall became engaged, the social scene in and around Tofino consisted of several different layers. Distinct groups of settlers, Norwegian, English and Scottish in origin, mingled and worked together, each group quietly convinced of its superiority over the others. At a cautious and polite distance, the Japanese occupied their parallel, hard-working world. The Indians lived in their nearby villages, a continual background presence, almost entirely separate from the growing community. Economic distinctions were clear in the town: there were those who held government jobs; those who fished, logged or operated businesses; those who—in the estimation of Walter Dawley or Mike Hamilton—paid their bills, and those who did not.

With the exception of the Japanese and the Indians, a significant number of Tofinoites occasionally invested in land with a view to selling at a profit. For a while Mike Hamilton owned an unnamed island in Tofino Harbour. Mabel, though she knew nothing about it, decided she liked it, even expressing the romantic desire to live there. Unfortunately, by the time he heard this, Mike had sold it.

> Regarding the Island. It is funny that you should mention it when you did. Only a short time ago it entered into a bargain involving 150 dollars which was to my credit. I couldn't wait to tell you about it as I had to say yes or no so I was jolly glad even to see 150 bucks as the island would have been a white elephant so I thought, perhaps your scheme would have made it different. Anyhow the bad burning it got last summer and the lack of water made it an undesirable place in my eyes... I hope you are not vexed I really thought you had forgotten about it. We can get lots more islands bigger and better ones and close to hand.

Mike never did purchase "lots more islands, bigger and better ones." He did not share the dream of island living that seemed, briefly, to entice Mabel—albeit

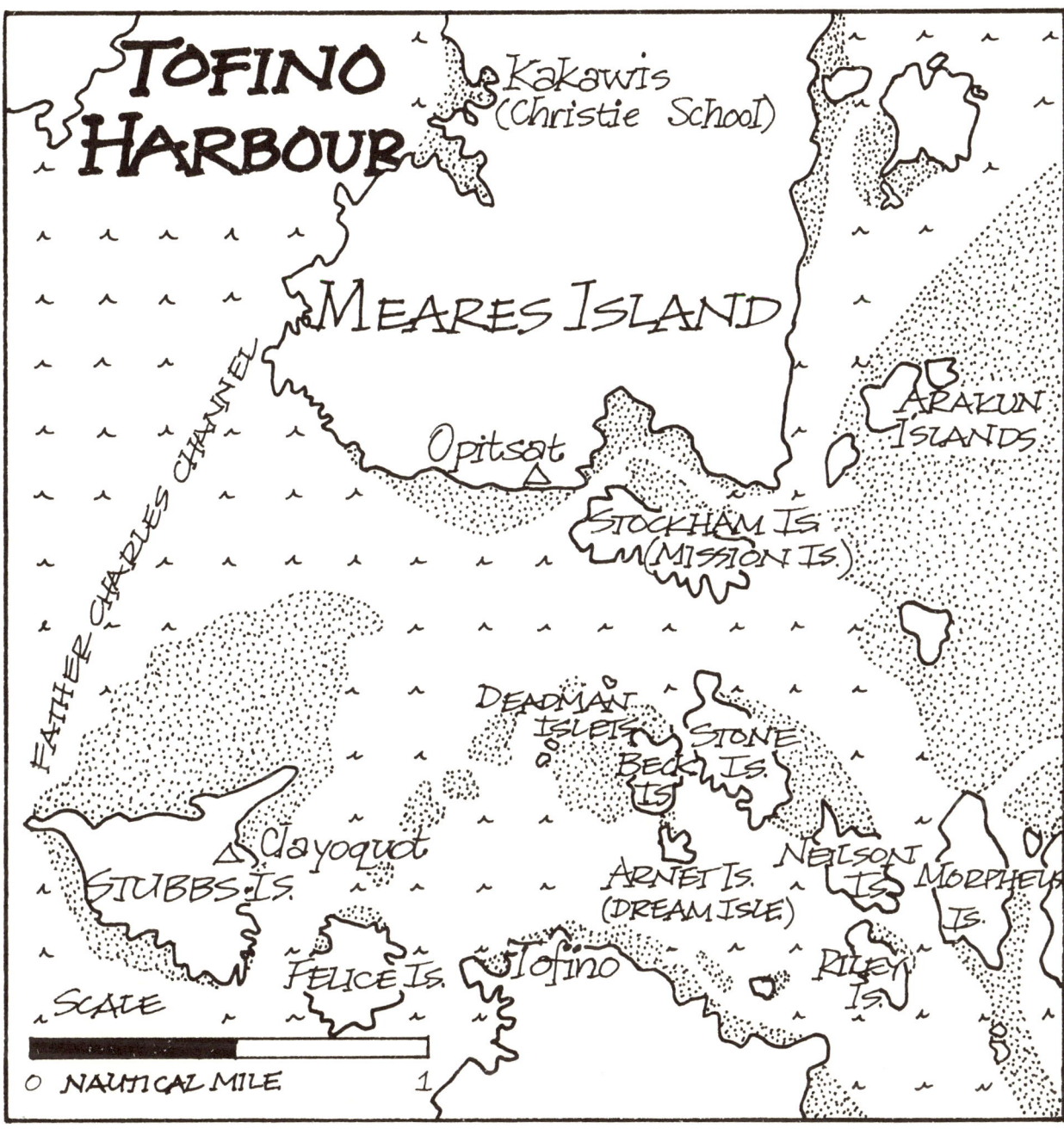

from the safe distance of Langley. Plenty of others did share that dream. The tiny islands scattered in the waters just in front of Tofino consistently charmed would-be settlers in the area, notwithstanding the tidal rips, the sandbars, the treachery of the sea, the lashing storms and the problems of water and moorage. As early as 1898, Mrs. Rolston commented in her diary that "on all or most of these lonely scattered islands a family or bachelor is struggling to clear the dense bush and have a patch ready for vegetables or garden."

On her visit to Tofino in 1923, Mabel Hall could not have missed Fred Tibbs's Dream Isle, that spectacularly exposed, clear-cut rock in the harbour, featuring the wooden castle Tibbs had built some ten years earlier. She would have heard stories of Tibbs, perhaps even the story of his will and the two local girls he favoured, for he was already becoming a legend in Tofino. She may have wondered what he was really like, what inspired him to pursue his idiosyncratic island dream. But Mabel would not have met Fred Tibbs on her visit. He died two years earlier.

After enlisting in 1917, Fred Tibbs served overseas until the end of the war, returning to Tofino in 1919 to pick up where he left off. He removed the boards on the windows of his dream castle and lived on his island once again, working in his garden and resuming local friendships. He continued climbing the ladder he had built to the top of his hundred-foot-high tree, and there, on the platform, he played his cornet or sat and wrote letters.

"No doubt you wonder what has kept me so infernally busy," he wrote to his niece on February 14, 1920, "the weather this winter has been so nice that it has been possible to work out of doors, so that when I come in, after having supper I fall asleep, or perhaps some people come over to hear the gramophone or I have to go over to Tofino for the mail or to have some music, as there are two or three damsels here who play very nicely." He told his niece that he tried to explode some dynamite on his tree platform—to "blow the old year to the four winds"—and that he made a hot-air balloon, "but the blighter caught fire just as it started off." Tibbs gained local renown for the risks he took with dynamite: "it was quite scenic," he

"I am glad that my love and your love proved true… ours is not an ordinary love affair," Mike wrote to Mabel. The Hamiltons are pictured here, probably after their wedding in 1924.

wrote, explaining his unsuccessful New Year's explosion on his tree platform, but "it failed to explode as it was frozen."

Fred Tibbs turned his attention to his new job. He was now responsible for tending the harbour lights, coal-oil lanterns mounted on tripods on flat wooden floats. They needed refuelling every other day, and Tibbs would row his skiff to the wooden floats and tie up, then clamber on and deal with the light. Everyone in Tofino could see him going happily about the harbour from light to light; except in really bad weather, this was pleasant-enough work.

On July 1, Tibbs took a party of friends up to the hatchery at Kennedy Lake for a picnic in his motorboat *Agnes*. "We spent a really wonderful day up there," recalled Trygve Arnet years later. "Then on the fourth of July we happened to look over in the afternoon and the Clayoquot Hotel was on fire. And boy, did she burn! And Tibbs, he went over. We saw him going across in his skiff to fight the fire." In his memoirs, Frank Garrard concurred, writing that "Tibbs with others, myself amongst the number had been very energetic in helping prevent the fire spreading to other buildings." Garrard also mentioned that in days prior to the fire, "[Tibbs] had been blasting some of the rock on the island, which he owned and on which he had built his house, with some old powder he had got badly powdered and had been quite ill from the effects."

"The next morning early he started out to look after these lights," Garrard continued, "but apparently after landing on one of the buoys on which the light was placed, his skiff and engine got away." Intending to swim after the skiff, Tibbs removed his clothes and dived in. This was his undoing. Accounts of what happened vary, but apparently an Indian saw the skiff drifting with no one in it and towed it back to Opitsat, not realizing Tibbs was in the water. Seeing this, and unable to make himself heard, Tibbs turned and swam for the nearest land, the long sandy spit on Stubbs Island, a considerable distance away. Although he was a strong swimmer, this proved too much for him, and as he neared land he became entangled in the long strands of seaweed lying thickly on top of the water. "He made the spit alright," Bill Sharp of Tofino recalled. "He crawled up on the sand and lay there." A Japanese man saw Tibbs and went to fetch Clarence Dawley. "Everything was done to revive him," the coroner later noted, "but without success." Fred Tibbs was buried in the Tofino cemetery, which was then on Morpheus Island.

His complicated will, leaving his dream castle to Olive Garrard and the island on which it stood to Alma Arnet, became the focus of much local gossip and speculation. The fathers of the two girls handled it, resolving that the Arnets would buy out the Garrard share of the assets. The Arnet family also acquired

Dream Isle, with the castle and "tree rig," around 1920.

Tibbs's cornet; it hung, disregarded, in the basement of their family home for decades. In 1992, Edward Arnet, Alma's nephew, donated it to the provincial museum in Victoria.

In 1922, a group of Tofino men went over and cut down Tibbs's "tree rig," as he called it, probably deeming it unsafe. Within a few years, Dream Isle greened over with new trees, and as time passed, Tibbs's castle disappeared from sight. The Arnets did not hold the property long before selling it; finding a buyer for the islands in Tofino Harbour has never been difficult.

Mabel Hall did not argue with Mike for her island. She had other arguments she wanted to win, a particularly pressing one being that Mike should learn how to dance. In January 1924 he commented nervously, "I don't really know what I'll do if I don't learn to dance because it appears that you are determined to learn." In April he admitted he had not yet learned to dance, and in May he said, "Now, Sweetheart, regarding your ultimatum as you call it. I was going to suggest even before I got that ultimatum that I learn to dance with you in our own home."

Mabel also did her best to encourage Mike to take a wedding trip following their marriage. She told Mike she was not at all keen to spend their honeymoon on the west coast, but he was determined they should go to Kennedy Lake, "a wonderful place, where there have been several honeymoons already." In another letter he elaborated: "We take launch for Kennedy Lake right from Tofino. We go to the cannery go up a short trail by Kennedy river rapids and then a fourteen mile launch ride on the lake. It is a big lake and a beautiful place I believe. The people there...will be tickled to death to have us."

Mike and Mabel were married in Fort Langley on August 18, 1924. They did spend their honeymoon at Kennedy Lake, and photographs show Mabel, outlined against the sunlit backdrop of the lake. This destination may not have been of Mabel's choosing, but the images that remain glow with the luminous beauty so characteristic of Mike Hamilton's pictures. To be in this remote and peaceful place was probably a great relief to the harried Mike—at Kennedy Lake he would not, after all, be required to dance.

The Hamiltons lived in Tofino for the first three years of their married life. Mabel astonished the locals by bathing in the sea every day, year round, and she aroused even more comment by the furniture she ordered. After two single beds were unloaded from the *Princess Maquinna*, Mabel began to realize what it meant to live in such a small and isolated community. Everyone in town knew the Hamilton's sleeping arrangements, or thought they did. Mabel attracted even more attention by becoming Tofino's postmistress for eight months in 1925.

"I am afraid you will find Tofino rather a dull place, during the winter anyhow, though we do have an occasional dance and whist drive," Mike told Mabel in a letter before they were married. Yet according to Dorothy Abraham, the social scene had greatly improved. "Do you know," she wrote, "they had NEVER had a bazaar, or even such a thing as a whist drive!! and no one even wore light coloured stockings! I was quite a freak! The first dance I went to in a semi-evening frock, almost everyone turned up in print frocks, and many of them wore high black boots, the kind our great-grandmothers wore. I felt an awful idiot all dressed up." She firmly declared, in her book *Lone Cone*, that *everyone* in town went to the dances, where local talent provided the music and "after a dance the men all sat on one side of the hall, and the ladies on the other. The Norwegians were the most wonderful dancers." A group of English bachelors could always be found at these social events, as well as the solid and respectable core of Tofino's population, the Scottish contingent and the Norwegians, described by Mrs. Abraham as "tall handsome women, with their lovely hardanger aprons; and taller handsomer men."

Mike Hamilton's technical wizardry added some zest to the social calendar in Tofino, particularly for the children. "We had movies in Tofino long before we had electricity," Anthony Guppy recalled in his book, *The Tofino Kid*. "Mike Hamilton had a movie projector he could set up in a hall. The projector had to be cranked by hand and the black and white pictures flickered wildly. He would usually show an old melodrama, then finish with 'Felix the Cat' or an 'Out of the Inkwell' comedy. We sat on wooden benches in a hall that was often a bit cold and drafty, but we loved every minute of it." At Kakawis, Mike serviced the

Mabel on honeymoon at Kennedy Lake, August 1924.

old movie projector, enabling the children there to enjoy the occasional Charlie Chaplin film.

The joyous action of boat days always revealed Tofino at its best and brightest. Children listened for the discordant screech of the whistle, restless for the moment they would be let out of school to run to the dock, little boys vying to be the lucky one who would catch the monkey's paw—that great round ball of knotted rope, attached to a thinner rope, which was thrown from the ship to the dock. Small boats converged from all around the harbour, including Indians in their canoes, "gay with colour" according to Dorothy Abraham. Everyone thronged to greet the *Princess Maquinna*, to eye the new arrivals, to collect whatever goods they had ordered. Groups of people waited around, chatting, while parcels and freight were unloaded. Because everything on board appeared on the manifest and was checked off when collected, no order was entirely private—it was easy, and often entertaining, to see what your neighbours were collecting from the ship. Those expecting deliveries from the mail-order catalogues would be ready to open the parcels immediately, check the contents, even try the clothes on their children right there and then; if it did not fit, the clothing was bundled up and sent straight back on the boat. Economically minded householders would receive bulk orders of groceries, as Anthony Guppy recalled: "Fifty pound sacks of flour and sugar, fourteen pound boxes of butter, five pound pails of shortening, large tins of Rogers' Syrup, a case of two dozen cans of Pacific milk, and so on. It was much cheaper to buy our groceries in bulk, saved endless trips to the store." And as Mike Hamilton pointed out, for those who had worked up a thirst since the previous steamer, there were "not infrequently mysterious crates, jars and packages." It was impossible to buy a drink in the village of Tofino; until the early 1950s, when the first beer parlour opened in town, the only liquor available in the area was over at the Clayoquot Hotel on Stubbs Island.

Tofino lifeboat crew, photographed by Mike Hamilton, mid-1920s.

Mike Hamilton wrote of the eccentric loners who lived on the coast on their pre-emptions or mining claims, "odd and weird individuals, bearded and long-haired who somehow lived hidden away in some remote location." Anthony Guppy also recalled these scattered and reclusive settlers and how, on boat days, even they made their way to Tofino for mail and supplies, sometimes finding a market for their garden produce amongst the townspeople or on board the steamer. "They would converge upon [the steamer] in canoes, skiffs and rowboats, from all directions," according to Mike's description. "But just as soon as the steamer had unloaded and taken its departure there would be a general exodus of the same skiffs, canoes and rowboats fanned out in their homeward direction. A period of semi-desolation would descend upon the scene until the next steamer arrived, and so it went on year in and year out."

In 1927, the Hamiltons left Tofino for Port Alberni, where Mike eventually became mayor. In later life, when he was writing his memoirs, Mike dwelled at length on his vivid years in Clayoquot Sound, striving to capture the grandeur and the isolation of the area, keen to share his love for "this wonderland of inland waters, bays, beaches and picturesque waterways backed by lofty mountains [that] never had a means of access, rail or road." He commented that "with some reasonable means of access it would immediately spring into prominence as a summer playground and resort unparalleled by anything on this coast." He was not alone in believing this.

18

Silences

September 6, 1926: Labor Day. After dinner the school band, Fr. Ildefonse included went per our launch first to Tofino wharf where we played 3 pieces, thence to Clayoquot wharf where we played several pieces. The Tofino store treated the boys with a box of plums and one of candy. At Clayoquot the boys got oranges, apples candies and orange crush. We (Fr. Ildefonse and myself) of course were treated in the beer parlor.

SEPTEMBER 1926 began well for Father Charles Moser with this musical interlude and the welcome refreshments. Other events also buoyed him up, including a visit from Mike Hamilton to install radios at Christie School: one in the girls' dormitory and one in the boys'. "We heard something from San Francisco," Father Charles remarked with evident pleasure. A few weeks earlier both Mike and Mabel Hamilton had paid another welcome visit to the school, and Mike had taken several pictures of the school and students.

Tofino Harbour, photographed by Mike Hamilton in the mid-1920s.

Even better, from Father Charles's point of view, construction had finally begun on the new church at Opitsat. Over a year earlier, in June 1925, a disastrous fire destroyed much of Opitsat village, including twenty-three homes as well as the church. Residents watched helplessly as a strong wind fanned the flames, and people from Tofino who rushed over to help could do nothing but offer relief afterward. In the ensuing months the village had gradually been rebuilt, and now, at last, work was underway on the church. Even though he sprained his ankle and smashed his thumb while shingling the walls, Father Charles was delighted by the new building. Soon the windows would be in, and the church would be ready. To add to his satisfaction, another church would soon be under construction, for Father Charles had successfully initiated a plan to build a church up at Port Alice. He visited this growing community frequently, and he now confidently awaited donations from the townspeople for the new church.

Another gratifying event claimed Father Charles's attention in the early autumn of 1926. He was about to become a published author. He pored over the proofs, recently arrived from the printer, and eagerly awaited arrival of the actual books. He had laboured long and hard on his *Reminiscences of the West Coast of Vancouver Island*, incorporating some of his own writings, parts of Father Brabant's diary and a number of photographs. This publication stands alone, for none of Father Charles's fellow Benedictines attempted to write a book about their time on the coast, contenting themselves with occasional articles, if they wrote anything at all. When the first box of books arrived, he noted, "My first book sold to a Clayoquot Indian," and he took one of the first copies up to Port Alice to show to the congregation there.

This burst of positive energy and encouraging events did not last. "Our big boys show bad humor," the priest commented in late September, and as the autumn progressed, his familiar tight-lipped unhappiness returned, souring his writing. Trouble dogged him, and he could not escape the school's difficulties. On October 2 he wrote: "Repaired a skylight on the roof which had been broken February 19 by a run away boy."

February 1926 had been a miserable month at Christie School. Repairing the damaged skylight months later could not obliterate the memory of all the disturbances and some children's repeated attempts to run away from school.

> *February 7, 1926:* Four run away boys broke into Dawley's store, stole and went to Long Beach. They were away a few days. Their Opitsat parents searched for and found them... The devil seems to be loose along the whole coast.

> *February 14:* Willie Harry and Louis Sabbas ran away from school either before or after supper. Some time after supper Fr. Ildefonse sent 2 big boys out to bring them back.
>
> *February 15:* By 10 AM neither the run away boys or the two sent after them had come back. Before noon the 2 sent returned. About 8 PM Fr. Ildefonse sent the launch with boys to get them at Opitsat—they brought them—they got a licking and were put in jail.
>
> *February 17:* One of the boys was let out of jail. A bag of bread being discovered by Sr. M. Elizabeth helped to discover another run away plot. Some more boys had planned to run away among them were two who had gone before and broken into Dawley's store. These two were locked up.
>
> *February 19:* About 5 PM the boys broke jail. One got out, broke skylight and going along the roof escaped by fire escape. He escaped in the direction of the village, though Fr. Ildefonse and boys were after him.

Such disappearances had become almost commonplace by 1926. Father Charles's diary speaks of runaways from the school as early as 1916, but the first detailed account comes in 1920:

> *January 19, 1920:* Four boys are on a diet without bread today for having been outside after supper yesterday. Two of them also had left the Dormitory by the fire escape ladder. In the evening three of these boys were missed about 7 o'clock. Investigation showed they had left the place by our small canoe.
>
> *January 20:* The run away boys had made the plan to run away already three days before Christmas:…they had along ½ sack of bread, ½ sack of spuds and cabbage and a blanket for each one.

Two days later, word reached Kakawis that these boys had arrived at Hesquiat. By the end of the month, one of them, Silvester, had been brought back to the school. "*January 28, 1920:* Silvester starts his punishment today bread and water diet; tomorrow the ordinary food, but no bread; the third day bread and water again."

Runaway children like Silvester never returned of their own accord. Concerted efforts involving several layers of authority generally brought them back.

As the years passed, ever more authorities became involved, and more enforcement. On August 31, 1926, the Indian Agent sent a telegram to the school with the assurance that the Department of Indian Affairs would "pay for launch hire whenever Constable Bradner goes out to get truant children in Clayoquot Sound." Father Charles noted that this constable arrived at the school the same evening in a Japanese motor launch, "bringing 2 truant girls from the cannery." The constable stayed overnight at the school "as we was going out tomorrow in search of truant boys."

School attendance became compulsory for all children in British Columbia in 1921. Although enforcement was erratic, truant officers and policemen had the power to force native and white children alike into school, regardless of their parents' wishes. The Rae-Arthur children at Boat Basin fell foul of such authorities in 1923. On March 5, Father Charles commented that "Ray Arthur came in the afternoon telling me of his troubles with his wife and family. They are getting crazy." Growing up in the complete isolation of Boat Basin, running wild when they were not working hard for their parents, the Rae-Arthur children took their schooling by correspondence, haphazardly. Word of this, of their impoverished conditions, perhaps of the "crazy" behaviour Father Charles mentions so obliquely, without any elaboration, must have became known to outside authorities. The long arm of the law reached out to remove the three eldest children from home. On April 25, 1923, Father Charles wrote that there had been "Visitors in the afternoon: the Principal of the BC Reform School at Vancouver, Constable Woods (Alberni) and Constable Anderson (Clayoquot). The first two had gone to Hesquiat by steamer came down to Clayoquot with 3 of Ray-Arthur's children by Indian launch. The children will be put to school." These three children, George, Frank and Margaret, unhappily spent the following five years at school in Vancouver, despite requests from their parents that they be returned home.

In the autumn of 1921, problems escalated at Kakawis. A group of the older boys rebelled, refusing to cooperate with the fathers or sisters. "When I go to punish

Students and staff of Christie School, probably on August 1, 1926, the day Father Charles wrote in his diary: "Mike Hamilton and his wife from Tofino paid us a visit. Mr. Hamilton took a picture of the school and another of all the inmates with his panorama camera."

them, they shake their fists in my face and try to fight me," Father Charles later explained to the Indian Agent. "They fight at the table and eat like animals... they take half a cup of tea in their mouths and then spit it on the table...[they] go rushing about...cursing and...interfering with punishments."

Escapes from the school became ever more ingenious and determined. "When I entered boys dormitory for inspection at 1:30 AM, lights were out of order," recounted Father Charles in his diary on November 3, 1921. "I got a flashlight and found four beds empty, canoe on the beach was gone." When the boys returned to the school, he found "one self-made pass key from one of the boys and found file and pass key in the pants pocket of another one." The rebellious boys made off again, but once more returned and "at 7 PM...electric lights went out, the boys had shut off the engine and in the darkness entered with self made [keys]." The boys then entered the girls' dormitory, and five girls ran away with them, pausing only to take two sides of bacon, bread, tea, a teapot and cooking pots from the kitchen before making off in a canoe.

This episode was the beginning of the end for Father Charles as principal of the school. Indian Agent Charles Cox had opposed his appointment from the outset, claiming in letters to his superiors that Father Charles was a lax disciplinarian who "lost his usefulness among the Indians through not having a regular system of rules." Now, with the big boys at Christie School in open revolt, Cox was less than impressed when he heard Father Charles explaining why he did not tackle the boys.

"If I go to whip them," Father Charles testified at the trial of the boys, all of whom were charged with theft, "they want to fight and I cannot fight with my light weight and height against several of the boys."

"Well, as I have told you before," Cox retorted when he addressed Father Charles at the trial, "you have lost control of the school, and I think that for all concerned it would be better if there was a change."

Father Charles was silent about these proceedings in his diary, noting only that all four boys were found guilty of theft and sentenced to two years in a reform school near Vancouver. He wrote nothing of the public dressing-down he received at the end of the trial, when the judge addressed him directly: "[The boys] are in your charge and you must control them. It is often necessary that you fight in order to subdue them...you are not severe enough in your punishments."

A few months later, in March 1922, Father Charles darkly declared, "The Evil One starts to work," adding, "Complaints have been made to the Indian Department at Ottawa." A file of administrative correspondence about the school reveals protracted disputes concerning the principalship of Christie School.

When Father Charles took on the position in 1919, no one in the Department of Indian Affairs approved of his appointment; only the abbot at Mount Angel and the bishop in Victoria spoke up in his favour. After three years had passed, Bishop Alex Macdonald of Victoria received a stern letter from Duncan Campbell Scott, of the Department of Indian Affairs in Ottawa, requesting Father Charles's removal and the appointment of a "competent principal." In April 1922, the priest wrote a long, aggrieved letter in his own defence: "I leave my post with the inward consolation that I am the victim of prejudice (perhaps slander also) judged and condemned by you without a hearing."

In this perturbed atmosphere, the abbot at Mount Angel seriously considered withdrawing all of his priests from the school and closing it down, but in the end he only reshuffled the personnel. Father Ildephonse Calmus, who had been at the school since 1919 as assistant to Father Charles, replaced him as school principal in May 1922. The bishop in Victoria reassured officials within Indian Affairs that Father Ildephonse was "reputed to be a strong disciplinarian." In mid-May, Father Charles left for a six-month break, travelling to Europe to visit his family.

The choice of Father Ildephonse as principal came at the same time that one of the boys at the school charged him with assault. "Scuffle between 2 boys and Fr. Ildefonse," Father Charles reported on April 11, 1922, at the height of the administrative uncertainties. The following day, "Constable Anderson came to serve papers to Fr. Ildefonse to appear before court tomorrow at 3 PM to answer charge of assault (for yesterday)." This is the only indication in the diary that any of the priests were ever officially charged for striking a student. "Court case was settled outside of court," wrote Father Charles, "Fr. Ildefonse paying expenses so far incurred, $5.50." Within a month, Father Ildephonse was in charge of Christie School.

On his return from Europe in November 1922, Father Charles took on new responsibilities: "My office is now Missionary from Clayoquot up to and including Kyuquot with Headquarters at Christie School." In other words, he would be on the move continually, travelling great distances, never in one place for long. His position at Kakawis was ambivalent; he spent a good deal of time there and did a lot of hard work, but he had no authority.

Although his years as principal of the school ended unhappily, with official censure, Father Charles was nonetheless the most senior and experienced priest on the coast, and in his new role he felt entirely unappreciated. At the same time, he was the one on whom the most difficult jobs always fell—or this is the impression given by his diary. He never flinched when faced with the dirtiest or most thankless tasks, and whenever he returned to Kakawis from long trips up the coast, more such work always awaited him. "In heavy rain I alone cleaned out a stopped up sewer pipe in the yard, worked from 1 PM to 4 PM," he wrote in October 1928. Only a few days prior to this he noted: "Last night after dishwashing I started to change hot water boiler in kitchen. Was finished at 3 AM." This was his lot throughout the 1920s. During these years, the enrolment at the school increased. Under Father Charles it had fallen to thirty-three, but now, with Father Idlephonse at the helm, it mounted gradually: back up to fifty, then sixty, then seventy-five. By 1928, eighty children were there.

An unusual entry appears in Father Charles's diary in the middle of September 1928. It occupies an entire page:

> Note: For sometime already, perhaps a year, I have left out certain happenings recorded in my diary—and this will be the case in future to the end of it. For the full story, therefore consult the original. This remark is made Oct. 2, 1946.

Father Charles signed this note "Chas." Careful reading of the different available versions of Father Charles's diary reveals that he edited his own recollections. The above note appears in the handwritten reproduction he made in 1946, copied from his original year-by-year journals. Only a few of these shabby little volumes now survive, and none for the year 1928, so Father Charles's cryptic comment about leaving out "certain happenings" cannot be verified against the original. What had been going on at Kakawis that Father Charles recorded in the original diaries and decided to omit when he copied the diary? Anyone can guess; no one can tell.

Another cryptic note appears in the diary at the beginning of the entry for November 28, 1928. "See Secreta." *Secreta* is Latin for "secret, or hidden." Father Charles used the word only this once. Given the context, it seems to imply a secret document, or a secret place where other material he had written could be found, but no such document or place is known. If he was referring to the original diary from which he made this handwritten copy, that original has not survived amongst his papers. His "Secreta" remains obscure to this day. From this point on, reading Father Charles's diary is like a game of hide-and-seek, with the reader wondering continually what has been left out, what left unsaid, what might be hidden in another, undiscoverable document.

Throughout his years at Kakawis, Father Charles periodically mentioned the punishments meted out to the children. The term "licking" appears in his diary, also the term "beating," and he referred once to the other fathers taking unspecified "severe measures." He often used the word "spanking." On January 21, 1928, he reported that "four big boys received a spanking this evening for having been at the girls' gym windows after supper. Two smaller boys get the same punishment for having gone to Opitsat without permission." Father Charles never went into detail about these punishments; he maintained a stern silence. Very rarely, other evidence surfaces, telling more about these punishments. In the case of one of the boys punished on January 21, 1928, more information is available.

Joseph Hayes was one of the four big boys "spanked" that day. His punishment, administered by Father Idlephonse, was severe. Afterward, as soon as he could, Joseph fled the school, going to his parents' home at Opitsat. Seeing the condition he was in, they took him to Ted Abraham, one of the local magistrates in Tofino, and Abraham sent the boy to Dr. Dixson for a medical examination. The doctor submitted a report to the Indian Agent.

> He was whipped on the naked skin with a one-ply strap, on his right thigh and buttocks, on the outer side of the right leg there are several blisters and abrasions, 6 or more. He received altogether a dozen or more lashes, and one blow on the back. He says he could not walk for one day after, nor could he get away from the school till the evening of the 23rd.

The doctor concluded that "the wounds are not serious, but must be considered excessive." Indian Agent Edward Frost concurred, as did the Indian Commissioner for British Columbia, W. E. Ditchburn. Eventually Father Ildephonse received an official rebuke from Mr. A. F. Mackenzie of the Department of Indian Affairs at Ottawa. "It is considered this punishment was too severe and that it was inflicted before the pupil was proven guilty of the particular offense," wrote Mr. Mackenzie, adding, "Corporal punishment should be administered in extremities only, and then with much care."

Father Idlephonse's methods of punishment had come under official scrutiny before. He received a similar letter from the Department of Indian Affairs in October 1924, from Mr. J. D. McLean. "Reverend Sir," the letter begins. "It is my duty to inform you that the Department cannot countenance severe disciplinary measures…in future resort to corporal punishment in moderation only after careful deliberation." In February 1925 the Indian Agent for the west coast wrote to the department concerning another incident: "[Father Ildephonse] is undoubtedly of a hasty temper, and I am convinced inflicted unduly harsh punishment on the boy." This followed the beating of a ten-year-old boy named Christopher; no other details are available. Father Charles does not mention that particular "spanking." He was not always at the school, and even if he were, these punishments were frequent events, only occasionally noted in his diary.

Charlie Mickie was a student at Kakawis from 1925 onward. "Yeah, I think there was a lot of them that got spankings," he recalled in an interview for the book *Indian Residential Schools: The Nuu-chah-nulth Experience*, published in 1996. "Every night there would be maybe a girl or a boy." Charlie Mickie joined the ranks of the runaways. He and three others lit out one night, regardless of the risk: "We went along the beach, there was a whole bunch of canoes along the beach…one had oars, two sets of oars in it. So we took that, we looked, it was getting foggy. We went along the shore. We started going to Ahousaht. Really foggy, I don't know how we made it…We got to Hesquiat…back at the school, punished, working, working, working…"

In November 1928, after three boys took Father Charles's own canoe at Kakawis and fled in the direction of Hesquiat—perhaps these boys were Charlie Mickie and his friends—students at the school were in turmoil:

> *November 4, 1928:* My name day. I said an early Mass…Trouble on the boys side, a lot of boys had to kneel in the upper hall. After supper when I visited the girls I found 7 of them in a bad spirit, the leader insulting Sr. M. Caroline. She was jailed, the others were mean and ugly. So I left them before bed time.

> *November 5:* One or two girls were spanked this morning. One of them fought Sr. Caroline, I heard something so I went to see what it was. Sister was glad I came—but Fr. Ildefonse soon followed me and fixed the girl alright. The devil seems to be loose here. Later in the day I was told that all those 7 girls were going to be spanked.

The northbound steamer arrived soon afterward and delivered to the school five crates of grapes, "which I had ordered as a treat for the children for my name's day yesterday," commented Father Charles, rather forlornly. No amount of grapes could ease the strained atmosphere. The following day Father Charles abruptly decided to leave for Victoria on the next boat, but before the southbound steamer arrived, everyone at Kakawis endured another bad day: "*November 7, 1928:* These are dreadful days. Spanking and crying. Sr. M.C. is spanking one a day; she claims she has not the strength for more than one a day. Is the spanking not overdone?"

The next day Father Charles escaped for Victoria. There he visited St. Ann's Convent, talked to the bishop and spent several days in hospital, having a cyst removed from his neck. To be granted the same hospital room that Father Brabant had occupied eased Father Charles's unquiet soul; he felt honoured to be there. While in Victoria, Father Charles met two families known to him from their days at the whaling station at Cachalot, and they treated him most kindly. Exuding from the pages of the diary written during these days in Victoria is a sense of overwhelming relief to be away.

He headed back to Kakawis on the night of November 23. At Port Alberni, in the early morning, the Indian Agent came aboard along with a truant officer. Later on, at Tofino, a policeman joined them: all three men were "bound for Kyuquot to get Canut Tom's daughter to our school. For several years this family had refused and defied the authorities." The end of that story came two weeks later. "Indian Agent, Policeman and truant officer returned from Kyuquot with one new boy for the school and Canut's daughter for Alberni (hospital or school I could not learn)."

Father Ildephonse Calmus with Christie School boys in the late 1920s.

By this time, Father Charles wanted only to return to Mount Angel. He went about his normal duties with a sense of marking time, continuing to write in his diary, perhaps comforted by his longstanding habit of recording everyday details. "I went aboard bound for Kyuquot. About 30 loggers aboard for Nootka Sound. Lots of rum and beer," he wrote in January 1929. On this northbound trip, he noted a piano being unloaded at Kyuquot, "the first piano bought by an Indian of this coast." A month later, taking the southbound steamer from Kyuquot to Kakawis, Father Charles saw the Napoleon family: "Stopped at Nootka all night. Margaret Napoleon was coming back to school after 6 weeks absence, because she cried her father came along with her."

When Father Idlephonse left Kakawis, apparently for health reasons, at the end of 1928, the event merited no comment in Father Charles's diary, but he had plenty to say when the younger Father Victor Rassiter took over as principal of the school. "He wants to be all at Kakawis. He wants to be Customs, PM [Post Master], and agent of Government Telegraph." An appeal to the abbot did little good. His reply was clear: "I must therefore ask you to turn over full control to Fr. Victor i.e. Post Office, Telegraph Office and Chapel." Doomed to be under the younger priest's authority, Father Charles commented caustically, "Poor Abbot to give like that to a young one. Will see how all will end."

It all ended in disarray, with Father Charles writing repeatedly to the abbot, asking to be allowed to return to Mount Angel. Nothing Father Victor did pleased Father Charles, and even allowing for the older priest's evident prejudice against this newcomer, Father Victor seems to have been a man of singularly little charm. Many months passed before he asked Father Charles to tell him about Father Brabant, about the pioneering days of the priests on the coast—subjects close to Father Charles's heart. He responded by spending as much time as possible up the coast at the missions, and he threw himself into finishing the church at Port Alice. He returned to Kakawis only sporadically, although he was always on hand to help escort children to and from their homes when school terms began and ended.

This could be the "orchestra of 5 instruments" Father Charles described in his diary in April 1928. They entertained passengers aboard the *Princess Maquinna* on their way home for the vacation.

April 14, 1928: Steamer Maquinna came at 6 AM. I left with 23 children who are going home for vacation. After leaving Gibson mill we gave on the steamer a musical entertainment, orchestra of 5 instruments, also some vocal pieces. We were applauded and complimented.

In accompanying the children on their various journeys, Father Charles had one great advantage over more recently arrived priests, partly because the parents of the children knew him from previous visits, but mostly because he spoke to them in their own language. Maurus Mclean, who first went to Christie School in 1925, remembered this clearly when interviewed for *Indian Residential Schools: The Nuu-chah-nulth Experience:*

> Father Charles was going around, from Kyuquot to Opitsaht, on *Princess Maquinna*. Father Charles, he was talking our language. *Aatsik tsiiktsiikas.* Talked to my parents, *suukwilth t'aanaakaat nanaachaktl maamaamalthna. Uushii-aktla uukwinkalth*...I said to my Dad and Mom, I'm willing, I'm willing to go to school to learn ABC.

Right to the end of his time on the coast, Father Charles continued going to the villages, talking to parents in their own language, recruiting children and bringing them back to the school. If he ever wondered about his role, shepherding children to the school from which so many would run away and where he himself felt increasingly ill at ease, he never expressed this openly.

In June 1929, Father Charles travelled hopefully to Oregon, summoned by the abbot, only to learn he must still remain at Kakawis. Disheartened, he returned to the coast, travelling directly up to Port Alice for a ten-day stint. Over the course of the following months, he found the atmosphere at Kakawis increasingly cold and unfriendly, and his sense of injury and exclusion grew. Small personal triumphs cheered him occasionally, especially when he celebrated his fifty-fifth birthday on board the *Maquinna* in the wireless cabin, with passengers and officers in attendance, and when the manager of the Nootka Packing Company donated ten cases of canned pilchards to the school. "Fr. Victor had asked me to order one case and I brought ten."

In early October he reported: "Mass wine getting sour. I mentioned this to Fr. Victor who replied he ordered a new supply." Meanwhile, Father Victor remained unfriendly, spurning an offer of some precious Swiss cheese sent from Switzerland by Father Charles's brother, sometimes not speaking when spoken to. Father Charles went to Hesquiat, overnighting on board the steamer as it unloaded freight at Gibson's mill at Ahousat en route, and arriving early in the morning. He said Mass in memory of his father, but only two people attended. The following day, in the pouring rain, he butchered a cow for Christie School and returned with the meat within a day, only to find the Kakawis meat house full, as they had butchered a cow when he left without telling him their plan. His diary notes waspishly that "it took them all day to finish the job."

By now there was no pleasing Father Charles. "*October 19, 1929:* Cut meat for tonight's supper and for tomorrow. After supper the 2 plumbers, Mr. Emelton and myself had a game of bridge. Fr. Victor brought us a bottle of spoiling Mass wine. Thanks!"

Soon off to Hesquiat again, he returned on November 7 aboard the *Princess Norah*. "I went on board…with 6 new school girls for Kakawis," he reported. "Big crowd on steamer—170 from Nootka alone, the cannery and fish reducing plant being closed down. Also plenty rum." These six girls from Hesquiat were the last new recruits he would ever escort to the school. Shortly afterward, Father Charles at last heard he could return to Mount Angel Abbey. He remained on the coast until early January 1930, spent his final Sunday up the coast at Nootka and then boarded the *Maquinna* for one final time.

> *January 7, 1930:* At 9 AM were at Kakawis. Two boys bring my trunks to the steamer, but no mail. When the Maquinna left and proceeded I blew 3 long whistles for goodbye. This with the permission of the Captain…
>
> *January 16:* Reached the Monastery, my home, at Mt Angel, 11:30 AM.

Father Charles's diary ends there, with the single word "Finis."

The Benedictines of Mount Angel Abbey continued working at Christie School and at the missions on the west coast for only eight years following Father Charles's departure. In 1938 they elected to withdraw, and another Roman Catholic order, the Oblates, took charge. Under the Oblates, Christie School continued operating until 1971.

Back amongst his confreres at the abbey, Father Charles became absorbed into the calm order of monastic life. From this mellow, agricultural setting in central Oregon, with distant Mount Hood rising over the Willamette Valley, he looked out onto an entirely different world, and the stresses of his life at Clayoquot Sound ebbed away.

Father Charles in later years.

Father Charles lived to a great age, renowned by his fellow monks for his stern piety and for his love of a good card game. Notably abstemious—"He just needed a jug of claret and his Italian cigars," recalled Father Stephen Hofman with a chuckle—he inspired respect amongst younger monks. As a novice, Father Stephen came to know Father Charles in the 1940s as he drove the older man to his occasional work in nearby parishes. Asked what the older priest was really like, Father Stephen deliberated for a moment and then replied, "He was—he was *Swiss*. He was very strict with himself and with others."

On January 16, 1968, at the age of ninety-three, Charles Moser died. He is buried at Mount Angel Abbey cemetery. He never returned to the west coast.

Apart from his extensive diary, Father Charles left few papers about his time on Vancouver Island. Unlike Father Maurus Snyder, he did not keep a hoard of photographs of the coast, nor did he write articles or give talks on the subject. When asked to contribute to a booklet to mark the golden jubilee of Christie School in 1950, Father Charles produced three brief paragraphs. Father Maurus wrote several pages. Father Charles's papers contain only a few letters from his time on Vancouver Island, whereas Father Maurus's papers are a treasure trove of such letters. Most notable in this collection are Father Maurus's letters from Father Brabant, letters from his fellow priests, letters from children at Christie School in 1912–13, and a sheaf of letters from Fred Thornberg.

Fred Thornberg and family in about 1905.

These letters from Thornberg predate Father Maurus's departure from Kakawis; most were written in 1909 and 1910. The last of them is dated November 1911, at which time Thornberg was in Victoria, wondering if he would ever return to Ahousat. He had been unwell and was still "shaky and weak." On the move continually between Ahousat and Victoria, his physical health was deteriorating and his mental state becoming ever more fragile.

Thornberg's mental instability had been evident for a number of years by then. Observers commented on this as early as 1903, when Thornberg tried to bring a charge of assault against the Presbyterian minister in Alberni, claiming that the minister attacked him and forcibly removed his daughter Hilda. Although both Hilda and her brother Andy said no such assault occurred, Thornberg complained to the police, the editor of the *Colonist*, the Indian Agent and the Attorney General. Despite his protests, the children were removed from his care, largely because of questions about his mental fitness. Hilda stated she preferred to be at residential school rather than with her father, concluding: "My father is not the same as he used to be he seems a little crazy at times now."

A few years later, Thornberg's letters to Father Maurus chronicle further mental deterioration. Obsessed with his daughter Hilda, who by then had returned to live at Ahousat, he wrote rambling accounts of men plotting to "defile" her and steal her from his home. When Hilda took up with a man Thornberg detested, he was consumed with disgust and convinced she was stealing from him and conspiring against him. These letters all harp on themes of defilement, abduction and betrayal; in one of them, Thornberg indicated that Hilda claimed publicly that he had "defiled" her. He mentioned this only once. The truth of such an assertion cannot be known.

As Thornberg aged, his family was hard-pressed to know how to deal with him. He was painfully thin and often highly agitated, and his behaviour became increasingly erratic over the years. Eventually, on March 5, 1921, Thornberg's son John committed him to the care of the provincial mental institution at Essondale in Coquitlam. The words "restless, talkative, delusional" appear frequently in the notes in Thornberg's hospital files. He talked ceaselessly: about his sons, about their efforts during the war, about his daughter, about people trying to poison him, about Christie School—"a splendid school…my children all went there, nothing wrong with that school." A heavy smoker and wildly excitable, Thornberg gesticulated dramatically with his cigarettes, jumping up and down while talking to others, convinced that evil outsiders were trying to kill him and his family, and terrified someone might come to take little Freddie away from him—a fear that continually plagued him in earlier years.

Freddie Thornberg Junior was the most beloved of Thornberg's children, and the youngest, born in 1900. As a small child he bravely resisted being sent to Christie School. When he was eight, according to his father, he declared that "if I compelled him to goe to a Catholick school = he would run away" because he had seen that his father was not always allowed to visit his older children at Kakawis. "If same was to happen to Little Fred = it would just kill me," Fred stated. "Since his Mother diet when he was only 14 months old, I have bean both a Father & Mother to him & I can not part with him the same as I had to do with the others." Yet in the end, Freddie Thornberg did attend Christie School, and he wrote from the school to Father Maurus in March 1912: "I was spading in the garden yesterday…My brother Andy got twenty-one mincks two weeks ago."

Freddie may have moved to Victoria with his father shortly after that, but he returned to the west coast, becoming a well-known figure in the Tofino area. He worked at the Clayoquot Hotel on Stubbs Island for many years, long after Walter Dawley had moved on. His father, Frederick Christian Thornberg, died at Essondale on May 19, 1924. The cause of death: "Exhaustion of Senile Dementia." He was eighty-three years old.

By the time of Fred Thornberg's death, an era had ended. Walter Dawley's papers show this very clearly, for as time passes, the entire tone of his incoming correspondence changes. Highly individual letters, alive with character and full of gossip, rarely appear in his files by the early 1920s. Idiosyncratic personalities seem to disappear, strange demands and comments diminish, peppery arguments between sparring businessmen fade away and far fewer letters fill the files. Indecipherable handwritten letters give way to typewritten correspondence; a more businesslike, infinitely less interesting, atmosphere begins to prevail.

By this time, Dawley ran his business differently, relying more on telegrams and the telephone, less on the mail. Improved communications meant that his domain was no longer the central hub for a large area of the coast; that role had disappeared along with the dream of commercial monopoly in the region. Now Dawley knew that the growing population over at Tofino could find pretty much everything it needed in the town—except what he supplied as proprietor of the one and only saloon in the region. As well, the needs of the area had greatly changed. Sealing was long gone as a major industry; hard-working fishermen and loggers easily outnumbered fly-by-night prospectors or would-be developers; respectable settlers dominated the local scene rather than wily entrepreneurs.

When George Nicholson went to work at Clayoquot in 1925, he discovered some surprises at Dawley's store. The place seemed dated, and a great deal of unsold merchandise hung heavy. "The upstairs storeroom was crammed with merchandise," Nicholson marvelled, "mostly vintage." His description is vivid: "There was black powder and buckshot by the hundredweight; wads, percussion caps and wooden ramrods, all for the muzzle-loaders which the Indians used to shoot fur seals... Piled high were boxes of button-up and elastic sided boots, and patent leather dress shoes with pointed toes. Broad-brimmed men's felt hats, long out of style, bell-bottom pants and other articles of clothing just as antiquated, were there." Nicholson believed Dawley acquired this glut of merchandise because he could not resist the temptation to "scour the wholesale houses in search of bargains."

Dawley was, by this time, often in Victoria at the family home on McClure Street. The boys from Clayoquot would sometimes pop in for a visit when they were in town. "Murdo McLeod goes up tonight," Dawley wrote to William

Walter Dawley, date unknown.

Simpson, his clerk at Clayoquot, "he and Ewen are here for dinner." Increasingly, Dawley relied on his employees to keep the store running day to day. His customers now often addressed their letters to his clerk rather than to Dawley. Yet Dawley remained in control, occasionally barking instructions in letters to his storekeeper. "I don't think we can sell them shirts even at the greatly reduced price…Re Bull I promised Joseph $25.00 he to have use of him free but bull belong[s] to me…If Murdo wants credit let him $50.00 worth, our limit to good reliable customers…Quicksilver is sold by the apothecaries weight. Will be up to relieve you on 1st."

Afflicted by gout and arthritis as the years passed, Dawley took on more help in running his business at Clayoquot. By the mid-1930s, his daughter Madeline and her husband, Pierre Malon, had moved to Stubbs Island to help run the hotel and store, and at various times his sons Walter and George both worked at Clayoquot. In 1937, George took over from his father as postmaster, but Dawley still held his position as mining recorder and as registrar of births, marriages and deaths that year. Ownership of all his assets, and of the Stubbs Island property, passed to the Malons around this time. Rumour has it that Dawley gave Madeline the island and all it contained as a belated wedding gift, but the transfer of title to her name was definitely a business transaction. According to her daughter Joan Nicholson, Madeline paid one dollar for her father's liquid dominion of Clayoquot—unquestionably the greatest bargain Walter Dawley ever allowed anyone in his life. Madeline and Pierre Malon remained at Clayoquot, running the store and hotel, until 1942, but according to their daughter Joan, who was born there in 1934, Madeline never much liked the place. She was a city person.

Perhaps the continued presence of her father unsettled Madeline, for despite handing over management of the business, Dawley never really relinquished control, nor did he ever truly leave Clayoquot. He remained a weighty influence around the place, permanently maintaining a room in the hotel for his own use and keeping a watchful eye on all proceedings. "He was grumpy," Joan Nicholson recalls. "Always grumpy." She never saw her grandmother at Clayoquot; Rose Dawley stayed in Victoria.

In 1944, at the age of eighty-four, Walter Dawley died in Victoria. He is buried at Royal Oak Cemetery. After his death, a ring he always wore passed first to his daughter Madeline and later to his granddaughter Joan. Designed specially for him, and made of gold sluiced from the sands at Bear River, the wide, thick band features a series of raised, and now heavily worn, letters.

They form the word "Clayoquot."

Epilogue

All of these people are now long gone. The storekeepers and the priests, the seal hunters and the schooner captains, the native schoolchildren, the entrepreneurs, prospectors and settlers who lived in Clayoquot Sound in the early twentieth century seem immeasurably distant now, and strange, almost obliterated in a sepia-toned past. Their lives are incongruous to imagine in the current west coast scene, in the contemporary chatter of Tofino, with its profitable bustle of coffee shops and kayak rentals, and its keen crowds of visitors.

Some three quarters of a million tourists currently visit Tofino every year, their numbers nearly overwhelming the small town with its permanent population of twelve thousand. Effusive articles about the beauties of the area appear regularly in newspapers and magazines, both nationally and internationally. The list of attractions grows continually: a whale festival, an oyster festival, a food and wine festival, winter storm watching, Clayoquot Days, a botanical garden, art galleries, surfing lessons, surfing competitions, the famous musicians who occasionally come to perform. Tour operators rhapsodize about unique wilderness experiences and extol the still-remaining tracts of old-growth rainforest; they take eager groups of visitors on whale- and bear-watching excursions, on trips to Hot Springs Cove or Meares Island, on short scenic flights, on visits to distant lakes and harbours.

The crowds keep coming: from far and wide, surfers converge to ride the waves on the outer coast; families camp at the consistently full campsites; others luxuriate in the growing number of high-end resorts; still others seek to discover the wilderness, sometimes on a generous budget, prepared to spend whatever it takes to revel in the genuine west coast. Restaurants are full, service can be slow, accommodation is often difficult to find and the cost of housing is high. The voices in the streets of Tofino speak in French, in German, in Japanese, in Cantonese and Mandarin, in every form and accent of English. Armed with cameras and often with rain gear, these visitors walk the beaches and explore the forest, awestruck by the scenery and generally undeterred by the weather. But in every language, at some point or other, visitors do find themselves talking about the weather—especially the rain.

Rain. This talk of rain never changes, for rain is a great leveller here, uniting everyone in one voice. This has always been so; everyone speaks of rain, and writes about it. The average rainfall in the Tofino area is well over 120 inches (over three metres) every year, most of it falling in winter deluges. Father Charles Moser took gloomy pleasure in measuring, even timing, such downpours:

> *January 29, 1910:* Last night from 8 pm till 8 am we had 2" rain; today from 8 am to 4 pm it rained 4 inches; and at 8 pm it was still pouring down…It rained from 8 pm to 8 pm 7.4 inches.

Time and distance never cease to play tricks in this west coast landscape, especially when the rain closes in. Then, in the dim pewter light, the horizon slowly disappears. Visibility changes, outlines become unclear, perceptions shift. Then, if the moment is right, time seems to dissolve.

Imagine yourself once again on the shoreline, in a blur of rain. Look over Tofino Harbour at that grey, indistinct expanse of water and those scattered islands. Imagine what is out there; imagine what was out there, and in the obscuring rain, wait. You might glimpse haunting reminders of the past: canoes racing toward the dock, a steamer coming into view. You might catch fleeting echoes: a shrill steam whistle, a distant cornet playing. Perhaps you will hear distant voices.

But abruptly, before your eyes can narrow and look carefully, before you can begin to listen with all your attention, the rain eases off. The light changes, visibility improves, and the present lurches back into focus, raucous and bright.

The roar of a float plane fills the air. A multi-hued group of kayakers flashes into sight. A shiny motorboat sweeps loudly across the harbour.

The images fade.

The voices are silenced.

The moment has gone.

Photo Credits

Most photographs in this book have never been published. In the credits below, abbreviations indicate the major sources of photographs. Dates are provided when possible; many are approximate.

About the sketches
All sketches in the book are by Briony Penn. Most are based on images in old photographs too damaged to be reproduced.

MAA (Mount Angel Abbey)
The West Coast Collection at Mount Angel Abbey Archives in Oregon contains hundreds of images from the early 1900s, both photographic prints and glass slides. Although uncatalogued, the glass slides are stored in special boxes, as are some of the prints. Other prints are with the papers of the priests who worked on the west coast. With a few exceptions, the photographs and glass slides are undated, and people and places unidentified. Many of the glass slides are damaged, but prints from some of them survive. A number of these slides were used in magic lantern shows, to assist fundraising for Christie School in Europe in 1900 and 1901.

Father Charles and/or Father Maurus probably took most of these photographs. The sisters may also have taken photographs; they certainly aided in developing and printing pictures at Christie School (see page 103 and related note on sources).

Some images from Mount Angel Abbey have been reproduced and are available in the Royal British Columbia Museum and through the BC Archives, but originals from Mount Angel were used in this book.

Photographed passages from Father Charles's diary come from the handwritten manuscript copy he made of his journals (see Notes on Sources). Photographed passages from letters to Father Maurus Snyder come from his personal papers in Mount Angel Abbey Archives.

SPA (Sister Protasia's Album)
At Queen of Angels Monastery at Mount Angel, the photograph album of Sister Protasia Schindler is a valuable resource. Sister Protasia collected many photographs relating to Christie School and the coastal missions. Some of these images also appear in the archives at Mount Angel Abbey.

MHP (Mike Hamilton Photograph)
Photographs taken by Mike Hamilton are reproduced courtesy of his daughter Joan Niblock. When specified, some Hamilton family material appears courtesy of Ken Gibson.

DP (Dawley Papers, BC Archives MS 1076 and MS 2430)
Most photographs of documents, signatures or place names from the Dawley papers are by Mark Kaarremaa. Peter Buckland also photographed a selection of these papers.

KGC (Ken Gibson Collection)
Ken Gibson's extensive collection of photographs from the west coast brings together many smaller collections from families and individuals. Ken has dedicated untold time and energy to gathering, cataloguing and identifying these photographs; his knowledge in this field is unsurpassed.

PHOTO CREDITS

Chung Collection

Several photographs are reproduced from CPR inspector Mr. H. Brodie's report on his trip aboard the *Princess Maquinna* in 1919. This report is in the UBC Library, Special Collections, Wally Chung Collection, Cat. #18823.

Chapter 1: Up the Coast

1. Thornberg letters, May 21, June 8, one undated, all 1899, DP.
2. Stockham Island from the northwest, Stone collection, KGC.
3. Hotel on Stockham Island, courtesy of Leona Taylor.
4. Thornberg portrait, reproduced with permission from Bossin, *Settling Clayoquot*.
5. Dawley portrait, courtesy of Joan Nicholson.
8. *Queen City*, BC Archives A-00305.
9. *Willapa*, photographer unknown, MAA.
10. Thornberg letter, January 12, 1899, DP.
12. Canoe loaded with goods, alongside *Queen City*, BC Archives A-06438.
17. Father Brabant portrait, BC Archives A-01432.

Chapter 2: A Hot Time in Ahousat

22. Sealing schooner *Favorite*, SPA.
22–23. Victoria Sealing Company letter and company stamps, January 11, 1901, DP.
26. Native girls wearing new shawls, MAA.
27. Thornberg's accounts for *Walter L Rich*, April 1, 1899, DP.
29. *Queen City* and two schooners, SPA.

Chapter 3: Kakawis

All images in this chapter probably date from 1900 to 1904. The original square shape of the school changed in 1904, when two new wings were added. The photographs on pages 40, 43, 46, 48, 55 (both), 56 and 60 (both) are from MAA; those on pages 42, 47, 50, 52, 54, 57 (both), 58, 59 and 61 are from SPA.

Chapter 4: Dear Mr. Dawley

62. Dawley portrait, courtesy of Joan Nicholson.
64. View of Clayoquot on Stubbs Island, probably 1905, Stone collection, KGC.
65. Invoices, May 29, 1897, and "Aug & Sept" 1901, DP.
69. Clayoquot Hotel on Stubbs Island, probably 1905, Stone collection, KGC.
70. Chesterman letter, November 7, 1910, DP.
74. Father Maurus letter to "Charley Store," August 28, 1901, DP.
76–77. Selection of letterheads: Stanfield's, September 1, 1909; Hudson's Bay Company, July 14, 1906; Turner, Beeton, December 20, 1905; E. G. Prior, November 23, 1915; P. Burns, August 31, 1910; Giant Powder, October 16, 1901; Frederick Buscombe, May 21, 1900; Weiler Bros., June 6, 1901; Popham Bros., November 29, 1915; James Maynard, March 9, 1906, DP.
78. Leiser letter, October 8, 1900, DP.
80. Billy August letterhead and signature, date incomplete, 1909, DP.
81. Pages from 1907 Dawley store ledger, DP.

Chapter 5: Priests at Sea

Photographs in this chapter come from MAA with the exception of:

84. Priests standing by canoe, SPA.
86. The village of Opitsat, 1919, Hamilton collection, KGC.
103. Three boys with their certificates, SPA.
106. Search warrant and signatures on warrant, July 15, 1905, DP.

Chapter 6: A Bunch of the Boys

108. Some of the boys outside the Clayoquot Store, date unknown, SPA.
109. James Jones's signature is taken from a different letter, dated January 22, 1901. The signature on the letter quoted on this page is unclear.
113. Stuart Stone, Stone collection, KGC.

PHOTO CREDITS

116 Oriental Hotel letterhead, Jones letter, January 22, 1901, DP.
119 Work crew around 1914, MHP.

Chapter 7: Around the Sound
127 Three Wing On letters, May 14, July 22 and September 30, 1903, DP.
129 From 1898 inventory of Stockham Island hotel, DP.
130 Title page of 1900 inventory for Clayoquot Hotel, Stubbs Island, DP.
131 Wong Tuck letter, January 13, 1905, DP.
138 Dawley letterhead, July 1, 1908, DP.

Chapter 8: Vital Events
144 Wedding photograph, MAA. This is undated, the couple unidentified. Judging by the clothing, this photograph could be from around 1906.
150–52 Photographs courtesy of Joan Nicholson.

Chapter 9: Liquid Dominion
159 Tibbs, blue paint order, September 26, 1909, DP.
161 Tibbs, pink paint order, undated, 1909, DP.
165 Two photos of Kyuquot whaling station, Brodie photographs, Chung Collection.
166 Whale baleen, MAA.
167 Humpback whale ashore at Echachis, MAA.
168 Nootka Marble Quarries letterhead, March 14, 1910, DP.
169 Wedding of Chief Napoleon and processional march, May 1908, SPA.
170 Chief Napoleon Maquinna and his bride, SPA.
170 Wedding feast inside the longhouse at Friendly Cove, May 1908, SPA.
172 Clubb letter, February 2, 1911, DP.
176 Tibbs's "tree rig," BC Archives F03431.
177 Dream Isle, BC Archives F03432.

Chapter 10: Hesquiat Days
The photographs throughout this chapter are from MAA, except for:

182 Church and priest's house at Friendly Cove, SPA.
184 Children at Hesquiat, SPA.

Chapter 11: A Winter's Tale
197 The steamship *Tees*, Reese Riley collection, KGC.

Chapter 12: Next Boat
210 *Princess Maquinna* at Tofino dock, probably 1913, photographer Bert Drader, MAA.
212 Steamer schedule, spring 1917, personal source.
213 The faithful and unpopular *Tees*, MAA.
214–15 On board the *Tees*, around 1912, D. Laval collection, KGC.
222 Captain Gillam with his wife, courtesy of Flora McCue.
223 Father Charles aboard *Princess Norah*, 1929, MAA.

Chapter 13: Dear Father
229–33 Cosmos Damian William letter; signature "From your poor Indian boys of Kakawis"; excerpt of Mamie Sam letter; and all signatures on these pages are reproduced from letters to Father Maurus Snyder, MAA.
235 Father Frowin Epper at Ahousat, around 1913, MAA.
240 Christie School, around 1913, MAA.

Chapter 14: A Go-Ahead Little Settlement
244 Tofino waterfront, 1913, Bert Drader collection, KGC.
245 White Wing Hotel letterhead, Fletcher Cleland letter, September 6, 1913, DP.
248 Clayoquot Cannery, courtesy of Nan Beere.
252 Willie Rae-Arthur, 1917, MAA.
258 Beach picnic, MacKenzie collection, KGC.

Chapter 15: Writing Under Difficulties
259 MacLeod letter, September 19, 1916, DP.

260 Censor and field post office stamps, courtesy of Nan Beere.
262, 264 Photos sent by Ray Brewster, then serving overseas, to his family, courtesy of Nan Beere.
265 Hopkins letter, July 2, 1916, DP.
275–76 Canoes and *Princess Maquinna* at Ahousat, Brodie photographs, Chung Collection.

Chapter 16: Affliction
277 Address and signature from William Aloysius letter to Walter Dawley, March 5, 1916, DP.
278 William Aloysius and family, MAA. He is identified on the back of the photograph, presumably by one of the priests.
279 Wedding portrait, William Aloysius and Josephine, SPA. Father Maurus identified them on another photograph of the couple at MAA.
280 "Return of death of an Indian" forms, BC Archives Vital Events registration numbers: Emil Howard (1917-09-001291/Roll b13359), Josephine (1918-09-002900/Roll b13359) and Sophie Aloysius (1917-09-001277/Roll b13359).
291 Pages from Dr. Dixson's diary, courtesy of Ron MacLeod.
293 Dr. Dixson rowing, source unknown, KGC.

Chapter 17: Dearest Girl
297 Mabel Hall, Hamilton collection, KGC.
298 Mike Hamilton, MHP.
299 Mabel at Tofino, 1923, Hamilton collection, KGC.
301 Telegraph line workers, MHP.
307 Mike Hamilton at work, mid-1920s, MHP.
308 Envelope and letter, courtesy of Joan Niblock.
310 "Self at Tofino April 1923," Hamilton collection, KGC.
312 Mike and Mabel, Hamilton collection, KGC.
314 Dream Isle, Mrs. W.E. Bond photograph, KGC.
315 Mabel on honeymoon, MHP.
316 Tofino lifeboat crew, MHP.
317 Letter courtesy of Joan Niblock.

Chapter 18: Silences
318 Tofino Harbour, MHP.
321 Students and staff, Christie School, 1926, MHP.
327 Father Ildephonse Calmus with boys, probably 1928, MAA.
328 "Orchestra of 5 instruments," probably 1928, MAA.
330 Father Charles in later years, MAA.
331 Fred Thornberg and family, source unknown, KGC.
334 Walter Dawley, courtesy of Joan Nicholson.

Signatures reproduced in the book
The following signatures come from documents at Mount Angel Abbey: Father A.J. Brabant; Fathers Maurus Snyder, Charles Moser, Ildephonse Calmus, Frowen (Froben) Epper; Mamie Sam, Cosmos Damian William, Emily Jacob, Mary Alphonse Swan.

The following are from private documents: Dorothy Abraham, Willie Rae-Arthur, Edward Gillam, Mike Hamilton.

The following are from the Dawley papers in the BC Archives. The original letters can be found by searching the database by date or by writer's name: William Aloysius (March 5, 1916); Billy August, (date incomplete, 1909, a signed order for "papers, letters and newspapers"); Harlan Brewster (June 3, 1901); Constant Charleson (January 26, 1911); John Chesterman (November 17, 1910); Walter Dawley (two signatures: one on a letter of July 19, 1904; the other on a document, date illegible, addressed to J.W. Smith); Joe Drinkwater (March 3, 1906); Thomas Gardhouse (July 6, 1902); John Grice (October 3, 1907); Harry Guillod (September 17, 1900); George Heater (January 2, 1916); Freeman Hopkins (May 27, 1916); James W. Jones (January 22, 1901); A.W. Neill (May 15, 1905); Wm. Netherby (August 14, 1900); J.W. Peppett (November 16, 1907); Sister M. Placida (July 11, 1901); Police George (undated, Box 7 File 21); James Sloman (May 1903); Frederick Stanley Spain (April 18, 1900); Thomas Stockham (January 16, 1901); Stuart Stone

(February 18, 1899); W.J. Stone (April 20, 1907); Fred Thornberg (May 22 and July 21, 1899); Fred Tibbs (September 26, 1909); Henry Varney (November 24, 1901).

Reproductions of place names and return addresses are all from the Dawley papers and can be located on the database for the collection by searching names, places or dates.

Photographs on the inside front and back covers are by Mike Hamilton from the mid-1920s and show the Clayoquot store on Stubbs Island and the *Princess Maquinna*.

On an excursion up Lone Cone Mountain, two sisters and a group of students from Christie School pose for a photograph. Date unknown. (MAA)

Notes on Sources

This book relies largely on primary sources: letters, diaries, unpublished memoirs. Some are in the public domain; many are not. In general, details concerning sources are provided within the text. Any direct quotations not explained within the text are detailed below, chapter by chapter. When more detail about any given source will help the reader's understanding, it appears in the notes below.

First, some explanation of the major sources for this book:

The Walter Dawley Papers

This collection is one of the largest in the BC Archives (MS 1076 and MS 2430), occupying a staggering 8.3 metres of shelf space. This includes some twenty boxes of inbound correspondence, with over 15,000 letters, as well as boxes containing ledgers, telegrams, accounts and other material. Catalogued by Leona Taylor, the letters within the Dawley papers are now listed on a database she created. Any letter can be searched by writer's name, date, location or subject.

Father Charles Moser's Diary

In 1946, Father Charles transcribed his own diaries, working from the originals. He copied by hand his year-by-year leather-bound journals (1900–30) creating a 1,132-page, unbound document. Most of the original journals are now lost, so this manuscript is the most authoritative, complete version of his diary that is available.

In this manuscript, mid-1928, Father Charles stated in a special entry that he was omitting certain events from the original diary in making this copy (see Chapter 18 for details). Because most originals are missing, this statement cannot be verified. The handwritten copy of the diaries, and the few surviving originals, are all at Mount Angel Abbey Archives.

Another version of the diary exists. At an unknown time (probably during the 1960s), Father Charles revised the diary with the help of Dorothy Abraham. She worked at his request, editing his diaries with a view to publication, producing a typescript on which the elderly priest's shaky handwriting appears, making corrections. He died in 1968. In 1971, Dorothy Abraham wrote to the BC Archives (see GR 1738) to say that the typescript had lain abandoned amongst her papers for some years. It was never published and is now in the BC Archives (MS 2172). This typescript differs substantially from, and is much shorter than, the copy of the diaries that Father Charles made in 1946.

Throughout this book, unless otherwise indicated, the diary entries quoted come from the handwritten manuscript copy.

The Papers of Father Maurus Snyder

In his unsorted personal papers, Father Maurus left a great many jottings, notes, half-written articles, scraps of memoir and other documents of uncertain origin or purpose, mostly undated. These papers, in the Mount Angel Abbey Archives, give the impression he was gathering information with a view to publishing something, but he never completed the task.

The most valuable papers he left, for the purposes of this book, are his letters from Father Augustin Brabant, from children and former pupils at Christie School, from the sisters at the school, from his fellow priests and brothers who worked on the west coast of Vancouver Island, and from Fred Thornberg. His own writings dealing directly with his west coast years are also of considerable interest.

The Archives at Mount Angel Abbey

The papers of every member of the abbey are preserved in these archives. I have examined the papers of Brother Leonard Niederpruem, Brother Gabriel Loerch, Father Frowin Epper, Father Ildephonse Calmus, Father Joseph Schindler, Father Victor Rassiter and Father Anthony Terhaar, as well as those of Father Charles Moser and Father Maurus Snyder. For information concerning the photographs in these archives, see the photo credits.

The Archives of Queen of Angels Monastery

The Benedictine sisters who worked at Christie School all came from Queen of Angels Monastery, at Mount Angel, Oregon. Many of their papers, letters and photographs remain in the archives there. For information concerning the photograph album of Sister Protasia Schindler, see the photo credits.

Father Augustin Brabant's Letters

Unless otherwise indicated, all quotations from Brabant's letters originate in correspondence addressed to Father Maurus Snyder.

Victoria Daily Colonist

Unless otherwise indicated, all newspaper quotations are from the *Colonist*. The database of west coast articles compiled by Leona Taylor from this newspaper is accessible at www.victoriasvictoria.ca.

The Earl Marsh Collection: British Columbia Coast Steamship Service Records

This collection of papers concerning steamship service on the coast contains much useful information and correspondence. It fills several boxes at the BC Archives (Accession # 93-7330) and is uncatalogued and unsorted.

NOTES

Chapter 1: Up the Coast

For information about sealing in this and the following chapter, I am indebted to Murray's *Vagabond Fleet* and Crockford's thesis "Nuu-Chah-Nulth Labour Relations in the Pelagic Sealing Industry, 1868–1911."

Indian Agents' annual reports to the Department of Indian Affairs are often valuable sources of information. Harry Guillod's are of particular interest. These reports are available online at www.collectionscanada.gc.ca/indianaffairs/index-e.html.

"[Stockham] told me that..." Dawley's undated scrap of memoir is amongst Father Maurus's papers.

The two hotels (on Stockham Island and Stubbs Island) are mentioned jointly in the *Victoria Daily Colonist*, February 26, 1899.

Population statistics for this era and area are open to much debate. Father Brabant estimated that on his arrival on the west coast in 1874, the total native population was 4,500. By 1893 he wrote that there were probably no more than 3,000 (see Lillard's *Mission to Nootka* and Brabant in *American College Bulletin*). He never specified the area or villages he included in these statistics, so they cannot be considered reliable.

Indian Agent Guillod's 1901 report counts people in the villages in Clayoquot Sound: Opitsat (Clayoquot), 240; Kelsemat, 71; Ahousat, 277; Hesquiat, 154. From these figures, I estimate a total of eight hundred native people in the Sound, but this figure is approximate at best.

For the white population, *Henderson's British Columbia gazetteer and directory* for 1902 states that Clayoquot (meaning the area) had 150 white people. The directories are notoriously imprecise, however, and many names listed are prospectors and itinerant workers. The 1901 Census provides another source of information, from which it is surprisingly difficult to glean reliable numbers. The figure of 100 should be taken only as an estimate.

The first mention of "Tofino" in Father Charles's diary is on March 23, 1904. In the *Colonist*, the term "Tofino" was not in regular use until 1909–10.

"This staunch little steamer…" Information about *Queen City* comes from papers of the Earl Marsh Collection, BC Archives. See also Sharcott's article in the *Colonist* of February 25, 1962.

Fred Thornberg's memoirs are in the Alberni Archives. Parts are reprinted in Bossin's *Settling Clayoquot*. See also Les Hammer's articles in the *Colonist*.

In his letter of April 10, 1899, about poisoned blood, Thornberg declares his intention to write to the Victoria newspapers about this alleged attempt to kill him and others in Ahousat. Either he or someone else informed the *Colonist*. On April 21, 1899, an article describing an "almost incredible story of Indian superstition" repeats a similar description of blood on door handles and in water. The paper does not name Thornberg. The article concludes: "There is a belief among the Indians that when this is done another contracts the disease and the [sick person whose blood is used] is cured, but the practice is not customary."

"The Ahousats cordially disliked…" For more on tensions in Ahousat surrounding Thornberg and the store see Murray's *Vagabond Fleet*, especially page 189.

Bishop Charles Seghers was the first to envision a mission on Vancouver Island's west coast. This followed his initial visit to the coast in June 1869, when he accompanied two Hesquiat men condemned to death for their alleged role in the *John Bright* affair (for more on this affair see Johnson's *Glyphs and Gallows*; Horsfield's *Cougar Annie's Garden*). The men were hanged on gallows erected for the purpose at Hesquiat. According to Father Maurus in an unpublished memoir, Seghers resolved then and there to return to the coast and establish a mission. In later years, Father Brabant vehemently asserted that the men had been innocent.

For Brabant and Seghers' visit to Thornberg, see Nicholson's *Vancouver Island's West Coast*, page 99. This event does not appear in Lillard's *Mission to Nootka*.

In this chapter, Brabant's cited writings are all from the version of his diary in Lillard's *Mission to Nootka*. See also Moser's *Reminiscences of the West Coast of Vancouver Island*.

Chapter 2: A Hot Time at Ahousat

The diocesan instructions for Hesquiat appear in Moser's *Reminiscences of the West Coast of Vancouver Island*.

Quotations from Brabant's diary come from Lillard's *Mission to Nootka*.

"$100 to $500 each in a successful season…" See Murray's *Vagabond Fleet*, page 223. See also page 24 for the bonanza 1880 season, when "some [natives were] making as much as $120 a day."

"I seen the Cpt and Mates…" is from Thornberg's memoirs.

"Two Schooners are in the harbour…" is from Brabant's article in *American College Bulletin*.

"The Indians cannot go to law about it…" This letter from Brabant is quoted in *Vagabond Fleet*, page 193.

"A tall, lean man…" See Kelley, "Nesika Illahee (Our Land)," in the *Colonist* of May 29, 1951.

"The decks of the schooners ran with blood…" See *Vagabond Fleet*, pages 10, 134–35.

"to protect and preserve the seals" is quoted in *Vagabond Fleet*, page 212.

The final trip of the *Bayard*, the loss of crew members and the adventures of the Kyuquot couple are described in the *Colonist* of September 13, 1908, and October 22, 1908.

The story of Captain Peppett and his gold watch is in the *Colonist* of April 12, 1913.

"rotten old hulks…" is a comment made by A. W. Neill, quoted in *Vagabond Fleet*, page 219.

Chapter 3: Kakawis

The opening passage is the beginning of Father Charles's diary.

"…a boarding school" and the following passage, "Their efforts to invade…," come from Father Brabant's diary, quoted in Lillard's *Mission to Nootka*.

"If we do not accept the grant…" Brabant quotes Bishop Christie's comments in his diary.

"The location is an ideal one…" is from Father Maurus's 1905 report to the Department of Indian Affairs.

Any letter cited from Father Brabant is amongst Father Maurus's papers.

For Father Maurus's anecdote about the "Indian brave," see his article "The Beginning of Christie School" in *Golden Jubilee of Christie Indian Residential School: 1900–1950*. (He writes in the third person throughout this article.)

"Everything was in order…," "The school was here…" and "…after much pow-wow…" are all from Father Maurus's article in the *Golden Jubilee* booklet.

"I outbluffed him…" is from an unpublished article/memoir of Father Maurus.

"The Sister matron rang the bell…" is from Father Maurus's article in the *Golden Jubilee* booklet.

Complaints concerning beds from Father Joseph Schindler's article in the *Golden Jubilee* booklet.

"The correct use of English…" is from the 1905 annual report by Father Maurus to the Department of Indian Affairs.

"Sunday evening we had a little programme…" is from a letter Mary Alphonse Swan wrote to Father Maurus in August 1919.

Quotations from *Indian Residential Schools: The Nuu-chah-nulth Experience* appear with permission of Ron Hamilton, who did the original interviews for the book.

Chapter 4: Dear Mr. Dawley

For more on Chesterman, see Adrienne Mason's article in *Tofino Time*.

"weathered wooden-framed building…" For the Guppy family's arrival on Chesterman's property, see Anthony Guppy's *Tofino Kid*, page 29.

"Eulogized in the newspaper.…" See *Colonist*, May 13, 1917. For more on Leiser see the article by Leonoff in *The Scribe*.

The Ahousat store was the focus of many disputes. See Murray's *Vagabond Fleet* for more on Billy August and the store. See also Fred Thornberg's memoirs, where he complains about unfair treatment from Dawley, Gardhouse, Indian Agent Neill and others.

Chapter 5: Priests at Sea

For more on building the church and house at Ahousat, see Brabant's memoirs in Lillard's *Mission to Nootka*. See also Fred Thornberg's memoirs and his letters to Father Maurus.

Brother Leonard's letter of February 19, 1911, to Father Maurus is in Father Maurus's papers.

"Both the Indians and myself had given up…" Brabant's description of his sea voyage is in Lillard's *Mission to Nootka*.

"fight the priest…" Brabant quotes William Netherby's comments in a letter to Father Maurus dated February 13, 1901.

Much information in this chapter comes from Brabant's lengthy letters to Father Maurus, most of them written in 1900 and 1901. During 1901, Brabant speaks in detail of events and people at Nootka, where he was then based. Of particular interest are his letters about the death of Chief Maquinna, the letters about the children he is sending to school, and the letter cautioning against the use of "bodily punishment."

Indian Agent A. W. Neill's annual report of 1905 describes the Ahousat school.

"I am not one of those who believe…" Brabant's comments about reading and writing appear in *American College Bulletin*, 1893.

Sister Mary Sophie's letter to Father Maurus Snyder concerning printing postcards is dated February 1912. A number of postcards made from photographs taken by the priests survive among their documents from Christie School. An envelope in Father Charles's papers indicates that some of the priests' photographs were developed professionally in Victoria.

Chapter 6: A Bunch of the Boys

James Jones appears frequently in the *Colonist*. See particularly April 7, August 21 and December 12, 1897.

"We all feel very sorry…" Stuart Stone's letter about Jones, dated February 10, 1900, contained an article he copied by hand, attributing it to the *Daily Star*. The source of the article is uncertain; the original has not been found.

For more on mining claims, see Department of Mines annual reports. See also the detailed article in the *Colonist* of February 7, 1907, and Walter Guppy's *Clayoquot Soundings*.

A typescript of a portion of Mrs. Rolston's diary was provided by Ken Gibson. She is also quoted in *Clayoquot Soundings*, page 13.

Articles cited about gold at Bear River are all from the *Colonist*; see particularly August 11 and 15, 1865; April 27, 1887; October 24, 1887.

For the Chinese at Alberni in the 1870s see the *Colonist* of July 19, 1878. See also Peterson's *Journeys*.

For articles about Port Hughes in the *Colonist* see particularly August 22, 1899; October 22, 1899; and December 13, 1899.

The increased personal possessions of native Indians are mentioned in the *Colonist* of October 20 and 21, 1899.

For details of Joe Drinkwater's travels see *When the Whistle Blew*.

"the largest cedar mill in the world…" is from the *Colonist*, August 20, 1905. Many other articles describe the Mosquito Harbour operation around this period.

Chapter 7: Around the Sound

The Clayoquot Hotel (Stubbs Island) inventory is dated October 22, 1900, two years before Stockham and Dawley took over the hotel.

The Earl Marsh Collection at the BC Archives contains a number of pamphlets outlining the different classes of fares and the deck-class restrictions over a period of many years.

Dawley's letters reveal no details of why Fred Thornberg stopped working at the Ahousat store.

Stanley Spain's letters to the Attorney General are dated November 22, 1900, and December 7, 1900. Both are at the BC Archives (GR 0429 Box 6). Chief Nokamis's letter is in the same collection and box.

For more on Stockham and his claim for compensation see Murray's *Vagabond Fleet*, page 219.

"Is Tom simmering down…" Guillod's letters about the Stockham-Dawley feud are dated November 12, 1905, and March 1906.

"I did not know a rat from a beaver…" The interview appeared in the *Victoria Daily Times*, December 4, 1926.

"I could not get them…" Sloman's letter to Dawley about otters is dated August 19, 1904.

Sloman's letter to Dawley suggesting they forge Maquinna's signature is from August 24, 1904.

Chapter 8: Vital Events

The surname "Andrews" often appears as "Andrew" in the priest's diary. Records in the BC Archives give the name as "Andrews."

NOTES ON SOURCES

Joan Nicholson provided information about the Dennan sisters; about her grandfather, Walter Dawley; and about her uncle, Clarence.

Reviews of the Pringle Company's theatrical offerings appear throughout November 1904 in the *Colonist*.

Varney's letter to Dawley about roses is dated October 24, 1908.

The *Colonist* article about Varney's produce is from October 1, 1898.

The phrase "salt salmon for the orient" and the description of Dr. Newcombe appear in the *Colonist*, October 29, 1911. "Salt dog salmon" (chum) is often mentioned in the paper, as it was shipped overseas from the west coast.

The story of James Jones's watch, and its history, comes from his great-great-nephew Hank Byington and his wife, Jill. They generously shared with me what they know of James Jones and showed me the family heirloom.

Chapter 9: Liquid Dominion

Unless otherwise indicated, all quotations from Fred Tibbs come from his letters in the Dawley papers.

Comments about Tibbs from Alma Arnet [Sloman], Olive Garrard [Broad], Winnie Dixson and Bill Sharp are from Bossin's *Settling Clayoquot*.

For more on Tibbs, see Mackie's article in *The Beaver*, especially for his family background. The comment from Tibbs's niece comes from this article.

In an interview with Bob Bossin for *Settling Clayoquot*, Madeline (Dawley) and Pierre Malon remembered the boys from Mosquito Harbour drinking up their paycheques.

Many articles about whaling and whale products appear in the *Colonist*; see, for example, April 6, 1905; January 5, 6, and 18, 1906; May 7, 1907.

For the 1911 total for whales killed, see Reksten's *Illustrated History of British Columbia*, page 161.

For statistics on production of whale products, see Brodie's 1919 report in the Wally Chung Collection, at the UBC Library, Special Collections.

Father Maurus wrote of Chief Napoleon's wedding in an undated typescript and in an undated memoir (an unfinished article?) found amongst his papers.

Mr. Clubb's letters are in the Dawley papers; see particularly April 26 and May 6, 1911; May 17, 1917.

The letter from Tibbs on Triangle Island, dated March 15, 1910, comes from Bossin's *Settling Clayoquot*.

Chapter 10: Hesquiat Days

This chapter draws on letters written by Father Brabant to Father Maurus, many in 1909, found in Father Maurus's papers.

For the story of the cow aboard *Tees*, see the article by Oliver in the *Colonist* of June 5, 1966.

Emma Gallagher (nee Dickinson), who was raised at Clo-oose, related the story of cows being forced to walk the plank.

For more on wild cattle see Horsfield's *Cougar Annie's Garden*, page 137 ff.

Chapter 11: A Winter's Tale

For the description of the *Tees* as "blunt nosed ugly duckling," etc., see the article by Wills in the *Colonist*, December 19, 1976.

Chapter 12: Next Boat

"The blamed steamer is expected…" is from one of Mike Hamilton's letters to Mabel Hall, 1924.

For information about *Maude's* early runs up the coast, see the Earl Marsh Collection, BC Archives.

"Some of the waters which…" and "Take the Tees…" This letter and memo from Troup are in the Earl Marsh Collection.

"Holy Roller" description of the *Tees* is in Oliver's article in the *Colonist*, June 5, 1966.

"3 cylinder triple expansion…" is from a memo in the Earl Marsh Collection, filed with other CPR documents about the construction and technical specifications of the *Maquinna*.

Suggestions that the Indians on the coast are a tourist attraction come from a CPR report on the *Norah's* inaugural trip and from a 1936 CPR brochure about the west coast route, both from the Earl Marsh Collection. The collection contains many similar reports and pamphlets.

"The steamer is quite often…" is from a 1922 publicity leaflet for CPR, in the Earl Marsh Collection.

Chapter 13: Dear Father

Father Joseph Schindler's comments about record keeping are in the *Golden Jubilee* booklet.

Chapter 14: A Go-Ahead Little Settlement

The chapter title comes from an article in the *Colonist* of May 18, 1913.

Unless otherwise indicated, all quotations from Frank Garrard here and in later chapters are from his unpublished memoirs (BC Archives, MSS 46). For more on Garrard see Scott's article in the *Daily Colonist*, July 21, 1974.

The White Wing Hotel letterhead was used by Fletcher Cleland of Vargas Island, writing to Dawley from Tofino on September 6, 1913. For details about this hotel, I am indebted to Ken Gibson.

See Gibson's *Bull of the Woods* for information about west coast industry before the First World War.

A 1912 Clayoquot Development League pamphlet, and further League information about the campaign for a road, is in the Longstaff Collection at the BC Archives (MS 0677).

I found Adrienne Mason's article about Vargas Island in *Tofino Time* helpful as I wrote this chapter.

Harold Monks provided information about early Vargas settlers.

"Lands Inspector's report…" See H.N. Clague, *Department of Lands Report 1914*, "Clayoquot and Nootka Districts."

The letter quoted from Ada Annie Rae-Arthur comes from private sources.

The quotation from John Oliver comes from Ormsby's *British Columbia: A History*, page 358.

Exaggerated claims about land development in BC are cited in Ormsby's *British Columbia: A History* and in Lillard's *Seven Shillings a Year*. The Quatsino information comes from the Longstaff Collection.

"…yell for a road" pamphlet is in the Longstaff Collection

For further information about Clo-oose, see Newitt's article in *Raincoast Chronicles*.

Emma Gallagher's (Dickinson's) memories about Clo-oose were helpful in this chapter.

Quotations about the Clo-oose development come from West Coast Development Company, "Canada's Greatest Pleasure Resort," in the BC Archives and from West Coast Development Company, "Canada's Only Real Pleasure Resort," at the University of Victoria's McPherson Library. There is also a copy of one promotional brochure about the development, in the Longstaff Collection.

For more on the Clo-oose men who enlisted, see the *Colonist* of March 20, 1917. Twenty-nine names are listed.

"No fields! No grass!…" is from Abraham's *Lone Cone*.

Chapter 15: Writing Under Difficulties

Attestation papers of soldiers of the Canadian Expeditionary Force in the First World War can be viewed online at www.collectionscanada.gc.ca/databases/cef/index-e.html. I was able to locate many, but not all, of the men listed in this chapter.

Harold Monks discussed his father's memories of Vargas Island and of the First World War. Adrienne Mason and Nan Beere also supplied information for this chapter.

Dr. Dixson's diary is quoted courtesy of Ron MacLeod.

For more on native soldiers in the First World War see Gaffen's *Forgotten Soldiers* and Summerby's *Native Soldiers, Foreign Battlefields*. For information on natives' contributions to the Canadian Patriotic Fund and for Chief Moo-Chew-Eines's letter see Dempsey's *Warriors of the King*, particularly pages 33–35.

"The ship was scheduled…" Brodie's report on the *Princess Maquinna* is in the Wally Chung Collection at UBC Library, Special Collections.

Chapter 16: Affliction

For information about patent medicines see Wikipedia (en.wikipedia.org/wiki/Castoria), Forgotten NY Ads (www.forgotten-ny.com/ADS/Castoria %20page/castoria.html), and Antique-Bottles.net (www.antique-bottles.net/forum/m-16199/mpage-1/ key-/tm.htm).

Dr Dixson's history comes from Bossin's *Settling Clayoquot* and Walter Guppy's *Clayoquot Soundings*. See also Abraham's *Lone Cone*.

Dr. Dixson's diary has been invaluable in this chapter.

For detailed information about tuberculosis among natives in BC, mortality statistics, the role played by Dr. Peter Bryce, and statistics showing the decline in native populations, see Kelm's *Colonizing Bodies*. See also Miller's *Shingwauk's Vision*. In 1922, after his resignation, Bryce published a tract entitled *The Story of a National Crime*.

The notion that native people might not survive was so common that when my mother attended school in Duncan, BC, in the early 1930s, she was taught that the Cowichan Indians were dying out and in a few years there would be none left.

Statistics for deaths in BC from Spanish influenza come from Francis, ed., *Encyclopedia of British Columbia*.

Chapter 17: Dearest Girl

For access to Mike Hamilton's memoirs, letters and photographs throughout the book, I thank his daughter Joan Niblock. Throughout this chapter, these are used extensively.

For the Riley's Cove story see Nicholson's *Vancouver Island's West Coast*, page 216, and the Hamilton memoirs. Some sources insist this was a herring saltery; others speak of Heater running a halibut operation in Riley's Cove. Mike Hamilton, who was there, describes it as a pilchard saltery.

"All the Reduction Plants had closed…" Father Charles's comments about pilchards come from the typescript version of his diary in the BC Archives (MS 2172). Dorothy Abraham, who prepared the typescript, may have had a hand in this passage, as Father Charles's handwritten copy of his original diaries does not give as much detail about the fish.

Japanese cutting cordwood are mentioned in a letter to Dawley from Bonthrone Barclay, dated December 12, 1899. The earliest letter to Dawley about Japanese fishing on the coast is from J. Tanaka in Nanaimo, dated July 20, 1904.

Fred Tibbs's letter to his niece comes from Bossin's *Settling Clayoquot*, as do comments by Winnie Dixson, Trygve Arnet, Bill Sharpe and Tommy Kimoto. See also Mackie's article about Tibbs.

Information about Robert Guppy comes from Anthony Guppy's *Tofino Kid*.

All quotations from Dorothy Abraham come from *Lone Cone*.

For descriptions of boat days, information came from Ken Gibson and Harold Monks, from memoirs by Alder Bloom and Mike Hamilton, and from many articles and unpublished sources.

Chapter 18: Silences

The year 1921 is only partially covered in the handwritten version of Father Charles's diary at Mount Angel. A significant number of pages from that year are out of order or missing. The typescript of the diary in the BC Archives contains some additional information concerning the events of November 1921, but not in great detail.

"This episode was the beginning…" For the rest of the chapter, unless otherwise indicated, all quotations by or about Father Charles and Father Ildephonse come from the correspondence file held at Library and Archives Canada in Ottawa. See "West Coast Agency — Christie Residential School — General Administration. 1911–1930." Finding Aid 10-17. RG10, vol. 6439, file 879-1, part 1. All of the letters concerning punishments at the school during the 1920s, and concerning the various principals at the school, come from this file.

"The Evil one starts to work…" This passage is from Father Charles's diary, as is "Scuffle between 2 boys and Father Ildephonse…"

Maurus Mclean's comments in his own language translate as: "It's good to learn to speak English," "I'm willing" and "I'll go along and learn the whiteman's ways."

Published articles by Benedictine priests about the west coast missions and Christie School include: Terhaar's "Romance of the Missions," a series appearing in *St. Joseph Magazine* from January to July 1940; the *Golden Jubilee Booklet*; Reverend Sister Theodore's article about Father Brabant in *Orphan's Friend*; and Father Nicolaye's lengthy article in the same publication about the early days of the coastal missions.

Comments about the Clayoquot store in 1925 are from Nicholson's article in the *Colonist* of November 1, 1964.

Joan Nicholson provided information about her family at Clayoquot in the 1930s and early 1940s, when she was a child, and related the story of Dawley's ring.

Princess Maquinna in Tofino Harbour, mid 1920s. Photograph by Mike Hamilton.

Select Bibliography

BOOKS

Abraham, Dorothy. *Lone Cone: A Journal of Life on the West Coast of Vancouver Island, B.C.* Victoria: privately printed, 1945.

Andersen, Marnie. *Women of the West Coast: Then and Now.* Sidney, BC: Sand Dollar Press, 1993.

Barman, Jean. *The West beyond the West: A History of British Columbia.* 1991. Revised edition, Toronto: University of Toronto Press, 1996.

Bossin, Bob. *Settling Clayoquot.* Sound Heritage Series #33. Victoria: Sound and Moving Image Division, BC Provincial Archives, 1981.

Busch, Briton Cooper. *The War against the Seals: A History of the North American Seal Fishery.* Montreal/Kingston: McGill-Queen's University Press, 1985.

Crockford, Cairn Elizabeth. "Nuu-Chah-Nulth Labour Relations in the Pelagic Sealing Industry, 1868–1911." MA thesis, University of Victoria, Department of History, 1996.

Dempsey, L. James. *Warriors of the King: Prairie Indians in World War I.* Regina: Canadian Plains Research Center, University of Regina, 1999.

Directory of Vancouver Island. Victoria: Provincial Publishing Company, 1909.

Drucker, Philip. *The Northern and Central Nootkan Tribes.* Washington, DC: US Government Printing Office, 1951.

Eckerstorfer, Andreas. "To Do Some Good among the Indians." Master's thesis, courtesy of Queen of Angels Monastery, 1994.

Francis, Daniel, ed. *Encyclopedia of British Columbia.* Madeira Park, BC: Harbour Publishing, 2000.

Gaffen, Fred. *Forgotten Soldiers.* Penticton, BC: Theytus Books, 1985.

Gibson, Gordon. *Bull of the Woods: The Gordon Gibson Story.* Vancouver: Douglas and McIntyre, 1980.

Golden Jubilee of Christie Indian Residential School: 1900–1950. Victoria: Acme Press, 1950, especially "The Beginning of Christie School" by Father Maurus Snyder.

Great Central Book Project Committee. *When the Whistle Blew: The Great Central Story.* Duncan, BC: Author and Alberni District Historical Society, 2002.

Greene, Ruth. *Personality Ships of British Columbia.* West Vancouver: Marine Tapestry Publications, 1969.

Guppy, Anthony. *The Tofino Kid: From India to this Wild West Coast.* Duncan, BC: Priority Printing, 2000.

Guppy, Walter. *Clayoquot Soundings: A History of Clayoquot Sound 1880s–1980s.* Tofino, BC: Grassroots Publication, 1997.

Henderson's British Columbia gazetteer and directory. Vancouver: Henderson Publishing Co., 1897–1905, 1910.

Henderson's Greater Victoria City and Vancouver Island gazetteer and directory. Vancouver: Henderson Publishing Co., 1910–11.

Horsfield, Margaret. *Cougar Annie's Garden.* Nanaimo, BC: Salal Books, 1999.

Johnson, Peter. *Glyphs and Gallows: The Rock Art of Clo-oose and the Wreck of the John Bright.* Surrey, BC: Heritage House, 1999.

Kelm, Mary-Ellen. *Colonizing Bodies: Aboriginal Health and Healing in British Columbia, 1900–50.* Vancouver: UBC Press, 1998.

Lillard, Charles. *Mission to Nootka 1874–1900: Reminiscences of the West Coast of Vancouver Island.* Sidney, BC: Gray's Publishing, 1977.

———. *Seven Shillings a Year: The History of Vancouver Island.* Ganges, BC: Horsdal and Schubart, 1986.

Miller, J.R. *Shingwauk's Vision: A History of Native Residential Schools.* Toronto: University of Toronto Press, 1996.

Moser, Father Charles. *Reminiscences of the West Coast of Vancouver Island.* Victoria: Acme Press, 1926.

Moses, John, with Donald Graves and Warren Sinclair. *A Sketch Account of Aboriginal Peoples in the Canadian Military.* Ottawa: Minister of National Defence Canada, 2004. http://dsp-psd.pwgsc.gc.ca/Collection/D61-16-2004E.pdf.

Murray, Peter. *The Vagabond Fleet: A Chronicle of the North Pacific Sealing Schooner Trade.* Victoria: Sono Nis Press, 1988.

Neitzel, Michael C. *The Valencia Tragedy.* Surrey, BC: Heritage House, 1995.

Newitt, Angela. "Some Childhood Memories of Clo-oose." In *Raincoast Chronicles: Forgotten Villages of the BC Coast,* edited by Howard White. Madeira Park, BC: Harbour Publishing, 1987.

Nicholson, George. *Vancouver Island's West Coast 1762-1962.* Victoria: Morriss Printing, 1963.

Nuu-chah-nulth Tribal Council. *Indian Residential Schools: The Nuu-chah-nulth Experience.* Port Alberni, BC: Author, 1996.

Ormsby, Margaret A. *British Columbia: A History.* Toronto: Macmillan, 1958.

Peterson, Jan. *Journeys: Down the Alberni Canal to Barkley Sound.* Lantzville, BC: Oolichan Books, 1999.

Peterson, Lester R. *The Cape Scott Story.* Langley, BC: Sunfire Publications, 1985. First published 1974 by Mitchell Press.

Reksten, Terry. *The Illustrated History of British Columbia.* Vancouver: Douglas and McIntyre, 2001.

Scott, R. Bruce. *People of the Southwest Coast of Vancouver Island.* Victoria: Morriss Printing, 1974.

Summerby, Janice. *Native Soldiers, Foreign Battlefields.* Ottawa: Veterans' Affairs Canada, 1993. http://www.vac-acc.gc.ca/content/history/other/native/natives_e.pdf.

Wells, R.E. *There's a Landing Today.* Victoria: Sono Nis Press, 1988.

Wright, E.D., ed. *Lewis & Dryden's Marine History of the Pacific Northwest.* 1895. Reprint, Seattle: Superior Publishing, 1967.

Wrigley's British Columbia Directory. Vancouver: Wrigley Directories, 1918, 1919, 1928.

ARTICLES

The following is a highly selective list. Of countless articles written about coastal steamers, only a few are included.

Abraham, Dorothy. "Father Charles," *Victoria Daily Colonist,* Islander section, September 4, 1966.

Bailey, Ruth Greene. "Marine Notebook: The Good Ship Maquinna," *Harbour and Shipping,* June 1963, p. 312 ff.

Boyce, Captain W.J. "Navigating Steamers in Fog on the BC Coast," *Canadian Merchant Service Guild Annual,* 1923.

Brabant, Father Augustin. *American College Bulletin,* July(?)1893. In the archives of the Roman Catholic Archdiocese of Victoria.

Brown, Nancy. "Last Residential School Closes for Good Today on Island's West Coast," *Victoria Daily Colonist,* June 20, 1971.

Dufour, Pat. "Ships 'Whistled' Their Way Homeward," *Victoria Daily Times,* May 30, 1970 (interview with Archibald Phelps).

Halkett, Captain H.D. "The Good Ship Maquinna," *Victoria Daily Colonist,* Islander section, May 18, 1980.

Hamilton, Jim. "The Traders' Route," two-part series, *Victoria Daily Colonist,* April 18 and 25, 1971.

Hammer, Les. "Trader Thornberg of Clayoquot," three-part series, *Victoria Daily Colonist,* June/July Sunday editions, 1974.

"History of British Columbia Coast Service," *Victoria Daily Times,* February 19, 1925; reviewed by

Comptroller-General and reprinted in a pamphlet in the Earl Marsh Collection, BC Archives (see below).
"Indian Children Give Up Their School in the Forest," *Vancouver Sun*, June 15, 1971.
James, Phyllis. "A Garden Never Dies," *Victoria Daily Colonist*, December 19, 1971.
Kelley, Frank. "Nesika Illahee (Our Land)," twelve-part series, *Victoria Daily Colonist Magazine*, February 25 to late August 1951 (see particularly May 29, 1951).
———. "Coast Trip Pleasant in Old Days," *Victoria Daily Colonist*, October 9, 1955.
Leonoff, Cyril E. "Simon Leiser: Principal Merchant of Vancouver Island," *The Scribe* (Journal of Jewish Historical Society of BC), February 1995.
Mackie, Richard. "The Short, Happy Life and Sad Death of Fred Tibbs," *The Beaver*, February/March 1991.
Maiden, Cecil. "The Other Side of the Island," twenty-part series, *Victoria Daily Times*, magazine section, November 10, 1950, to March 24, 1951.
Mason, Adrienne. "What's in a Name," series of articles in *Tofino Time*. See particularly the articles on Arnet, Chesterman, Tibbs and Vargas (March, April, July and October 2004); Monks (October 2007).
Moore, Bill. "The Forest around Us," *British Columbia Lumberman*, June 1977.
Nicholson, George. "The Ladies Leave Romantic Island," *Victoria Daily Colonist*, November 1, 1964.
———. "Gallant Old Maquinna: Her Glorious Memories," *Victoria Daily Colonist*, July 8, 1982.
Nicolaye, Father J. "Reminiscences of Early Days on Vancouver Island," *Historical Number of British Columbia Orphans' Friend*, undated. In the archives of the Roman Catholic Archdiocese of Victoria.
Old Timer. "Old Timer Tells of 13 Day Trip to Zeballos," *West Coast Advocate*, July 7, 1955.

Oliver, Sidney M. "Tees' arrival was social event," *Victoria Daily Colonist*, June 5, 1966.
"Rev. Father Charles Moser of West Coast Fame Is to Leave after Long Service," *Victoria Daily Colonist*, January 7, 1930.
Scott, R. Bruce. "Stormy Landing," *Victoria Daily Colonist*, March 9, 1971.
———. "Garrard of Tofino," *Victoria Daily Colonist*, July 21, 1974.
Sharcott, Margaret. "The *Queen City*: Gallant Little Ship," *Victoria Daily Colonist*, February 25, 1962.
———. "Bad Luck Dogged the Little Ship: The Story of the *Maude*," *Victoria Daily Colonist*, August 19, 1962.
Simmons, Vic. "Whistle's Echo Guided Ships in Fog," *Victoria Times Colonist*, October 8, 1989.
Sismey, Eric. "Jim Merrix Had Salt Water in His Veins," *Victoria Daily Colonist*, November 7, 1971 (describes navigation in fog).
Terhaar, Anthony, OSB. "Romance of the Missions," a series of articles about the west coast missions, *St Joseph Magazine*, January to July 1940.
Theodore, Reverend Sister. "The Late Very Rev. Augustus J. Brabant: A Sketch of his Life and Work," *Historical Number of British Columbia Orphans' Friend*, undated. In the archives of the Roman Catholic Archdiocese of Victoria.
Tonkin, Doris Farmer. "King of Dream Isle Castle," *Victoria Daily Colonist*, November 5, 1972.
"Vast Areas Staked as Timber Limits," *Victoria Daily Times*, May 29, 1907.
"When Fashion Calls for Sealskin Coats West Coast Indians Cash-In on Monopoly," *Victoria Daily Times*, December 4, 1926 (interview with James Sloman).
Wills, Archie. "In the Days of Sealing," *Victoria Daily Colonist*, June 28, 1970.
———. "Worst Run in the World" *Victoria Daily Colonist*, December 19, 1976.
———. "West Coast's Best Friend Died on World's Worst Run," *Victoria Daily Colonist*, March 13, 1977.

PRIVATE DOCUMENTS

Alder Bloom's unpublished memoirs, courtesy of Ken Gibson.

Ray Brewster's letters to his sisters, courtesy of Nan Beere.

Dr. D.S. Dixson's diary for 1916–17, courtesy of Ron MacLeod.

Captain Edward Gillam's letter to his wife, dated March 21, 1906, courtesy of Flora McCue.

Mike Hamilton's letters to Mabel Hall, courtesy of Joan Niblock.

Mike Hamilton's unpublished memoirs, courtesy of Ken Gibson and Joan Niblock.

Mike Hamilton's memories of his years on the West Coast, recorded in an interview and transcribed for his daughters, courtesy of Joan Niblock.

ARCHIVAL MATERIAL

BC Archives:

Abraham, Dorothy. Correspondence with W.E. Ireland, June 26, 1971, onward, regarding Father Charles Moser's diary, GR 1738.

BC Department of Mines. Annual Reports. *Sessional Papers*, D-24, D-25.

Brabant, Father Augustin. Letters and Papers, MS 2742.

———. Miscellaneous Papers, E/D/B72.4A.

Dawley, Walter. Papers, MS 1076 and MS 2430.

Earl Marsh Collection, Accession 93-7330.

Garrard, Frank. Papers, MS 46.

Justice, Clive. Papers, MS 2428.

Longstaff, Frederick. Papers, MS 0677.

Malon, Madelaine [Madeline Dawley] and Pierre. 1979? Interview by Bob Bossin. Tape recording. Part of Bob Bossin (Tofino-Clayoquot) oral history collection, T3878:0065-0066.

Moser, Father Charles. Memoirs, based on his original diary, edited by Dorothy Abraham, MS 2172.

Nokamis, Chief. Letters to the Attorney General, GR 0429, Box 6, Attorney General inbound letters.

Stanley Spain, Frederick. Letters to the Attorney General, GR 0429, Box 6, Attorney General inbound letters.

West Coast Development Company. "Canada's Greatest Pleasure Resort," 1913? 35 pp, NW 971.24 W522.

Other archives:

Brodie, H. Report on the *Princess Maquinna*, 1918. Wally Chung Collection. UBC Library, Special Collections (Vancouver), Cat. Number 18823.

Department of Indian Affairs and Northern Development. Annual Reports 1864–1990 (these contain reports from Indian Agents and from the principals of residential schools, financial summaries for residential schools and much more). http://www.collectionscanada.gc.ca/indianaffairs/index-e.html.

———. "West Coast Agency—Christie Residential School—General Administration. 1911–1930." Finding Aid 10-17. Library and Archives Canada (Ottawa) RG10, vol. 6439, file 879-1, part 1.

Library and Archives Canada. "Soldiers of the First World War" (an online collection of attestation papers and other information on soldiers in the Canadian Expeditionary Force during the First World War). http://www.collectionscanada.gc.ca/databases/cef/index-e.html.

Thornberg, Fred. Memoirs. Alberni District Historical Society Archives.

University of Victoria. Victoria's Victoria (the "Newspaper Indexes" tab provides access to specialist newspaper databases, including the one Leona Taylor compiled for the *Victoria Daily Colonist*, which contains articles about the west coast of Vancouver Island from 1859 onwards). www.victoriasvictoria.ca.

West Coast Development Company. "Canada's Only Real Pleasure Resort," Colonist Presses, Victoria, 1913? McPherson Library, University of Victoria, CIHM/ICMH Microfiche series no 9 – 90134 ISBN 065990134X.

Index

Locators in **bold** indicate a map; those in *italics* are photographs or drawings

Aaronson, A.A. 171
Abraham, Arthur 260, 261
Abraham, Dorothy 228, 293: in Tofino 307, 315; on Vargas Island 257
Abraham, Ted 257, 260
Active 30
Ahousat **93**, 276: Catholic church 45; Chief Billy's store 80; First World War 261; Gibson shingle mill 222; grave robbing 134–36; religious competition 94–95; schools 48, 95, 97, 99, 241; sealing crews 5, 23, 24; steamer facilities 11
Ahousat people: and Fred Thornberg 16; rumours about Christie School 103
Ahousat store 3, 6: prices and merchandise 28. *See also* Gardhouse, Thomas; Netherby, William; Thornberg, Frederick Christian
Alberni 64, 82, 175, 254: school 48, 241; transportation 225, 255
alcohol: in Clayoquot Sound 161–63, 316; medicine 289–90, 305; sold to native people 135, 137; on steamers 220
Aloysius, Josephine 278–79, *279*
Aloysius, Maggie 278
Aloysius, Sophie 278
Aloysius, William 277–78, *278*, *279*, 288
Amoda, Stanish 46

Andrews, Alice Yaksouse 145–46, 286–88
Andrews, Benedict 287
Andrews, Chief Eustace 46, 278, 286–87: death 287–88; wedding 145–46
Andrews, Jessie 46
Andrews, Lawrence 287
Andrews, Maurus 287
Anglican church 244, 245
Anton's Point 94, 184, **194**, 197, 198
Arnet, Alma 176–77
Arnet, Edward 314
Arnet, Jacob 68
Arnet, Trygve 313
Arnet Island 176, **311**, 312, 313–14, *314*
arson, at schools 241–42
August, Chief Billy 25, 80, 171

Baker & Son 76
Balcom, Sprott 82
Barnes, Mrs. F.M. 249–50
BC Good Roads League 255
Bear River 111, 118–19, 131, 190, 246
Beavan, Annie Louise 266
Beavan, Bertha 266–67
Beavan, Robert Arthur 260, 265, 266–67
Beavan, Walter 266
Bedwell River. *See* Bear River
Beere, Nan Brewster 216, 261
Bering Sea 29–30, **31**, 35–36. *See also* sealing industry

Bird, George 215–16
Blakstad, Hans 139
Boat Basin **194**, 252, 305
boat day xiii–xiv, 316
Boer War 111–12
Boyce, W.J. 221
Brabant, Father Augustin 16, 17, 104: at Ahousat 94–95; arrives on the west coast 16–17; attempted murder of 18; canoe voyages 92; cattle 188, 189, 190–91, 195; cautions against corporal punishment 103–4; Chief Maquinna 95–97; Christie School 41–42, 51, 53, 55–57, 59–61, 102–3; control of native people 17–18, 28–29, 32, 183; death 186; dictionary 179, 273; Father Maurus 51, 54, 107; fears for Catholic missions 182–82; Fred Thornberg 17, 18, 185; fundraising in Europe 43–44, 49; gold fever 117–18; at Hesquiat 17, 31, 88, *178*, 182, 183; *John Bright* 344; last years 185; medical skills 32, 280; at Nootka 95; parts of diary published (1926) 319; Protestants 42, 49, 58, 59, 95, 97; saving souls 42, 58; sealing industry 28, 29, 30, 31–32; steamers 213; visits Hesquiat in 1911 179–82, 184–85
Brewster, Harlan 50, 216, 261
Brewster, Marjorie 261
Brewster, Raymond 261

355

British Columbia Coastal Steamship Service 215–16. *See also* Canadian Pacific Railway, *Princess Maquinna*, *Princess Norah*, *Queen City*, *Tees*, *Willapa*
Brodie, H. 165, 225–26, 273–74, 276, 302
Browne, H.A. 171
Bryce, Peter 283
Bucholz, Otto 194–95
Burns Meats 76
Byington, Emily Jones 157
Byington, Hank 157

Cachalot. *See* Kyuquot whaling station
Calmus, Father Ildephonse 323, 325, 326, 327, 328
Cameron Lumber Company 163
Canadian Pacific Navigation Company 10, 214–15. *See also Maude*, *Queen City*, *Tees*, *Willapa*
Canadian Pacific Railway 215: promotes west coast tourism 225–27, 228 (*see also* Brodie, H.). *See also Princess Maquinna*, *Princess Norah*, *Queen City*, *Tees*, *Willapa*
canneries 9, 202, 219, 222, 296: Chinese workers 128; Clayoquot Cannery 50, 111, 246, 248; Kennedy Lake 314; native workers 183, 223, 274, 278, 283; Nootka Cannery 219, 240, 330; pilchards 302; Quatsino Cannery 219; tuberculosis 283, 284
Cape Scott 254
Carelmapu 222
Carolan, Allan 261, 265
Carolan, Helen 261, 265–66
Carrie C W 23, 33
Carter, Lawrence 149, 151, 155, 175

Carusi, Samuel Pollard 115
cascara bark 174
Catholic church: Ahousat 97–97; competition with Protestants 94–95, 97–98; death rituals 49–51, 281–82; Echachis 88; establishes presence on west coast 16–18, 45; Hesquiat 17, 45, *178*, *183*, 204, 240, 243; loses dominance on west coast 183; Nootka 95, *182*; Opitsat 86–87, 319; Port Alice 319; voyages by canoe 90–94; west coast missions 45, 183–84. *See also* Brabant, Father Augustin; Christie School; Moser, Father Charles; Snyder, Father Maurus
cattle 188–96, 300
Cecil, Susan 106
Charles, Father. *See* Moser, Father Charles
Charleson, Constant 80, 180
Charleson, Eudoxia 46
Charlie, Philip Chester 284
Chesterman, Elizabeth Anne Adams 70–71
Chesterman, John 67–71, 151, 162, 245, 247
Chesterman's Beach 71, **160**
childbirth 288–89
Childs, Sydney 123
Chinese: entrepreneurs 132, 174; head tax 130–31; prospectors 118, 131–32; workers 127–32, 133. *See also* Sing Lee
Christie, Alexander 42, 43
Christie School 41–42, *42*, 50, 56, 213, 240: annual reports 47, 238; arson attempts 240–42; assault charges 323; brass band *40*, 54, 170, 318, 328, 329; Brodie's comments on 274, 276; cattle 189–91;

chores 57, 89, 92, 98, 186; closure considered 323; curriculum 51–52, 57, 101–2; deaths of students 49–51, 56, 235, 237, 282, 283–88, 289; dental care 293; description 42, 47–48; discipline 104; disruptions 230–31, 232, 233, 238–39, 242–43, 319, 321–22, 323, 326–27; disruptions blamed on sisters 239; English language 46, 52–54; expansion 105–6, *105*; Father Augustin Brabant 41–42, 49, 51, 53, 54–57, 59–61, 97, 102–3, 107; Father Charles Moser 86–87, 88, 94, 105, 107, 188–89, 236, 328–29 (*see also* Moser, Father Charles: at Christie School); first death at school 48–49; first pupils 45–46, *46*, *47*; food from Father Charles 188–89; garden 42, 54, 100, 105, 237; identities of students 46–47; medical checkups 292; movies 315–16; Oblates 330; original staff 42–45; orphans 57; parent visits 61, 233; parents' reluctance to send children 45–46, 60, 61, 99–100, 104, 235; penmanship 102–3, *103*, 229, 232, *232*; "poor Indian boys of Kakawis" 230, 233; punishment 103–4, 230, 231, 233, 238–39, 242, 275, 320, 325–26, 327; radios 318; rumours of mistreatment 103–4; shoemaking *101*, 102; sick students 51, 56; Spanish influenza 295–96; Stockham and Dawley 50, 72–74; student pictures *40*, *46*–*47*, *46*, *47*, *48*, *50*, *52*, *54*, *55*, *57*, *60*, *61*, *89*, *92*, *98*, *100*, *101*, *102*, *103*, *103*, *105*, *321*; students resist attending 100–1, 105–7,

INDEX

274–75, 319–21, 326; support from Tofino settlers 50; used for meeting with Protestants 58. *See also* Calmus, Father Ildephonse; nuns; Rassiter, Father Victor; Snyder, Father Maurus

Clayoquot 7, 10, 26, 29, 64, **311**: in 1909 164; sealing crews 23, 24; surpassed by Tofino 245; telegraph connection 66–68. *See also* Stubbs Island

Clayoquot Cannery 50, 111, **160**, 246, 248

Clayoquot Development League 245, 255

Clayoquot Hotel 8, *69*, *130*: burns down 163, 313; Chinese workers 127–28, 130; inventory 130; only licensed establishment 163, 316

Clayoquot Island. *See* Stubbs Island

Clayoquot Sound: development 18, 222, 333; dominant community 7–9, 65–66, 143, 245; industry 111, 156, 164–68; newspaper coverage 9–10; population 8, 18, 159–60, 283, 343; resources 6, 9; settlement 8–9, 111, 249–54, 255–57

Clayoquot store 7, 15, 66, *108*: bought by Stockham and Dawley 65. *See also* Carter, Lawrence; Nicholson, George; Simpson, William

Cleland, Fletcher 250, 260, 261, 262, 264

Clo-oose 48, 214, 256–57

Clubb, W.J. 172–73

Codfish, Jimmy (Nootka Jimmy) 90–91, 181–82

Cole, Lou 193, 298, 301, 302–3

Cole, Minnie Hamilton 298, 301, 302–3

colonization, and religion 16–17

Conservative Association 161, 175

Coomes, F.C. 162

Cougar Annie. *See* Rae-Arthur, Ada Annie

Cox, C.A. "Charles" 241–42, 272, 322

Curzon Brothers 75

Danish settlers 17, 254

Dawley, Clarence 116, 148, 271: Clayoquot Hotel 162; marriage 147, *150*, *150*; mining interests 120–21

Dawley, Clarence (Bud) 151, *152*

Dawley, George 151, *151*, *152*, 334

Dawley, Lydia 151, *151*, *152*, 152

Dawley, Madeline. *See* Malon, Madeline Dawley

Dawley, Mamie Dennan 150, *150*: life on Stubbs Island 149; marriage 147, 148

Dawley, Rose Angela Dennan 334: children 151–52, *151*, *152*; life on Stubbs Island 149; marriage 147, 148; moves to Victoria 152

Dawley, Walter 3, 5, 6, 62, 66, 148, *334*: attitude toward missionaries 58–59; bulls 191; cascara bark 174; Chief Billy August 80; children 151–52, *151*, *152*; Chinese workers 127–31, 133; Christie School 50, 72–74; Christmas gifts 72, 74, 159, 160; clothing 153; competition 7–8, 80, 132–33, 140–41 (*see also* Tofino); correspondence 1, 3–4, 23–24, 63–64, 74–79, 333; credit 27–28, 124, 277, 334; customer complaints and demands 63, 72; customers buying elsewhere 70, 73, 78, 80, 265–66; final years 333–34; First World War 269–70; fur trade 6, 80, 82, 270; home in Victoria 152, 333; Indian handicrafts 170–74; James W. Jones 114, 115, 124–26; Japanese 309, 310; John Chesterman 68–70; Justice of the Peace 7, 136; land speculators 253; marriage 147; mining 7, 110, 111, 116; natives 78, 79–80, 81, 82–83, 170–74; nursery stock 149–50; overdue accounts 123, 263, 264–67; patent medicines 290–91; politics 161, 175–76; sealing industry 11, 23–24, 25–27; sealing schooners 139; sells Clayoquot establishment 334; "sick and destitute" natives 80, *81*, 82–83; Sing Lee's store 132–33, 138–39, 140; Thomas Stockham partnership 6, 66, 138–39 (*see also* Stockham and Dawley); Vargas Island 250; Vargas oxen 249–50; weight 153–54. *See also* Clayoquot Hotel; Clayoquot store; Stockham, Thomas

Dawley, Walter Jr. 151, *151*, *152*

death: Catholic rituals 49–51, 280–82; of children 279–280, 294; at Christie School 49–51; native death rate 56, 282–83; ; native deaths recorded 237, 278, 280; native rituals 51, 95–97, 134–35, 279; students 49–51, 56, 235, 237, 282, 283–88, 289. *See also* smallpox, Spanish influenza; tuberculosis

Della Falls 122

Dennan, Marie 147, 149

dental care 292–93

Department of Indian Affairs 280, 291, 292: censures Father Ildephonse Calmus 325–26; Father Charles's principalship 322–23;

McKenna-McBride Royal Commission 299–300; "sick and destitute" natives 80, *81*, 82–83; tuberculosis 283. *See also* Cox, C.A.; Frost, Edward; Guillod, Harry; Neill, A.W.

Dewdney, Edgar 115, 116, 126, 154

Dick, Leo 46

Didac 237, 282

Dionys (Dennis Jacob) 46, 106

Ditchburn, W.E. 325

Dixson, Charlie 258, 260

Dixson, Douglas Scott 224, 291–95: boats 293–94, *293*; Christie School punishments 325; diary 291–92, *291*; First World War 269; medical care for natives 292

Dixson, Winnie 177

dogfish oil 5, 14, 79

Dominion Government Telegraph Service 7, 246–47, *301*: to Clayoquot 66–68; construction workers *119*; to Hesquiat 299, 300–1; to Nootka 211, 299, 300–3. *See also* Chesterman, John; Cole, Lou; Cole, Minnie; Hamilton, Walter Charles "Mike"; MacLeod, Murdo

Dora Sieward 23, 38, 78, 98

Drader, C. Wilbert A. (Clarence or Bert) 261, 262

Dream Isle. *See* Arnet Island

Drinkwater, Della Fayette, 121, 122

Drinkwater, Joe 69, 121–23

Earle, Thomas 7–8, 65

Earle's Hotel. *See* Clayoquot Hotel

earthquake 296

Eby, Jacob 249–50

Echachis *87*, 88, **160**

English language, at Christie School 46, 52–54

Epper, Father Frowin (Froben) 235: Christie School principal 230, 238; complaints from students and nuns 230–31, 232, 233, 235–36

Esowista Peninsula 7, 8, 132. *See also* Tofino

Estevan Point 90, 162, **194**

Estevan Point lighthouse 181

Evans, Thomas Howard 260

farming 248, 249, 251–52, 254. *See also* cattle; gardening

Favorite 22, 301–2

First World War 258, 296: Clo-oose 257; Dawley's suppliers 269–70; enlisted men from Clayoquot Sound 260–62, 303; letters to Dawley 259–60, 262–68, 269–72; native people 272–73; Vargas Island 257

fishing industry 9, 126, 222, 246, 333. *See also* canneries; pilchard fishery

Fletcher, F.W. 77

Fletcher's Castoria 277, 278

Forsythe, Donald 250, 261, 271

Forsythe, William 261, 262, 269, 271

Frank, Dan 46

Fraser, George 247

Friendly Cove 95, *169*: Catholic church *182*; tourism 225–26, *226*. *See also* Nootka

Frost, Edward 325

Frowin, Father. *See* Epper, Father Frowin (Froben)

Fung Ma 129

fur trade 5, 6, 7, 80, 82, 132, 139, 141, 270. *See also* sealing

Gabriel, Brother. *See* Loerch, Brother Gabriel

Gaffen, Fred 272

gardening 149–50, 176, 188, 222, 248, 252, 257, 304, 312: Christie School 42, 54, *100*, 105, 237. *See also* farming

Gardhouse, Thomas 80, 171, 262

Gardiner, D.W. 262

Garrard, Annie 246, 293

Garrard, Burdett 246, 247–48, 260, 261–62

Garrard, Edward 248

Garrard, Ethel 246, 247–48

Garrard, Frank 194: First World War 260, 268; Fred Tibbs 313; Labour Day picnic 258; land development schemes 249, 251; Lennard Island lighthouse 247–48; Tofino in 1910s 244–45, 246; Vargas Island 248–49

Garrard, Lilly 247, 260, 268

Garrard, Noel 246, 247, 260, 261, 268

Garrard, Olive 176–77, 246, 247

Garrard, W.B. 125

Gault Brothers 76

Gibson, Gordon 227

Gibson family 222

Gillam, Betty 222

Gillam, Edward 215, 222: *Carelmapu* 222; death 224; groundings in 1911 202, 207; navigation 221–22; priests 223; *Princess Maquinna* 220, 222; *Princess Norah* 223–24; service on west coast 219–20

gold rushes 116–22

Goss, John W. 6, 32, 137

grave robbing 134

Grice, John 50, 71, 99, 149, 247: coroner 224; Justice of the Peace 135, 136

Grice, Joseph 260, 261

INDEX

Guillod, Harry 82: Christie School 46, 53; grave robbing 134; native consumers 5, 20; population statistics 283, 343; potlatches 19–20; Protestant-Catholic disputes 58–59; provisions for natives 82–83; Stockham and Dawley split 139; tuberculosis 56; William Netherby 134, 135
Guillod, Mrs. Harry 64–65
Gullin, Victor 64
Guppy, Anthony 315, 316
Guppy, Robert 71

Hackett, Fred 139
Hackla, Chief 50
Haikala, Arvo 261, 262
Haikala, Eino 262–63
Hall, Mabel. *See* Hamilton, Mabel Hall
Hamilton, Addie 298, 303
Hamilton, Harry 298, 303, 304
Hamilton, Mabel Hall 297, 299, 308, *310*, 312: correspondence with Mike Hamilton 297, 306–9; island living 310; meets Mike Hamilton 298; Tofino 314–15; wedding 314
Hamilton, Mabel Wade 304
Hamilton, Sarah 298, 303–4
Hamilton, Walter Charles "Mike" 220, *298*, 304, *307*, 312: background 297–98; Christie School 315–16, *318*, 321; correspondence with Mabel Hall 297, 298, 306–9; credit 308–9; Father Charles 304–6; First World War 270; machine shop 306, 307, 308–9; McKenna-McBride Royal Commission 300; memoirs 317; movies 315–16; owns island 310; photography *119*, 301, 314, 315,

316, *318*, *321*; Port Alberni 317; *Princess Maquinna*'s whistle 220–21; steamer schedules 213; *Tees* 216; Tofino 306–7, 308, 315–17; tourists 227–28; Vargas Island 250, 251; wedding 314; wild cows 195; works on telegraph line 299, 301, 302
Harris, Harry 261, 265
Hayes, Joseph 325
head tax 130–31
Heater, George 139, 140, 151: natives 38; pilchard fishery 301–2; sealing 38–39, 184
Helmcken, J.S. 9
Henderson, William 67
Hesquiat **93**, *180*, *184*, *186*, **194**: after Father Charles's departure 240, 243; cannery work 278; Catholic church 17, 45, *178*, *183*, 204; cattle 188–89, 194–96; "Christian dwellings" 31; deaths in village 294; dogs 187–88; fate of mission 183–84; land speculators 253–54; local stores 80; McKenna-McBride Royal Commission 299–300; sealing crews 5; sealing industry 29, 30; steamers 212; telegraph line 300–1. *See also* Anton's Point; Brabant, Father Augustin; Moser, Father Charles
Hesquiat Land Co. 253
Hesquiat Peninsula **194**
Hilton, Henry 250
Hofman, Father Stephen 331
Home-is 93, **194**
Hooper, Thomas 59
Hopkins, Esther 261, 264–65
Hopkins, Frank Elliott 260, 266
Hopkins, Freeman 250, 260, 266, 264, 265, 270–71

Hopkins, Lillian 261
hotel inventories 129–30
Hot Springs Cove. *See* Refuge Cove
Hovelaque, Pierre 248–49
Howard, Emil 294
Hudson's Bay Company 65, 69, 74, 80, 162

Ildephonse, Father. *See* Calmus, Father Ildephonse
illness: native people 229–30, 234, 237, 277–79, 281; treated by priests 280–81. *See also* Dixson, Douglas Scott; medicine; smallpox; tuberculosis
Indian Agents. *See* Cox, C.A.; Frost, Edward; Guillod, Harry; Neill, A.W.
Indian Chief group 110
Indian Residential Schools: The Nuuchah-nulth Experience 53, 326, 329
Indians. *See* native people
islands 310, 312. *See also* Arnet Island; Meares Island; Morpheus Island; Stockham Island; Stubbs Island; Vargas Island

Jackson, Joseph 146
Jacob, Dennis (Dionys) 46, 106
Jacob, Emily 234
Jacob, Harry 106
Jacobsen, Filip 7, 71
Japanese, in Clayoquot Sound 309–10
Jay and Company 149
Jenner, Roxburgh & Company 75
Jessie 39, 184
Jim, Jimmy 24, 25, 89, 217, 279, 289
John, Mrs. Adolph 289
John, Nonat 46
John Bright 344

Johnston Brothers Dry Goods Wholesale 80
Jones, James Warren 13, 109: Boer War 109, 111–15; family 114, 115, 156–57; mining interests 110, 115–16; reappears 154; removal of testicle 125; reports of death 112–13; suicide 155–57; Walter Dawley 110, 111, 114, 124–25
Jones, Ray 219, 220
Jones, William 46
Joseph, Chief 45, 46, 235
Justices of the Peace 7, 50, 66, 135–36

Kakawis 42, **93**, **160**, **311**. *See also* Christie School
Kelley, Frank 32
Kelly Douglas & Company 75, 265
Kelsemat (Yaksis) 8, 30, 90, **160**
Kennedy Lake 314, *315*: salmon hatchery 176
Kenyon, W. N. 123–24
Kimoto, Tommy 309–10
Kincaid, James 110, 111
Kitla, Boss 25, 27
Kyuquot: Catholic church 45; whaling station 164, *165*, *165*, *166*, 202

land, clearing 42, 56, 71, 176, 249–50, 251–52. *See also* land development schemes
land development schemes 249, 251–54, 255–57
Lane, Gerald 261, 263, 265
language: Brabant's dictionary 179, 180–81, 273; English only used at school 46, 52–54; white people speaking native language 17, 49, 54, 137, 141, 281, 329
Leebro 207

Leiser, Simon 77–79, 132–33
Lemmens, Father John 45, 87, 94
Lennard Island lighthouse 247–48
Leonard, Brother. *See* Niederpruem, Brother Leonard
Liberal Association 161, 175
Ling, Dan Yuk 140
Loerch, Brother Gabriel 48
Logan, Captain 201, 205
logging industry 9, 126, 132, 210, 222, 246
Lomp, Joseph 269
Long Bay 136, 159, **160**, 162, 176: tourism 225. *See also* Long Beach; Tibbs, Frederick G.
Long Beach 120, 159, **160**, 225, 254–55. *See also* Long Bay
Lourdes 49
Love, A. R. 253
Lucas, John 288
Luckovitch, Anton 80, 106, 193
Luckovitch, Gussie 181
Luckovitch, Mrs. Anton 194–95
Lyford, P. L. 173

Macaulay, D. G. 33
Macdonald, Alex 323
Mackenzie, A. F. 325
Mackenzie Beach 258
Mackintosh, Donald 271
MacLeod, Alex 267
MacLeod, Ewan 267, 334
MacLeod, John 267
MacLeod, John 260, 261, 265, 267, 269
MacLeod, Murdo 246, 260, 333: First World War 259–60, 262, 267–68, 269
Malon, Helen 261
Malon, Madeline Dawley 151, *151*, 152, 334
Malon, Pierre 334

Maltby, George 136
Maquinna, Chief 60: canoe to Philadelphia 173; Christie School 104; death of 95–97, *96*; and potlatches 19–20; and religion 95; totem poles 54
Maquinna, Chief Napoleon 97: Nootka store 142–43; son's grave 169, 226; wedding 169–70, *169*, *170*
marble 168, 169
Mary, Queen 45, 235
Matlahaw, Chief 18
Matthew, Georgie 99
Maude 10, 214–15, 224
Maurus, Father. *See* Snyder, Father Maurus
McClary Manufacturing Company 75, 143
McDougall, Daniel 66, 106, 149
McGregor, Moses 119
McKenna, John 140
McKenna-McBride Royal Commission on Indian Affairs 299–300
McKeon, W. J. 113
McKinley, Dr. 65, 66
McLean, J. D. 325
Mclean, Maurus 53–54, 329
McPhee, Captain 25–26
Meares Island **160**, **311**
measles 292
medicines: administered by priests 280, 282, 288–89; native 174; patent 278, 290–91. *See also* illness; smallpox; Spanish influenza; tuberculosis
Mellor, J. W. 73
Methodists 48, 59, 65, 66, 86–87: at Clayoquot 98–99; at Opitsat 99
Michael, Felix 46, 50
Michael, Katie 46

INDEX

Michael, Mike (first death at Christie School) 46, 49–51
Mickie, Charlie 326
mining 7, 9, 13, 110–11, 116, 124, 214, 246: copper 110; First World War 270; gold 116–22; Sydney Inlet 157–58. *See also* Chinese: prospectors; Drinkwater, Joe; Jones, James Warren
Mission Island. *See* Stockham Island
missionaries: and colonization 16–17; Protestant 66. *See also* Catholic church; Methodists; Presbyterians; Protestants
Monks, Harold 260, 261, 262
Morpheus Island **311**, 313
Moser, Father Charles 43, *84*, *85*, *220*, *328*, *330*: arrives on west coast 43; background 86; battles Protestants 98; Brabant's visit in 1911 179–82, 184–85; butchering cattle 188–89, 200–1, 295, 330; canoe travels 89, 90–94, *93*; cattle 188, 189, *190*, 192–94, 196; Chief Eustace Andrews 286–88; Christie School 88, 240–43, 318, 319–21; condemns adultery 285; daily routine 179–80, 185; death of Brabant 185–86; deaths of native people 98, 278–80, 281–86, 287–88, 294; diary 43, 88–89, 324–25; difficulty getting students 86, 99; dogs 179, 187–88; Edward Gillam 223–24; escorts Christie School students 94, 105, 328–29, 330; Father Frowin Epper 236; Father Victor Rassiter 328, 329–30; final years on coast 323–30; first death at school 48–50; First World War 272, 273, 296; Hesquiat 88, 183–84, 186–89, *187*, 197–98, 205–7, 208–9, 295; hike to school in thunderstorm 85–86; Japanese 309; land speculators 253, 254; leaves Hesquiat for Christie School 240; Lou and Minnie Cole 302–3; McKenna-McBride Royal Commission 299–300; medical skills 280, 282, 288–89; Mike Hamilton 304–6, 318; missionary at Opitsat 86–88; native ceremonies 209, 286; Opitsat church 319; Port Alice church 319; *Princess Maquinna* 218; *Princess Norah* 223–24, *223*; principal of Christie School 243, 322–23; problems at Christie School 238; providing food for Christie School 188–89; publishes book 319; reluctant students 101, 105, 107; returns to Mount Angel Abbey 330–31; saving souls 279, 281, 284–86, 306; seasickness 90, 91; Spanish influenza 295–96; steamers 197, 198, 205–6, 211–12; Stockham and Dawley 139; Sydney Inlet 157–58; telegraph line at Hesquiat 299, 300–1; tourists 227; travels on coast 87–88, 184, 323; travels to Switzerland 179, 187, 323; water pipes 197, 205–8; weddings 145–47; whaling 165–67; wine freezes in sacristy 294; "workhorse" 86
Mosquito Harbour 126, 132, **160**, 246
Mount Angel Abbey 43, 231, 330: abbot visits Hesquiat 300; baby whale 167; Christie School 43, 323, 330
movies 315–16

Munro, George 136
Munsie, William 25, 26–27, 33
Murphy, James 162–63

Napoleon, Chief. *See* Maquinna, Chief Napoleon
Napoleon, Mamie 285–86
native people: baptisms 146; cash economy 5–6, 19–20, 28, 31, 183; Catholic church 17–18, 146, 183, 242, 284–86; consumer demands 5–6, 31, 79; corporal punishment 103–4; credit 308; death rituals 51, 96–97, *96*, 134–35, 169, 226, *226*, 279; deaths of children 279; deaths recorded 237, 278, 280; dogs 187, 188; English language 52–54; First World War 272–73; handicrafts 5, 170–74, 223, 226–27 (*see also* totem poles); illness 229–30, 234, 237, 277–79, 281, 282–83 (*see also* smallpox, Spanish influenza, tuberculosis); "loath to part with children" 46; medical care 292; medicinal plants 174; pants 28–29, 45, 142; photos of children 103; population in Clayoquot Sound 8, 282–83, 343; potlatch 13, 19–20, 99, 208–9; provisions for "sick and destitute" 80, *81*, 82–83; reluctance to send children to school 45–46, 60, 61, 99–100, 104, 235; sealing industry 5–6, 23–25, 27, 33, 34–35; social structure changing 183; Spanish influenza 296; as tourist attraction 225–27; travel on steamers 214, 215, 227, 274; travel to jobs 183, 278; tuberculosis 56–57, 229; villages 8 (*see also* Ahousat, Hesquiat, Kelsemat, Opitsat);

weddings 144, 145–47, 169–70, 169, 170, 183, 279, 284; whaling 166–67, 167; wolf dance 208, 209, 286. *See also* Christie School
navigation 221–22
Neill, A. W. 82–83, 142
Netherby, William 19, 95, 133, 136: accused of grave robbing 134–36; Ahousat 21, 133–34, 136, 137; Chinese worker 129; Father Brabant 32; potlatches 19
Newcombe, C. F. 156
Niblock, Joan 306
Nichols, F. P. 122–23
Nicholson, George 333
Nicholson, Joan 148, 150, 334
Nicolaye, Father Joseph 45
Niederprucm, Brother Leonard 48, 55, 89, 102
Nokamis, Chief 135–36
Nootka **93**: Catholic church 45; first students to Christie School 60–61; schools 97; sealing crews 5
Nootka Cannery 219, 240, 330
Nootka Marble Quarries 168
Nootka Sound marble 168, 169
Nootka store 3, 6: burns down 141, 142–43. *See also* Goss, John W.; Netherby, William; Sloman, James; Smith, H.; Vaughan, Alfred
Norwegian settlers 68, 160, 245, 260, 310, 315
nuns, on west coast 48, 57, 58, 59: Christie School problems blamed on 239; complaints about Father Frowin 230–31; miss Father Maurus 230, 232; Sister Mary Clara 231, 232, 234, 236, 239; Sister Mary Clotilde 41, 239; Sister Mary Elizabeth 230, 232, 243; Sister Mary Frances 41, 217, 235; Sister Mary Placide 41, 43, 44, 46, 47, 57, 190; Sister Mary Scholastica 231; Sister Mary Sophie 232, 235, 236; staying at Kakawis 273

Oliver, John 252
Opitsat 6, 86, **93**, **160**, **311**: Catholic church 43, 45, 319; religious competition 87; schools 86, 87, 99; sealing crews 5, 24
ore. *See* mining
Ormsby, Margaret 253
orphans, at Christie School 57
Orth, Bishop 48
Otto 24, 25, 26, 27, 33
Owen, George N. 76

Pacific Whaling Company 82, 164–65
Palmer, Austin 102
Palmer Method of handwriting 102–3
Park, Arthur 258, 260, 262, 263
pelican, stuffed 129, *130*
Peppett, J. W. 23, 24, 36–37, 39: loss of *Active* 30; Thornberg writes about 2
Peter, Emma 101, 284
phthisis 292. *See also* tuberculosis
pilchard fishery 301–2
Police George 25, 27
policing 7, 66, 136–37: truants 106–7, 321, 327. *See also* Beavan, Robert Arthur; McDougall, Daniel; Stanley Spain, Frederick
Pollock, Robert 162
"poor Indian boys of Kakawis" 230, 233
population statistics 8, 159–60, 282–83, 343

Port Alberni 215, 244, 317
Port Alice 319
Port Gillam 250
Port Hughes 111, 119
Port Vargas. *See* Port Gillam
post office 7, 66, 111, 119, 143, 223
potlatches 13, 19–20: ban 19; popular gifts 13, 26
pre-emptions 251–52. *See also* land, clearing
Presbyterians 48: Ahousat 95; Nootka 95; schools 97–98, 99
Price, Frederic Sydney 251, 260, 261, 269
Princess Maquinna 90, 210, 217–19, 275: schedule 219. *See also* Gillam, Edward
Princess Norah 223–24
Pringle, Florence 147–48
Pringle Company 147–48
Protestants: hospital 65; missionaries 66; presence on coast 41–42, 87, 94–95, 97–98; west coast schools 48. *See also* Anglican church, Methodists, Presbyterians
Ptarmigan Mine 246, 270

Quatsino 150, 172, 189, 253–54, 278
Queen City 8, 10–11, 12, 29, 200, 205–6, 215: officers comment on schooners 34; runs aground 207

Rae-Arthur, Ada Annie 222, 252: childbirth 288–89; children taken to school 321
Rae-Arthur, Willie 72, 222, 252, 288, 304, 321
railway 215, 244
rain 336
Rassiter, Father Victor 328, 329–30
Raynor, H. 98, 99

Refuge Cove 93
Remington Arms 270
Reminiscences of the West Coast of Vancouver Island 319
Rennie and Company 75
residential schools: arson 241–42; English language 53; tuberculosis 56–57, 234, 283. *See also* Bryce, Peter; Catholic church; Methodists; Presbyterians; Protestants
Riley's Cove 301–2
Rolston, Mrs. William 117, 221, 312
Rolston, William 50, 66, 135, 136
Ross, Jack 261
Ross Bay Cemetery 157, 186, 224
Round, H.A. 270
Royal Oak Cemetery 334
Russell, John 48, 58, 95, 121

Salvor 199, 200, 201, 203, 205
Sam, Mamie 233–34, 285
Scharschmidt, B.J. 269
Schindler, Father Joseph 237: Christie School principal 238–39, 243; *Princess Maquinna* 218
Schindler, Ted 275
schools 48, 88: Ahousat 48, 97, 99, 241; Clo-oose 48; compulsory attendance 321; correspondence 252; Nootka 97; Opitsat 86; Tofino 248. *See also* Christie School
Scott, Duncan Campbell 323
Scottish settlers 160, 245, 310, 315
sea otter 35, 37, 141
sealing industry: accounts at Ahousat 27; Bering Sea 29–30, 31, 35–36; captains travel up coast 34; compensation for sealers 39, 139; decline 20, 37, 36–39; importance on coast 5–6; international moratorium 36, 39; native crews 1, 5, 23–27, 29, 30, 31–32, 37; natives in Victoria 33; offshore 4–5, 29; prices 139; unsustainable 35. *See also* sealing schooners

sealing schooners: *Active* 30; *Carrie CW* 23, 33; *Dora Sieward* 23, 38, 78, 98; *E. B. Marvin* 24; *Favorite* 22, 301–2; *Florence M Smith* 26; *Ida Etta* 23; *Jessie* 39, 184; *Otto* 24, 25, 26, 27, 33; shipping freight 11; *Surprise* 4, 16, 17; *Thomas F Bayard* 37–38, 139; *Triumph* 26; *Umbrina* 23, 24, 36–37, 38, 39; *Vera* 38; *Victoria* 23; *Viva* 26; *Walter L Rich* 27
search warrants 106
Searle, J. 37
Sechart 164, 165, 202
Seghers, Charles 16, 17, 344
Service, Charles 66
Sharp, Bill 176, 313
Shaughnessy, Thomas 216
"sick and destitute" natives 80, 81, 83
Sidney Inlet. See Sydney Inlet
Sieward, Captain 2, 24
Simpson, William 131, 334
Sing Lee 132–33, 138–39, 140
Sloman, Harold 260
Sloman, James 140–43
smallpox 18, 32, 280, 282
Smith, H. 168–69, 212
Snyder, Father Maurus 43, 47, 84, 104, 231: annual reports 47, 54, 101–2, 104; arrives on west coast 44; background 42; cattle 190, 192, 195; Chief Napoleon Maquinna's wedding 169–70; children's unhappiness 100; comments on curriculum 51–52; corporal punishment 104;

Father Brabant 54, 107, 191; first death at school 48–49; fundraising in Europe 52; leaves Christie School 229–30, 231–32; letters from nuns and students 229–31, 232–37, 243, 331; problems after departure from Kakawis 230–31, 232, 233, 235–36; runaways 106; students' penmanship 103; students running stores 80; Walter Dawley 74
Sobry, Father Emil 45, 209
Spanish influenza 295–96
Spring, William 4
St. Clair, A.K. 63
Stadthagen, H. 172
Stanley Spain, Frederick 50: complains about Clayoquot JPs 136; difficulties of policing 137; grave robbing 134–36
steamship service 7, 8, 9, 10–11, 18: Hesquiat 11–14; loading and unloading 11–15, 117, 141–42, 156, 192–93, 197–99, 212, 213, 218, 275, 276, *276*; schedules 11, 198, 199, 211–14, *212*; stops, **xviii**; stormy weather 198; Tofino 316; tourism 224, 226 (*see also* Brodie, H.); whistle 220–22. *See also* BC Coastal Steamship Service; Canadian Pacific Navigation Company, *Maude*, *Princess Maquinna*, *Queen City*, *Tees*, *Willapa*
Stern, Father Aloysius 45
Stevens, Maggie 234
Stewart and McDonald 153
Stockham, Agnes McKenna 138
Stockham, Thomas: background 6; buys sealing schooners 37, 39, 139; buys Sing Lee's store 140; marriage 137–38; mining

interests 120; personality 66; politics 161; telegraph line 66–67, 68; Walter Dawley 6, 138–39; Wreck Bay 120. *See also* Stockham and Dawley

Stockham and Dawley 6–8: best store on west coast 64–65; buy store and hotel on Clayoquot 65; communication and transport hub 5, 65, 67–68; competition 7–8, 79, 132–33; hotels 3, 7; native people 5, 27–28; partnership ends 138, 139; sealing industry 5, 27–28; stores 2, 3, 6. *See also* Ahousat store; Clayoquot Hotel; Clayoquot store; Dawley, Thomas; Nootka store; Stockham Island hotel; Stockham Island store; *individual storekeepers*

Stockham Island 2, 3, 65, **160**, **311**: hospital (Mission Island) 98–99

Stockham Island hotel 7, 225, 309: Chinese workers 128–29; inventory 129

Stockham Island store 2, 3, 6

Stone, Gwendolyn Hoop-Kwis-Tuck 214

Stone, Stuart 112–13, *113*: steamers 213–14; Stockham's marriage 138

Stone, William 48, 98, 138, 175, 213–14, 281

Stubbs Island 7, 149, **160**, **311**. *See also* Clayoquot

Stuermer, George 290

Surprise 4, 16, 17

Sutton, William 210–11

Swan, Mary Alphonse 284

Swartout, Melvin 48, 95

Sydney Inlet 13, 110, 116, 154, 155, 157–58, 246, 276. *See also* Jones, James Warren; mining

Tahoma 201

Taylor, Dominic 53, 57

Tees 197, 213, 215: grounding in Kyuquot Sound 197–205, 208–9; inadequacy 202, 215–16, 218; replaced 216, 218; rough weather 192, 202, 216; schedule 181, 211

telegraph. *See* Dominion Government Telegraph Service

theatre 147–48

Thomas F Bayard 37–38, 139

Thompson, Alex 202–3, 204

Thompson, G. R. 82

Thomson, James 69, 76, 113, 140, 151, 168, 171, 211, 269

Thornberg, Andy 261, 331, 332

Thornberg, Freddie Junior 15, 261, 332

Thornberg, Frederick Christian 4, 6, *331*: Ahousat people 15–16, 79; business methods 20–21; Catholics 94; describes freight and loading 11–15; dogfish oil 14–15; family 15, 331–32; Father Brabant 17, 18, 185; "Jones Oare" 13–14; letter writer 4; loss of *Active* 30; mental instability 331–333; native deaths 283; patent medicines 290, 291; poor customer service 28; potlatches 13, 19; sealing industry 1, 2, 27–28; sets up his own store 133–34, 171

Thornberg, Hilda 331–32

Thornberg, John 261

Thornberg, Lucy 15, 332

Tibbs, Frederick G. 312, 260: death 313; Dream Isle 176–77, *176*, *177*; First World War 177, 312–13; Long Bay 159–61, 176; Triangle Island light 174–75; will 177, 313–14

Tidewater Copper 158

Tlaghshiet 98

Tofino 9, **160**, 210, 244, 247, 335–36: automobiles 245; boat day xiii–xiv, 316; dominant community 143; First World War 260, 261; harbour **311**, *318*; land speculators 310; lifeboat crew 245, *316*; in 1913 245; rain 336; rivalry with Clayoquot 245; road to Alberni 255; road to Ucluelet 9, 246, 255; school 248; social scene 245, 315, 306–7, 308, 310; telegraph line 67. *See also* Esowista Peninsula; Garrard, Frank; Hamilton, Walter Charles "Mike"; Sing Lee

Tofino cemetery 313

Tofino store 132–33, 140. *See also* Sing Lee; Sloman, James

totem poles 54, 156, 172, 173, 225–26

tourism 224–28, 256–57, 273–74, 276, 317

transportation 8, 9: freight 11, 12; passenger *8*, 10; road link 9, 246, 255; sealing schooners 11; small boats *91*; waterborne 94. *See also* BC Coastal Steamship Service; Canadian Pacific Navigation Company; railway; steamship service

tree rig 176, *176*, 314, *314*. *See also* Tibbs, Frederick G.

Triangle Island 174–75

Troup, J. W. 215, 216

tuberculosis 56–57, 282–83, 292

Turner, Beeton & Company 76, 82, 133, 143

Tyee Copper Company 157–58

Uchuckleset 202

Ucluelet 9, 254: Protestant school 48; road to Alberni 255; road

to Tofino 9, 246, 255; sealing crews 26
Umbrina 23, 24, 36–37, 38, 39

Valencia 200
Van Nevel, Father 45, 87, 95, 289
Vancouver Island, west coast **xviii**: development 215–16; gold rush 117–18; population 8, 18, 282–83, 343; scattered settlements 219, 252, 257, 312, 317; tourism 165, 172, 223, 224–28, 273–74, 276. *See also* Catholic church; Clayoquot Sound; *Victoria Daily Colonist*
Vancouver Island Development League 245
Vargas Island **160**, 248–49, 250–51, 258: First World War 257–58, 260, 261; tourism 225. *See also* Port Gillam
Varney, Henry 149–50, 171–72
Vaughan, Alfred 168
Vera 38
Victoria: gold fever 116; sealing industry 5, 29–30, 34; theatre 147–48. *See also Victoria Daily Colonist; Victoria Daily Times*

Victoria Daily Colonist: Chief Maquinna 96; Chinese workers 131–32; Clayoquot Hotel fire 163; Clayoquot Sound 9–10, 11, 126, 168; First World War 264, 268, 272; James W. Jones 109–10, 113, 155–56; mining 13, 111, 117, 118, 119; native artefacts shipped to U.S., 173; Presbyterian schools 97–98; sealing industry 6, 20, 30, 34, 39; Sing Lee 132, 140; steamers 215, 217–18; Stockham and Dawley 7, 65, 68, 138; *Tees* 1911 grounding 200–5; telegraph 68; Tofino 245; Ucluelet 254–55; Victoria theatre 147–48; West Coast cow 195; west coast tourism 224–25; whaling 164, 165; Wreck Bay 120
Victoria Daily Times, interview with James Sloman 141
Victoria Sealing Company 25–26, 38

Wah Yun 130
Walter L Rich 27
weddings: Andrews, Eustace 145–47; Dawleys 147; Hamiltons 297, 308, 314; Maquinna, Chief Napoleon 169–70, *169, 170*; native people 52, 144, 146, 183, 279, 284, 285–86; Stockham, Thomas 138
West Coast Development Company 255–57
whaling 126, 164–67, *165, 166, 167*, 202, 222
Wheeler, Arther 305
Wheeler, Helen 305
White Wing Hotel 245
Willapa 9, 10, 43
William, Cosmos Damian 229–31, 236–37, 295
William Jolliffe 199, 201, 203, 205
Wing On 127–28, 130
wolf dance 208, 209, 286
Wong Tuck 131
Wreck Bay 119–20, 131, 132
Wrotnowsky, Mr. 254

Yaksis **160**. *See also* Kelsemat (Yaksis)
Yaksouse, Alice. *See* Andrews, Alice Yaksouse
Yaksouse, Harry 146, 287
Yet Wo Lung 174
Yuquot. *See* Friendly Cove

Sister M. Placida

I remain Yours truly

Your's truly
F. C. Garrard

Stuart Stanley Stone

P. Maurus

Respectfully yours
William Aloysius

From everloving husband
E. Gillam

Respy yours H.C. Brewster   With lots & lots of love
from
I am your little
Police George   Your Michael